MW01627315

GUM

Grammar, Usage, and Mechanics

Conventions of Standard English

ZB Zaner-Bloser
A Highlights Company

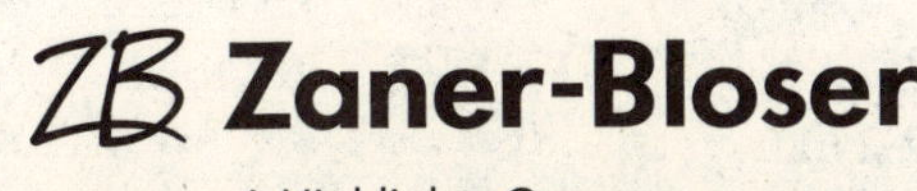

Grade Level Consultants

S. Elaine Boysworth
Lincolnton, North Carolina

Linda Crawford
Calhoun, Georgia

Martha Swan Novy
Florissant, Missouri

Heather Stanton
Colorado Springs, Colorado

Jaqueline Xavier
Cleveland, Ohio

Illustration: Tom Kennedy, Tracy Greenwalt

ISBN: 978-1-4531-1212-0

This book is printed on paper certified by third-party standards for sustainably managed forestry.

Zaner-Bloser, Inc.
800.421.3018
zaner-bloser.com

Printed in the United States of America

6 7 8 9 10 11 12 13 14 27950 24 23 22 21 20

ZB Code 16

Table of Contents

Unit 1 Sentence Structure

Beasts & Critters: Astounding Animals

Unit 2 Sentence Structure

The World Outside: Changes in the Natural World

Unit 3 Parts of Speech: Nouns, Pronouns, Adjectives, and Adverbs

Timeless Tales: Myths and Legends

Unit 4 Parts of Speech: Verbs and Conjunctions

Looking Back: American Journeys

Unit 5 Usage

Grab Bag: High-Tech Highlights

Unit 6 Grammar

Great Getaways: Rivers of the World

Unit 7 Mechanics

Unforgettable Folks: Problem Solvers

Appendix

Unit Pretests

Extra Practice

Unit Posttests

Read and Analyze

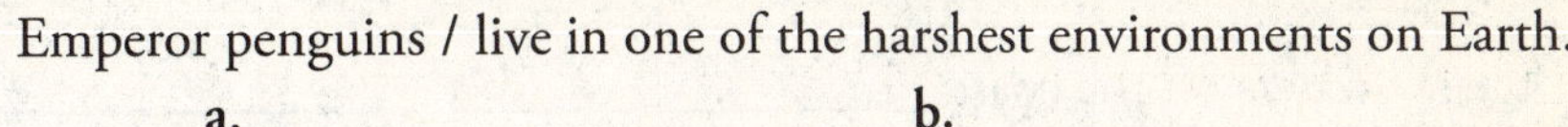

Emperor penguins / live in one of the harshest environments on Earth.
a. b.

Which part of this sentence (*a* or *b*) tells whom or what the sentence is about? ________

Which part of this sentence (*a* or *b*) tells what happens? ________

Every sentence contains a subject and a predicate. The **complete subject** in a sentence is made up of a noun or pronoun and words that tell about it. The **complete predicate** in a sentence is made up of a verb and words that tell what the subject is, has, or does.

See Handbook Sections 11, 12

Practice

Underline the complete subject in each sentence once. Underline each complete predicate twice.

1. This species of penguin survives in the extreme conditions of Antarctica.
2. Antarctica is the coldest and windiest continent on Earth.
3. Colonies of Emperor penguins live along the Antarctic coast.
4. Groups of penguins huddle together on the ice.
5. This action protects the penguins against the cold and wind.
6. The body of an Emperor penguin contains a large amount of fat.
7. This body fat provides insulation against the cold.
8. Emperor penguin chicks are born during the long Antarctic winter.
9. The female penguin lays a single egg in mid-May.
10. She goes on a two-month journey to the sea in search of food.
11. The female leaves the egg with her mate.
12. The male penguin balances the egg on his feet.
13. A fold of skin on the male's abdomen covers the egg.
14. This fold protects the egg from the harsh environment.
15. The male penguin eats nothing during this time.
16. The female returns in mid-July from her journey.
17. The male transfers the egg back to his mate.
18. The egg hatches soon after this transfer.
19. The mother penguin feeds her newly hatched Emperor chick.

Emperor penguins endure the severe weather in Antarctica.

Name ____________________

Apply

Add a subject or a predicate to each phrase to make a sentence. Underline the complete subject in each sentence you write. Circle the complete predicate in each sentence.

20. the icy waters off the coast ____________________

21. eat fish and squid ____________________

22. study the penguins' habits ____________________

23. strong Antarctic winds ____________________

Reinforce

Complete subjects and predicates may be very short (*Penguins / swim*) or very long. Short sentences can make a paragraph seem direct and can help focus readers' attention on actions and events. Long sentences in a paragraph can create a smooth flow that carries the reader along from one idea to the next while providing clear descriptions and explanations.

On the lines below write a short paragraph about an unusual animal. Make the subjects and predicates in your sentences short and concise. Then rewrite your paragraph on another sheet of paper, adding words and phrases to make the subjects and predicates longer and more informative. For what purpose might the more concise paragraph be better? For what purpose might the more descriptive paragraph be better?

Read and Analyze

Scientists in New Zealand study the habits of the kiwi, an unusual bird.

The complete subject of the sentence above is in boldfaced type. Draw a box around the most important word in the complete subject. Circle the verb that tells what the subject does.

Do some research on this fascinating creature.

Can you find a subject at the beginning of this sentence? ________

Which word below would fit as the subject of the sentence? Circle it.

you research kiwi bird

The **simple subject** is the most important word or words in the complete subject. It is a noun or pronoun that tells whom or what the sentence is about. By identifying the simple subject in a sentence, you can determine whether the subject is singular or plural and choose the correct verb form to use with it. The subject of a request or a command (an imperative sentence) usually is not named. The person being spoken to, *you,* is the **understood subject**. The **simple predicate** is the verb that tells about the subject. It may tell what the subject did or what was done to the subject; or, it may link the subject to words that tell about it.

See Handbook Sections 11, 12

Practice

Draw a box around the simple subject in each sentence. If the subject is the understood *you,* write *you* on the line. Then underline the simple predicate.

1. The tiny kiwi scurries quickly from place to place. _____
2. The wings of this flightless bird are very small. _____
3. The kiwi has nostrils at the end of its long beak. _____
4. The feathers of the kiwi look much like hair. _____
5. Describe the kiwi's physical appearance. _____
6. The oropendola is another interesting type of bird. _____
7. This member of the Icterid family lives in Central and South American rainforests and grasslands. _____
8. The nest of the oropendola resembles a long hanging sack. _____
9. Notice those long nests hanging from tree branches. _____
10. That male bowerbird has built a nest with sticks, leaves, and moss. _____
11. He is decorating the nest with pebbles, berries, and shells. _____
12. The elaborate nest will attract a female bowerbird's attention. _____

The kiwi is a flightless bird native to New Zealand.

Name ______________________________

Apply

Write five sentences about birds with unusual characteristics. You may use nouns and verbs from the word bank as simple subjects or simple predicates. Use the understood subject *you* in one of your sentences.

researchers	fly	beak	hunt	habitat	lives
builds	nest	eats	branches	study	rainforest

13. ______________________________

14. ______________________________

15. ______________________________

16. ______________________________

17. ______________________________

Reinforce

See Handbook Sections 35, 36, 37

Use the Internet or an encyclopedia to research another unusual bird. Then write an e-mail to a friend or family member describing this bird. Begin with the reason you are e-mailing. Use proper etiquette, such as typing a clear subject line; avoiding special type features and emoticons and using only uppercase letters; and including a detailed salutation (full name and e-mail address). When you have finished your first draft, read your e-mail from beginning to end. Did you achieve your purpose for writing? Proofread for errors in capitalization, punctuation, and spelling. Then print out a hard copy of your final draft. Circle the simple subject in each sentence. Underline each simple predicate.

___ Many Australian zoologists and veterinarians study marsupials.

___ A marsupial carries and nurses its young in a pouch on its stomach.

Write *S* next to the sentence that contains two or more simple subjects.

Write *P* next to the sentence that contains two or more simple predicates.

A **compound subject** is two or more subjects joined by a coordinating conjunction (examples: *and, but, or*). A **compound predicate** is two or more verbs joined by a coordinating conjunction.

See Handbook Sections 11, 12

Practice

Each sentence below has either a compound subject or a compound predicate. If a sentence has a compound subject, underline the nouns that are the simple subjects. If a sentence has a compound predicate, circle the verbs that are the simple predicates.

1. Koalas, kangaroos, and wallabies are three kinds of marsupials.
2. Koalas live in trees and sleep up to 20 hours a day.
3. They survive on a diet of eucalyptus leaves and drink very little water.
4. Australia and Papua New Guinea are home to kangaroos and wallabies.
5. These marsupials have powerful hind legs and hop from place to place.
6. Baby koalas, kangaroos, and wallabies are called joeys.
7. A joey crawls into its mother's pouch after birth and receives nourishment from her.
8. Wombats and Tasmanian devils are two other kinds of marsupials.
9. Wombats dig and live in burrows.
10. Native grasses and shrub roots are part of the wombat's diet.
11. Tasmanian devils hunt and eat small mammals and birds.
12. The appearance and sound of the Tasmanian devil frightens some people.
13. Tasmanian devils look fierce and screech while eating.
14. Wombats and Tasmanian devils have backward-facing pouches.
15. The newborn wombat makes its way into its mother's pouch and stays there for up to ten months.
16. The Tasmanian devil joey enters its mother's pouch after birth and remains there for about four months.

The Tasmanian devil looks ferocious and has an eerie cry.

Name ______________________________

Apply

Combine each pair of sentences to form one sentence that has either a compound subject or a compound predicate.

17. Opossums are marsupials. Numbats are marsupials, too. ______________________________

____

18. The opossum grasps branches with its tail. The animal also carries nesting material with its tail.

____

____

19. Baby opossums develop inside their mother's pouch. Later they ride on their mother's back.

____

____

20. Numbats live in the woodlands of western Australia. They eat termites. ______________________________

____

21. Dogs prey on the numbat. Foxes prey on this marsupial, too. ______________________________

____

Reinforce

It is possible to have both a compound subject and a compound predicate in the same sentence. (*The boys and girls talked and laughed together.*) However, both parts of the compound subject must be performing both actions of the compound predicate. Avoid sentences like this one: *The birds and dogs chirped and barked.* This sentence might make the reader think that the dogs chirped and the birds barked.

On the lines below, rewrite the incorrect sentence as two separate sentences. Write *C* beside the sentence that uses compound subjects and predicates correctly.

22. The campers and counselors swam and splashed in the lake. _____

____

____

23. The stars and the wind sparkled brightly and blew softly. _____

____

____

Read and Analyze

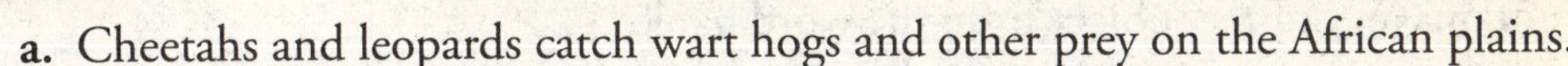

a. Cheetahs and leopards catch wart hogs and other prey on the African plains.

b. Zookeepers give visitors information about these predators.

Circle the nouns in sentence *a* that tell what cheetahs and leopards catch. Circle the noun in sentence *b* that tells what zookeepers give visitors. Draw a line under the noun in sentence *b* that tells *to whom* they give it.

A **direct object** is a noun or pronoun that receives the action of the verb. To find the direct object, say the verb and then ask "What?" or "Whom?" An **indirect object** is a person or thing to whom something is given, told, or taught. The indirect object is a noun or pronoun, and it comes before the direct object. To determine whether a word is an indirect object, move it after the direct object and put the word *to* or *for* in front of it. Example: *Zookeepers give information to visitors.* A sentence may have more than one direct object or indirect object.

See Handbook Section 21

Practice

Circle each direct object in the sentences below. Underline each indirect object. Be careful. Not all sentences contain indirect objects.

1. The zookeeper gave us a short lecture about cheetahs and leopards.
2. The cheetah hunts its prey during the daytime.
3. This swift predator catches creatures using its strong claws.
4. It holds the doomed animal by the neck.
5. The cheetah must eat its catch quickly.
6. Other predators may steal its food.
7. A cheetah cannot defeat a lion or a pack of hyenas.
8. The mother cheetah brings her cubs meat from her catch.
9. The leopard most often stalks prey at night.
10. This carnivore can kill animals larger than itself.
11. The leopard keeps its catch from other predators in an effective way.
12. It climbs a large, thick-branched tree with its catch in its jaws.
13. The leopard then eats its meal in the branches, safe from lions and hyenas.
14. The zookeeper gave adults and children more details about differences between cheetahs and leopards.
15. Many people asked the zookeeper questions after her speech.

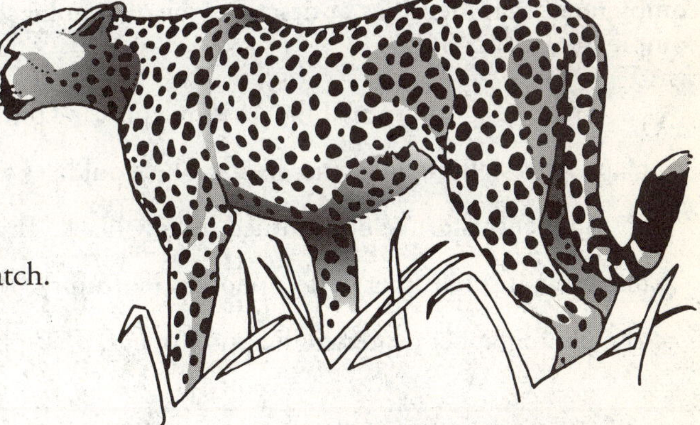

The cheetah is the fastest land animal on Earth.

Name ______________________________

Apply

Complete each sentence with a direct object or an indirect object from the word bank. Write *DO* next to each sentence that contains a direct object from the word bank. Write *IO* next to each sentence that contains an indirect object from the word bank.

teacher	water	class	us	cubs	fur

16. Our teacher gave ______________ information about the world's wild cats. ________
17. Wild cats groom their ______________. ________
18. Mother cats carry their ______________ with their mouths. ________
19. One student asked the ______________ a question about wild cats' dislike of water. ________
20. He gave the ________________ a surprising answer. ________
21. Tigers, leopards, and jaguars like ________________ and are good swimmers. ________

Reinforce

See Handbook Section 21

An *object complement* is a noun, pronoun, or adjective that follows a direct object and identifies or describes the direct object. An object complement is often used with verbs that create or nominate, such as *make, name, elect, paint, call,* and so on. In the sentence *He painted the fence white*, for example, the adjective *white* is the object complement, since it describes the direct object *fence*. In the sentence *The team elected her captain,* the noun *captain* is an object complement; it identifies what the direct object *her* has been elected to.

Read the passage below. Find each direct object and underline it. Then put a box around each object complement that identifies or describes the direct object. Be careful. Not all sentences contain object complements. (22–36)

The setting sun turned the African landscape pink. The wildlife photographer spied a cheetah across the plain. This sighting made her happy. She would get a perfect photo of the graceful animal!

Suddenly, storm clouds turned the sky black. This change in the weather made the photographer unhappy: it spoiled her perfect photo opportunity. The cheetah gave a high-pitched call and sprinted away. The photographer expressed disappointment. That photo could have made her an award winner!

Predicate Nouns and Predicate Adjectives

Unit 1: Lesson 5

Read and Analyze

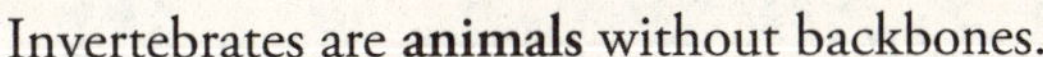

Invertebrates are **animals** without backbones.

Most terrestrial invertebrates are **small**.

Find the simple subject and the linking verb in each sentence above. Put a box around the boldfaced noun that tells who or what the subject of its sentence is. Circle the boldfaced adjective that gives descriptive information about the subject of its sentence.

A **predicate noun** follows a linking verb and tells more about who or what the subject is. A **predicate adjective** follows a linking verb and describes the subject.

See Handbook Section 12

Practice

Underline the linking verb in each sentence. Put a box around each predicate noun. Circle each predicate adjective.

1. Cephalopods are an ancient group of marine invertebrates.
2. They are also a class of mollusks.
3. Mollusks are animals with soft bodies and, in most cases, shells.
4. Some marine biologists are experts on cephalopods.
5. According to these experts, a cephalopod's brain is relatively large.
6. These creatures are the most intelligent of the invertebrates.
7. Squid and octopuses are one variety of cephalopod.
8. Giant squid and colossal squid are two species of squid.
9. In the past, people were awestruck by tales of giant sea monsters.
10. Marine biologists became curious about the existence of gigantic squid.
11. Antarctica's Ross Sea was the site of a major discovery in January 2007.
12. John Bennett is the captain of a New Zealand fishing boat.
13. He was amazed at the sight of a colossal squid tangled in his fishing lines.
14. The adult male squid was enormous—the largest one ever recovered.
15. The creature's weight was about 1,000 pounds.
16. The squid's length was 33 feet.
17. Bennett's capture of the colossal squid was a major contribution to our knowledge of cephalopods.

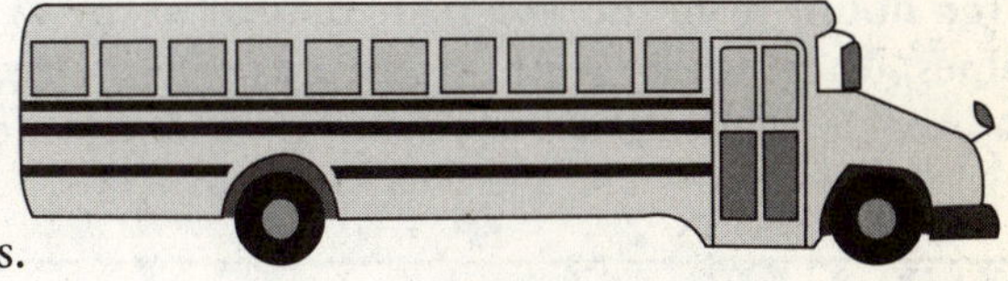

school bus
length: 40 feet

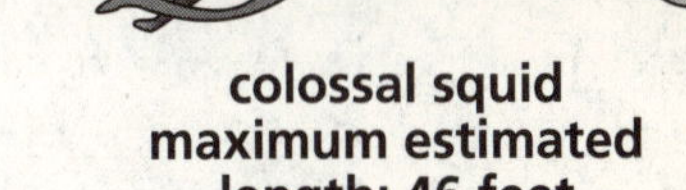

colossal squid
maximum estimated
length: 46 feet

Name ______________________________

Apply

Write a predicate noun or a predicate adjective to complete each sentence.

18. When I look at the ocean, I feel ______________________________.

19. My favorite sea creature is the ______________________________.

20. Invertebrates are ______________________________.

21. Octopuses are ______________________________.

22. Two species of squid are ______________________________.

23. When the researcher saw the giant squid, he became ______________________________.

24. When marine biologists learned of the discovery of the colossal squid, they felt ______________________________.

Reinforce

Ten nouns from the lesson are hidden in the word search puzzle below. Circle them and list them on the lines. Then use some of these words to write two sentences, one with a predicate noun and the other with a predicate adjective. Do this on another sheet of paper.

C	E	P	H	A	L	O	P	O	D	S	D	B
L	Z	K	R	N	S	C	T	J	M	Q	E	I
A	J	Y	H	I	A	T	L	D	A	U	R	O
S	V	T	D	M	B	O	Q	F	H	I	J	L
S	H	E	L	L	S	P	Z	M	L	D	P	O
D	S	M	O	L	L	U	S	K	S	R	C	G
P	V	C	L	S	C	S	M	Y	H	F	L	I
I	N	V	E	R	T	E	B	R	A	T	E	S
A	N	I	M	A	L	S	L	P	X	Q	V	T
Z	A	Y	I	B	A	C	K	B	O	N	E	S

Nouns

25. ____________________

26. ____________________

27. ____________________

28. ____________________

29. ____________________

30. ____________________

31. ____________________

32. ____________________

33. ____________________

34. ____________________

Read and Analyze

The hummingbirds flew around the garden.

Where did the hummingbirds fly? ______________________________

A **prepositional phrase** can tell *how, what kind, when, how much,* or *where.* A prepositional phrase begins with a **preposition,** such as *about, around, at, by, from, in, into, of, on, over, to,* or *with*. It ends with a noun or pronoun that is the **object of the preposition**. The words between the preposition and its object are part of the prepositional phrase. A prepositional phrase can appear at the beginning, middle, or end of a sentence.

See Handbook Section 20

Practice

Underline each prepositional phrase. Circle the preposition that begins each phrase. Put a box around the object of the preposition. There may be more than one prepositional phrase in each sentence.

1. We are learning about different bird species in science class.
2. Last week, a guest speaker from the bird sanctuary visited our class.
3. Our science teacher introduced the guest speaker to us.
4. The speaker gave an interesting talk on his favorite subject—hummingbirds.
5. He is an expert on these tiny, colorful birds.
6. Hummingbirds are the size of a thumb; their wings can beat 80 times per second.
7. The needle-like beak of a hummingbird can reach into long flower blossoms.
8. Hummingbirds can hover in the air and can fly backward.
9. A hummingbird extracts nectar from flowers with its long, thin tongue.
10. This species of bird is found only in North America and South America.
11. The speaker described his recent trip to Ecuador with a research team.
12. Ecuador is located in northwestern South America.
13. This country has 163 species of hummingbird—the largest number in any one country.
14. The speaker gave us information about Ecuador's hummingbird species.
15. The Esmeraldas Woodstar is a rare hummingbird species found in western Ecuador in a fog forest.
16. This tiny bird is dangerously close to extinction.

Hummingbirds fly from flower to flower in search of nectar.

Name ______________________________

Apply

Rewrite each sentence. Add at least one prepositional phrase to make the sentence give more information. Use prepositional phrases from the work bank, or think of your own.

above the treetops	from the United States	in their natural habitat	in Ecuador
during the day	toward the researchers	near the campground	by plane

17. The researchers traveled to South America. ______________________________

____

18. They explored the tropical rainforest. ______________________________

____

19. The colorful hummingbirds flew. ______________________________

____

20. The researchers observed the hummingbirds. ______________________________

____

Reinforce

See Handbook Section 20

A prepositional phrase can modify, or tell more about, a noun or pronoun. Prepositional phrases that modify nouns or pronouns are called *adjectival prepositional phrases*. An adjectival prepositional phrase usually comes after the noun or pronoun it modifies. A prepositional phrase can also modify a verb, an adverb, or an adjective. This type of prepositional phrase is called an *adverbial prepositional phrase*. Many adverbial prepositional phrases tell *when, where, how,* or *how long* something was done.

Circle the prepositional phrase in each sentence. Draw an arrow to the word or words it modifies. Then, on the line next to each sentence, write whether the phrase is an adjectival prepositional phrase or an adverbial prepositional phrase.

21. In 2004, many scientists visited Germany. ______________

22. A zoologist from Frankfurt presented his findings. ______________

23. The discovery of a possible hummingbird fossil astounded the scientists. ______________

24. The delicate bones of hummingbirds rarely fossilize. ______________

25. The bird fossils were found in southern Germany. ______________

26. The tiny skeletons were unearthed with extreme care. ______________

a. Lonesome George was a Galapagos giant tortoise.

b. Lonesome George, a Galapagos giant tortoise, lived on an island off the coast of Ecuador.

Draw a box around the phrase in sentence *b* that tells who or what Lonesome George is. What punctuation marks separate this phrase from the rest of the sentence? ______________

An **appositive** is a phrase that identifies a noun. An appositive follows the noun it identifies and is usually separated from the rest of the sentence by commas. (The appositive is set off with commas when it is a nonrestrictive element. A phrase is considered a nonrestrictive element when it gives information that is not essential to the meaning of a sentence.)

See Handbook Section 24

Practice

Underline the appositive in each sentence. Draw a box around the noun it identifies.

1. The Galapagos Archipelago, a group of islands in the Pacific Ocean, is located on the equator.
2. Galapagos, a province of Ecuador, is home to a large variety of plants and animals.
3. *Archipelago* comes from the term *galapago,* the Spanish word for *saddle.*
4. The shells of some tortoises on the islands resemble a *galapago,* a type of British riding saddle.
5. Giant tortoises, perhaps the most famous animals in the Galapagos, can weigh over 500 pounds and can live for more than 150 years.
6. One male Galapagos giant tortoise, Lonesome George, was from Pinta Island in the Galapagos.
7. Lonesome George, one of the last known survivors of his species, was thought to be between 60 and 90 years old when he died.
8. Giant tortoises are also found in the Seychelles, a group of islands in the western Indian Ocean.

The Galapagos giant tortoise is one of the largest tortoises on Earth.

9. The Seychelles are located about 1,000 miles east of Kenya, a country in East Africa.
10. The Aldabra Atoll in the outer Seychelles is home to about 152,000 giant tortoises, the world's largest population of the animal.
11. Adwaitya, a giant Aldabra tortoise, died in March 2006 at the age of 255.
12. The tortoise had been living at the Alipore Zoo in Kolkata, an Indian city formerly known as Calcutta.
13. Subir Chowdhury, director of the Alipore Zoo, said records show that the tortoise was born in 1750.
14. The giant tortoise was given as a gift to Robert Clive, one of the founders of British rule in India, in 1875.
15. The tortoise's name, *Adwaitya,* comes from a Sanskrit word meaning "the only one."

Name ______________________________

Apply

Rewrite each pair of sentences as one sentence. Change the underlined sentence into an appositive.

16. Haller Park is an animal sanctuary in Mombasa, Kenya. Haller Park is home to a giant Aldabra tortoise. ______________________________

____

17. Dr. Paula Kahumbu is the manager of Haller Park. Dr. Kahumbu described how an orphan baby hippo befriended the tortoise. ______________________________

____

18. Owen is a baby hippopotamus. Owen lost his mother in the devastating tsunami of December 2004.

____

19. Owen was brought to Haller Park by Dr. Kahumbu and Stephen Tuei. Stephen Tuei is the sanctuary's chief animal caretaker. ______________________________

____

20. Owen was released in Haller Park and ran to Mzee. Mzee is the park's 130-year-old giant Aldabra tortoise. ______________________________

____

Reinforce

See Handbook Section 24

The appositives studied so far have been separated from the rest of the sentence by commas. These appositives give more information about the nouns they describe. However, some appositives should *not* be set off by commas. If an appositive is essential to the meaning of a sentence, it should not be set off by commas. Appositives that are essential to the meaning of a sentence are called *restrictive appositives*. Those that simply provide more information about the nouns they describe are called *nonrestrictive appositives*.

Example

Jeremy Aguilar, my cousin, wrote a report on giant tortoises.
(The nonrestrictive appositive *my cousin* is not essential to the sentence; it gives more information about Jeremy Aguilar and should be set off by commas.)
My cousin Jeremy Aguilar saw giant tortoises at the San Diego Zoo.
(The restrictive appositive *Jeremy Aguilar* is necessary to explain which cousin is meant.)

If necessary, add commas around the appositives in the following sentences. If no commas are necessary, write *C* on the line next to the sentence.

21. My sister Tamara is the youngest of all my sisters. _____
22. Tamara my youngest sister plans to visit the Galapagos Islands someday. _____

Read and Analyze

Walking through the dense Asian forest, the elephants search for food.

Circle the two verbs in the sentence above. Which verb tells what the subject of the sentence does? ______________

Which verb begins a descriptive phrase? ________________

Sometimes a verb does not act as the simple predicate of a sentence. A **verbal** is a word formed from a verb that plays another role in the sentence. One type of verbal is a **participle**. A participle may be a present participle (*covering*) or a past participle (*consumed*). A **participial phrase** is made of a participle and other words that complete its meaning. A participial phrase can act as an adjective. In the sentence above, *Walking through the dense Asian forest* is a participial phrase that describes *elephants*.

See Handbook Sections 18d, 25a

Practice

Underline each participial phrase. Then circle the participle.

1. Visitors traveling to Africa and certain parts of Asia might see elephants.
2. Identified as the largest living land mammal, the African elephant is found in the wild only in Africa.
3. Weighing about 12,000 pounds, an adult male African elephant stands approximately 11 feet tall at the shoulder.
4. Zoologists researching African elephants have determined that there are two different types: bush elephants and forest elephants.
5. The type of African elephant known as the bush elephant is found in most countries south of the Sahara.
6. Inhabiting the countries of central and western Africa, forest elephants live in forests, grasslands, and mountains.

Elephants are highly intelligent and social animals.

7. The type of elephant called the Asian elephant is smaller than the African elephant.
8. Standing 9 to 10½ feet tall at the shoulder, an adult male Asian elephant can weigh up to 8,000 pounds.
9. Found in parts of India and Southeast Asia, Asian elephants are light gray and may have pink or white spots.
10. Two humps located just above the Asian elephant's ears give the animal a distinctive appearance.
11. Scientists studying elephants have discovered many amazing things about them.
12. Experts observing wild elephants have documented their highly complex societies.
13. Possessing special receptors on their feet, elephants can pick up underground vibrations.
14. The animals can sense vibrations indicating potential danger.
15. Elephants living in seaside areas ran to safety in advance of the deadly Indian Ocean tsunami of December 2004.

Name ______________________________

Apply

A participial phrase should be placed near the noun or pronoun it modifies so it does not create confusion for the reader. The participial phrase in each sentence below is misplaced. Rewrite each sentence so that it makes sense.

16. Called one of the most scenic places in Africa, my aunt, uncle, and cousins went on a trip to Kenya. ______________________________

17. Located near the beaches of Kenya's South Coast, they visited an elephant sanctuary. ______________________________

18. Grazing in the tall grass, my cousins Bettina and Kent spied a baby elephant. ______________________________

19. Rolling in the mud, my uncle snapped a picture of a baby elephant. ______________________________

Reinforce

See Handbook Section 25b

An absolute phrase consists of a noun or noun phrase followed by a descriptive word or phrase. Like a participial phrase, an absolute phrase may contain a verbal form ending in *–ing* or *–ed*. It may also contain an adjective, an additional noun phrase, or one or more prepositional phrases.

noun phrase + present participle
The elephants bathed in the river, their mother watching.

noun phrase + adjective + prepositional phrase
A hippo swam upstream, its nose visible above the water.

noun phrase + prepositional phrases
A lioness lay under a tree, her cubs in the grass near her.

Each sentence below is formed incorrectly. Cross out the form of *be* in the second clause to turn the clause into an absolute phrase. Then rewrite each sentence.

20. Sue paddled down the river, her brother was sitting quietly beside her.

____

21. Crocodiles slithered along the bank, their bodies were covered in mud.

____

22. Juan photographed the giraffe, its neck was almost too long for the shot.

____

23. The elephants huddled together, the babies were in the center of the group.

____

a. Lizards belong **to a class** of animals called reptiles.

b. Horned lizards have a unique way **to escape from predators.**

Look at each boldfaced phrase. In which phrase is the word *to* followed by a verb? ________

In which phrase is the word *to* followed by an article and a noun? ________

An **infinitive** is a phrase made up of the word *to* followed by the present form of a verb (*to escape*). Infinitives may act as adjectives, adverbs, or nouns. An **infinitive phrase** is made up of an infinitive and any other words that complete its meaning. In sentence *b* above, *to escape from predators* is an infinitive phrase.

See Handbook Section 25a

Practice

Underline the infinitive phrase in each sentence.

1. I went to the local library to do research on lizards.
2. The librarian helped me to learn the distinguishing characteristics of lizards.
3. I used the library computer to look up information about several lizard species.
4. The largest species of lizard, the Komodo dragon, is able to climb trees.
5. The Komodo dragon's keen sense of smell helps it to find food.
6. When a Komodo dragon bites its prey, deadly bacteria in the lizard's mouth are transmitted to the prey, causing it to die of infection.
7. The flexible skull of the lizard allows it to swallow large chunks of food.
8. Komodo dragons are able to withstand the harsh environment of their habitat.
9. I was amazed to discover that a horned lizard can squirt blood from its eyes.
10. This ability enables the horned lizard to protect itself from predators.
11. The lizard's coloring allows it to blend in with its desert surroundings.
12. The horned lizard's camouflage makes it difficult to spot.
13. During the early part of the day, horned lizards may flatten themselves against rocks to bask in the sun.
14. At night, the lizard uses its spines to dig a hole for itself in the sand.
15. The horned lizard uses its long, sticky tongue to catch ants, its main source of food.

The horned lizard heats itself by basking in the sun.

Name ______________________________

Apply

Write an infinitive from the word bank to complete each sentence.

to pursue	to focus	to discover	to become	to study

16. Someone who wants ____________ a herpetologist, a scientist who studies reptiles and amphibians, must take many science classes.
17. Subjects that herpetologists need ____________ in college include biology and chemistry.
18. A person who wishes ____________ this career needs persistence and determination.
19. Many herpetologists find it exciting ____________ new things about reptiles and amphibians.
20. Herpetologists may want ____________ their research on just one species of reptile or amphibian.

Reinforce

See Handbook Section 25a

A sentence may contain more than one participial phrase (*Caught off guard and flattered by the attention, she thanked us for the surprise party*) or infinitive phrase (*I like to sing and to go fishing*). Using two verbals of the same type to express similar ideas is using *parallel structure*. Using two verbals of different types to express similar ideas—for example, *I like singing and to go fishing*—is considered poor style. In your writing, use parallel structure when expressing two or more similar ideas.

Read the two sentences below. Rewrite the sentence that is not parallel in structure to make it parallel. Write *C* beside the sentence that is parallel in structure.

21. Observing the lizards and taking notes, Graham began the research for his report. ____________

____

____

____

22. Iris likes to hike in the woods and riding her bicycle. ____________

____

____

____

Subjects and Predicates in Sentences With Verbals

Unit 1: Lesson 10

a. Yasmin travels to wild areas to photograph large mammals.

b. She is following tracks made by a grizzly bear.

Which underlined verb in sentence *a* tells what the subject does? _______________ What type of verbal phrase in sentence *a* is the other verb a part of? _______________ Which underlined verb in sentence *b* tells what the subject is doing? _______________ What type of verbal phrase in sentence *b* is the other verb a part of? _______________

Every sentence has at least one **subject-verb relationship**. The subject tells what the sentence is about. The verb tells what the subject does or what the subject is doing, or links the subject to more information about it. Some sentences also contain verbs that are not part of a subject-verb relationship. These verbs are called **verbals**. **Participles** and **infinitives** are types of verbals. Participles and infinitives usually are parts of phrases that describe.

See Handbook Sections 11, 12, 25a

Practice

Draw one line under the simple subject in each sentence. Draw two lines under the simple predicate. Draw a box around each participial phrase. Circle each infinitive phrase.

1. Living mostly in Alaska and western Canada, grizzlies are a type of brown bear.
2. Weighing around 500 pounds, an adult male can be 6 feet in length.
3. A grizzly standing on its hind paws is surveying the surrounding area.
4. Mother bears carefully supervise their cubs to protect them from other predators.
5. These massive creatures hunt small mammals, hoofed animals, and fish, and gather berries, leaves, and roots to eat.
6. Scientists studying grizzly bears have identified more than 100 plants in western North America as parts of these bears' diet.
7. Feeling hunger, a grizzly will use its sensitive ears and nose to locate food.
8. Concerning locations of past food sources, these bears have excellent memory.
9. Observers studying grizzly bears have described them as intelligent and curious.
10. A grizzly uses its long claws to dig up roots.
11. The hump of muscles extending across the grizzly's shoulders provides extra strength for a dig.
12. To accumulate fat for winter, a grizzly eats up to 90 pounds of food each day.
13. Bears living in very cold climates spend the winter inside their dens or caves.
14. Dens are shelters made of branches or dug out of the ground.
15. Grizzlies typically try to avoid contact with humans.
16. A single attack on a human by a grizzly causes many people to regard these bears as ferocious predators.

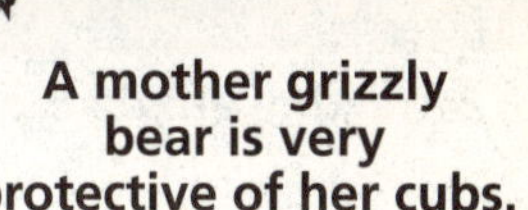

A mother grizzly bear is very protective of her cubs.

Name ______________________________

Apply

Write the correct verbal from the word bank to complete each sentence.

to protect	co-existing	according	respecting	to destroy

17. ______________________ with Native Americans, grizzly bears thrived in North America for thousands of years.

18. ______________________ grizzly bears, Native Americans admired their intelligence and strength.

19. European settlers killed grizzly bears for their fur and began ______________________ their habitat in the mid-1800s.

20. ______________________ to biologists, fewer than 1,000 grizzly bears roam the continental United States today.

21. ______________________ those few that remain, conservationists added the grizzly bear to the endangered species list in 1975.

Reinforce

When a writer uses a verbal phrase instead of a proper subject-verb relationship, the result is a sentence fragment. Identify the sentence fragments below by writing *fragment* on the line. If possible, use a computer's grammar checker to help you do this.

22. Several ways for humans to protect themselves from grizzly bears. ______________________

23. Campers should store all food in bear-resistant containers to keep bears away. ______________________

24. Attracting grizzly bears, scented items such as chocolate, candy, or toothpaste. ______________________

25. To avoid surprising a grizzly bear, hikers should talk or sing songs. ______________________

26. Never approach or feed a bear crossing your path. ______________________

27. Being responsible, keeping both humans and bears safe. ______________________

a. Hippopotamuses do look cute. However, they are aggressive and dangerous.

b. Many people see hippopotamuses as cute, humorous, even lovable creatures. In reality, though, hippos are among the most aggressive of all creatures; and, because of their enormous size and considerable speed, they are among the most dangerous.

Which paragraph presents more key information? _____ What are some of the differences between the sentences in paragraph *a* and the sentences in paragraph *b* above? ____

____

____

Sentences that include details, descriptive words, and words with precise meanings **give more information.** Sentences that combine connected facts or ideas **make clear important relationships.** Just adding more words to a sentence doesn't make it more effective, however. When you write, **expand or combine sentences** to help readers better understand what you are discussing.

See Handbook Sections 13, 16, 19, 20, 22

Practice

Draw a star by the paragraph in each item that more effectively presents key information.

1. The name *hippopotamus* means "river horse" in Greek. Hippos resemble pigs, but they are most closely related to whales, dolphins, and porpoises.

The ancient Greeks gave this remarkable creature the name *hippopotamus*, meaning "river horse." Many of the hippo's physical features, including its girth, teeth, and toes, resemble those of pigs. Advanced scientific analysis has shown, however, that the hippo's closest relatives are not land animals; they are sea creatures—whales, dolphins, and porpoises!

2. Hippos are the third-largest land creature in size and weight; only elephants and rhinoceroses are larger. Hippos live in warm regions of Africa and spend their days submerged in rivers, lakes, or ponds; the water keeps them cool and helps support their enormous weight.

Hippos are huge. They live in warm parts of Africa. They stay underwater during the day.

3. Hippos emerge from the water at dusk each evening to feed. These herbivores prefer to graze on short grasses, but they eat many other types of plants as well. A feeding session can last as long as six hours.

At the end of the day, hippos leave their watery homes and trot across the land to find grassy areas to graze on. They don't just grab a quick bite; they may spend four, five, or six hours eating before they return to the water. Also, they don't just eat grass. A hungry hippo will eat a wide variety of plants.

Name ______________________________

Apply

Work with a partner to search the Internet to find more information on hippopotamuses in zoos. Then rewrite the paragraph below, expanding and combining sentences so that it gives more information and makes clear important relationships.

Hippos have been popular animals in zoos for a long time. A hippo in a zoo was kept in a small cemented area with a pool and a patch of grass. Now some zoos have created areas for hippos that are more like their homes in the wild. The Toledo Zoo is one of these.

____

____

____

____

____

____

____

____

____

____

____

____

Reinforce

On the lines below, rewrite a paragraph from a report or story you have written recently. Expand and combine sentences so the paragraph helps readers better understand what you are discussing.

____

____

____

____

____

____

____

Read and Analyze

Read this paragraph. It contains the four kinds of sentences.

Will gorillas be able to survive in the wild? Their numbers have declined sharply in recent years. What a tragedy it would be to have these gentle, intelligent creatures become extinct! Think about what the world's people can do to help ensure gorillas' survival.

Circle the sentence that makes a statement. Draw a box around the sentence that asks a question. Draw two lines under the sentence that gives a command. Draw one line under the sentence that expresses strong emotion.

A **declarative sentence** makes a statement and ends with a period. An **interrogative sentence** asks a question and ends with a question mark. An **imperative sentence** gives a command and ends with a period or an exclamation point. An **exclamatory sentence** shows excitement and ends with an exclamation point. Begin every sentence with an uppercase letter.

See Handbook Section 10

Practice

Add the correct punctuation mark to each sentence. Then label it *declarative, interrogative, imperative,* or *exclamatory.*

1. Where is the region known as Equatorial Africa ____________
2. It is in the part of Africa nearest the equator ____________
3. Find the nations of Uganda, Rwanda, and Democratic Republic of Congo on a map of Africa ____________
4. Eastern lowland gorillas, one of four subspecies of gorillas, live in these nations ____________
5. Consider the likelihood of survival for the 5,000 Eastern lowland gorillas that remain in the wild ____________
6. How scarce Eastern mountain gorillas have become ____________
7. Are there fewer than 1,000 of this subspecies remaining in the world ____________
8. This tiny population lives in the Virunga mountain area, where the three nations come together ____________
9. Western lowland gorillas face many threats, but their numbers remain in excess of 150,000 ____________
10. Will the other subspecies, the Cross River gorilla, be enabled to survive ____________
11. Picture a population of only 300 gorillas ____________
12. Thank goodness international organizations such as WWF Global are working to protect gorillas and their habitats ____________

Name ______________________________

Apply

Rewrite each sentence so it is the type of sentence indicated in parentheses.

13. You should read this article about gorilla behavior. (imperative)

____

14. Gorillas' arms are longer than their legs. (interrogative)

____

15. Do gorillas often use both arms and legs in walking? (declarative)

____

16. Gorillas are shy. (exclamatory)

____

17. Do gorillas live in groups of six to twelve, with a large male as the leader? (declarative)

____

18. What great responsibilities the leader has as decision-maker and protector of the group! (interrogative)

____

Reinforce

Each kind of sentence can be structured in different ways to achieve different effects. Read the statement below by gorilla researcher Dian Fossey.

The more you learn about the dignity of the gorilla, the more you want to avoid people.

19. What type of sentence is this? ______________________________

20. What does Fossey compare in this sentence? ______________________________

21. How does the structure of the sentence emphasize the comparison and increase its impact?

____

____

____

____

Subjects and Predicates

Underline the complete subject in each sentence. Circle the simple subject. If the understood subject is *you*, write *you* on the line.

1. Come with us to the marine animal park. ________
2. The star of the show is a bottle-nosed dolphin. ________

Underline the complete predicate in each sentence. Circle the simple predicate.

3. These acrobats of the marine world leap in formation.
4. Dolphins swim in large groups in the wild.

Draw one line under each compound subject in these sentences, and circle each simple subject in the compound subject. Draw two lines under each compound predicate, and draw a box around each simple predicate in the compound predicate.

5. A dolphin breathes and expels water through a blowhole on its head.
6. Herring, sardines, and other fish are favorite dolphin foods.
7. Agile dolphins swim very fast and leap high out of the water.
8. Happy passengers and members of the crew spot dolphins in front of their ship.

Objects, Predicate Nouns, and Predicate Adjectives

Circle the term in parentheses that correctly describes the boldfaced word in each sentence.

9. Many varieties of tuna are **valuable** to fishermen. (direct object/predicate adjective)
10. Dolphins often accompany the **schools** of tuna. (direct object/predicate noun)
11. One of the tools used to ensnare dolphins is a **net**. (direct object/predicate noun)
12. New kinds of nets give **dolphins** an escape route. (indirect object/direct object)

Appositives

Underline the appositive in each sentence.

13. The sound waves bounce off the object and return to the dolphin, a creature sensitive to such waves.
14. From the echoes, the returning sound waves, the dolphin can tell an object's size, shape, and location.
15. Bats, flying mammals, use a similar system.

Unit 1 Review Name ______________________

Prepositional Phrases

Underline the prepositional phrase or phrases in each sentence. Circle each preposition. Draw a box around its object.

16. Humans have been very fond of dolphins for a long time.
17. Our relationship with dolphins is featured in many stories.
18. In one ancient Greek story, a dolphin saves a drowning boy.

Circle each adjectival prepositional phrase. Underline each adverbial prepositional phrase. Draw a box around the word each phrase modifies.

19. Dolphins communicate without any vocal cords.
20. A dolphin's whistles, squeaks, and clicks apparently transmit information to other dolphins.
21. Sounds waves from a dolphin's clicks move outward toward objects.

Verbals

Draw one line under the simple subject in each sentence. Draw two lines under the simple predicate. Draw a box around each participial phrase. Circle each infinitive phrase.

22. You can learn to tell alligators and crocodiles apart.
23. To see the main difference between a crocodile and an alligator, you must compare the animals' snouts.
24. Looking at the snouts, you will notice a broader snout on the alligator than on the crocodile.
25. Dining mostly on fish, alligators also occasionally eat crustaceans, insects, and small animals.

Sentences

Expand and combine these sentences so they tell more and make relationships clearer.

26. Sloths move slowly. Predators consider them unappetizing.

____

27. Porcupines move slowly. Their quills discourage most predators.

____

Add the correct punctuation mark to each sentence. Then label it *declarative, interrogative, imperative,* or *exclamatory.*

28. What an awesome sight a moose is ______________________
29. Have you visited Glacier National Park ______________________
30. Hikers often see moose there ______________________
31. Bring binoculars and a camera if you go ______________________

Spelling Practice

Read and Analyze

The speed a running cheetah can achieve is **extraordinary.** This lightning-fast cat can sprint at up to 75 miles per hour.

What is the suffix in the word in bold type? ___________ What does the word mean? ___________

Adding Suffixes: *-ary, -ory*

The suffixes *-ary* and *-ory* can be added to the ends of roots and base words to create adjectives, as in *primary* and *satisfactory*. The spelling of the base word sometimes needs to be changed before these suffixes can be added. For example, the silent **e** at the end of *imagine* is dropped before *-ary* is added to form *imaginary.*

Word Sort

Use the words below to complete the word sort.

momentary	honorary	circulatory	preparatory	secondary	advisory
auditory	contrary	sensory	legendary	migratory	customary

Suffix *-ary*	Suffix *-ory*

Name ______________________________

Pattern Practice

advisory	legendary	mandatory	customary	literary	migratory
momentary	sensory	involuntary	elementary	contrary	complimentary

Add *-ary* or *-ory* to each base word. Change the spelling of the base word as needed.

1. custom ____________________
2. compliment ____________________
3. advise ____________________
4. migrate ____________________
5. moment ____________________
6. element ____________________
7. legend ____________________
8. sense ____________________

Write the word from the word bank above that best completes each sentence.

9. My sister's ____________________ school is two blocks from here.
10. The school has a ____________________ fire drill once a month.
11. These ducks are ____________________ birds that summer in the north.
12. Your information is ____________________ to everything else I've heard.
13. Anne's ____________________ club reads and discusses books.
14. It is ____________________ for Rob's family to eat dinner at 6:00.
15. Quinn's kind remarks were very ____________________.

Use the Dictionary

Circle the word in each pair that best completes the sentence. Use a print or an online dictionary to confirm word meanings.

16. Kyle listens well and is more of an auditory/sensory learner.
17. Arteries and veins are part of the subsidiary/circulatory system.
18. I prefer contemporary/involuntary writing to the classics.

(you) | Diagram | sentences

See Handbook Section 41

A **sentence diagram** is a picture of a sentence that shows how the parts of the sentence fit together. Diagramming sentences can help you understand how the words in a sentence are related.

Diagramming Subjects and Verbs

A short sentence consisting of a simple subject and a simple predicate is diagrammed this way:

Owls hoot. Owls | hoot

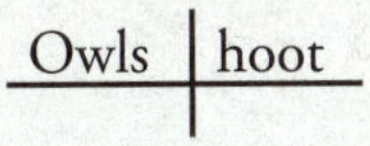

Look at the structure of the diagram. Based on its structure, complete these sentences.

1. The simple subject and simple predicate go on a ________________ line.
   horizontal/vertical
2. A ________________ line separates the subject and predicate.
   horizontal/vertical
3. The subject goes to the __________ of the vertical line, and the predicate goes to the
   left/right
   __________.
   left/right

Use what you have learned to diagram these sentences. Include only the simple subject and the simple predicate. Ignore all the other words in the sentences.

4. The sun disappeared.
5. The owls awoke.
6. Rodents scurried.

Diagramming Adjectives and Articles

An adjective (describing word) or an article (*a, an, the*) goes on a slanted line below the word it modifies. Look at the way this sentence has been diagrammed.

The bright sun disappeared. sun | disappeared (The, bright on slanted lines below sun)

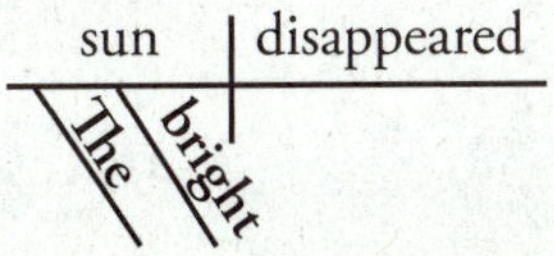

Now diagram these sentences.

7. The sleepy owls awoke.

Name ____

8. Hungry rodents scurried.

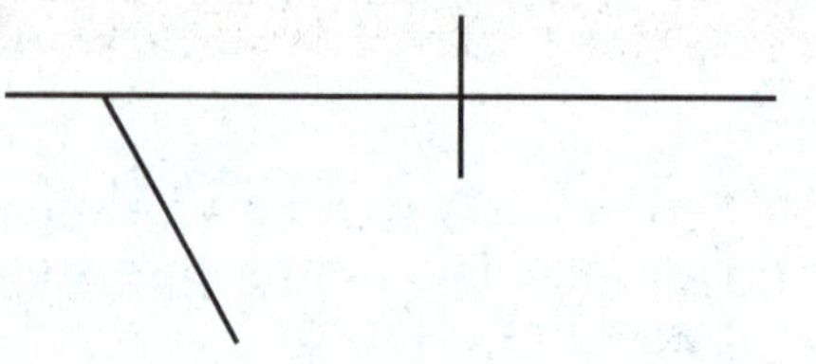

9. A full moon shone.

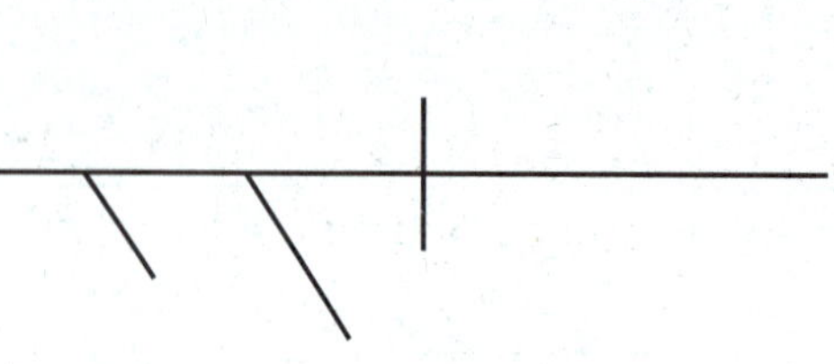

Diagramming Direct Objects

A direct object (a noun or pronoun that receives the action of the verb) is placed on a horizontal line to the right of the verb. Notice how the diagram changes when a direct object is added.

Most owls eat **rodents**.

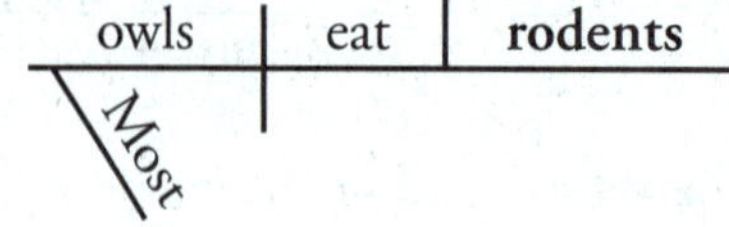

How is the vertical line that separates the direct object and the verb different from the vertical line that separates the subject and predicate?

____

____

Use what you have learned to diagram the simple subjects, simple predicates, adjectives, articles, and direct objects in these sentences.

10. The owl hears the busy rodents.

11. Sharp ears locate prey.

12. Two beady eyes watch the prey.

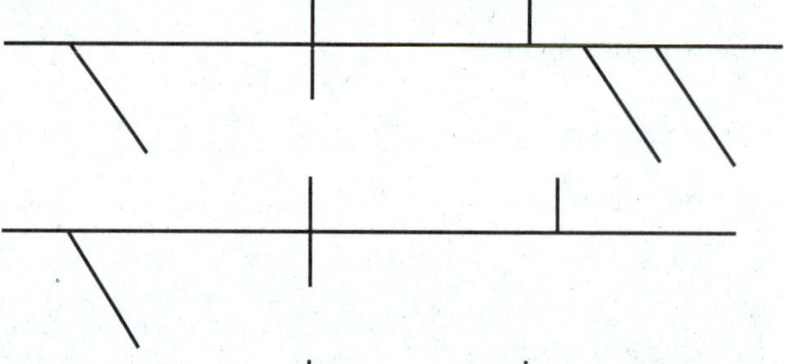

Now diagram these sentences on another sheet of paper.

13. Many owls have special silent wings.

14. Soundless owls surprise their prey.

15. These stealthy hunters swallow the entire creature.

16. The owl regurgitates the indigestible matter.

17. Indigestible matter includes fur.

18. Owls eject the bones.

19. Tree holes make good nests.

20. Brown feathers camouflage owls.

These sentences need your help. Rewrite each one so it is clearer and makes better sense.

1. Our city's new aquarium offers amazing sights and sounds, more of them than any other attraction in the area. ______________________________

2. Visitors find themselves staring down into a pond filled with twenty huge alligators entering the building. ______________________________

3. In one large gallery visitors can pick up and listen to starfish and the songs of humpback whales. ______________________________

4. A rare opportunity to see nature's marine marvels up close is offered at this wonderful new facility; you should definitely visit it soon. ______________________________

5. In another room they can stand in the middle of a great hollow glass cylinder, and big fish swim around and around. ______________________________

All the sentences in a paragraph relate to a single topic. A paragraph should have a topic sentence, at least two supporting sentences, and a concluding sentence. Notice these kinds of sentences in this model paragraph. Also notice its purpose: it is trying to persuade readers to do something.

topic sentence (states the main idea you are making)

supporting sentences (give details to support your main idea)

concluding sentence (summarizes the paragraph or restates the topic sentence)

No living room is complete without a fish tank full of guppies. Guppies are energetic, colorful fish that breed easily. Because there are many colors of guppies, you can create an aquarium with a unique look. You can choose blue or red guppies to contrast with your green plants. If you put different colors of guppies together, you will soon have a tank full of multicolored baby guppies. **If you want a truly striking aquarium that catches everyone's eye, you should fill it with guppies.**

Name ______________________________

Writing a Paragraph

The sentences you repaired on page 39 can be reordered to make a persuasive paragraph. Decide which sentence is the topic sentence, which are the three supporting sentences, and which is the concluding sentence. Reorder the sentences, and write the paragraph on the lines below.

Think of a great place for people to go to see astounding animals. Write a paragraph that would convince people to visit that place. Describe some amazing things they might experience there. Be sure to include an enticing topic sentence, at least two vivid supporting sentences, and an enthusiastic concluding sentence.

Read your paragraph again. Use this checklist to make sure it is complete and correct.

- ❑ My paragraph has a topic sentence.
- ❑ My paragraph has at least two supporting sentences.
- ❑ All my sentences are clear and make sense.
- ❑ I have used prepositional phrases correctly.
- ❑ My paragraph has a concluding sentence.

Proofreading Practice

Read this passage about whales and find the mistakes. Use the proofreading marks to show how the mistakes should be fixed. Use a dictionary to check and correct spellings.

Proofreading Marks

Mark	Means	Example
℘	delete	Baleen whales ~~have~~ have no teeth.
^	add	Baleen whales ^have no teeth.
≡	make into an uppercase letter	baleen whales have no teeth.
/	make into a lowercase letter	Baleen Whales have no teeth.
⊙	add a period	Baleen whales have no teeth⊙
(sp)	fix spelling	Baleen wails have no teeth.

Whales

The whale may look like a giant fish but, it is not a fish at all. It is a mamal, like a mouse or a human being. This means that it has to come up to the ocean's surface to breathe, which it does through a blowhole located at the top of it's head. Some whales can hold their breathe for up to two hours!

Scientists place whales into two major groups: the baleen whales and the toothed whales. Toothed whales, as they're name suggests, have teeth baleen whales do not have teeth. Instead, they have hundreds of tall, thin plates. Hanging from the upper jaw. These plates are made of the same material as human fingernails. The plates, together called the baleen, filter food from water. baleen whales eat mostly plankton, small plant and anamal organisms that float around the ocean. Most toothed whales, on the other hand, eat fish or squid their diet might even include octopuses or crabs.

Both kinds of whales have a layer of fat, or blubber, under there skin. This blubber can be up to 20 inches thick, it helps to keep them warm in cold waters. Because blubber is stored enenrgy, whales are able to go a long time without eating. They do this especially when migrating or breeding.

Name ____________________________

Proofreading Checklist

You can use the checklist below to help you find and fix mistakes in your own writing. Write the titles of your own stories or reports in the blanks at the top of the chart. Then use the questions to check your work. Make a check mark (✓) in each box after you have checked that item.

Proofreading Checklist for Unit 1

Titles				
Does each sentence have a subject and a predicate?				
Have I used appositives correctly?				
Have I used prepositional, participial, and infinitive phrases to make my writing more precise?				
Have I varied the length and type of sentences to add variety to my writing?				
Do all my sentences state complete thoughts?				

Also Remember...

Does each sentence begin with an uppercase letter?				
Does each sentence end with the right end mark?				
Have I spelled each word correctly?				
Have I used commas correctly?				
Did I use a dictionary to check and correct spellings?				

Your Own List

Use this space to write your own list of things to check in your writing.

Community Connection

In Unit 1 of *Grammar, Usage, and Mechanics,* students learned about **different types of sentences and sentence structures** and used what they learned to improve their own writing. The content of these lessons focuses on the theme **Astounding Animals.** As students completed the exercises, they learned about numerous creatures with remarkable attributes. These pages offer a variety of activities that reinforce skills and concepts presented in the unit. They also provide opportunities for students to make connections between the information presented in the lessons and animal-related activities going on today in the community.

A Pal to a Pet

Find out which pet care facilities in your area allow students to volunteer. You may be able to volunteer at a local Humane Society to play with pets and take them for walks. Dogs and cats need regular human attention and can become stressed and unhappy if left alone for too long. You'll have fun as you perform a valuable service.

Watch the Birds

Go on a bird-watching expedition. Wherever you live, you can easily find somewhere to observe birds. In dense urban areas, birds congregate at places they might find food and water, such as parks, outdoor café tables, and public fountains. In the country, you don't need to look far to find birds. Different types of birds live in fields, scrubby brush, and wetlands. You may even have a bird feeder at your own house. Wherever you go bird watching, take a notebook and a pencil with you and write descriptive information about each bird you see.

Internet Creatures

The Internet contains a vast network of information about nearly every possible topic. Conduct a Web search for "unusual animals" and bookmark your most interesting results. Whenever you find amazing animal pictures, copy the pictures to your desktop. Make an online photo album with these photos to share with friends and family. To make the album instructional, look up each animal in an online encyclopedia and write a short caption to go with each picture.

Habitat Helper—Animal Careers

Learn about job opportunities for people who love animals. Such opportunities may include careers in biology and other life sciences, forestry and park management, veterinary medicine, and pet training, grooming, breeding, and showing. Organizations that can give you more information about animal careers include your local Humane Society, your State Department of Wildlife (which may also be called the Department of Fish and Game), and your nearest zoo. Choose one occupation that interests you and learn more about it.

- What skills are required to do this job?
- What education and training would I need for this job?
- How can I get this education and training?
- How long does it take to become proficient at this work?
- What is a typical working day like in this profession?

If possible, interview an adult you know who has a job working with animals. Take notes during the interview, and share the results of the interview with your class. Use the planning guide on the next page to help you plan the interview and organize your notes.

Name ____________________

Interview Planner

Person I am interviewing:

Name ____________________

Age ____________________

Occupation ____________________

Number of years employed in that field ____________________

Date of interview: ____________________

Questions to ask:

1. ____________________
2. ____________________
3. ____________________
4. ____________________
5. ____________________
6. ____________________
7. ____________________
8. ____________________

Notes:

____

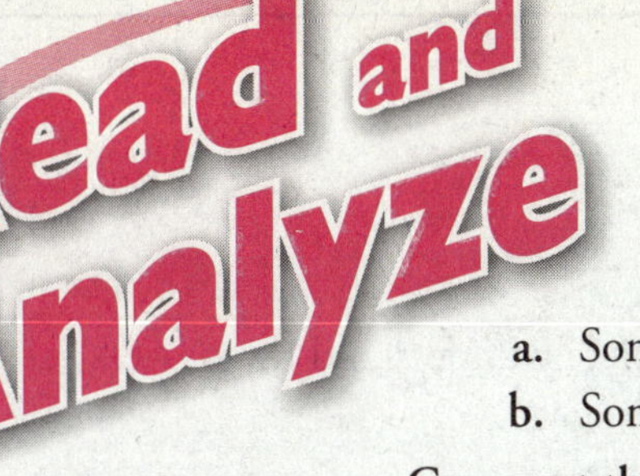

a. Some deserts were once forests **or** lakes.
b. Some dry lands are becoming deserts, **and** some deserts are spreading.

Cross out the boldfaced conjunction in each sentence. Which sentence could be written as two separate sentences? _______

A **simple sentence** is made up of a subject and a predicate and expresses only one complete thought. It is an *independent clause*. A **compound sentence** is made of two closely related independent clauses. The two clauses can be joined by a comma and a coordinating conjunction (*and, but,* or *or*) or by a semicolon (;).

See Handbook Sections 8, 13, 22

Practice

Write *S* next to each simple sentence. Write *CD* next to each compound sentence. Circle the comma and conjunction or the semicolon in each compound sentence.

1. Not all dry regions are deserts, but all dry regions are fragile ecosystems. _____
2. A dry, fragile ecosystem may be threatened by excessive human activities such as cultivation, irrigation, and industry, and it becomes vulnerable to desertification. _____
3. *Desertification* refers to the process of dry areas becoming deserts. _____
4. Water is lost off the land instead of soaking into the soil to provide moisture for plants; this leads to reduced plant and animal life. _____
5. Areas with fewer plants cannot sustain existing animal populations; these populations then begin to disappear. _____
6. The dry heat also affects the delicate ecosystem. _____
7. The hot sun heats the exposed rocks, and the rocks eventually crack and crumble. _____
8. Wind picks up and smashes the rock pieces, and they become sand. _____
9. Desertification exists on every continent except Antarctica, but many people are fighting it. _____
10. Desertification can be fought with new plantings of hardy, native trees and shrubs. _____
11. Water conservation and wise use of resources by humans can stop desertification in some areas. _____

Camels scavenge for vegetation as a result of desertification in Sudan, Africa.

Name ____________________

Apply

Rewrite each pair of simple sentences as one compound sentence.

12. Scientists have studied the formation of deserts. They do not completely understand the process yet.

13. Some deserts form because of human activity. Others form naturally.

14. Forests once covered much of North Africa. Now, the Sahara desert exists in that same area.

15. The lands in Death Valley National Park in California are bone-dry now. In prehistoric times a huge lake existed there.

16. The earth's climate grew warmer over time. The lake dried up.

Reinforce

See Handbook Sections 36, 37

Use the Internet or an encyclopedia to research the Dust Bowl period of the 1930s in the United States. Then write three compound sentences about this event.

17.

18.

19.

Read and Analyze

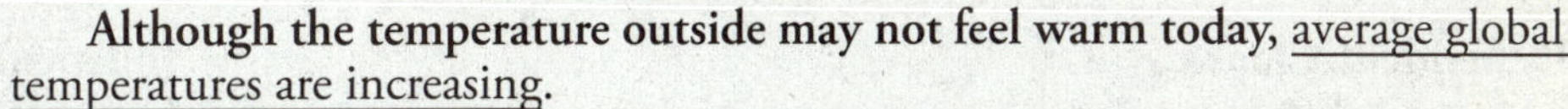

Although the temperature outside may not feel warm today, average global temperatures are increasing.

Look at the two parts of this sentence, the boldfaced part and the underlined part. Which part makes sense by itself? ______________________________

An **independent clause** is a group of words with a subject and a predicate that makes sense by itself. A **dependent clause** has a subject and a predicate, but it does not express a complete thought by itself. It needs—or is dependent on—an independent clause. Often a dependent clause begins with a subordinating conjunction such as *although, because, if, as,* or *when*. When a dependent clause is an introductory element in a sentence, use a comma to separate it from the rest of the sentence.

See Handbook Sections 8, 13, 22

Practice

Draw one line under each independent clause. Draw two lines under each dependent clause. Circle the subordinating conjunction that begins each dependent clause.

A polar bear on sea ice watches for seals that come to the surface to breathe.

1. Because average global temperatures are increasing, the earth is experiencing global warming, or climate change.
2. Scientists labeled recent temperature increases abnormal after they studied temperature data from the past 1,000 years.
3. Although some temperature fluctuations are normal, human activities almost certainly are accelerating the recent increases.
4. When the temperature rises, changes to the environment can be significant.
5. Glaciers and sea ice melt when temperatures increase.
6. Polar bears could be harmed by this melting since sea ice is a critical habitat for them.
7. These hunters spend much of their time on the sea ice where they stalk seals.
8. Because sea ice now melts sooner in spring and forms later in fall, polar bears have fewer good hunting months.
9. Many polar bears apparently are thinner than normal because the sea ice now melts three weeks earlier.
10. Although Alaska remains a cold region, average temperatures there have risen.
11. Even though an increase of 5.4 degrees sounds small, it can cause big changes.
12. When temperatures in the Arctic increase, permanently frozen ground called permafrost thaws.
13. The ground becomes unstable and uneven as the permafrost layer softens.
14. As the ground shifts, it can twist railroad tracks and damage the foundations of buildings.
15. While scientists document these changes, some people are working on solutions.

Name ______________________________

Apply

Draw a line to match each dependent clause with an independent clause. Then write the new sentences you have created on the lines. Be sure to add punctuation. (16–20)

Dependent Clauses	Independent Clauses
when scientists studied climate changes	polar bears may go hungry
as the planet warms up	they found that average global temperatures have increased rapidly recently
if permafrost thaws	a small increase in temperature can have big effects
if sea ice melts early	disruptive events are occurring
because the environment is so delicate	structures can be damaged

21. ______________________________

____

22. ______________________________

____

23. ______________________________

____

24. ______________________________

____

25. ______________________________

____

Reinforce

On the lines below, write three dependent clauses about climate change. (Example: *if the temperatures in Antarctica increase significantly*) Trade papers with a partner. Complete your partner's sentences by writing an independent clause to go with each dependent clause. Trade papers again and read the sentences your partner completed.

26. ______________________________

27. ______________________________

28. ______________________________

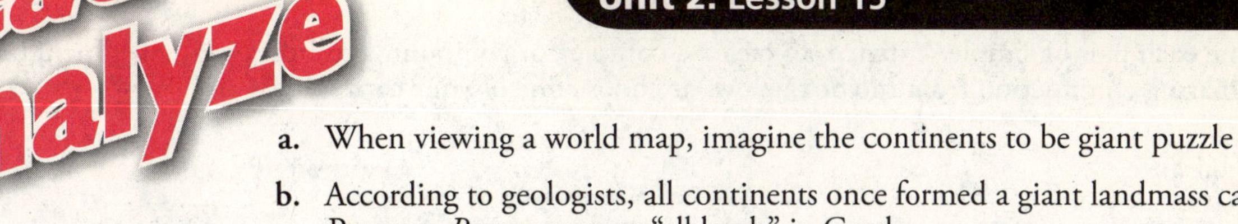

a. When viewing a world map, imagine the continents to be giant puzzle pieces.

b. According to geologists, all continents once formed a giant landmass called Pangaea; *Pangaea* means "all lands" in Greek.

Cross out the comma in sentence *a* and the semicolon in sentence *b*. Which sentence begins with words that would *not* be a sentence if a period replaced the crossed-out comma or semicolon? _______ Which sentence would become two separate sentences if a period were added at the end of its first clause? _______

A dependent clause must be joined with an independent clause to become a sentence. A sentence made up of an independent clause and a dependent clause is a **complex sentence**. A sentence made up of two independent clauses and a dependent clause is a **compound-complex sentence.**

See Handbook Sections 8, 13, 22

Practice

Write *CD* next to each compound sentence. Write *CX* next to each complex sentence. Write *CCX* next to each compound-complex sentence. Then underline each dependent clause and draw a box around each independent clause.

1. Pangaea apparently existed about 200 million years ago; it was surrounded by one ocean, which scientists call Panthalassa. _____
2. After Pangaea had existed for a long time, it split into two separate continents. _____
3. The northern continent included present-day North America and Europe, and most of present-day Asia; this ancient continent has been given the name Laurasia. _____
4. The southern continent has been given the name Gondwanaland; it included present-day Africa, Antarctica, Australia, South America, and India. _____
5. Landmasses move around the globe because they are situated on slabs of rock called plates. _____
6. When German scientist Alfred Wegener first proposed the idea of drifting continents in 1912, his peers ridiculed it; however, Wegener had evidence supporting his theory. _____
7. Because fossils in South America match fossils in Africa and Australia, South America probably was connected to those continents long ago. _____
8. After two other scientists refined Wegener's theory of continental drift, more researchers found it convincing. _____
9. Scientists Harry Hess and Robert Dietz added information about changes in the lands beneath the ocean; according to Hess and Dietz, seafloors spread and continents shift because plates under the ocean floor move against or away from each other. _____
10. When plates move, they can cause earthquakes or create volcanoes. _____

Name ______________________________

Apply

Combine each pair of simple sentences to create a complex or compound-complex sentence. Include a subordinating conjunction from the box below, or choose one of your own.

because	after	since	although	if

11. It may not feel like it. Continents continue to shift today. ______________________________

12. You feel an earthquake. You are sensing plate movements. ______________________________

13. Many scientists believe Africa and South America must have been interlocked. The geological structures of rock in southwest Africa and southeast Brazil are identical. ______________________________

14. The theory that Pangaea existed is now widely accepted. Extensive geological evidence supports it.

____

15. According to some scientists, the continents may drift back together. That day, if it comes, would be very far in the future. ______________________________

Reinforce

Write a paragraph about a place in your area where you could go to see evidence of Earth's constant change. Describe what you might see there and what these sights might reveal about change over time. Include at least one complex or compound-complex sentence in your paragraph.

____

Read and Analyze

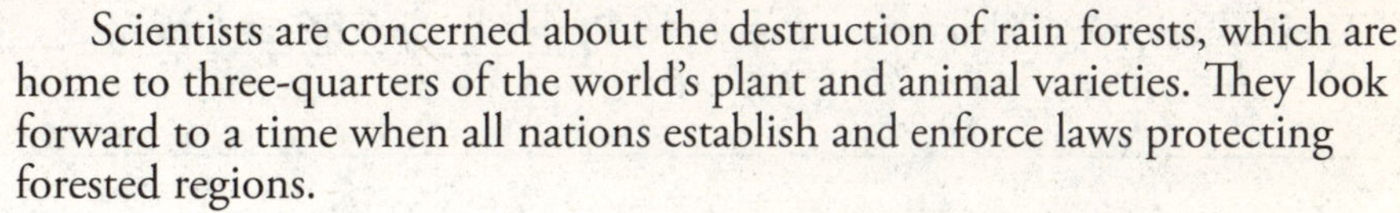

Scientists are concerned about the destruction of rain forests, which are home to three-quarters of the world's plant and animal varieties. They look forward to a time when all nations establish and enforce laws protecting forested regions.

Draw one line under the dependent clause that gives descriptive information about rain forests. Circle the first word in this clause. Draw two lines under the dependent clause that explains what sort of time scientists hope will come. Draw a box around the first word in this clause.

An **adjective clause** is a **dependent clause** that describes a noun or a pronoun. An adjective clause can begin with a **relative pronoun,** such as *that, who, whom,* or *which;* or it can begin with a **relative adverb,** such as *when, where,* or *why.*

See Handbook Sections 8, 13, 17g, 19

Practice

Underline the adjective clause in each sentence. If the first word in the clause is a relative pronoun, circle that word. If the first word in the clause is a relative adverb, draw a box around the word.

1. Rain forests, which cover about 2 percent of the earth's surface, are being destroyed.
2. Logging and clearing land for agriculture are two reasons why rain forests are being cut down.
3. Destruction of rain forests means loss of habitat for the creatures that live there.
4. Tree-dwelling animals cannot remain in areas where all vegetation has been removed to create pasture land.
5. When loggers harvest rain forest timber, birds that nest in trees must move to other areas.
6. After its big trees have been logged, a forest that had been thick and humid becomes thin and dry.
7. Forests where large healthy trees have been cut are more vulnerable to fire.
8. *Deforestation*, which means "the removal of forests," also affects the soil.
9. Soil in areas where rain forest vegetation has been removed loses its nutrients.
10. One reason why many scientists oppose rain forest destruction is the loss of potentially valuable plant species.
11. According to botanists whose research focuses on tropical plants, many varieties of plants there are undiscovered.
12. Plants that grow only in rain forests have yielded several important anti-cancer drugs.

Deforestation causes many changes to the environment and landscape.

Name ______________________________

Apply

Rewrite each pair of sentences as one complex sentence. Change the underlined sentence into an adjective clause.

13. Deforestation can also devastate people. People live in the rain forests. ______________________________

____

14. These people rely on the forest for food and shelter. The forest is the place where they live. ______________________________

____

15. Sometimes loggers damage places. These places are very important to local people for religious reasons.

____

____

16. In some cases, though, forest communities want more contact with the modern world. The modern world can offer them jobs, roads, schools, and medical care. ______________________________

____

____

Reinforce

When a dependent clause acts like a noun, it is called a noun clause. The noun clause can be the subject or object of a verb. Words often used to begin noun clauses include *that, whichever, who, what, where, when,* and *why.*

I have learned that rain forests are in danger.

The dependent clause *that rain forests are in danger* functions as a noun: it is the direct object of the verb *have learned.*

Underline each dependent clause in the sentences below. Then write *noun* if the clause is a noun clause, and write *adjective* if the clause is an adjective clause.

17. Scientists have shown that deforestation can cause landslides. ______________________________

18. Without the trees that normally keep a hillside stable, rocks and soil can easily slide down. ______________________________

19. Scientists say that continued deforestation will cause the extinction of certain species. ______________________________

20. I will join an organization that opposes harmful deforestation. ______________________________

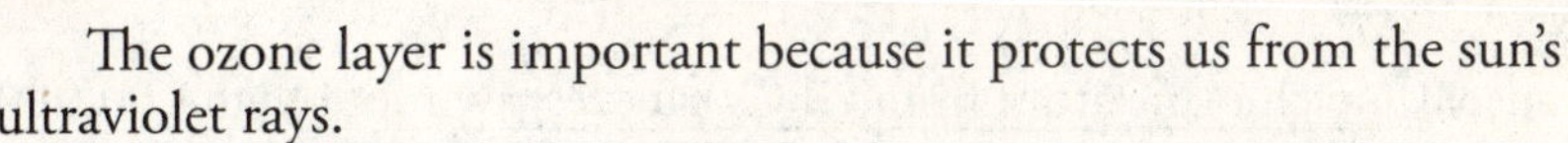

Read and Analyze

The ozone layer is important because it protects us from the sun's ultraviolet rays.

Underline the dependent clause that tells why the ozone layer is important. Does this part of the sentence make sense by itself? ________

An **adverb clause** is a dependent clause that tells about a verb, an adjective, or an adverb. Adverb clauses tell *where, when, why,* or *how much*. They often begin with a subordinating conjunction such as *than, although, because, if, as, as if, while, when,* or *whenever*.

See Handbook Sections 8, 13, 22

Practice

Underline the adverb clause in each sentence.

1. Although you cannot see it, the ozone layer exists about 31 miles high in the atmosphere.
2. When the sun is shining, it is sending harmful ultraviolet rays toward Earth.
3. The ozone layer protects us because it absorbs some of these ultraviolet rays.
4. When scientists discovered a thinning of the ozone layer above Antarctica, they called it the ozone hole.
5. The ozone hole occurs every August, when it is winter in the Southern Hemisphere.
6. When there is less ozone in the atmosphere, more ultraviolet rays hit Earth.
7. Ultraviolet rays are a health concern because they can cause skin cancer.
8. Eyes can also be damaged when they are exposed to ultraviolet rays.
9. If ultraviolet rays increase, animals will experience more health problems too.
10. Although it seems that animals in the ocean are safe from the harmful rays, they are not.
11. Crop production can drop when ultraviolet radiation is strong.
12. Humans, plants, and animals are more at risk at high altitudes because less atmosphere exists overhead.
13. When scientists investigated the ozone hole, they concluded that chlorofluorocarbons (CFCs) were destroying the ozone layer.
14. Because these chemicals were widely used in aerosol sprays, large amounts of toxins were swept up by the wind into the atmosphere.
15. When chemicals such as these rise through the atmosphere, they destroy the ozone in the ozone layer.

The ozone layer protects living things from ultraviolet rays.

Name ______________________________

Apply

Rewrite each pair of simple sentences as one complex sentence. Use the word in parentheses to change the underlined sentence into an adverb clause.

16. (because) One chlorine atom from CFCs can destroy more than 100,000 ozone molecules. The ozone layer was being destroyed quickly. ______________________________

17. (as) People realized that chemicals were harming the ozone layer. They sought solutions to the problem.
____

18. (before) They decided to stop making chlorofluorocarbons. It was too late. ______________________________

19. (when) Countries around the world signed a treaty called the Montreal Protocol in 1987. They agreed to limit the manufacture of CFCs. ______________________________

20. (because) Scientists expect the ozone layer to heal itself by around 2050. So many countries have limited the production of CFCs. ______________________________

Reinforce

In this activity, you will distinguish among adverbs, adverb phrases, and adverb clauses. Draw a line from each sentence to the correct description of the boldfaced word or words.

21. The ozone layer started disappearing **because chemicals harmed ozone.**	adverb (one word)
22. The ozone layer started disappearing **quickly.**	adverb phrase (no verb)
23. The ozone hole started appearing **in the 1970s.**	adverb clause (has a verb)

24. The sun shines **during the day.**	adverb (one word)
25. The sun shines **although there are some clouds.**	adverb phrase (no verb)
26. The sun shines **brightly.**	adverb clause (has a verb)

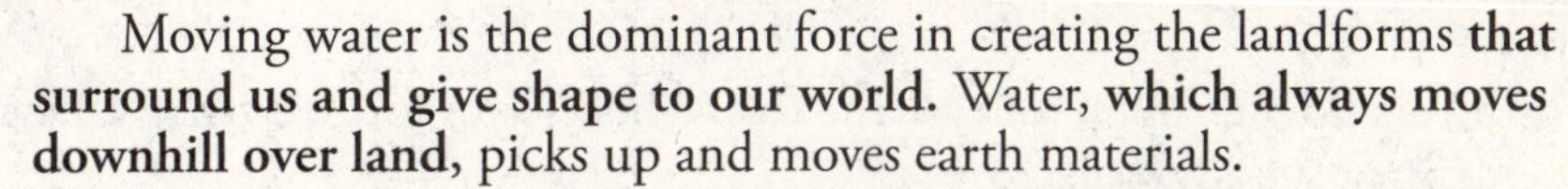

Read and Analyze

Restrictive and Nonrestrictive Clauses

Unit 2: Lesson 18

Moving water is the dominant force in creating the landforms **that surround us and give shape to our world.** Water, **which always moves downhill over land,** picks up and moves earth materials.

Which boldfaced clause gives information that is essential in its sentence? ______________________ Which boldfaced clause gives information that is not essential in its sentence? ______________________ ________ What punctuation marks are used to set off this clause from the rest of the sentence? ______________

A **restrictive clause** is a dependent clause that is essential to the meaning its sentence conveys: it gives information about the noun it modifies that is critically important. A **nonrestrictive clause** is a dependent clause that is not essential to the message its sentence conveys: if this clause were left out, the sentence would still convey its message effectively. A nonrestrictive clause is set off from the rest of its sentence by one or two commas, depending on its place in the sentence.

See Handbook Sections 8, 17g

Practice

Read each sentence. Draw a line under the adjective clause and circle the noun it modifies. Write *RC* if it is a restrictive clause and *NC* if it is a nonrestrictive clause.

1. Rainwater that falls on hills and mountains moves downslope. ____
2. The sheets of water concentrate into rills, which then join together to form creeks. ____
3. Creeks join together to form small rivers, and these join to form the great rivers that eventually flow into the ocean. ____
4. Each stream carries solid material with it; some of the material that is picked up is deposited elsewhere as the water moves across the land, and some of it is carried all the way to the ocean. ____
5. Water that is concentrated in linear flows erodes the land beneath it when it flows swiftly. ____
6. A slight increase in the speed of a creek's flow, which typically happens when rain falls or snow melts, significantly increases the creek's ability to transport material. ____
7. A creek swollen by heavy rains can move large rocks as well as massive amounts of sand and gravel; this process, which occurs most frequently in winter and spring in many parts of the United States, reshapes the landscape. ____
8. Over time, streams that flow swiftly carve deep channels for themselves. ____
9. Another factor that affects the amount of material carried by a stream is the nature of the land beneath it. ____
10. A stream flowing over bedrock, which is relatively smooth and solid, will not pick up much material. ____
11. A stream moving at the same pace that flows over land with loose soil will pick up and transport a much greater amount of material. ____
12. A river that spreads out and slows down will drop much of its load; a swiftly flowing river will carry solids much farther. ____

Name ________________________________

Apply

Combine each pair of sentences into one complex sentence. If the dependent clause in the sentence is a nonrestrictive clause, use one or two commas to set it off from the rest of the sentence.

13. Most rivers flow through valleys. The rivers themselves formed these valleys. ________________________________

____

14. These valleys reflect the size of the rivers in them. The valleys have been formed over long periods of time. ________________________________

____

15. The course of a river changes over time. This river flows through a valley. ________________________________

____

16. This process is quite predictable and happens in stages. The process is called the erosion cycle.

____

____

17. Over time, a river changes its course from a straight line to a sequence of S curves. These curves become more pronounced as time passes. ________________________________

____

Reinforce

Eleven words for natural waterways of various sizes are hidden in the puzzle below. Write these words on the lines provided. Then, on another sheet of paper, write two sentences using some words from the puzzle. Include a restrictive clause in one sentence and a nonrestrictive clause in the other.

W	F	R	E	S	H	E	T	G
S	O	R	C	R	E	E	K	X
T	R	I	B	U	T	A	R	Y
R	K	V	R	N	R	I	L	L
E	B	U	A	N	I	A	Q	B
A	Z	L	N	E	V	H	C	L
M	S	E	C	L	E	D	W	G
M	J	T	H	B	R	O	O	K

Across

18. ____________

19. ____________

20. ____________

21. ____________

22. ____________

Down

23. ____________

24. ____________

25. ____________

26. ____________

27. ____________

28. ____________

a. Plants and animals can threaten established ecosystems by **becoming invasive.**

b. **Controlling invasive species** can be a difficult task.

Circle the simple predicate in each sentence. Draw a box around each verb form ending in *-ing*. Is either *-ing* form part of a simple predicate? ____

Is the boldfaced phrase in sentence *a* the sentence subject, an indirect object, or the object of a preposition? ____________________

Is the boldfaced phrase in sentence *b* the sentence subject, a predicate noun phrase, or the object of a preposition? ____________________

A **gerund** is a verbal that acts as a noun. All gerunds are verb forms that end with *-ing*. A **gerund phrase** is made up of a gerund and the other words that complete its meaning. In the sentences above, *becoming invasive* and *Controlling invasive species* are gerund phrases.

See Handbook Section 25a

Practice

Underline each gerund phrase. Draw a box around the gerund itself.

1. Non-native species become invasive by taking over resources and by harming native species.
2. Competing with native species for food is one example of how invasive species can unbalance an ecosystem.
3. Non-native tree frogs called *coqui* are skilled at hunting Hawaii's snails, insects, and spiders.
4. These tree frogs may impact native Hawaiian birds by consuming the birds' preferred prey.
5. The frogs may also harm native birds by sustaining large populations of the birds' predators.
6. Introduced predators can reduce populations of native animals by preying on them.
7. The brown tree snake has negatively impacted the ecology of Guam by eating large numbers of lizards and birds.
8. Hanging on power lines is another way brown tree snakes cause damage.
9. Invasive plant species can harm native plants by blocking their sunlight.
10. The salvinia plant presents a threat by covering the surfaces of ponds and lakes.
11. The salvinia kills underwater plants by blocking off all light.
12. Sometimes scientists can find animals that are ideally suited for controlling an invasive species.
13. Scientists have used salvinia weevils to control salvinia by introducing the weevil to heavily infested areas.
14. The weevil larvae kill the salvinia plants by burrowing into their buds and stems.

The salvinia weevil eats only the salvinia plant, so it is safe to introduce as a biological control agent.

Name ______________________________

Apply

Imagine that you need to warn a friend about releasing a goldfish into the wild. Plan your argument by completing each sentence with a gerund from the word bank.

adopting	releasing	endangering	contacting	competing	breeding

15. I know you want to give your goldfish a larger home, but ______________________ it could cause problems.
16. By ______________________ with other fish for survival, your goldfish could harm the ecosystem.
17. Your goldfish may even start a new invasive population by ______________________.
18. There are ways to give your fish a better home without ______________________ the ecosystem.
19. Members of local pet clubs may help you out by ______________________ your fish.
20. ______________________ them would be a much better solution.

Reinforce

Using gerund phrases is a good way to add variety to the sentence structures in your writing.

Read the sentences below. Rewrite each pair of sentences as a single sentence containing at least one gerund phrase.

21. Zebra mussels can change a lake's ecosystem. They can carpet the bottom of the lake and use up nutrients. ______________________

____

____

22. Zebra mussels suffocate native mussel populations. This is just one of the zebra mussel's destructive effects on lake ecosystems. ______________________

____

____

Earth's mountains were created by plate tectonics. _____

Plate tectonics created the earth's mountains. _____

Circle the simple subject in each sentence. Write *X* by the sentence in which the subject does something. Write *O* by the sentence in which something is done to the subject.

If the subject performs an action, the verb is said to be in the **active voice**. (*Plate tectonics created.*) If the subject is acted upon by something else, the verb is said to be in the **passive voice**. (*Mountains were created.*) Many sentences in the passive voice have a prepositional phrase that begins with the word *by* and follows the verb.

See Handbook Sections 18g, 20

Practice

Circle the simple subject in each sentence. Draw a box around the simple predicate. Be sure to include helping verbs. Write *A* if the verb is in the active voice. Write *P* if it is in the passive voice.

1. *Plate tectonics* refers to the movement of chunks of the earth's crust. _____
2. The earth's plates constantly are moving into, away from, or against each other. _____
3. The land is reshaped drastically at the plates' boundaries. _____
4. Many of the earth's mountains were formed by the force of plate movements. _____
5. These movements can push rocks upward. _____
6. A plate also can slide beneath a neighboring plate. _____
7. The top plate can be pushed upward to a great height by the bottom plate. _____
8. Plates also can compress and expand. _____
9. The process of compression and expansion creates breaks, or faults, in the rock layers. _____
10. Mountain ranges can be formed by faults in the middle of plates, far from their colliding edges. _____
11. Parts of the Rocky Mountains were created by compression folds and faults. _____
12. In the southwest United States, the earth's crust has been stretched by the movement of plates. _____
13. Because of this extension, the Basin and Range region is covered by fault-block mountains. _____
14. The stretching crust broke the rocky plates into pieces. _____
15. Downward-sliding chunks formed valleys. _____
16. The steep sides of the remaining rocks stood as mountain ranges. _____
17. The process of extension has been forming these rugged features since the Miocene epoch 25 million years ago. _____

Name ____________________

Apply

Look again at each sentence in the Practice section that has a verb in the passive voice. Rewrite each sentence so the verb is in the active voice.

18. ____________________

19. ____________________

20. ____________________

21. ____________________

22. ____________________

23. ____________________

24. ____________________

Reinforce

The active voice communicates action briefly and powerfully. Some writers believe that the passive voice should be used only when an action is done by an unknown or unimportant agent—for example, *The ridge had eroded.*

Read the passage below. Notice that all of the sentences are in strong active voice. Then underline each verb in the active voice. (25–26)

At transform plate boundaries, plates grind past each other side by side. This type of boundary separates the North American plate from the Pacific plate along the San Andreas fault, a famous transform plate boundary that is responsible for many of California's earthquakes.

Write a sentence about an earthquake that has its verb in the passive voice. Then rewrite the sentence so the verb is in active voice.

27. ____________________

Analyzing Phrases and Clauses

Unit 2: Lesson 21

a. A large asteroid entered Earth's atmosphere **on June 30, 1908.**

b. This burning chunk of rock, **which was more than 100 feet across,** was headed directly toward our planet.

c. **Traveling at a speed in excess of 30,000 mph,** the meteor had the potential to do unimaginable damage if it collided with Earth.

d. **Although it exploded before striking Earth,** the Tunguska Fireball (as it came to be called) caused more destruction than any other space object in modern times.

Which sentences above contain boldfaced phrases? ______ Which contain boldfaced clauses? ______ In which sentences do the boldfaced words tell more about a noun? ______ In which do they tell more about a verb? ______

A **phrase** is a group of words that functions as a part of speech. For example, a participial phrase typically functions as an adjective by modifying, or telling more about, a noun. A phrase does not contain a subject-verb combination. A **clause** is a group of words that contains a subject-verb combination. A dependent clause—a clause that cannot stand alone as a sentence—functions as a part of speech also. For example, a dependent clause can function as an adverb by modifying a verb.

See Handbook Sections 13, 17g, 19, 20, 25

Practice

Look at the boldfaced group of words in each sentence. Circle the word or words it modifies. Then identify the structure and function of these words by writing *adjective phrase, adverb phrase, adjective clause,* or *adverb clause.*

1. The Tunguska Fireball is classified as a meteoroid; a meteoroid is a chunk **of space rock** that enters Earth's atmosphere but does not reach its surface. ________________________
2. The energy of its explosion was a thousand times more powerful than that of the atomic bomb **that was dropped on Hiroshima.** ________________________
3. The meteoroid exploded **near the Podkamennaya Tunguska River** in a thinly inhabited part of Siberia. ________________________
4. **If it had occurred in a populous area,** the explosion would have caused a tragedy too terrible to imagine. ________________________
5. The area **where the explosion occurred** was so sparsely populated that no deaths are known to have resulted from the blast. ________________________
6. The blast did flatten trees **over an 800-square-mile area.** ________________________
7. The heat **from the blast** was so intense that a worker in a trading post 40 miles away felt that his shirt had caught fire. ________________________
8. **Because the site was so far from transportation routes and is so frequently affected by severe weather,** no researcher reached it until 1927. ________________________

The Tunguska fireball damaged many trees when it hit Earth.

Name ______________________________

Apply

Combine each pair of sentences into a single sentence. If the sentence you create contains an adjective phrase, an adverb phrase, an adjective clause, or an adverb clause, underline it and write which it is. (You only need to mark one phrase or clause in each sentence you write.)

9. There is no impact crater at the epicenter of the Tunguska blast. The meteor did not strike Earth.

____

____

10. Asteroids enter Earth's atmosphere. These asteroids are called meteors. ______________________________

____

11. When a meteor burns up in Earth's atmosphere, it is called a meteoroid. Most meteors do burn up in Earth's atmosphere. ______________________________

____

12. A few meteors do strike Earth. These are called meteorites. ______________________________

____

13. A meteorite struck a spot in northern Arizona about 49,000 years ago. It created a huge crater there.

____

____

14. This crater is known as the Barringer Meteor Crater. It is almost a mile wide and more than 500 feet deep.

____

____

Reinforce

Write four sentences about meteors. Include an adjective phrase in one sentence, an adverb phrase in another sentence, an adjective clause in another, and an adverb clause in the remaining sentence. Be prepared to tell what word or words each phrase or clause modifies.

____

____

____

____

____

a. Fujiyama is a volcano, and so is Mauna Loa.
b. Fujiyama and Mauna Loa have different shapes.
c. Although Fujiyama and Mauna Loa are both volcanoes, they were formed in different ways.
d. Although Fujiyama and Mauna Loa are both volcanoes, they have different shapes, and they were formed in different ways.

Which sentence is made up of one independent clause? ____ Which sentence is made up of two independent clauses? ____ Which sentence is made up of one independent clause and one dependent clause? ____ Which sentence is made up of two independent clauses and one dependent clause? ____ Which of these sentences conveys the most information in an effective manner? ____

Simple sentences, compound sentences, complex sentences, and **compound-complex sentences** offer a writer a variety of ways of stating information and showing relationships. When you write, choose sentence types that enable you to express your ideas clearly and show how they are related to one another.

See Handbook Section 13

Practice

Read each pair of sentences. Mark a star beside the one that more effectively expresses the idea and shows relationships. If the sentence you choose is a simple sentence, write *S* in the blank. If it is a compound sentence, write *CD*. If it is a complex sentence, write *CX*. If it is a compound-complex sentence, write *CCX*.

1. Many landforms are created when processes occur within Earth; these are called tectonic processes. ______
   Tectonic processes create many of Earth's landforms. ______
2. Diastrophism is the name of a process that changes Earth's surface. ______
   Diastrophism, which is the change of Earth's surface resulting from movements of tectonic plates, is one tectonic process that creates landforms. ______
3. Vulcanism produces volcanoes, which are mountains formed by volcanic eruptions; the material that pours forth from a volcano builds up the volcano so it becomes higher than the surrounding land. ______
   Vulcanism is the term for the other tectonic process that creates landforms; volcanoes are the most noticeable products of volcanism. ______
4. While some volcanoes are shaped like cones, others are shaped like shields; these different shapes are the result of different processes of formation. ______
   Cone-shaped volcanoes are formed in one way, and shield-shaped volcanoes are formed in another way. ______
5. Cone volcanoes like Fujiyama result from explosive eruptions that typically lay down alternating layers of lava, and of ash and cinders. ______
   Explosive eruptions produce cone volcanoes, and Fujiyama is a cone volcano. ______
6. Nonexplosive flows of lava create shield volcanoes like Mauna Loa. ______
   Shield volcanoes like Mauna Loa are created when lava flows but does not explode; shield volcanoes can be many miles wide. ______

Name ______________________________

Apply

Rewrite each group of sentences as one sentence. Choose a type of sentence that makes clear the relationships between ideas.

7. The Pacific Ring of Fire is a horseshoe-shaped region. It stretches from the west coast of South America northward to Alaska's Aleutian Islands and then southward off the coast of Asia all the way to Indonesia.

____

____

____

8. Three-quarters of the world's volcanoes are located along the Pacific Ring of Fire. Some of these volcanoes are active, and others are dormant. ______________________________

____

9. Japan is home to ten percent of the world's active volcanoes. Japan occupies an area in the Ring of Fire where Earth's crust is particularly unstable. ______________________________

____

10. The Hawaiian Islands are not located on the Ring of Fire. They rise in the western Pacific Ocean over a hot spot in Earth's upper layers. ______________________________

____

Reinforce

Different circumstances call for different kinds of sentences. Read these two reports about the eruption of Krakatoa, the most violent eruption in modern times. The first is from the log of a captain whose ship was in the vicinity of the eruption. The second is from the report a British official in the area sent to his superiors in London.

A fearful explosion. A frightful sound. I am writing this blind in pitch darkness. We are under a continued rain of pumice-stone and dust. So violent are the explosions that the ear drums of over half my crew have been shattered.

—Captain Sampson, from the log of the Norham Castle

The present [volcanic] outburst commenced on Sunday last, and on that night the inhabitants of nearly the whole of Java and Sumatra were alarmed by loud noises resembling the reports of heavy artillery, which continued through the night and at rarer intervals during Monday. . . .

—Consul Alexander Patrick Cameron, dispatch to Lord Granville

On another sheet of paper, write a paragraph comparing the sentence structure, tone, and purpose of the two reports. Explain whether you think each writer used kinds of sentences appropriate for his purpose.

Read and Analyze

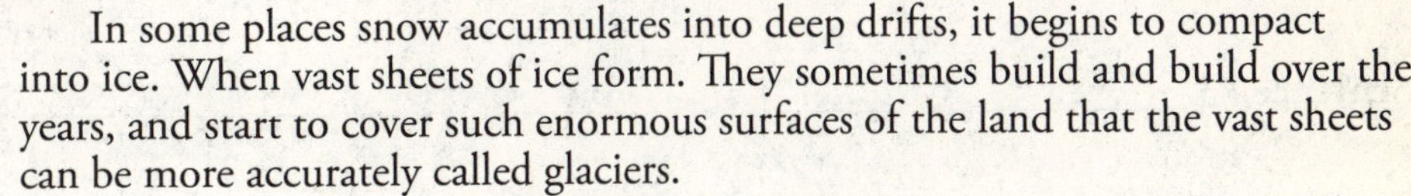

In some places snow accumulates into deep drifts, it begins to compact into ice. When vast sheets of ice form. They sometimes build and build over the years, and start to cover such enormous surfaces of the land that the vast sheets can be more accurately called glaciers.

Circle the dependent clause that is missing an independent clause. Underline the sentence that is written incorrectly because it is made up of two independent clauses without a conjunction. Write *X* at the beginning of the sentence that contains unnecessary words and phrases.

A **fragment** does not tell a complete thought. A **run-on sentence** is a compound sentence that is missing a comma and a conjunction. A **comma splice** is a run-on sentence that has a comma but is missing a conjunction. A **ramble-on** sentence is correct grammatically but contains unnecessary words and phrases or includes too many ideas. Avoid fragments, run-ons, comma splices, and ramble-ons in the final versions of your written work.

See Handbook Sections 8, 14, 22

Practice

Write *F* after each fragment. Write *RO* after each run-on. Write *CS* after each comma splice. Write *RA* after each ramble-on sentence.

1. There are two different types of glaciers they are not hard to distinguish. _______
2. Alpine and continental glaciers. _______
3. Alpine, or mountain, glaciers occur in high, cold mountain valleys, over time these glaciers slowly slide down the mountains. _______
4. Continental glaciers cover large, flat areas around the earth's poles, it is cold enough for snow to fall throughout the year. _______
5. You may be surprised to learn that, like alpine glaciers, continental glaciers, which cover large areas that are often basically just open ocean, are frozen fresh water because they are made by snow falling from above instead of sea water freezing from below. _______
6. During colder eras, these glaciers expanded they spread over the Antarctic and Arctic regions like pancake batter. _______
7. Alpine glaciers are one of the strongest forces the earth has ever seen; with their might, these powerful glaciers have carved and shaped landforms of all kinds in many parts of our planet. _______
8. There are two national parks called Glacier National Park one is in Canada and the other is in the United States. _______
9. Glaciers once covered the land in both parks even today there are glaciers for visitors to see. _______
10. Carved extraordinary formations out of the land there. _______
11. These big, heavy rivers of ice, like sandpaper and chisels as they move across the land. _______

Name ______________________________

Apply

Rewrite the sentences from the Practice section that are listed below. Correct the fragments, run-ons, and comma splices. Shorten the ramble-ons. There is more than one way to correct each sentence. (12–19)

Sentence #3 ______________________________

____

Sentence #4 ______________________________

____

Sentence #5 ______________________________

____

Sentence #6 ______________________________

____

Sentence #7 ______________________________

____

Sentence #9 ______________________________

____

Sentence #10 ______________________________

____

Sentence #11 ______________________________

____

Reinforce

This monster ramble-on sentence contains more than 60 words. Cross out unnecessary words, phrases, and clauses to make the sentence as short as possible. Write your revised sentence below.

In some cases, where the rocks contain important clues as to the early geological processes of the earth in past eras, glaciers can come through the area and scrape away rocks, shear rocks in half, and expose whole cliff faces with the result that scientists can access these rocks and find important geological information that they would never have been able to access without the glacier.

20. ______________________________

____

Read and Analyze

Natural, Inverted, and Interrupted Order

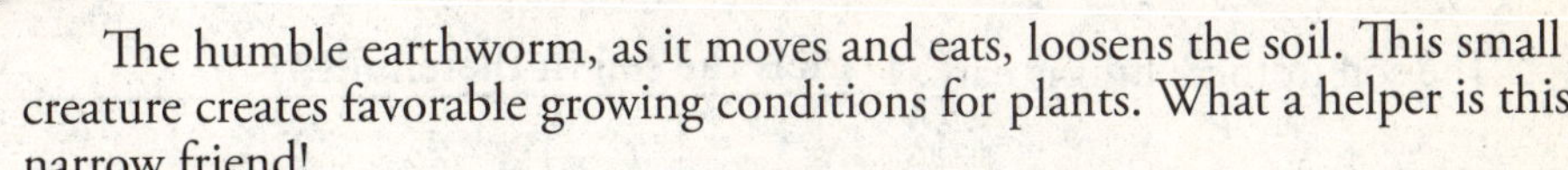

The humble earthworm, as it moves and eats, loosens the soil. This small creature creates favorable growing conditions for plants. What a helper is this narrow friend!

Underline the sentence in which the natural order of subject followed by verb is reversed. Draw a box around the clause that interrupts a subject-verb-object pattern. Put a check mark over the sentence that has the subject, verb, and object in that order, with no clause interrupting it.

A sentence with **natural order** follows the subject-verb pattern, with any direct object, predicate noun, or predicate adjective coming after the verb. In a sentence with **inverted order,** a verb, direct object, predicate noun, or predicate adjective comes before the subject. A sentence with **interrupted order** breaks up the subject-verb pattern with a dependent clause.

See Handbook Section 13

Practice

Write *N* after each sentence with natural order. Write *IV* after each sentence with inverted order. Write *IT* after each sentence with interrupted order.

1. Soil, which is necessary for most plant life, is a complex mix of ingredients. ___
2. Thousands of kinds of soils cover the surface of the earth. ___
3. Fortunate are those families with farms on fertile soil! ___
4. All soils contain organic matter, rocks, minerals, air, and water. ___
5. Organic matter, which comes from decaying plants and animals, adds to the soil's fertility. ___
6. Earthworms hasten the decomposition of organic matter. ___
7. How odd it seems that a creature would eat soil! ___
8. Soil earthworms do devour. ___
9. Their castings they leave on the surface. ___
10. Earthworms, as farmers do with plows, turn over soil. ___
11. Earthworms make tunnels and burrows. ___
12. These passageways let air and water into the soil and so improve its ability to sustain plant life. ___
13. Without burrowing creatures, how desolate the earth would be! ___
14. Human activity can also affect soil quality. ___
15. Cutting down plants, which help to sustain life on Earth, can cause soil to blow or wash away. ___

Earthworms enrich the soil by breaking down organic matter, aerating the soil, and acting like tiny plows.

Name ____________________

Apply

Rewrite each sentence below as an inverted sentence. The first one has been done for you.

16. The soil in these hills is dark. **Dark is the soil in these hills.**

17. The days are long during early summer. ____________________

18. The first shoots of vegetables are green. ____________________

19. The rabbits that raid our garden are clever. ____________________

20. The farmer who buries fencing to keep rabbits out is wise. ____________________

21. The plants in this fertile soil are so healthy! ____________________

Reinforce

If inverted sentences are overused, they can make a piece of writing sound unnatural. Because inverted sentences are so unusual, though, they can be effective: They draw the reader's attention to the sentences. Many great writers have used inverted sentences to create interesting effects.

Read the two quotes below. They are from works by William Shakespeare. Notice that each of these lines uses an inverted pattern. Rewrite each in natural sentence order. Then decide whether the inverted or the natural sentence order sounds better.

But, soft! what light through yonder window breaks?
—from *Romeo and Juliet,* II, ii

22. ____________________

Thus sometimes hath the brightest day a cloud;
—from *King Henry VI,* Part II, II, iv

23. ____________________

Clauses and Sentence Types

Write *S* next to each simple sentence. Write *CD* next to each compound sentence. Write *CX* next to each complex sentence. Write *CCX* next to each compound-complex sentence.

1. Vikings settled in Iceland and Greenland between A.D. 800 and 1200. _____
2. These settlers, who came from northern Europe, were called the Norse; they were looking for farmland, and Iceland and Greenland resembled their home region. _____
3. Farms could be established in those places because their climates were considerably warmer then. _____
4. The warmer temperatures melted dangerous sea ice, and this made voyages to and from these islands faster and safer. _____
5. After the Vikings arrived in Iceland and Greenland, they raised cattle and crops; they also gathered berries and seaweed and caught fish. _____

Draw one line under the independent clause in each sentence. Draw two lines under the dependent clause.

6. After the Vikings had lived in Iceland and Greenland for several centuries, some unwelcome changes occurred.
7. Crops failed frequently because the climate was becoming colder.

Underline the adjective clause in each sentence. Then circle the noun it modifies.

8. The crops that they raised fed their cattle.
9. Their cattle, which were given less and less food, started dying.
10. The areas where survival was becoming most difficult were in Greenland.

Underline the adverb clause in each sentence.

11. Because the climate was colder, dangerous drift ice appeared more frequently in the sea.
12. Although Europe was not far away, the drift ice made voyages there very dangerous.

Gerund Phrases

Underline each gerund phrase.

13. The Little Ice Age lasted from about 1400 to 1850; being cold for 450 years was certainly no fun!
14. Shortening the growing season was one effect of the Little Ice Age.

Active and Passive Voice

Write *A* after each sentence with a verb in active voice. Write *P* after each sentence with a verb in passive voice.

15. Entire villages and nearby farms were covered by expanding glaciers. _____
16. The cold temperatures reduced the yields of farms. _____

 Name ______________________________

Fragments, Run-ons, Comma Splices, and Ramble-ons

Identify each item as a fragment, run-on, comma splice, or ramble-on by writing *F, RO, CS,* or *RA*.

17. Why the Little Ice Age occurred. _____
18. Some scientists say that the sun was not shining as brightly during that period of time as it does in normal periods of time, and so it was not providing as much warmth to Earth as it usually provides. _____
19. The sun put out less heat energy, weather on Earth became colder. _____
20. Some scientists believe ash sent into the atmosphere by erupting volcanoes caused temperatures to drop the ash blocked the sun's rays and kept them from reaching Earth. _____

Natural, Inverted, and Interrupted Order

Write *N* next to a sentence if the sentence has natural order. Write *IV* next to a sentence if the sentence has inverted oder. Write *IT* next to a sentence if the sentence has interrupted order.

21. The "year without a summer" 1816 was called. _____
22. Frost and snow were on the ground in Europe during the summer months. _____

Clauses, Phrases, and Sentence Structures

Draw a line under the dependent clause in each sentence. If it is a restrictive clause, write RC after the sentence. If it is a nonrestrictive clause, write NC after the sentence.

23. The cold temperatures of 1816 may have been caused by a volcano whose eruption blasted a huge amount of material into the atmosphere. _____
24. That volcanic eruption, which occurred on an island in present-day Indonesia, lowered the world's average temperature by almost one degree Celsius. _____

Read each sentence. Circle the word or words modified by the boldfaced phrase or clause. Then identify the boldfaced words as an adjective phrase, an adverb phrase, an adjective clause, or an adverb clause.

25. Krakatoa's eruption affected worldwide temperatures **in a similar way.** ______________________
26. The material **that the eruption poured into the atmosphere** blocked some of the sun's rays.

    ____

Read each pair of sentences. Mark a star beside the sentence that more effectively expresses ideas. Then label that sentence *S* (simple sentence), *CD* (compound sentence), *CX* (complex sentence), or *CCX* (compound-complex sentence).

27. Because it poses a threat to the communities on its slopes, Mauna Loa has been carefully monitored for more than a century. _____

    Mauna Loa is a threat. It has been monitored for more than a century. _____
28. Scientists involved in the Decade Volcano project study Mauna Loa and other dangerous volcanoes. _____

    Mauna Loa is now included in the Decade Volcano project, which promotes the study of the world's most dangerous volcanoes; it is one of 16 volcanoes being observed. _____

Spelling Practice

With global warming, the polar ice caps we once thought were permanent are melting slowly.

Underline the word in the sentence that means "lasting." Circle the suffix in the word.

Adding Suffixes: *-ant, -ance, -ent, -ence*

The suffixes *-ant* and *-ent* can be added to the ends of roots and base words to create adjectives, as in *abundant* and *evident.* The suffixes *-ance* and *-ence* can be added to the ends of roots and base words to create nouns, as in *abundance* and *evidence.*

Word Sort

Use the words below to complete the word sort.

confidence	competent	relevant	permanent	competence	observant
significant	relevance	permanence	observance	significance	confident

Suffix *-ant*	**Suffix *-ance***

Suffix *-ent*	**Suffix *-ence***

Name ____________________

Pattern Practice

Write the word in each pair that is spelled correctly. Use a dictionary to check the spellings.

1. intelligance, intelligence ____________
2. permanence, permanance ____________
3. abundent, abundant ____________
4. inconveniant, inconvenient ____________
5. observance, observence ____________
6. significant, significent ____________
7. competance, competence ____________

Add *-ant, -ent, -ance,* or *-ence* to each base word given. Write the new word in the sentence. Change the spelling of the base word as needed.

8. The ____________ cat notices every tiny noise. (observe)
9. Yoshi has won an award for perfect ____________. (attend)
10. The Browns still live at this ____________. (reside)
11. It seemed so insignificant that she questioned its ____________. (relevant)
12. Did the detective find any ____________ at the crime scene? (evident)
13. That store is closed for the ____________ of the holiday. (observe)
14. That's just our ____________ cricket chirping away. (reside)
15. Living near train tracks can be an ____________ to many people. (annoy)

Use the Dictionary

Add *-ant, -ent, -ance,* or *-ence* to each base word and write the new word. Check your spellings in a print or an online dictionary.

16. dominate + ance = ____________
17. expect + ant = ____________
18. converge + ent = ____________

See Handbook Section 41

Diagramming Compound Sentences

You have learned that a compound sentence is made of two independent clauses joined by a comma and a coordinating conjunction or by a semicolon.

A compound sentence is diagrammed this way:

Some cities bury trash, and others burn it.

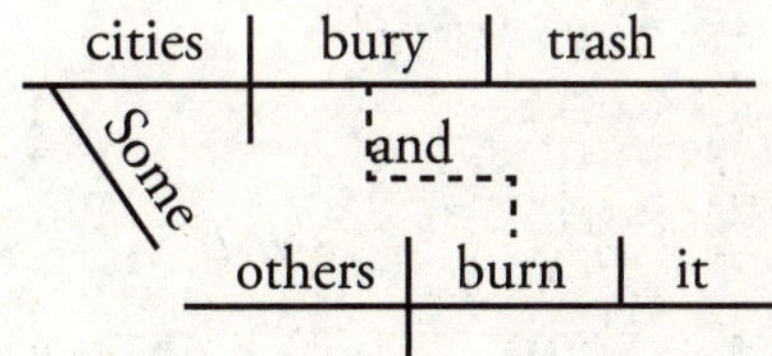

Try diagramming these compound sentences.

1. I visited the dump, but it had closed.

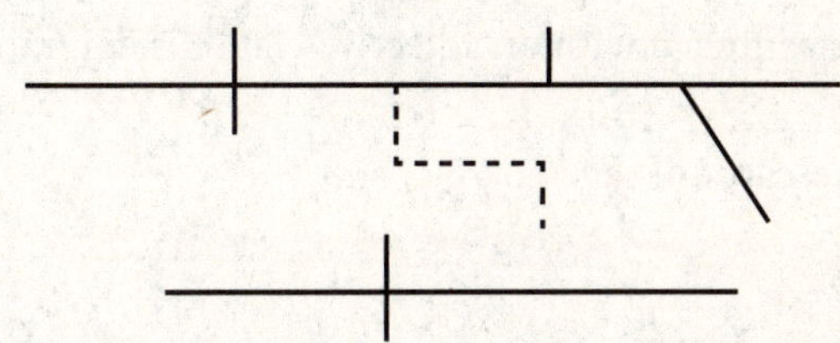

2. Rosa saved newspapers, and Tio recycled them.

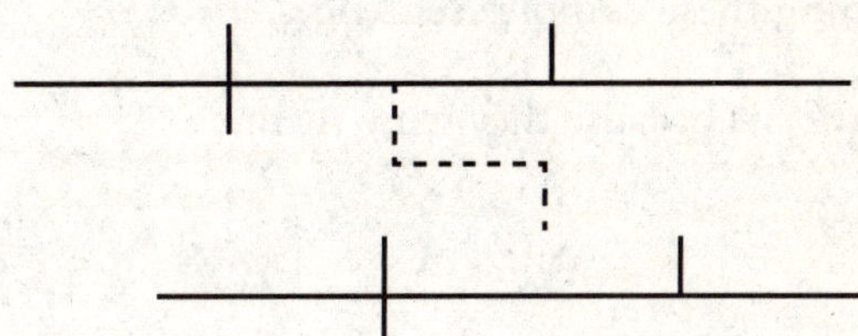

3. Recycling helps, but reducing helps more.

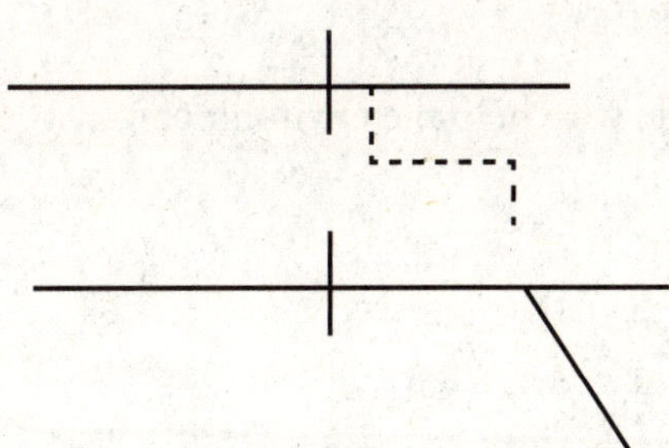

4. Rohit once used many napkins daily, but now he uses just a few.

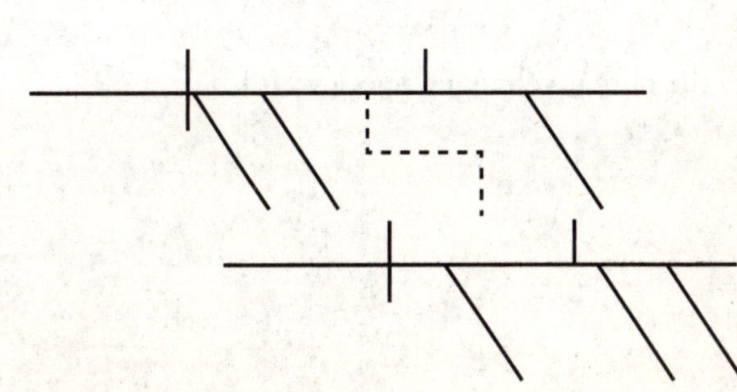

Name ____________________

Diagramming Complex Sentences

You have learned that a complex sentence is made up of an independent clause and a dependent clause. The dependent clause may be an adjective clause that begins with a relative pronoun such as *who, whom, whose, which,* or *that.* Or, it may be an adverb clause that begins with a subordinating conjunction such as *although, if,* or *because,* or a relative adverb such as *when* or *where.*

A complex sentence with an adverb is diagrammed this way:

When people carpool, they save energy.

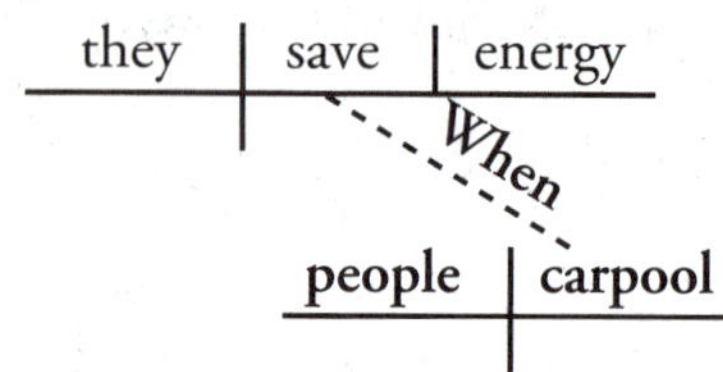

A complex sentence with an adjective clause is diagrammed this way:

People **who carpool** save energy.

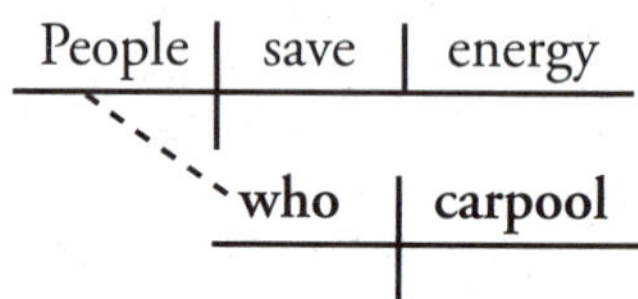

Try diagramming these complex sentences.

5. They save jars because they reuse them.

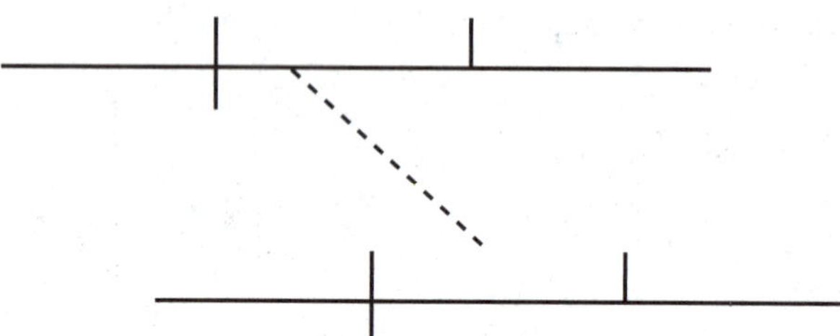

6. I respect people who help the environment.

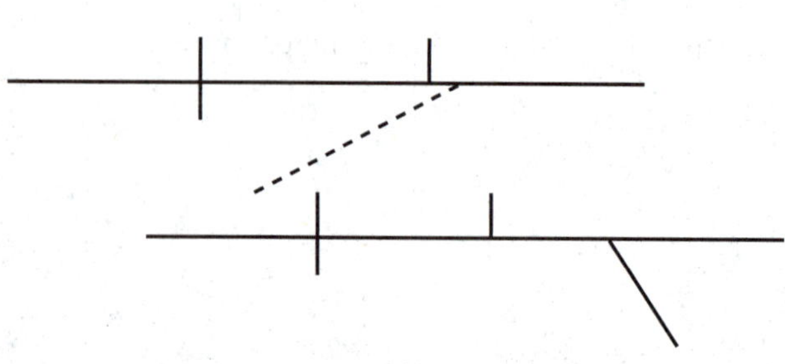

7. As the climate changes, species vanish.

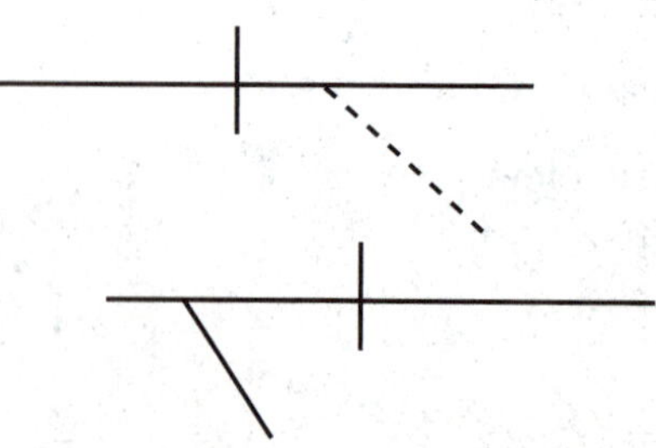

Writing Sentences

The writer of these sentences has tried to include too many ideas. Rewrite each sentence as two or three shorter, clearer sentences. Make sure each sentence you write is complete.

1. The Gulf Stream is a strong current of warm water that flows northward along the eastern coast of North America, and, once it reaches North Carolina, heads to the east to form part of a large clockwise circulation of water in the North Atlantic, although one branch of the Gulf Stream continues north and joins another major current known as the North Atlantic Drift.

____

____

____

____

____

2. Together, the Gulf Stream and the North Atlantic Drift help warm northern Europe by giving off the heat they carry to the surrounding environment, and today, many scientists are concerned that global warming may change the circulation patterns of these currents, and, consequently, cause temperatures in northern Europe to drop; some even predict a mini Ice Age!

____

____

____

____

____

There are four kinds of sentences—a statement, a question, a command, and an exclamation. Any of these sentences may be simple, compound, or complex. Notice the different types of sentences in this model paragraph.

imperative sentence (gives a command and ends with a period or an exclamation point)

declarative sentence (makes a statement and ends with a period)

interrogative sentence (asks a question and ends with a question mark)

exclamatory sentence (shows excitement and ends with an exclamation point)

Imagine a great river running through the ocean. This "river" carries warm water from the central Pacific Ocean, passes between Australia and the southern tip of Africa, and then proceeds up to the North Atlantic before looping back and retracing its course south and back to the central Pacific. *What is this "river"?* It is an ocean circulation pattern that is so effective at transporting heat energy that it's sometimes called the Great Ocean Conveyor Belt!

Name ______________________________

Writing a Paragraph

The sentences you repaired on page 75 can be used to make a paragraph. Decide what order the sentences should be in. Then revise at least two of the sentences so your paragraph has a variety of sentence types. Use the model on page 75 as a reference. Write the paragraph on the lines below.

Think of some event or process that has changed the area in which you live. This might be a flood, a fire, an earthquake, or the encroachment of an invasive species. Write a paragraph describing this event or process and its effects. Be sure to include a topic sentence, supporting sentences, and a concluding sentence. Also include at least two different kinds of sentences.

Read your paragraph again. Use this checklist to make sure it is complete and correct.

- ☐ My paragraph has a topic sentence.
- ☐ My paragraph has at least two supporting sentences.
- ☐ All my sentences are clear and make sense.
- ☐ I have used at least two types of sentences and punctuated them correctly.
- ☐ My paragraph has a concluding sentence.

Read this passage about waste management and find the mistakes. Use the proofreading marks to show how the mistakes should be fixed. Use a dictionary to check and correct spellings.

Proofreading Marks

Mark	Means	Example
	delete	Landfill is a waste management options.
^	add	Landfill ^is a waste management option.
≡	make into an uppercase letter	landfill is a waste management option.
/	make into a lowercase letter	Landfill is a Waste management option.
⊙	add a period	Landfill is a waste management option⊙
(sp)	fix spelling	Landfill is a waste managment option.

Responsible Waste Management

Landfill a method of spreding and compacting solid waste on land and covering it with soil is not a good long-term waste management solution. Landfill generates the greenhouse gases Methane and Carbon dioxide, leakage from landfill can puloot groundwater. population growth requires more and more wild land to be used as dumping grounds. For all these reasons cities across the country are trying to reduce the amount of material that winds up in landfill.

Many cities now offer curbside recycling of used paper, glass, alumanum, steel, and plastic bottles. Recycling offers numerous benafits. Recycling paper products saves trees. Which absorb Carbon Dioxide from the air. Manufacturing with recycled materials uses much less energy than manufacturing with raw materials does, and for example, it takes four to eight times as much energy to extract and process petroleum to make plastic goods as it takes to make plastics from recycled plastic materials.

Many cities also have drop-off centers for the disposal of hazardous waste such as paint and expired medicines. Some comunities even provide drop-off centers for old computers and electronics.

Composting of food scraps and yard trimmings offers another solution composting is the process of decomposing organic matter into a rich soil called compost.

By working together to divert recyclible and compostable materials from landfill. Cities and individuals can play an important role in protecting the environment.

Name ______________________________

Proofreading Checklist

You can use the checklist below to help you find and fix mistakes in your own writing. Write the titles of your own stories or reports in the blanks at the top of the chart. Then use the questions to check your work. Make a check mark (✓)in each box after you have checked that item.

Titles

Proofreading Checklist for Unit 2

Have I used phrases and clauses correctly?				
Have I used a comma and coordinating conjunction or semicolon to join independent clauses?				
Have I avoided run-on sentences, comma splices, fragments, and ramble-on sentences?				
Is each simple sentence an independent clause, and does each complex sentence have an independent clause and a dependent clause?				

Also Remember...

Does each sentence begin with an uppercase letter?				
Did I use a dictionary to check and correct spellings?				
Have I used commas correctly?				

Your Own List

Use this space to write your own list of things to check in your writing.

Community Connection

In Unit 2 of *Grammar, Usage, and Mechanics,* students learned about **different types of sentences, phrases, and clauses** and used what they learned to improve their writing. The content of these lessons focuses on the theme **Changes in the Natural World.** As students completed the exercises, they learned about the forces of change that have altered, and may continue to alter, our planet. These pages offer a variety of activities that reinforce skills and concepts presented in the unit. They also provide opportunities for the student to make connections between the information presented in the lessons and their modern surroundings.

Even Small Changes Count

Continents drift, mountains rise and fall, glaciers carve the land, and rivers change course. How have these forces of nature changed your area over the centuries? To find out, take a trip to your local library and ask a librarian for help researching what your area was like in the distant past. Find or draw a picture to show this. Then find or draw a picture of the same area as it looks today. Finally, write a paragraph in which you compare and contrast the two landscapes.

Water Under the Bridge

Water is necessary for all life. It is one of the most powerful agents of change on Earth. Water is constantly shaping the land through erosion. Too little water can also change the land and affect the plants and animals living there. What do you know about the water that is supplied to your community? To find out more, visit your local water department or utilities commission online or in person. Try to find answers to the following questions:

- Does the water in your home come from far away or nearby?
- Does acid rain fall in your area? What contaminants are in your water?
- Does your area experience droughts often? What have been the results of these dry periods?
- What are some things you can do to conserve water?

Preventing, Controlling, Reversing

Some changes, like meteorite hits, seismic activity, and magnetic field reversals, happen to Earth regardless of human existence. Other changes are directly brought about by humans. Learn how humans affect the earth and what people can do to slow down negative changes such as global warming and habitat loss. Search the Internet for websites of organizations that combat global warming, habitat loss, or other negative human impacts on the natural world. Choose one organization that you admire, and prepare a brief speech about how the organization is working toward its goals.

Name ______________________________

How Do We Know About Changes?

How do scientists find out what the natural world was like long before humans existed on Earth? If possible, interview a science teacher, a science museum curator, or another adult who is knowledgeable in the field of geology, paleontology, or natural history. Before you conduct your interview, collect some questions to ask about how scientists learn about what the earth was like long ago. Use the following list of questions to get started:

- Where can scientists find evidence of how the earth looked long ago?
- Is there anywhere nearby where you can see evidence of geologic changes?
- What kinds of tests can scientists do to learn the age of rocks?
- Does all of our knowledge about extinct species come from fossils?

Use the planning guide below to help you plan the interview. Take notes during the interview, and share the results of the interview with your class.

Interview Planner

Topic of interview: ______________________________

Date of interview: ______________________________

Name: ______________________________

Occupation: ______________________________

Experience in field of interest: ______________________________

Questions to ask:

1. ______________________________
____
2. ______________________________
____
3. ______________________________
____
4. ______________________________
____
5. ______________________________
____

Many **cultures** around the **world** have rich story-telling **traditions.**

Circle the boldfaced noun that names a single person, place, or thing.

A **singular noun** names one person, place, thing, or idea. A **plural noun** names more than one. Most nouns add *-s* or *-es* to form the plural. A small number of nouns have **irregular plurals.** Some nouns change spelling in the plural form (*woman, women*). Some nouns have the same singular and plural form (*deer*).

See Handbook Section 29

Practice

Circle each singular noun. Underline each plural noun.

The myth of Orion tells how the hunter ended up in the sky.

1. For centuries, groups across our planet have told and retold myths and legends.
2. Myths recount the great feats of supernatural beings, ancestors, and heroes.
3. Ancient groups invented myths to explain the world around them, or to explain the relationship between gods and humans.
4. The Greeks were fascinated by the stars, so they named each of the constellations and invented stories about them.
5. Many cultures have myths that offer supernatural explanations of how land, animals, and humans were created.
6. Mythical tales are fantastic and unbelievable.
7. However, they reflect the values of the times in which they were created.
8. Like a myth, a legend is an unverifiable popular story handed down from earlier times.
9. Some legends are based on real individuals or true events.
10. When stories about these folks and events are retold, facts are often embellished and exaggerated.
11. Johnny Appleseed was a real man who became legendary.
12. Paul Bunyan and his ox, Babe, were imaginary figures.
13. Real boys don't grow so quickly that they wear the clothes of their father within five days!
14. Real oxen don't straighten rivers by tugging on them!
15. People are still inventing myths and legends today; only time will tell which ones will be retold a century from now.

Name ____________________

Apply

Write the plural form of each singular common noun you identified in the Practice section. (Names of people or animals are not common nouns.)

16. ____________________
17. ____________________
18. ____________________
19. ____________________
20. ____________________
21. ____________________
22. ____________________
23. ____________________
24. ____________________
25. ____________________
26. ____________________
27. ____________________

Reinforce

See Handbook Section 15

A **collective noun** names a group of people or things that act as a unit. *Class, flock,* and *team* are collective nouns. Most often, a collective noun is treated as a singular subject:

The track *team is* the strongest one we've had in years.

Sometimes, if a writer wants to emphasize the different members of a group, he or she may treat the noun as a plural subject:

The track *team are* congratulating one another on their fine performances.

Circle the words below that are collective nouns. Then use three of them in sentences.

family	animals	centuries	class	audience
gods	myths	group	team	company

28. ____

____

____

29. ____

____

____

30. ____

____

____

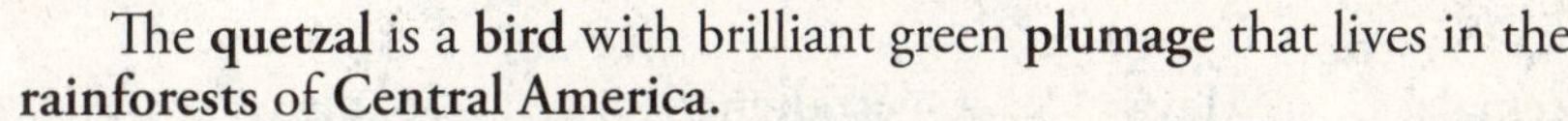

The **quetzal** is a **bird** with brilliant green **plumage** that lives in the **rainforests** of **Central America**.

Circle the boldfaced words that name a particular person, place, thing, or idea.

A **common noun** names any person, place, thing, or idea. A **proper noun** names a particular person, place, thing, or idea. Proper nouns must be capitalized. A proper noun made of several words (*United Nations* or *Martin Luther King High School*) is considered one proper noun.

See Handbook Section 15

Practice

Circle each common noun in the sentences below. Underline each proper noun.

1. Long ago, the Maya considered the quetzal sacred.
2. They believed that the bird would spread its green wings and use them as a shield to protect their warriors in battle.
3. In the years after the voyage of Christopher Columbus, the Spanish tried to conquer the Maya and seize their gold.
4. Pedro de Alvarado led an attack on Quetzaltenango, a city in the mountains of what is now Guatemala.
5. The Maya fought with spears, clubs, and shields woven out of wicker.
6. The Spaniards fought with swords and guns, and wore thick armor to protect themselves.
7. The chief of the Maya fought against Pedro de Alvarado.
8. As the two men fought, a quetzal darted above them, trying to protect the chief, Tecún Umán.
9. Tecún Umán was ill-equipped to defend himself against the superior arms of his opponent.
10. Pedro de Alvarado wounded Tecún Umán seriously, and the leader of the Maya fell to the ground.
11. It is said that at that moment, the quetzal fell upon Tecún Umán and spread its brilliant green plumes over his chest.
12. The next morning at dawn, the people of Quetzaltenango saw the quetzal rise up from the chief's body.
13. The feathers of the breast of the quetzal were stained with the blood of Tecún Umán.
14. Ever since then, all quetzals have had crimson breasts.
15. Today these exotic birds of Central America are endangered.

The quetzal is the national bird of Guatemala.

Name ______________________________

Apply

Proper nouns specify whom and what you are talking about. Rewrite each sentence, and replace each common noun with a proper noun from the word bank. You may also need to change other words in your sentences.

Guatemala	Maya	Quetzaltenango	Spanish	*A Guide to Central American Parks*

16. I'm planning a trip to that country. ______________________________

17. The traditions of that indigenous group really interest me. ______________________________

18. Outside that city, there's a rainforest that I would like to visit. ______________________________

19. I read all about it in a book. ______________________________

Reinforce

See Handbook Sections 1, 3

To correctly capitalize a proper noun made up of two or more words, capitalize the first word, the last word, and each important word in between. (Don't forget to underline or italicize book and movie titles and to put story titles in quotation marks.)

The National Baseball Hall of Fame

Around the World in Eighty Days

Rewrite these sentences by correctly capitalizing proper nouns.

20. I read a book called aztec and maya myths. ______________________________

21. I saw a model of the pyramid of the sun at the national museum of anthropology. ______________________________

22. Students at john f. kennedy middle school put on plays about the history of mexico. ______________________________

Concrete, Abstract, and Collective Nouns

Unit 3: Lesson 27

Read and Analyze

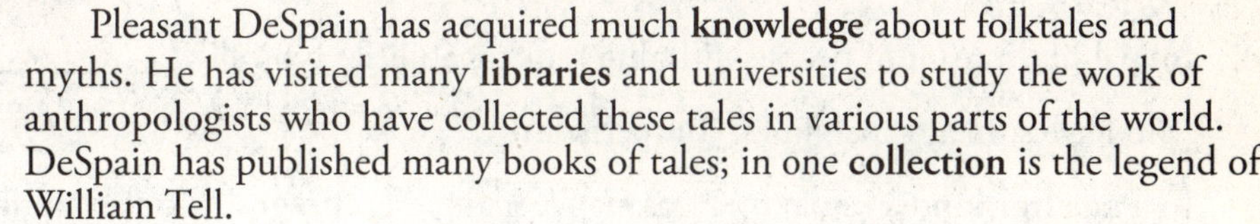

Pleasant DeSpain has acquired much **knowledge** about folktales and myths. He has visited many **libraries** and universities to study the work of anthropologists who have collected these tales in various parts of the world. DeSpain has published many books of tales; in one **collection** is the legend of William Tell.

Circle the boldfaced word that names a group of things. Draw one line under the boldfaced word that names things that can be seen and touched. Draw two lines under the boldfaced word that names an idea.

A **collective noun** names a group of people or things. In most cases, a collective noun that is singular in form should be treated as a singular noun for verb agreement. A **concrete noun** names something you can see, touch, hear, smell, or taste. An **abstract noun** names an idea.

See Handbook Section 15

Practice

Read each sentence. Circle the boldfaced word that is the type of noun listed in parentheses.

1. William Tell had great **skill** with the **crossbow.** (concrete noun)
2. He was a successful hunter, bringing home to his **cottage** food for his **family** regularly. (collective noun)
3. The **people** of the region in which William Tell lived were then ruled by an Austrian governor who was notorious for his **cruelty.** (abstract noun)
4. This governor levied high taxes on the **population** and threw those who could not pay into **jails.** (collective noun)
5. The governor had a red hat placed atop a **pole** in the village near the home of William Tell; the governor said that the hat was a **symbol** of the king of Austria, who then ruled over Switzerland. (concrete noun)
6. The governor then issued an order that everyone had to bow before the **hat** to demonstrate **fidelity.** (abstract noun)
7. One day William Tell walked into the **town** with his son; neither was aware of the **rule,** and both walked past the hat without bowing. (concrete noun)
8. The **pair** was immediately ordered by an Austrian **guard** to bow before the hat. (collective noun)
9. William Tell refused to perform this gesture of **submission,** so the guard blew a **whistle** and several soldiers responded. (abstract noun)
10. William Tell and his son were forced by the **group** to stand before the cruel **governor.** (collective noun)
11. The governor had heard of William Tell's **prowess** as an archer; he asked William Tell whether he could hit an apple with an **arrow** from a distance of 100 yards. (abstract noun)
12. The wicked **governor** then told William that the apple would be placed on his son's head; if William hit the apple, he and his son would regain their **freedom,** but if William missed, the son would be killed. (concrete noun)
13. Showing not just courage but also masterful skill and perfect **concentration,** William sent the arrow right through the **apple.** (abstract noun)

Name ______________________________

Apply

Read each sentence. Choose the correct present-tense form of the verb in parentheses. Write it in the blank to complete the sentence.

14. In real life, a team of people with different capabilities typically ________________ a group of people who have similar capabilities. (outperform)
15. In a tale from India retold by Pleasant DeSpain, a group of dissimilar animals ________________ the ability to solve a variety of problems. (demonstrate)
16. This band of comrades—a crow, a turtle, and a stag—________________ a very determined hunter by using individual talents and collective wisdom. (thwart)

Reinforce

William Tell overcame the cruel challenge he faced by performing well under pressure. Think of a time when you performed well under pressure. Write a paragraph describing that situation and telling what enabled you to succeed in that difficult situation. Use at least one abstract noun, one concrete noun, and one collective noun in your paragraph.

____

____

____

____

____

____

____

____

____

____

____

____

____

____

____

____

Read and Analyze

Singular Possessive and Plural Possessive Nouns

According to Norse mythology, natural phenomena were the results of the **gods'** actions. Thunder was caused by the banging of **Thor's** hammer. The sound of that **god's** hammer usually indicated he was fighting evil-doers.

Circle the part of each boldfaced word that shows ownership.

A **possessive noun** shows ownership or close relationship. **Singular** nouns add an apostrophe and *-s* to form the possessive (*giant, giant's*). Most **plural** nouns add an apostrophe after the *-s* to form the possessive (*giants, giants'*). Plurals that don't end in *-s* (*children, geese*) add an apostrophe and *-s* (*children's, geese's*) to show possession.

See Handbook Sections 7, 30

Practice

Underline each singular possessive noun. Circle each plural possessive noun. There may be more than one possessive noun in each sentence.

1. One morning everyone in Asgard was awakened by Thor's mighty shout; someone had stolen the thunder god's hammer!
2. Thor's first thought was that the theft might be one of his friend Loki's mischievous pranks.
3. Loki said he knew nothing about the hammer's disappearance, however.
4. Loki suggested that he himself should borrow the goddess Freyja's magic feather coat and use it to fly to the homeland of the giants, the prime suspects.
5. Loki traveled there and discovered the thief to be Thrym, the frost giants' king.
6. Thrym had taken a fancy to the goddess Freyja and refused to return the hammer without a promise of the goddess's hand in marriage.
7. Loki took the giant's message back to Asgard, but Freyja flatly refused to marry Thrym.
8. Thor and Loki hatched a plan: Thor would wear Freyja's dress and cover his face with a veil.
9. Upon the plotters' arrival to the giants' homeland, a great banquet was prepared.
10. Imagine the king's surprise when his bride-to-be ate a whole ox, eight salmon, and many sweets!
11. The fair damsel's maid told Thrym that her lady had not been able to eat for some time because of her excitement about the wedding.
12. Thrym lifted his beloved's veil to peek at her, but dropped it when he saw her eyes' fiery red color.
13. When the ceremony began, Thor's hammer was fetched so the couple could swear vows upon it.
14. Thor immediately grabbed the weapon's handle and used it to smite his enemy; then he and Loki returned victoriously to Asgard.

Name ______________________________

Apply

Rewrite each sentence, shortening the underlined section by using a possessive noun.

15. The hammer belonging to the thunder god was made by dwarves. ______________________________

____

16. Loki the troublemaker is the favorite Norse god of many people. ______________________________

____

17. The homeland of the giants was called Jotunheim. ______________________________

____

18. Thor wore the necklace belonging to the goddess. ______________________________

____

19. Loki was the friend of Thor, although he often made Thor angry. ______________________________

____

Reinforce

Circle six nouns hidden in the puzzle. Write each one in the column where it belongs. Then write the possessive form of each noun.

L	E	G	E	N	D	S
R	Q	I	U	E	W	T
H	W	A	C	Q	A	C
O	T	N	Y	J	R	H
U	P	T	V	G	V	O
S	E	W	O	M	E	N
E	O	Z	K	F	S	Y
Z	G	O	D	S	N	T

Singular Nouns	Possessive Forms
20. ________	________
21. ________	________

Plural Nouns	Possessive Forms
22. ________	________
23. ________	________
24. ________	________
25. ________	________

Use one of the possessive forms above in a sentence about Thor or Loki.

26. ______________________________

____

____

Read and Analyze

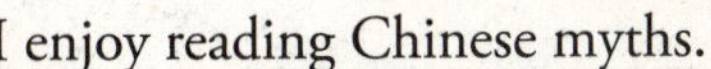

I enjoy reading Chinese myths.

Circle the word in the sentence above that shows who is speaking.

A **pronoun** can take the place of a noun. **Personal pronouns** can be used to stand for the person speaking, the person spoken to, or the person spoken about. **First person** pronouns refer to the speaker (*I, me*) or include the speaker (*we, us*). **Second person** pronouns refer to the person being spoken to (*you*). **Third person** pronouns refer to the person, place, or thing being spoken about (*he, him, she, her, it, they, them*). **Remember to use this information when you speak, too.**

See Handbook Section 17a

Practice

Circle each personal pronoun. Write *1* if it is a first person pronoun, *2* if it is second person, or *3* if it is third person. Hint: If a sentence has more than one personal pronoun, all are in the same person.

1. Have you read any Chinese myths? _____
2. Dad just gave me a book about Chinese gods and goddesses. _____
3. I learned about an important figure in Chinese mythology. _____
4. She was named Nuwa, and she was much loved by ancient people. _____
5. Nuwa was the mother goddess; she could change shape and appear in different forms. _____
6. Myths describe her as half-human and half-dragon. _____
7. Long ago before we humans dwelled upon Earth, Nuwa felt very lonely. _____
8. One day, while walking along the great Yellow River, she scooped up some mud and used it to form shapes of people. _____
9. She breathed life into them, and they danced around her, giving praise. _____
10. After she had made many figures, she took a piece of cane and rolled it in the mud and then shook it out. _____
11. Small drops of mud fell off, and they, too, turned into men and women. _____
12. Some myths say that the people she formed by hand became aristocrats, or privileged people. _____
13. They say that the people she made by shaking the mud off the cane became people who were less fortunate in life. _____
14. Dad and I have asked the librarian to find us more books about Chinese myths. _____

In Chinese mythology, dragons were gods who had special powers.

Name ______________________________

Apply

Write four sentences about a hero of yours, using the types of personal pronouns indicated.

15. first person: ______________________________

16. second person: ______________________________

17. third person singular: ______________________________

18. third person plural: ______________________________

Reinforce

The word *he* once was accepted as a universal pronoun that could refer to anyone, male or female, if a generalization about people was being made.
Example: Myths make a person think about his own cultural beliefs.

Now most writers try to avoid the use of universal *he*. Here are two ways the sentence above might be revised.

Solution #1:

Make the noun and the word it refers to plural.	Myths make people think about their own cultural beliefs.

Solution #2:

Replace *his* with *his or her*.	Myths make a person think about his or her own cultural beliefs.

Try both of these solutions for replacing the universal *he* in these sentences.

19. Each student chose a myth to write his report about.

____

____

20. The myths a person enjoys depend on his personal taste.

____

____

Read and Analyze

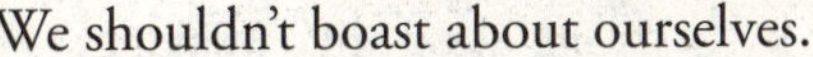

We shouldn't boast about ourselves.

I myself am a talented singer, but I don't brag about it.

Circle the pronoun in the first sentence that refers back to the subject. Underline the pronoun in the second sentence that is used for emphasis.

Words such as *myself, herself, itself,* and *themselves* are **compound personal pronouns.** When a compound personal pronoun is used as an object in a sentence and refers back to the subject or another noun, that pronoun is called a **reflexive pronoun.** When a compound personal pronoun is used to emphasize the identity of the sentence subject or another noun, it is called an **intensive pronoun.**

See Handbook Sections 17c, 17e

Practice

Read the sentences below. Underline each compound personal pronoun that is used as a reflexive pronoun. Circle each compound personal pronoun that is used as an intensive pronoun.

1. If you lived in ancient Greece, you would know better than to think yourself superior to a god or goddess.
2. A young weaver named Arachne, however, was as foolish as she was talented; she openly declared that the goddess Athena could not weave as well as she herself could.
3. Athena, upon hearing Arachne's words, pulled herself away from important business on Mount Olympus and came to Earth to punish Arachne.
4. Athena offered the girl a chance to prove herself and survive—the two would have a weaving contest.
5. On the fateful day, people came from all over the land to squeeze themselves into the meadow near Arachne's home.
6. Zeus himself did not deign to attend the match, but he undoubtedly watched it from above.
7. Arachne was sitting at her loom in front of her cottage when Athena appeared through the clouds and seated herself high on a nearby hilltop.
8. Arachne was the first to weave her tapestry, and so swiftly and deftly did her fingers move that they themselves seemed to be part of the loom.
9. The crowd made itself heard as it applauded the beauty of Arachne's work.
10. When Athena began weaving, the web in which Arachne had trapped herself became all too clear.
11. Athena's tapestry was breathtaking: The goddess used the sky itself to color her threads.
12. That tapestry foretold how we mortals would destroy ourselves through our pride and willfulness.
13. When Athena finished, the people threw themselves to the ground in a demonstration of respect, and Arachne knew she had lost.
14. Rather than end Arachne's life, Athena turned her into a spider that could spin webs for itself.

Name ______________________________

Apply

Rewrite each sentence, replacing the underlined word or words with a reflexive or intensive pronoun.

15. Arachne got <u>Arachne</u> into trouble by boasting about her weaving. ______________________________

____

16. Do you sometimes boast about <u>you</u>? ______________________________

____

17. The gods considered <u>the gods</u> to be far superior to mortals. ______________________________

____

18. Zeus<u>—yes, Zeus—</u>was prideful about his own mighty powers. ______________________________

____

Zeus is the king of the Greek gods.

Reinforce

Imagine that you yourself did something to offend Athena. Write a paragraph telling how you got yourself into and out of trouble. Include at least two reflexive pronouns and one intensive pronoun in your paragraph.

____

____

____

____

____

____

____

____

____

Read and Analyze

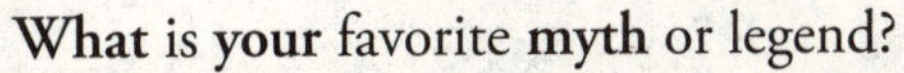

What is **your** favorite **myth** or legend?

Circle the boldfaced word that shows ownership or indicates a relationship.

Possessive pronouns show ownership or close relationship. The possessive pronouns *her, his, its, their, my, our,* and *your* can replace possessive nouns. (*The queen's* dress is blue.—*Her* dress is blue.) The possessive pronouns *hers, his, theirs, mine, ours,* and *yours* can replace both a possessive noun and the noun that is a possession. (The blue dress is *the queen's*—The blue dress is *hers*.)

See Handbook Section 17d

Practice

Circle the possessive pronouns. There may be more than one in each sentence.

1. King Midas lived with his young daughter in a palace in Greece; theirs was a peaceful, happy life.
2. One morning King Midas was walking in his garden when he stumbled upon a strange creature—its top half was like that of a man, but its bottom half looked like that of a goat.
3. King Midas thought the creature might be ill, so he sent it to his court physician.
4. Shortly thereafter, the god Dionysus appeared and told King Midas he would grant him one wish for helping his friend, a satyr by the name of Silenus.
5. Midas murmured, "Anything I want can be mine!"
6. The king thought to himself, "After my daughter, the thing I love best is gold," and it was thus that he wished that all he touched would turn to gold.
7. "Your wish is a bit rash," Dionysus exclaimed, "but I will honor it all the same."
8. The king ran to touch several fig trees in his garden, and each one turned to gold!
9. Laughing with glee, the king ordered a great feast to be prepared in celebration, and soon his servants entered the dining hall, their arms laden with huge platters of delicious food.
10. King Midas lifted a fig from a tray, but as soon as he touched it, its skin turned to gold!
11. The king also discovered that water turned to solid gold as it touched his lips.
12. Then his daughter ran inside and, before he could stop her, she hugged him and turned to gold.
13. Weeping inconsolably, Midas cried out that he wished his terrible curse could be washed away.
14. At that moment, Dionysus reappeared and told Midas he would grant his second wish if Midas washed himself in the river Pactolus.
15. Let this story be a lesson to all of us: our loved ones are worth far more than gold!

Name ____________________

Apply

Rewrite each sentence, replacing each group of underlined words with a possessive pronoun.

16. The legend's moral is "Be careful what you wish for." ____________________

17. King Midas's flaw was that he was too greedy. ____________________

18. The gods' lessons were sometimes painful ones. ____________________

19. My book is over here, and the one belonging to you is over there. ____________________

Reinforce

Use what you know about possessive pronouns to complete the puzzle.

Across

1. I wrote ____ own myth!
4. We turned in ____ homework.
5. A peaceful life was ____.
6. The dress is ____.
8. The dog licked ____ paw.

Down

2. Which myth is ____ favorite?
3. They walked in ____ garden.
6. Midas loved ____ young daughter.
7. That gold is ____, not yours!

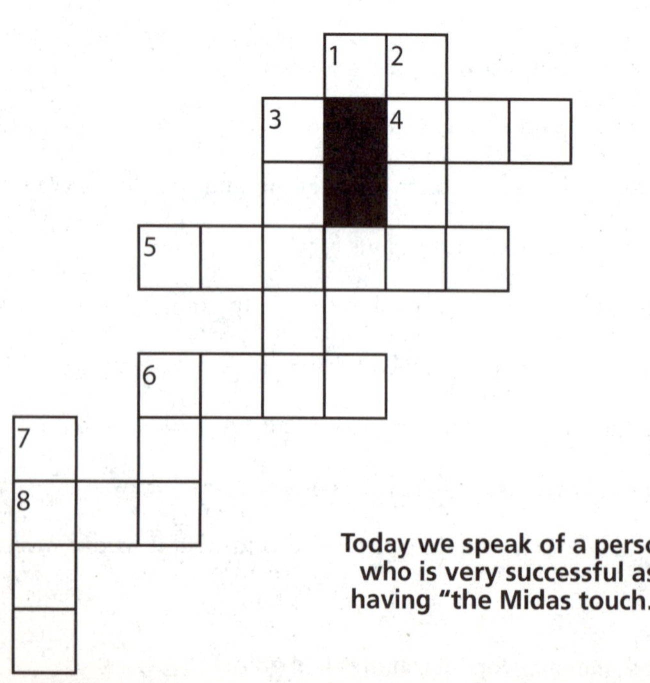

Today we speak of a person who is very successful as having "the Midas touch."

Read and Analyze

Does anyone know all the facts behind this American legend?

Circle the pronoun that refers to an unspecified person.

Indefinite pronouns refer to persons or things that are not identified. Indefinite pronouns include *all, anybody, both, either, anything, nothing, everyone, few, most, one, no one, several, nobody, someone,* and *something*.

See Handbook Section 17f

Practice

Circle the indefinite pronouns in these sentences. There may be more than one in each sentence.

1. Have all of you heard of Johnny Appleseed?
2. Most have heard the name, but few if any know the real story behind the legend.
3. Everybody believes that Johnny Appleseed was a scatterer of seeds, but he was actually a nurseryman.
4. A nurseryman is someone who plants seeds, tends plants, and provides young plants to others.
5. Does anybody know Johnny Appleseed's real name?
6. His name was John Chapman, and almost nothing is known about his early life.
7. Practically everything written about him is based on guesswork.
8. Something we do know, however, is that he was born in Leominster, Massachusetts, on September 26, 1774.
9. We also know that John Chapman had two passions—planting apple trees and being a missionary—and he pursued both.
10. Something else we know is that for almost 50 years, John Chapman traveled through Ohio, Indiana, and Pennsylvania preaching and establishing apple orchards.
11. Chapman was not the only nurseryman to plant trees and sell them to settlers, but he is the only one who achieved legendary stature.
12. Someone who always walks barefoot, even in the snow, wears a tin pan as a hat, and makes a sack into a shirt makes a colorful figure for a legend.
13. Some claim that he always slept out in his apple nurseries, confident in the belief that nothing could harm him as long as he lived in harmony with nature.
14. Because there is such limited information on Chapman's life, everyone is free to paint his or her own picture of this colorful American legend.

Johnny Appleseed planted thousands of trees in Ohio, Indiana, and Pennsylvania.

Name ____________________

Apply

Complete each sentence by writing an indefinite pronoun.

15. Can ____________________ tell me anything about Johnny Appleseed?
16. We know some facts about his adult life but ____________________ about his early childhood.
17. Don't believe ____________________ you hear about him!
18. I'll tell you ____________________ I learned about him, if you promise not to tell anyone else.
19. It's likely that ____________________ will ever know the entire truth behind the legend.

Reinforce

Circle the indefinite pronoun in each sentence. Then write each letter of the pronoun on the lines provided.

20. There are many stories about Johnny Appleseed, but few are true!

___ ___ ___
1 (first line), 5 (third line)

21. According to legend, everyone who met Johnny Appleseed liked him.

___ ___ ___ ___ ___ ___ ___ ___
3 (fourth line), 2 (sixth line), 9 (eighth line)

22. Often Johnny Appleseed would give settlers trees without charging anything.

___ ___ ___ ___ ___ ___ ___ ___
6 (first line), 4 (fourth line)

23. Many say that Johnny Appleseed never hunted animals or ate meat.

___ ___ ___ ___
8 (third line), 7 (fourth line)

Use the numbered letters to answer this question:

Where is John Chapman buried?

___ ___ ___ ___ ___ ___ ___ ___ ___, Indiana
1 2 3 4 5 6 7 8 9

Read and Analyze

Relative and Interrogative Pronouns

Unit 3: Lesson 33

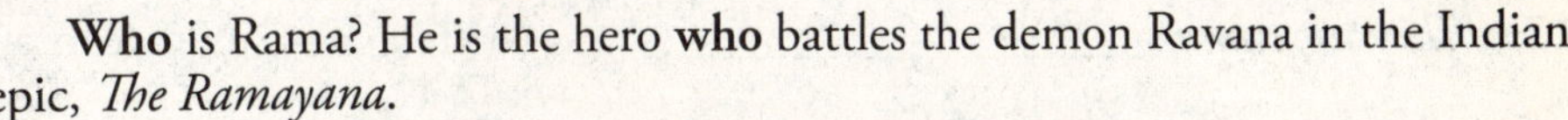

Who is Rama? He is the hero **who** battles the demon Ravana in the Indian epic, *The Ramayana*.

Draw a box around the boldfaced word that asks a question. Circle the boldfaced word that refers to the noun just before it.

When the pronouns *who, whom, whose, which,* and *that* are used to introduce an adjective clause, they are called **relative pronouns**. A relative pronoun always follows the noun described by the adjective clause it begins. When the pronouns *who, whom, whose, which,* and *what* are used to begin a question, they are called **interrogative pronouns**.

See Handbook Sections 17g, 17h

Practice

Circle each relative pronoun. Underline the noun the adjective clause is describing. Draw a box around each interrogative pronoun.

1. Who knows the story of *The Ramayana*?
2. Rama is the earthly form that the god Vishnu took in order to slay the demon Ravana.
3. Ravana kidnapped Rama's wife Sita and took her away to his home in Lanka, which was across a vast ocean.
4. Rama sent an army of monkeys, which was led by Hanuman, to go in search of Sita.
5. The army couldn't cross the ocean, but Hanuman, whose father was the wind god Pavana, could fly.
6. When Hanuman found Sita, she gave him a jewel that would assure Rama she was still alive.
7. Ravana's men captured Hanuman and set his tail on fire, but Hanuman had a blessing that protected him.
8. What did that clever monkey do next?
9. He leapt from roof to roof using his tail, which was still aflame, to set fire to the city of Lanka.
10. When Hanuman returned to Rama, Rama demanded to build a bridge that would reach Lanka.
11. The bridge, which was built in five days, allowed Rama and his army to cross into Lanka.
12. Ravana's army was led by his son, Indrajit, who had the power to make himself invisible.
13. Indrajit was about to perform a ceremony that would give him the power to kill Rama.
14. Rama's brother attacked and killed him, an act that brought Ravana to the battlefield.
15. Ravana and Rama fought intensely until Rama hurled a powerful weapon that he'd been given.
16. Ravana was vanquished, and Rama flew with Sita back to Ayodhya, whose people made Rama king.

Name ______________________________

Apply

Complete each sentence by writing a relative pronoun or an interrogative pronoun.

17. *The Ramayana,* ____________________ was written over 2,000 years ago, has been read by millions of people all over the world.
18. Rama is the character around ____________________ *The Ramayana* centers.
19. ____________________ is the main conflict in the story?
20. The main conflict ____________________ drives the story is the kidnapping of Rama's wife, Sita.
21. Ravana is the villain ____________________ kidnaps her.
22. ____________________ is Hanuman?
23. He is the son of Pavana, the god ____________________ controls the winds.
24. He's also the one ____________________ ability to fly helps save Sita.

Temples to honor Hanuman have been built in India and Japan.

Reinforce

Circle the pronoun that is used incorrectly in each sentence. Then rewrite each sentence with the appropriate relative pronoun.

25. My favorite part of *The Ramayana* is the part what tells how Hanuman sets fire to Lanka.

____

____

26. Rama's battle with Ravana, that happens at the end of the story, is also very exciting.

____

____

27. People that enjoy *The Ramayana* may also enjoy reading Chinese or Aztec myths.

____

____

Read and Analyze

Adjectives and Adverbs

Hercules was a noble and mighty warrior.

He labored diligently and fought valiantly.

Circle the two words in the first sentence that tell what kind of warrior Hercules was. Draw a box around the short word that precedes these descriptive words. Underline the two words in the second sentence that tell how Hercules labored and fought.

Adjectives modify nouns, pronouns, and other adjectives. Some adjectives tell what kind. Others tell how many or which one. The articles *a, an,* and *the* are also adjectives. **Adverbs** modify verbs, adjectives, and other adverbs. They tell how, when, where, or to what extent (how much). Many adverbs end in *-ly.* Other common adverbs are *first, very,* and *often.*

See Handbook Sections 16, 19

Practice

Circle each adjective and draw an arrow to the word it modifies. Draw a box around each adverb and draw an arrow to the word or words it modifies.

1. Hercules submissively presented himself to the king of Mycenae.
2. The wily king assigned Hercules a series of seemingly impossible tasks.
3. One of these labors began when a messenger suddenly entered the royal palace.
4. He breathlessly reported that a huge snake was terrorizing the countryside.
5. The snake was called the Lernaean Hydra; it had nine heads, and one head was immortal.
6. The king sent Hercules to search for this monster, and Hercules departed with his young nephew Iolaus.
7. In a dense forest Hercules found the dark cave where the Hydra lived.
8. He fired three arrows into the cave, and the malevolent Hydra emerged.
9. Its nine heads angrily bobbed and hissed; Hercules obliterated one head, but two heads immediately grew in its place!
10. Hercules desperately turned to Iolaus and gave him instructions.
11. Iolaus ignited a long branch and quickly ran to his uncle's side.
12. Hercules demolished head after head; Iolaus placed the red-hot branch on each open wound, searing it so no new heads could grow.
13. Hercules buried the immortal head under a huge rock to prevent it from causing more harm.
14. Hercules's reappearance surprised and angered the king; he had firmly believed he was sending Hercules on a fatal mission.

One of the Hydra's nine heads was immortal.

Name ______________________________

Apply

Expand each sentence below by adding one adjective and one adverb. You can use words from the word bank, or use your own words.

likely	continually	only	certainly
fierce	dangerous	valiant	hideous

15. The Lernaean Hydra terrorized residents. ______________________________

____

16. This monster seemed invincible. ______________________________

____

17. Without the help of his nephew, Hercules would have lost his battle with the Hydra. ______________________________

____

18. This task was one of twelve that the king assigned to Hercules. ______________________________

____

Reinforce

A noun can also be used to describe another noun.

mountain road　　*computer* class　　*school* principal

Circle four adjectives and four nouns in the puzzle. Then use the four nouns you circled as noun modifiers in your own sentences.

V	K	B	N	I	G	D	Z	S	A
I	M	M	O	R	T	A	L	H	P
C	S	D	B	U	J	N	V	E	P
T	C	Q	L	R	Z	G	F	C	L
O	L	U	E	V	V	E	B	N	E
R	A	X	J	U	Y	R	L	S	H
I	S	H	I	S	T	O	R	Y	X
O	S	Y	N	W	I	U	G	Y	W
U	Z	K	P	A	B	S	W	X	K
S	W	A	M	P	E	U	K	E	D

19. ______________________________

____

20. ______________________________

____

21. ______________________________

____

22. ______________________________

____

Read and Analyze

Demonstrative Pronouns and Demonstrative Adjectives

Unit 3: Lesson 35

This picture shows Popocatépetl and Iztaccíhuatl.

Those are two of the tallest mountains in Mexico.

Circle the word that modifies the noun *picture* and tells *which one*. Underline the word that stands for the noun *mountains*.

This, these, that, and *those* are **demonstratives**. **Demonstrative adjectives** describe nouns and tell which one. **Demonstrative pronouns** take the place of nouns. *This* and *these* refer to a thing or things close by. *That* and *those* refer to a thing or things farther away. **Remember to use this information when you speak, too.**

See Handbook Sections 16, 17i

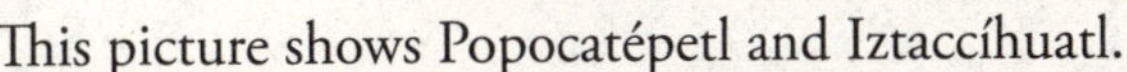

Practice

Underline each demonstrative pronoun. Circle each demonstrative adjective. Draw an arrow from each demonstrative adjective to the noun or pronoun it modifies.

1. Those two mountains in the picture are both volcanoes.
2. This smaller one nearby is Popocatépetl, and that larger one in the distance is Iztaccíhuatl.
3. A legend explains how both of these were formed.
4. This legend features a great Aztec warrior by the name of Popocatépetl.
5. This young warrior fell in love with an Aztec princess by the name of Iztaccíhuatl, but soon after, he learned he had to leave for battle.
6. That was sad news indeed, but before leaving, our hero received permission to marry the princess upon his return from war.
7. Many men had sought the princess's affections, and one of these was quite jealous of Popocatépetl for winning the right to wed the princess.
8. That cunning suitor approached the princess and told her Popocatépetl had been killed in battle.
9. The princess, saddened by this report, died from grief!
10. When Popocatépetl returned and learned this, he ordered a great tomb be built for her.
11. Legend has it, in those days, it was much easier to move land than it is today, so ten hills were brought together to form one great mountain.
12. No sooner had Popocatépetl laid the dead princess on the top of that mountain, than the mountain took on the shape of a sleeping woman.
13. As this warrior kneeled before his princess, snow began falling and soon covered both of them.
14. Popocatépetl and Iztaccíhuatl were transformed into those two volcanoes that we see today.

Name ______________________________

Apply

Rewrite each sentence, replacing the underlined words with a demonstrative pronoun or with a demonstrative adjective and any other words needed. Answers may vary.

15. The drawing I'm pointing to shows Popocatépetl. ______________________________

____

16. The mountains shown in the photograph are in Mexico. ______________________________

____

17. The smoke rising from the volcano is called the plume. ______________________________

____

18. The type of volcano shown in the picture is a cone volcano. ______________________________

____

Reinforce

Circle the demonstrative pronoun in each of the following quotations.

I also grew up, thankfully, with a love of language. That may have happened because I was bilingual at an early age.

—Amy Tan, interview with the Academy of Achievement

I am not one of those who in expressing opinions confine themselves to facts.

—Mark Twain, "Wearing White Clothes" speech

Whose woods these are I think I know.

—Robert Frost, "Stopping by Woods on a Snowy Evening"

Now explain what the demonstrative pronoun refers to in each quotation above.

19. ______________________________

____

20. ______________________________

____

21. ______________________________

____

Ordering Adjectives

Unit 3: Lesson 36

a. Trieu Thi Trinh was a **female brave** warrior said to have lived in the third century.

b. Trieu Thi Trinh was a **brave female** warrior said to have lived in the third century.

c. Her **extraordinary, inspirational** leadership in Vietnam's effort to resist invaders from China has earned her **widespread, long-lasting** admiration.

Read sentences *a* and *b*. Which sentence has the boldfaced adjectives in an order that sounds natural? __________ Read sentence *c*. What punctuation mark is used to separate each pair of boldfaced adjectives? __________

When you use more than one adjective to describe a noun, put the adjectives in an **order that sounds natural.** When you use **coordinate adjectives**—a pair of adjectives of a similar kind—to describe a noun, place a comma between the adjectives.

See Handbook Sections 8, 16

Practice

Underline the adjectives in parentheses that are written correctly.

1. According to legend, Trieu Thi Trinh stood nine feet tall and had a (loud, clear/loud clear) voice.
2. Some tales say that she rode into battle on an elephant; others claim that she fought atop (an enormous gray/a gray enormous) hippopotamus.
3. Her (older protective/protective older) brother tried to dissuade her from becoming a warrior.
4. She told him she had no intention of being a (submissive typical/typical submissive) female.
5. "I wish to ride the tempest, tame the waves, kill the sharks," she said, and she led her troops to (thirty consecutive/consecutive thirty) victories over the invaders.
6. Legends say that she wore (gold bright/bright gold) armor and carried a sword in each hand.
7. Her opponents feared her (fierce, penetrating/fierce penetrating) gaze; they said, "It would be easier to fight a tiger than to face Lady Trieu in battle."
8. Eventually the invaders sent in such a (well-armored huge/huge well-armored) fighting force that Trieu Thi Trinh could not prevail.
9. Although Lady Trieu perished in that battle, she lives on in (numerous thrilling/thrilling numerous) tales.
10. Most researchers believe that the legends of Trieu Thi Trinh are based on the exploits of a (female real/real female) warrior who led Vietnamese soldiers to victory nineteen centuries ago.

Trieu Thi Trinh is celebrated as a noble hero by the Vietnamese people.

Name ______________________________

Apply

Expand each sentence below by writing two adjectives on the line. Use an appropriate article in front of the adjectives, if one is needed. Be sure to use the adjectives in a natural-sounding order. If the two adjectives are of a similar kind, use a comma to separate them.

11. An army led by ______________________ individual has the best chance of success.
12. Even ______________________ army can be defeated by a clever leader and a disciplined group of fighters.
13. Many cultures tell ______________________ stories about female warriors.
14. Today ______________________ female soldiers help protect their nations as members of military units.
15. Perhaps the ______________________ accomplishments of some of these women will inspire legends that will be told and retold in future centuries.

Reinforce

Which of the legendary characters described in this unit do you think is most inspiring? Write a paragraph in which you describe this individual's traits, talents, and accomplishments, and explain why you admire him or her. Use a pair of adjectives with one of the nouns you include.

____

____

____

____

____

____

____

____

____

____

____

____

Spelling Practice

Read and Analyze

a. Myths offer explanations for things in the **universe.**

b. They have a **dual** purpose of amusing and teaching.

Which sentence contains a word with a prefix meaning "two"? _______
Which sentence contains a word with a prefix meaning "one"? _______

Prefixes: *uni-, mono-, duo-, bi-*

Prefixes are word parts added to the beginnings of words to change their meanings. Some prefixes indicate numbers. The prefixes ***uni-*** and ***mono-*** mean "one," as in *unicycle* and *monorail.* The prefix ***duo-*** means "two," as in *duet,* and the prefix ***bi-*** means "two" or "twice," as in *bisect.*

Word Sort

Use the words below to complete the word sort.

duplication	universe	uniform	biplane	dual	monocle
monopoly	binoculars	monotony	university	biennial	duplex

Prefix *uni-*	**Prefix *mono-***
Prefix *duo-*	**Prefix *bi-***

Name ______________________________

Pattern Practice

monotonous	bisect	unique	monotone	bimonthly	unify
monocle	biannual	unison	duplex	duo	monorail

Write the word from the word bank above that solves each riddle.

1. I'm one-of-a-kind. What am I? ______________
2. I come around every two months. What am I? ______________
3. I'm a group of two. What am I? ______________
4. I'm many voices sounding as one. What am I? ______________
5. I'll cut something in two. What am I? ______________
6. I'm a single lens for seeing. What am I? ______________
7. I'm two connected apartments. What am I? ______________
8. I'm one thing over and over. What am I? ______________

Write the word from the word bank above that best completes each sentence.

9. The class recited the pledge in perfect ______________.
10. The shelter has a ______________ fundraiser in March and October.
11. The poor presenter spoke in a quiet ______________.
12. ______________ the blueberry muffin and give me half.
13. We rode a ______________ to the next airport terminal.
14. This agreement is meant to ______________ the two countries.

Use the Dictionary

Circle the prefix that best completes each word. Use a print or an online dictionary to check your work.

15. I have the opening **mono/duo**logue in the play!
16. Shaun flexed his **uni/bi**ceps as he lifted the weights.

(you) | Diagram | sentences

See Handbook Section 41

Diagramming Understood *You*

Imperative sentences (commands) usually contain the understood *you* as the subject. When the subject is understood, write (*you*) in the sentence diagram, like this:

Close the door.

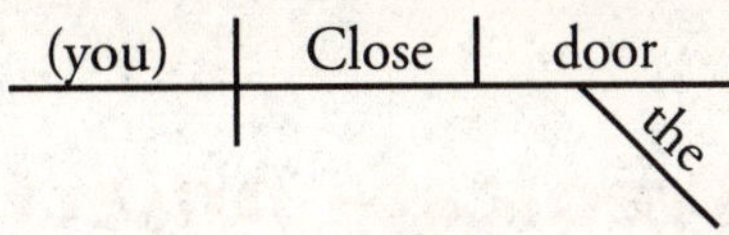

Try diagramming these sentences.

1. Read this book.

2. Do your homework.

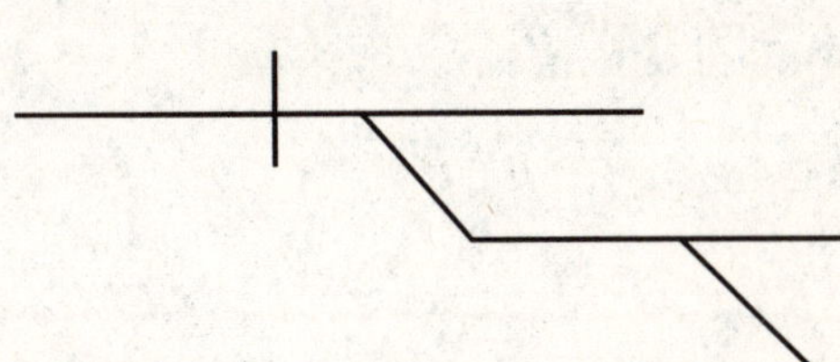

3. Come to the party!

Diagramming Possessive Pronouns

Look at the way the possessive pronouns *my* and *their* are diagrammed in these sentences.

My aunt coaches soccer.

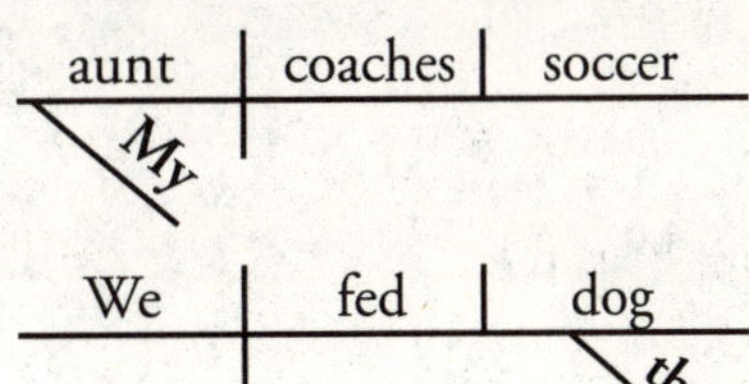

We fed **their** dog.

Now diagram these sentences.

4. They joined my class.

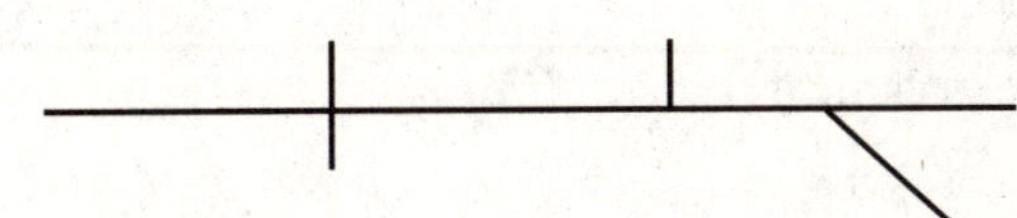

5. His story and her drawings won awards.

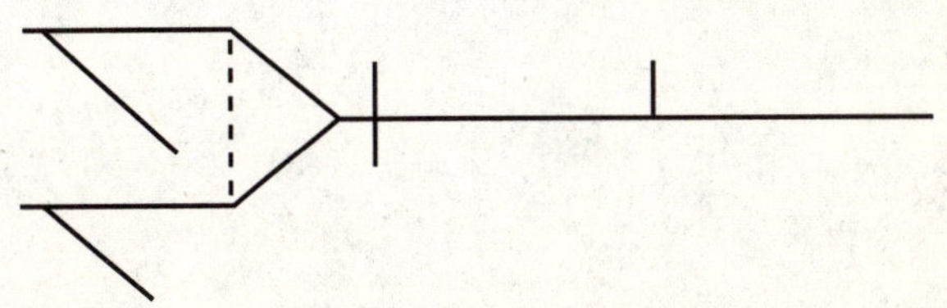

Name ____

6. Our class read a legend.

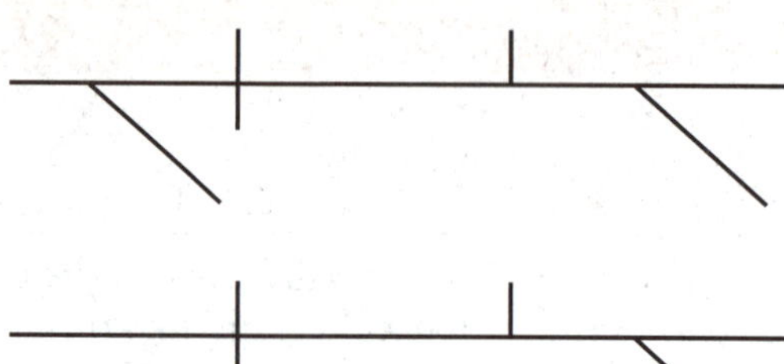

7. I loved your gift.

Diagramming Predicate Adjectives and Predicate Nouns

A linking verb, such as *be*, can link the subject of a sentence to an adjective or noun in the predicate. Look at the way *noble* and *a warrior* are diagrammed in these examples:

Predicate adjective:
Hercules was **noble**.

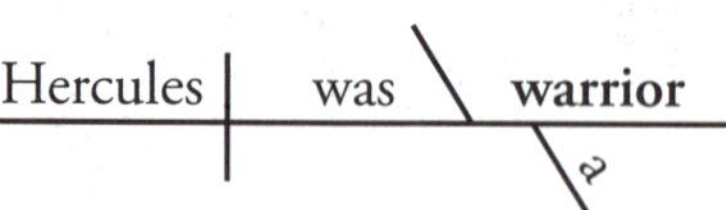

Predicate noun:
Hercules was a **warrior**.

Hercules | was \ **warrior**
a

Try diagramming these sentences.

8. Midas was a king.

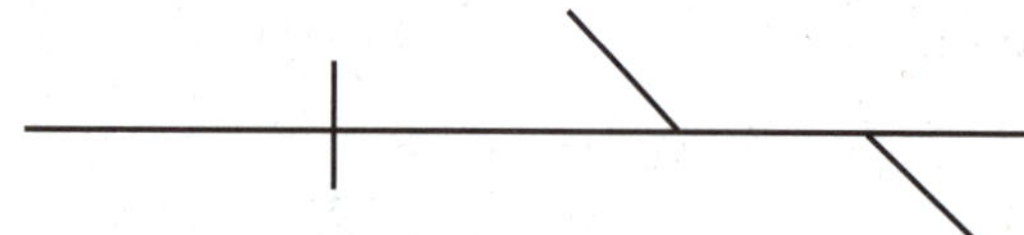

9. Midas was unwise.

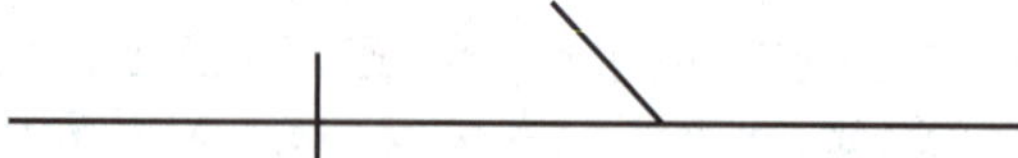

10. Arachne was skillful but boastful.

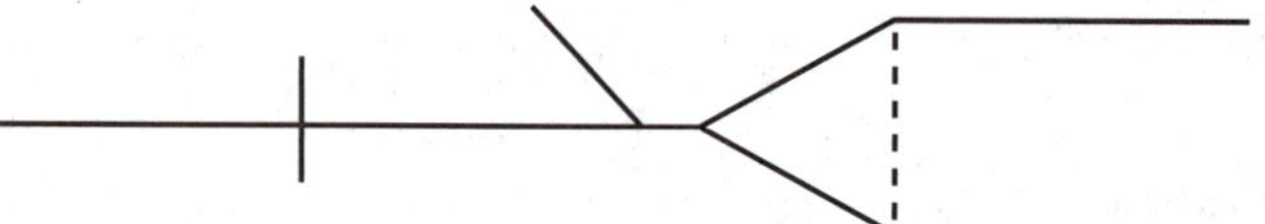

11. Arachne became a spider.

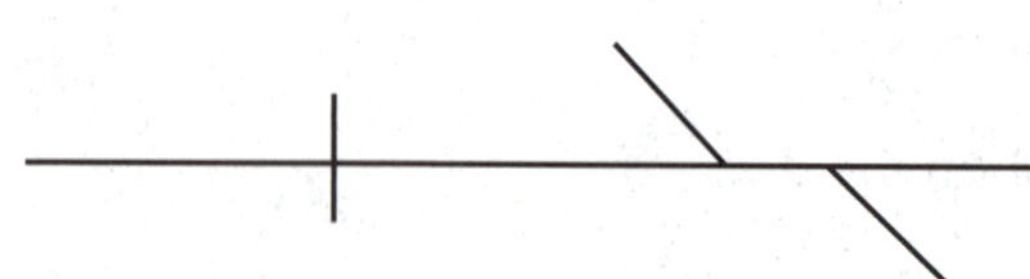

These sentences need help! Rewrite them so they give more information about Johnny Appleseed. Refer to Lesson 32 if you need to.

1. Everyone loves the legend. ______________________________

____

2. John Chapman was a real-life nurseryman. ______________________________

____

3. He bought up land and planted trees. ______________________________

____

4. Some stories were quite outlandish. ______________________________

____

5. Most mention his clothes. ______________________________

____

When you write a paragraph, always include a topic sentence, two or more supporting sentences that add details about your topic, and a concluding sentence. Your reader will enjoy your paragraph more if you include colorful adjectives and use pronouns and possessives appropriately. Notice how this model paragraph is written.

topic sentence

supporting sentences

colorful adjectives

pronouns and possessives

concluding sentence

My **favorite** *myth is "Theseus and the Minotaur."* The Minotaur was a **half-bull, half-human** creature ***that*** lived in a labyrinth. **Fourteen young** men and women were to be given to the Minotaur as a sacrifice. Theseus offered to be ***one*** of the victims. The princess Ariadne, ***who*** was in love with Theseus, told ***him*** to unwind a ball of thread behind ***him*** as ***he*** entered the maze. ***Everything*** worked out as planned. Theseus killed the **savage** Minotaur and found ***his*** way back out of the maze. *This myth has it all–monsters, drama, and adventure!*

Name

Writing a Paragraph

The sentences you revised on page 111 can be used to write a paragraph. Decide what order the sentences should be in. Write the paragraph on the lines below. Add other words and a concluding sentence, if necessary.

Write a paragraph about your favorite myth or legend. You might write about one you studied in Unit 3 or about another one you know. Refer to the model paragraph on page 111 if you need help. Be sure to include a variety of interesting adjectives. Use pronouns and possessives when appropriate.

Read your paragraph again. Use this checklist to make sure it is complete and correct.

- ❑ My paragraph has a topic sentence.
- ❑ My paragraph has at least two supporting sentences.
- ❑ All my sentences are clear and make sense.
- ❑ I have included colorful adjectives.
- ❑ I have used pronouns and possessives correctly.
- ❑ My paragraph has a concluding sentence.

Proofreading Practice

Read this passage about the legendary John Henry and find the mistakes. Use the proofreading marks to show how the mistakes should be fixed. Use a dictionary to check and correct spellings.

Proofreading Marks

Mark	Means	Example
ℓ	delete	John Henry is an ~~old~~ American legend.
∧	add	John Henry is ∧(an) American legend.
≡	make into an uppercase letter	John Henry is an american legend.
/	make into a lowercase letter	John Henry is an American Legend.
⊙	add a period	John Henry is an American legend⊙
(sp)	fix spelling	John Henry is an American legund.

The Mighty John Henry

John henry worked on a Chesapeake and Ohio Railroad crew. The crew was divided into teams of four, and it was each teams job to drive the long iron spikes that connected the rails to the wooden ties. Standing in a circle, the men would take turns swinging there long-handled hammers until each spike was sunk in place.

Once, the crew was working in the Mountains of west virginia. they had to blast dynamite to carve a tunel through the mountain. The railroad boss, whose thought the work was going too slowly, brought in a speicial machine what could drive spikes as it rode along the rails. The men became worried that they would lose their jobs if those machine could do faster work. Than they could.

John Henry picked up hammer and began racing against the machine, people say he swung his hammer so hard that sparks shot out as it hit each iron spike. John Henry won the contest; he laid himself fourteen feet of track and the machine only laid nine. However, John Henry's heart burst from the strain and he died on the spot, hammer in hand. The mens buried him their, and to this day when the trains pass through this tunnel, they blow their whistle's soft and low in solem tribute to the mighty john Henry.

Proofreading Checklist

You can use the checklist below to help you find and fix mistakes in your own writing. Write the titles of your own stories or reports in the blanks at the top of the chart. Then use the questions to check your work. Make a check mark (✓) in each box after you have checked that item.

Proofreading Checklist for Unit 3

Titles				
Have I capitalized proper nouns?				
Have I written plural forms of nouns correctly?				
Have I written possessive forms of nouns correctly?				
Have I used correct forms of personal pronouns?				
Have I used possessive pronouns correctly?				
Have I used appropriate relative pronouns?				

Also Remember…

Does each sentence begin with an uppercase letter?				
Did I use a dictionary to check and correct spellings?				
Have I used commas correctly?				

Your Own List

Use this space to write your own list of things to check in your writing.

Community Connection

In Unit 3 of *Grammar, Usage, and Mechanics,* students learned about different kinds of **nouns, pronouns,** and **adjectives,** and used what they learned to improve their own writing. The content of these lessons focuses on the theme **Myths and Legends.** As students completed the exercises, they learned about myths and legends from many cultures. These pages offer a variety of activities that reinforce skills and concepts presented in the unit. They also provide opportunities for the student to make connections between the information presented in the lessons and their modern surroundings.

Name That Mythological Character

Greek and Roman myths have been a part of our culture for so long that many words have been derived from mythological characters' names. For example, Arachne's name gave rise to the scientific word for spider: *arachnid.* Collect a list of words and expressions that are derived from Greek and Roman myths; then ask a classmate to guess which mythological character each came from.

Brand New Traditional Tales

Since many myths have no one official version, people are free to reuse plots, themes, and characters, and to retell the myths in new ways. Look for elements of a Greek or Roman myth in modern media. You may consider comic books, movies, television, and recent books and novels. Share your results with the class.

Discovering More Myths and Legends

Choose a region other than Greece or Italy, such as North America, China, India, Peru, West Africa, Mexico, Scandinavia, or the Caribbean. Search for myths and legends from that region. Print out or copy some stories that you particularly like. Arrange to visit a hospital, senior home, or elementary school to read the myths or legends aloud. Alternatively, you can take part in your local library's read-aloud program.

Release Your Inner Mythologist

Try writing a myth or legend in the style of an established mythological tradition. To get yourself started, choose a character from a myth you have read, and imagine a new adventure. To give your myth an interesting plot, you may want to include a problem or moral dilemma that the main character solves at the end. When you have finished your myth, share it with friends and family.

Celebrating Myths and Legends

In this unit, you read summaries and retellings of different myths and legends. Which did you find most interesting? Try to find a published version of that myth or legend. Ask your classmates to find published versions of their favorite myth, as well. Then plan a celebration at which everyone reads aloud his or her favorite myth or legend. Begin by making these decisions:

- When and where will you hold the celebration?
- Which myths and legends, out of those you and your classmates gathered, will be read aloud at the celebration?
- Who will you invite to the celebration, and how will you distribute invitations or announcements?

Use the planning guide on the next page to help you plan your Myth and Legend Celebration.

me ______________________________

Myth and Legend Celebration Planner

When the celebration will take place: ______________________________

Where it will take place: ______________________________

List of myths and legends to be retold at the event:

1. ______________________________
   ____
2. ______________________________
   ____
3. ______________________________
   ____
4. ______________________________
   ____

List of people who will read each aloud:

1. ______________________________
   ____
2. ______________________________
   ____
3. ______________________________
   ____
4. ______________________________
   ____

List of celebration invitees:

____

____

____

____

____

List of places to announce the event:

1. ______________________________
2. ______________________________
3. ______________________________
4. ______________________________
5. ______________________________

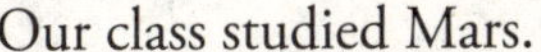

Our class studied Mars.

Mars is the fourth planet from the sun.

Underline the verb that shows action. Circle the verb that links the subject of the sentence to words in the predicate that rename and describe it.

An **action verb** shows action. It usually tells what the subject of a sentence or clause is doing, will do, or did. An action verb may include one or more helping verbs in addition to the main verb. A **linking verb** does not show action. It connects the subject of a sentence to a word(s) that describes or renames the subject. Linking verbs are usually forms of *be*. Some common linking verbs are *am, is, are, was, were, been,* and *will be*. The verbs *become, seem, appear,* and *look* can also be used as linking verbs. A linking verb may include one or more helping verbs in addition to the main verb.

See Handbook Sections 18a, 18c

Practice

Underline each action verb. Circle each linking verb.

1. In 1976, the United States made history when *Viking 1* and *Viking 2* arrived at Mars.
2. NASA launched *Viking 1* on August 20 and *Viking 2* on September 9, 1975.
3. The two parts of each spacecraft were an orbiter and a lander.
4. The spacecraft traveled for nearly a year on their way to an orbit around Mars.
5. Once in orbit around that planet, each lander separated from its orbiter.
6. They descended to the surface of the planet.
7. The "brain" of each lander was a specially designed computer.
8. The computers commanded the lander's actions.
9. During the mission, the two landers took photographs.
10. They also collected scientific data on the planet's surface.
11. They conducted biology experiments in search of signs of life.
12. The experiments provided important information about the chemical composition of the soil.
13. The soil was devoid of living microorganisms.
14. Scientists designed the spacecraft for 90 days of operation.
15. After several years, though, both spacecraft were still active!

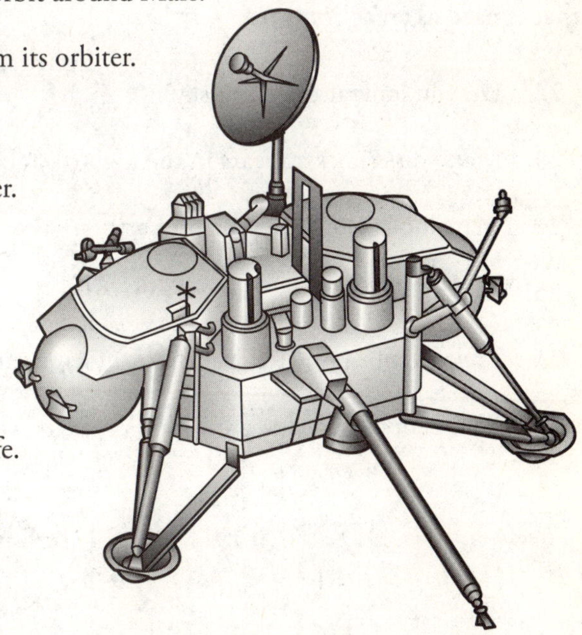

The *Viking* lander was about 10 feet across and 7 feet tall.

Name ____

Apply

Complete each sentence with a verb or phrase from the box. Underline each action verb you use. Circle each linking verb.

lies	is	may be	explore	want	offers

16. Mars ________________ a cold desert planet.
17. Even so, the planet ________________ exciting possibilities for exploration.
18. Because water is the key to finding out whether there is life on Mars, researchers ________________ more information about the planet.
19. NASA missions ________________ planetary features that might suggest the presence of water.
20. We know that no water ________________ on the surface of this planet.
21. However, large amounts of ice ________________ underground.

Reinforce

Some verbs, such as *appear, look, smell, feel, grow,* and *taste,* can be either action verbs or linking verbs, depending on how they are used in a sentence. You can test whether a verb is a linking verb by substituting a form of the verb *be* (*am, is, are, was, were, being* or *been*) in its place. If the form of *be* makes sense, the verb probably is a linking verb.

In the sentences below, circle each boldfaced verb that is used as a linking verb. Underline each boldfaced verb that is used as an action verb.

22. Do you **look** at the night sky?
23. Mars sometimes **appears** in the night sky above the United States.
24. Mars **looks** red to viewers on Earth.
25. In photos, this planet **appears** very dry.
26. I **felt** a replica of a red Mars rock in a museum.
27. Will people someday **grow** food on Mars?

Read and Analyze

Four days into its maiden voyage, the ocean liner *Titanic* **hit** an iceberg. Two hours and forty minutes later, it **sank** to the bottom of the sea.

Which boldfaced verb says an action the subject did by itself? ______

Which boldfaced verb tells about an action the subject did to something else? ______

A **transitive verb** is an action verb that transfers its action to a direct object. (*The captain steered the ship.*) An **intransitive verb** does not have a direct object. An intransitive verb shows action that the subject does alone. (*A ship floats.*) Many verbs can be either transitive or intransitive, depending on whether there is a direct object.

See Handbook Section 18b

Practice

Underline each transitive verb and draw a box around its direct object. Circle each intransitive verb.

1. As a young boy, Robert Ballard read stories about the sinking of *Titanic.*
2. Many years later, he worked as an oceanographer.
3. In 1985, Ballard and a French scientist took ships to the area of *Titanic's* collision.
4. For several weeks, they scanned the ocean floor with high-tech tools.
5. They sent an underwater craft on a picture-taking expedition along the ocean floor.
6. After several days, metal objects and then a ship's boiler appeared on the craft's video screen.
7. The underwater craft had discovered *Titanic*!
8. Ballard explored the site for several days.
9. Then he returned the following year with a different crew.
10. He took *Alvin,* a tiny submarine, down to the ocean floor.
11. From the submarine, Ballard sent a small, video-equipped deep-sea robot to the site of the wreck.
12. Ballard called the robot *Jason Junior,* or *J.J.*
13. The robot's camera peeked into many parts of the ship.
14. Ballard left a plaque in honor of the victims of *Titanic.*
15. He took nothing from that huge underwater museum.

The crew onboard *Alvin* were able to control the robot *J.J.* by means of a long cable.

Name ____

Apply

Write a verb from the word bank to complete each sentence. For each transitive verb you use, write *T*. For each intransitive verb you use, write *I*. Circle the direct object of each transitive verb.

swam	explored	remove	stole	grew	discovered

16. Robert Ballard and Jean-Louis Michel ________________ *Titanic* in 1985. _____
17. They ________________ the sunken ship with great care. _____
18. Fish ________________ among the ruins of the wreck. _____
19. A sea plant ________________ on a crystal chandelier. _____
20. The researchers did not ________________ anything from the ship. _____
21. Explorers who came in later years ________________ many objects from the site. _____

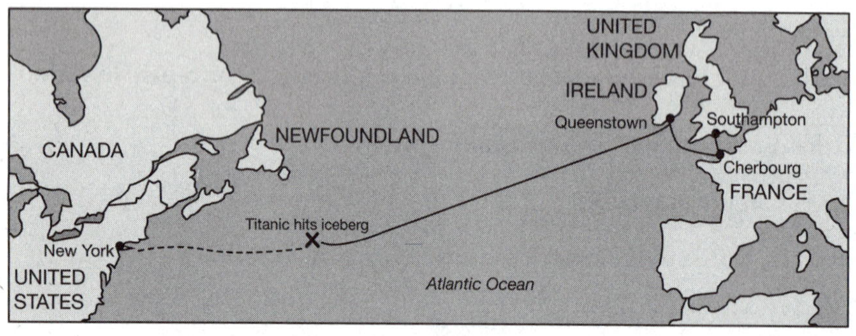

Titanic **hit an iceberg about 400 miles off the coast of Newfoundland.**

Reinforce

Many verbs can be transitive or intransitive, depending on whether they are used with a direct object.

D.O.

The iceberg *sank* the ship. (transitive)

Titanic sank in about three hours. (intransitive)

Use the verb *sailed* in two sentences. In one sentence, use the verb as a transitive verb with a direct object. In the other, use it as an intransitive verb. Circle the direct object of the transitive verb.

22. sailed (transitive): ____

____

____

23. sailed (intransitive): ____

____

____

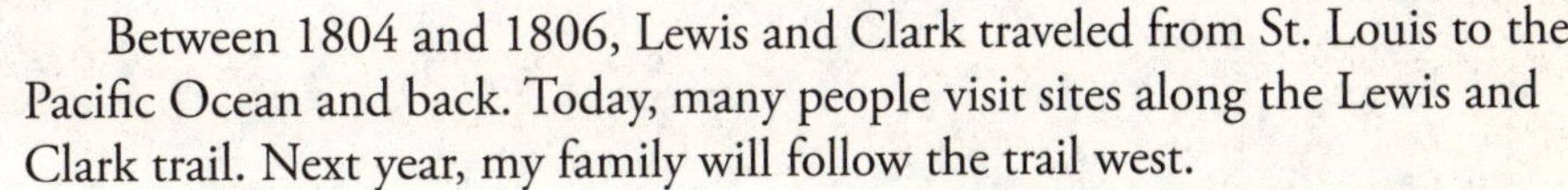

Read and Analyze

Between 1804 and 1806, Lewis and Clark traveled from St. Louis to the Pacific Ocean and back. Today, many people visit sites along the Lewis and Clark trail. Next year, my family will follow the trail west.

Circle the verb phrase that tells about something that will happen in the future. Underline the verb that tells about something that happened in the past. Draw a box around the verb that tells about something that happens regularly or is true now.

A **present tense verb** indicates that something happens regularly or is true now. A **past tense verb** tells about something that happened in the past. Regular verbs form the past tense by adding *-ed* (*watch, watched*). The spelling of most irregular verbs changes in the past tense (*know, knew*). A **future tense verb** tells what will happen in the future. Add the helping verb *will* to the present tense form of a verb to form the future tense (*visit, will visit*). **Remember to use this information when you speak, too.**

See Handbook Sections 18d, 18e

Practice

Circle the verb in each sentence. (Don't forget to include helping verbs.) Write whether the verb is in the *present, past,* or *future* tense.

1. President Jefferson sent Meriwether Lewis and William Clark on an exploratory journey into the new western territory of the United States. ___________
2. President Jefferson also asked for meetings with Native American groups from this area. ___________
3. Lewis and Clark kept detailed journals of their journey. ___________
4. They made notes about the people, plants, and animals along the way. ___________
5. The Lewis and Clark National Historic Trail extends through eleven states, from Illinois to the Pacific Ocean. ___________
6. Lewis and Clark journeyed roughly 3,700 miles from St. Louis to the Pacific Ocean. ___________
7. Thousands of people travel the Lewis and Clark National Historic Trail each year. ___________
8. Today, a journey along the entire westward route takes at least two weeks. ___________
9. Many lovely parks lie along the route of the trail. ___________
10. Next summer, my family and I will camp at Lewis and Clark Trail State Park. ___________
11. The park is approximately 25 miles northeast of Walla Walla, Washington, in the southeastern corner of the state. ___________
12. Meriwether Lewis and William Clark passed through southeastern Washington in the fall of 1805 and the spring of 1806. ___________
13. My family will spend about a week at this historic park outside Walla Walla. ___________

Name ______________________________

Apply

Write the past, present, or future tense form of a verb from the word bank to complete each sentence. Use a helping verb to form each future tense verb.

keep	take	record	be	learn	present

14. Some history websites ________________ journal entries from the Lewis and Clark expedition.
15. Lewis and Clark ________________ extensive notes and drew diagrams and sketches of what they saw.
16. Several sergeants on the expedition also ________________ observations in journals.
17. Visitors to these sites ________________ about the expedition from primary source materials.
18. It's likely that all expedition journals ________________ available online soon.
19. One day I will make a cross-country journey of my own, and I ________________ a journal of my adventures.

Reinforce

See Handbook Section 37

Write the opening paragraph for a brochure about the Lewis and Clark National Historic Trail. Do research on the Internet to learn about this trail. Use past, present, and future tenses in your entry.

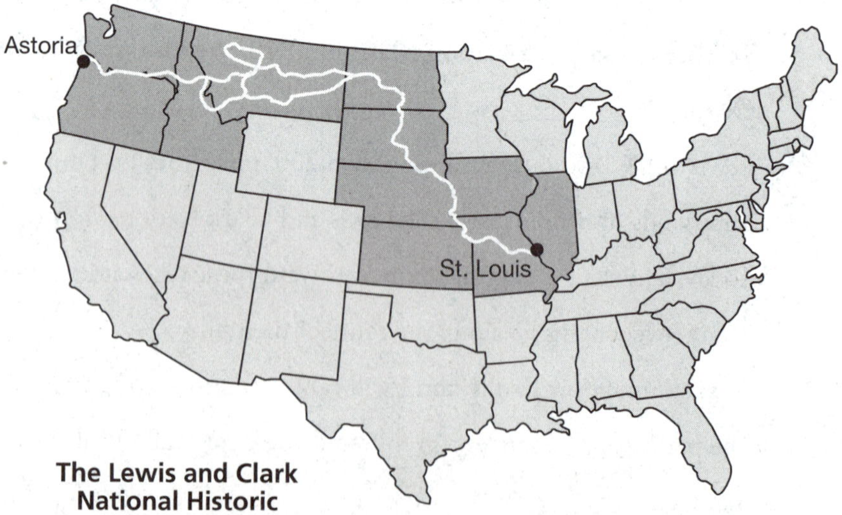

____

____

____

____

____

____

____

____

____

____

____

____

The Lewis and Clark National Historic Trail passes through eleven states.

Read and Analyze

Before the beginning of the twentieth century, no one **had made** an expedition all the way to the North Pole. Since the first successful journey there, nearly 200 people **have explored** the region. Who knows how many people **will have journeyed** the area by the end of this century?

Circle the boldfaced verb phrase that tells about an action that began in the past and continues today. Draw a box around the boldfaced verb phrase that tells about actions that will be complete before a certain time in the future. Underline the boldfaced verb phrase that tells about an action that was completed by a certain time in the past.

The **present perfect** tense (*have explored*) shows an action that started in the past and was recently completed or is still happening. The **past perfect** tense (*had made*) shows action that was completed by a certain time in the past. The **future perfect** tense (*will have journeyed*) shows action that will be complete by a certain time in the future. To form perfect tenses, use a form of *have* with the past participle of a verb. **Remember to use this information when you speak, too.**

See Handbook Sections 18d, 18e

Practice

Circle each verb in the present perfect tense. Underline each verb in the past perfect tense. Draw a box around each verb in the future perfect tense.

1. My history teacher has asked the class for facts about American explorers.
2. Many people have heard of Commander Robert E. Peary's expedition to the North Pole in 1908–1909.
3. Fewer people have read about Matthew Henson, an assistant to Peary on several historic journeys.
4. Henson had met Peary in Washington, D.C., in 1887, during Peary's preparations for an expedition to Nicaragua.
5. Peary had hired Henson as an expedition member.
6. Henson had acquired seafaring experience as a young ship worker.
7. By the beginning of the North Pole expedition in July 1908, Henson had spent more than twenty years with Peary as an explorer.
8. He, Peary, and four Inuits had reached either the North Pole or a place very near it by the end of the day on April 6, 1909.
9. The National Geographic Society has awarded Matthew Henson the Hubbard Medal posthumously.

Matthew Henson was admired by the Inuit.

10. Winners of this award have earned distinction in exploration, discovery, and research.
11. In 1906 President Theodore Roosevelt had presented Robert E. Peary with the same award.
12. Once I finish my notes on Matthew Henson, I will have created data files on about a dozen explorers.
13. How many explorers will my classmates have researched by the end of the year?

Name ____

Apply

Write the present perfect form (*has* or *have* + past participle), the past perfect form (*had* + past participle), or the future perfect form (*will have* + past participle) of the verb in parentheses to complete each sentence correctly.

14. Soon it ______________________ 110 years since Henson and Peary made their historic North Pole expedition. (be)

15. Some scholars ______________________ whether they reached the exact location of the North Pole. (question)

16. Others ______________________ whether Henson and Peary were the first to make it so far north. (dispute)

17. Perhaps the Inuit ______________________ the North Pole long before Peary and Henson. (explore)

18. In 1909 Frederick Cook claimed that he ______________________ the North Pole in April of the previous year. (reach)

19. Most people ______________________ that Cook's claim was false. (conclude)

Reinforce

Look at the timeline of Matthew Henson's life. Then use the information to write three sentences about him. Use a past perfect tense verb in each sentence to make clear that each event happened before another past time or event.

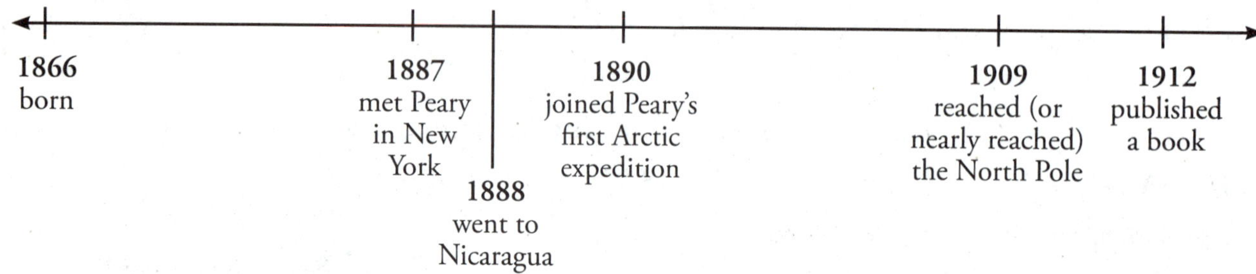

20. ____

____

21. ____

____

22. ____

____

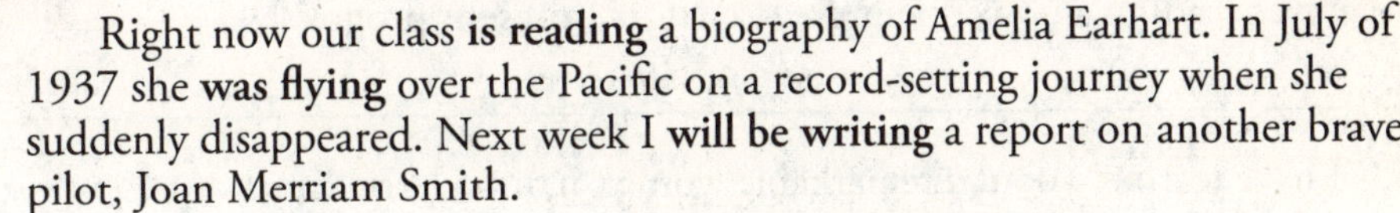

Read and Analyze

Right now our class **is reading** a biography of Amelia Earhart. In July of 1937 she **was flying** over the Pacific on a record-setting journey when she suddenly disappeared. Next week I **will be writing** a report on another brave pilot, Joan Merriam Smith.

Circle the boldfaced verb phrase that tells about an action that is going on now. Underline the boldfaced verb phrase that tells about an action that was happening for a while in the past. Draw a box around the verb phrase that tells about an action that will happen in the future.

Progressive forms of verbs show continuing action. To form a **present progressive** verb, add *am, is,* or *are* to the present participle of a verb (usually the present form + *ing*): *is snoring*. To form a **past progressive** verb, add *was* or *were* to the present participle: *was playing*. To form a **future progressive** verb, add *will be* to the present participle: *will be ringing*. **Remember to use this information when you speak, too.**

See Handbook Sections 18d, 18e

Practice

Underline each progressive verb form. After the sentence, write whether the verb is a *past progressive, present progressive,* or *future progressive* form.

1. The year was 1964, and Joan Smith was planning a solo flight around the world. ____________
2. My computer is listing all successful round-the-world fliers as of January 1, 1964. ____________
3. No woman's name is showing on the list. ____________
4. Joan Smith was retracing Earhart's 1937 round-the-world route. ____________
5. On the day of her disappearance, Earhart was flying over the South Pacific on the final one-third of her journey. ____________
6. On March 17, 1964, friends were waving to Joan Smith on her takeoff from Oakland, California. ____________
7. We are studying a map of Smith's eastward route to Florida. ____________
8. Thunderstorms were raging on her flight from Brazil to Africa. ____________
9. Smith was traveling with nothing but the hum of the plane engine for company! ____________
10. Most likely, people were cheering at the completion of Smith's round-the-world flight on May 12, 1964. ____________
11. I will be studying for my pilot's license at this time next year. ____________
12. I am practicing on flight simulators now. ____________
13. Maybe one day I will be flying over Brazil on a great journey like Smith's. ____________

Name ______________________________

Apply

Rewrite each sentence. Change the verb to the progressive form specified.

14. I was reading a book about great aviators. (present progressive)

____

15. I have learned about a remarkable woman named Jerrie Mock. (present progressive)

____

16. Mock flew around the world at the same time as Joan Smith. (past progressive)

____

17. She and Smith had taken different routes. (past progressive)

____

18. Each woman hoped for success on her potentially historic flight. (past progressive)

____

19. I will finish the chapter on Jerrie Mock tonight. (future progressive)

____

Reinforce

Circle the progressive verb form in each clue. Then write the answers in the puzzle.

Across

2. This is the direction that Smith was heading.
4. Many people are doing this in the sky right now.
5. She was trying to retrace Earhart's flight route.

Down

1. When Smith was flying from ________ to Africa, storms were raging.
3. She was hoping to fly around the world in 1937.
6. This woman was circling the globe at the same time as Smith.

Joan Merriam Smith flew 27,000 miles around the world.

Read and Analyze

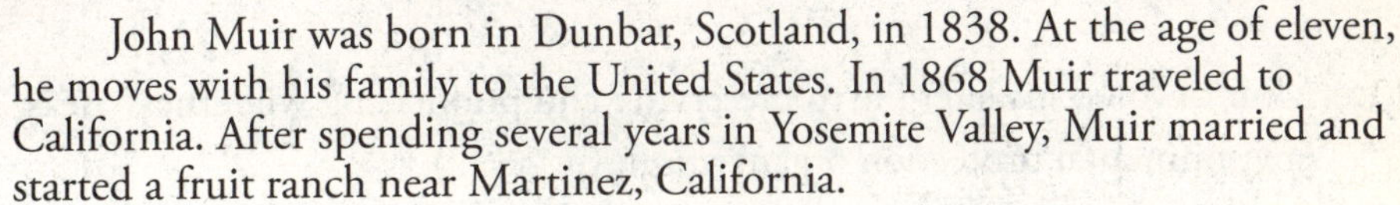

Avoiding Inappropriate Tense Shifts

Unit 4: Lesson 42

John Muir was born in Dunbar, Scotland, in 1838. At the age of eleven, he moves with his family to the United States. In 1868 Muir traveled to California. After spending several years in Yosemite Valley, Muir married and started a fruit ranch near Martinez, California.

Which verb in this paragraph shifts the time frame in a way that doesn't make sense? ____________ How should its sentence be rewritten so it stays in the time frame established in the previous sentence?

____

Choose **verb tenses** carefully so that the verb forms you use work together to indicate time accurately and consistently. When you describe events that happen in the same time frame, do not shift tenses. When you describe events that happen at different times, use verbs in different tenses to indicate the order in which the events happened.

See Handbook Section 18e

Practice

Read these paragraphs. If the verb in a sentence creates a time shift that doesn't make sense, mark an *X* through the verb. (1–5)

At the age of twenty-nine, John Muir set out on a journey that was to change his life. He had resigned from an industrial engineering job in Indianapolis, Indiana, because that profession did not interest him. He first walks 1,000 miles south to Florida. Then he sails to Cuba. He had planned a journey onward to South America, but he changed his plan because he had read about the natural wonders of a place in California.

On March 28, 1868, Muir arrived in San Francisco. Soon after, he travels east to Yosemite Valley. Four years earlier, conservationists had convinced Congress to set aside Yosemite as public land. Even so, with more settlers coming to California, those wild lands were being cleared and used for grazing. Muir joins the fight to preserve this land as wilderness. He publishes articles, essays, and books about the area. Eventually his efforts led to the creation of Yosemite National Park on October 1, 1890.

Write the correct tense form for each of the crossed out verbs above on the lines that follow.

6. ____________

7. ____________

8. ____________

9. ____________

10. ____________

John Muir is known for his conservational efforts.

Name ______________________________

Apply

Rewrite the following sentences so the verbs preserve the time frame established in the first clause of sentence 11. Add the time expressions in parentheses to the sentences to make the time progression clear.

11. Muir devoted his later life to preserving and publicizing wilderness areas; he cofounds the Sierra Club, an environmental protection organization. (in 1892)

____

____

12. The club leads a fight against a proposed reduction in the size of Yosemite National Park. (that same year)

____

____

13. Muir serves as president of the Sierra Club. (until his death in 1914)

____

____

14. Muir is being honored by having his picture appear on United States stamps. (issued in 1964 and 1998)

____

____

15. The California Legislature establishes April 21 of each year as John Muir Day. (in 1988)

____

____

Reinforce

Ask someone in your family to tell you about an important or memorable journey that she or he took long ago. Write a paragraph describing this journey. Be sure to use correct verb tenses and include helpful time-order words.

____

____

____

____

____

____

____

____

a. The 1840s was a time when Americans began following trails westward in search of new opportunities.

b. Study this map of pioneer trails.

Which sentence represents something as a fact? __________ What is the main verb in this sentence? __________ Which sentence gives a directive? __________ What is the main verb in this sentence? __________

In English, verbs express **mood** as well as tense. Mood as an aspect of grammar has to do with the way different forms of verbs reflect the speaker's attitude toward the information he or she is conveying in a sentence. The most common mood in English is the **indicative mood**. Verbs in the indicative mood represent actions or situations that the speaker believes to be factual or at least close to reality. Verbs in questions that seek real information are usually considered to be in the indicative mood also. (Interrogative sentences are sometimes said to be in the interrogative mood.) Another common mood in English is the **imperative mood**. Commands, requests, warnings, and other directives have verbs in the imperative mood.

See Handbook Section 18h

Practice

Read each sentence. Write whether the boldfaced verb is in the indicative mood or the imperative mood.

1. **Find** Salt Lake City on a map of the United States. __________
2. Mormon pioneers first **arrived** there in 1846. __________
3. The church **encouraged** immigration to this new Western community. __________
4. **Consider** the cost of a covered wagon, oxen, horses, food, and supplies for a journey across half a continent. __________
5. Many church members **were** recent arrivals from Europe. __________
6. Their resources **were** insufficient for purchasing a wagon and animals. __________
7. **Give** thought to possible solutions to this problem. __________
8. In 1855, church leaders **developed** a plan for emigration from the East without the use of costly wagons and animals. __________
9. The new pioneers **put** their belongings and supplies into wooden handcarts. __________
10. **Picture** yourself on a thousand-mile walk, pushing a handcart. __________
11. An ox **carried** food and provisions for every hundred pioneers. __________
12. Ten handcart brigades **made** the trip to Salt Lake City between 1856 and 1860. __________

A crossbar makes it possible to push or pull a handcart.

Name ______________________________

Apply

Fill each blank with an appropriate verb from the word bank. Circle each verb you write that is in the indicative mood. Draw a box around each verb you write that is in the imperative mood.

put	supplied	meant	faced	gathered	consider

13. Mormon pioneers ________________ in Iowa City.
14. Officials ________________ them with food and supplies for the journey.
15. ________________ yourself in the place of someone at the beginning of a hike across the plains and mountains.
16. A late start ________________ traveling through the mountains in severe weather.
17. ________________ the difficulty of pushing a handcart up a steep trail covered with snow.
18. Few pioneers ________________ more severe hardships than did members of the handcart brigades.

Reinforce

Imagine you are a worker in Iowa City in the days when emigrants gathered there to prepare to travel westward. Write six sentences with verbs in the imperative mood in which you direct people to prepare properly for the long and difficult journey.

____

____

____

____

____

____

____

____

____

____

____

____

____

____

____

____

____

The Subjunctive Mood

Unit 4: Lesson 44

a. Rafaela **plans** auto excursions for her family.

b. Her cousin has recommended that Rafaela **plan** a trip along Route 66.

c. "If I **were** you, I would begin your road trip in Chicago," said Alice.

d. "When I **was** in Chicago last year," she continued, "I stood at the corner of Lake Shore Drive and Jackson Boulevard, where Route 66 began."

Look at the boldfaced verb in each sentence. Which sentence has a present tense verb in the indicative mood? _______ Which has a present tense verb that has an unusual form? _______ Which sentence has a past tense verb in the indicative mood? _______ Which has a past tense verb that has an unusual form? _______

In English, verbs express **mood** as well as tense. Mood has to do with the way different forms of verbs reflect the speaker's attitude toward the information she or he is conveying. Verbs in the **subjunctive mood** (called the conditional mood in certain cases) are used to express conditions contrary to fact (*If I were you . . .* [but I could never be you]). They are also used after verbs of suggesting, representing, or commanding. (*Her cousin Alice has* recommended *that Rafaela* plan *a trip along the path of Route 66.*) Only the present tense has a special subjunctive form (for example, *plan* instead of *plans* as the form that goes with a singular noun). The one exception is the verb *be*: It has both a special present tense form (*be* instead of *is*) and a special past tense form (*were* instead of *was*).

See Handbook Section 18h

Practice

Read each sentence. Write whether the boldfaced verb is in the indicative mood or the subjunctive mood.

1. "If I **were** a car in 1929, I would have loved Route 66!" said Alice. _______________
2. "That **is** a silly thing to say," replied Rafaela. _______________
3. Alice asked that Rafaela **picture** a paved highway with many gas stations and motels. _______________
4. "In the 1920s, many roads in America **were** unpaved and did not have facilities for travelers," Alice explained. _______________
5. Rafaela proposed to her family that they **drive** from Chicago to Flagstaff, Arizona, along the roadways that once were part of Route 66. _______________
6. "If my vacation **were** longer than a week, I would love for us to take that trip," Rafaela's mother told her. _______________
7. "The highway to the Grand Canyon **runs** north from Flagstaff," she continued, "and I have always wanted us to see its grandeur!" _______________
8. "I suggest that your family **travel** as far as Oklahoma City," Alice said to her aunt. _______________
9. "Your suggestion **makes** good sense," said Rafaela's mother, "because we can drive there and back in a week and have plenty of time for side trips." _______________
10. "If time **were** not an issue," she continued, "I would take us all the way to Los Angeles—the western terminus of America's Mother Road!" _______________

Route 66 was the first great highway from the Midwest to the West Coast.

Name ____

Apply

Fill each blank with an appropriate form of a verb in the word bank. You can use a verb form more than once. Circle each verb you write that is in the subjunctive mood.

visit	see	stop	be	tour

11. "If I ______________ in Oklahoma right now, I would have us visit the Will Rogers Memorial Museum," said Jerome.
12. "I propose that we ______________ there when we take our Route 66 road trip," Rafaela responded.
13. "The George Washington Carver National Monument in Missouri ______________ my first choice for a side trip," said Brandon.
14. "If Dr. Carver ______________ still alive, I would want to visit him in his laboratory," Alice commented.
15. "This guidebook recommends that every Route 66 traveler ______________ Meramec Caverns, which is also in Missouri," said Jerome.
16. "I ______________ not a fan of caves," said Rafaela, "but if everyone else wants to visit that attraction, I will go along."

Reinforce

Complete each contrary-to-fact statement below. Use your imagination.

17. If I were ____,
    I would ____.
18. If I were a ____,
    I would ____.
19. If I were in ____,
    I would ____.
20. If I were the ____,
    I would ____.

a. Start in San Diego. Head north on the San Diego freeway. Exit that freeway at the turnoff for Doheny Beach.

b. Start in San Diego. Head north on the San Diego freeway. You should exit that freeway at the turnoff for Doheny Beach.

Which paragraph has all verbs in the imperative mood? _______ Which paragraph has a verb that is not in the imperative mood? _______ What is this verb? ___________________________

Be careful to **keep the mood of verbs consistent** in clauses that have a similar structure. Do not shift from imperative to subjunctive mood when you are giving instructions. (The modal auxiliaries *should, could, might,* and *may* can be joined with main verbs to create a form of the subjunctive that suggests rather than tells someone what to do.) Do not shift from indicative to subjunctive mood, or from subjunctive to indicative mood, in a compound structure.

See Handbook Section 18h

Practice

Read each sentence. Circle each boldfaced verb that is in the indicative mood. Underline each boldfaced verb that is in the subjunctive mood. Draw a box around each boldfaced verb that is in the imperative mood. If a paragraph contains an inconsistent shift of mood, mark an *X* beside it.

1. "I always recommend that a visitor **rent** a car and **drives** north along Highway 1," said Erlinda. _____
2. "**Stop** at Doheny Beach, **remove** your shoes, and then you **should stroll** on the wet sand," she continued. _____
3. "We **love** ocean beaches, and we **find** marine mammals fascinating," said Ms. Barbaro. _____
4. "I suggest that a family **pause** at Laguna Beach, and **strolls** around the old beachside area," Erlinda said. _____
5. "From there, **drive** through Newport Beach, Huntington Beach, and Seal Beach, **navigate** through Los Angeles as quickly as possible, and then you **might stop** for a walk at Santa Monica," instructed Erlinda. _____
6. "The beauty of unspoiled coastal land **is** visible to a traveler once she **passes** Point Dume," Erlinda continued. _____
7. "If I **were** able to take you with us, you **will direct** us to so many amazing spots!" exclaimed Ms. Barbaro. _____
8. Erlinda smiled and said, "If I **were** on vacation, I **could accompany** you all the way to Eureka!" _____
9. "**Stay** overnight somewhere in Big Sur, **linger** at beaches between Santa Cruz and Half Moon Bay, and you **should hike** in Mount Tamalpais State Park," Erlinda added. _____
10. "We **appreciate** all your wonderful advice," Ms. Barbaro said to Erlinda, "and we **will e-mail** you photographs of our trip!" _____

California's Highway 1 offers travelers many dramatic views of the Pacific Ocean.

Name ______________________________

Apply

Rewrite each sentence below to correct the inconsistent moods of the verbs in it.

11. "I insist that a newcomer visit Point Reyes National Seashore and then walks out to the lighthouse there," said Erlinda.

____

____

12. "Wear sensible shoes, carry a bottle of water, and you should bring a jacket, because the wind can be strong and cold," she continued.

____

____

13. "If I were able to build a house anywhere in the world, I will build it atop that cliff," said Ms. Barbaro, pointing to a picture of the coast near the town of Mendocino.

____

____

14. "I recommend that a traveler drive all the way to the Oregon border and then decides what spot was most inspiring," Erlinda responded.

____

____

15. "Fill your gas tank, wear sunglasses, and you should watch out for road hazards," called Erlinda as she waved goodbye.

____

____

Reinforce

Think of a scenic route in your area that you believe a visitor should take. On your own sheet of paper, complete the sentence below with information about that route; use verbs in the subjunctive mood. Then write a second sentence telling three things a traveler on that route should do; use three verbs in the imperative mood in this sentence.

I recommend that a traveler ______________________________.

Avoiding Voice Shifts

Unit 4: Lesson 46

a. Sailors must chart their course precisely so that their destination is reached by them.

b. Sailors must chart their course precisely so that they reach their destination.

Which sentence has both verbs in active voice? ___ Which sentence has one verb in active voice and one verb in passive voice? ___ Which sentence sounds awkward? ___

If the subject of a clause or a sentence performs an action, the verb is said to be in the **active voice**. If the subject of a clause or a sentence is acted on by something else, the verb is said to be in the **passive voice**. In many cases, using one verb in the active voice and one verb in the passive voice in the same sentence can produce an awkward-sounding statement. Be careful to avoid these voice shifts in your writing.

See Handbook Sections 18g, 20

Practice

Read each sentence. Circle each boldfaced verb that is in the active voice. Draw a box around each boldfaced verb that is in the passive voice. If the sentence sounds awkward because of a voice shift, mark an *X* beside it.

1. Ever since Ferdinand Magellan **set** sail in September of 1519, the goal of circumnavigation **has been pursued** by adventurous sailors. _____
2. Late in the 20th century, Marvin Creamer and a small crew **embarked** on such a journey, but no navigational aids **were carried** by them. _____
3. Modern sailors **rely** on electronic equipment such as GPS devices to determine location; in previous centuries, compasses, sextants, and clocks **were used** by sailors for this purpose. _____
4. Creamer **believed** that he **could circumnavigate** the globe without any of these devices. _____
5. In December 1982, a 30-foot cutter named the Globe Star **was launched** by Creamer at National Park, New Jersey; he **stopped** in several ports in the succeeding months to conduct maintenance on it. _____
6. Creamer **had sailed** for many years, and he **relied** on ambient cues to keep the boat on course. _____
7. He regularly **noted** the position of the stars, the sun, and the planets; the cloud formations, the waves, and the color of the water **were observed** by him as well. _____
8. He **used** landmarks and the horizon line as navigational aids, and bird sightings also **were noted** by him. _____
9. Emergency navigational equipment **was carried** on the boat below deck, but Creamer never **used** it. _____
10. Creamer **returned** to National Park in May of 1984 after seventeen months at sea; he **proved** that sailors can navigate successfully using nothing more than sharp eyes. _____

Marvin Creamer taught at the college where he himself had gone to school.

Name ____

Apply

Rewrite each sentence below to correct the awkward voice shift in it.

11. Marvin Creamer sailed his boat around the world without navigational devices, demonstrating that boats also could have been sailed long distances by ancient mariners using just ambient cues.

____

____

12. The ancient Phoenicians sailed their ships around the Mediterranean Sea and beyond, and boats were guided by the Polynesians across vast expanses of the Pacific Ocean long ago.

____

____

13. Creamer and his crew sailed to South Africa, Australia, and New Zealand without serious mishaps; even treacherous Cape Horn was rounded by them successfully.

____

____

14. Other sailors recognized the significance of Creamer's accomplishment, and he was awarded the Blue Water Medal, sailing's highest honor, by them.

____

____

Reinforce

In the puzzle, circle seventeen words for types of boats and ships. Then, on another sheet of paper, write a compound or complex sentence with two of these words. Make sure your sentence does not have a shift in voice.

C	H	S	P	E	E	D	B	O	A	T	C	E	F
G	K	K	V	I	D	I	N	G	H	Y	A	R	R
S	A	I	L	B	O	A	T	R	Y	L	R	O	I
L	Y	F	E	R	R	Y	B	A	X	C	A	W	G
O	A	F	T	S	Y	N	S	F	H	A	V	B	A
O	K	B	R	I	G	A	N	T	I	N	E	O	T
P	G	A	L	L	E	O	N	R	J	O	L	A	E
A	R	K	O	U	T	R	I	G	G	E	R	T	Z

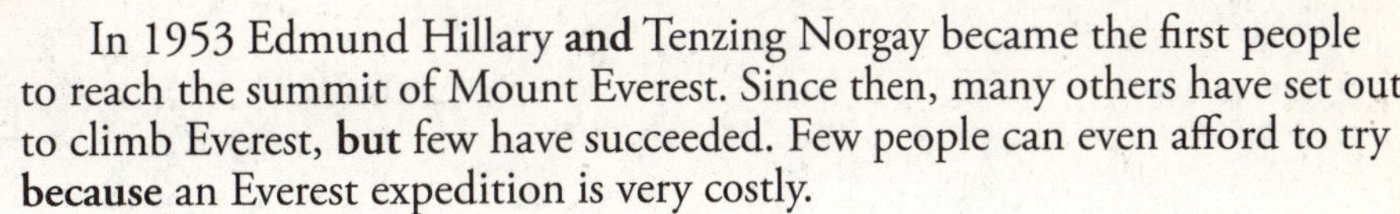

In 1953 Edmund Hillary **and** Tenzing Norgay became the first people to reach the summit of Mount Everest. Since then, many others have set out to climb Everest, **but** few have succeeded. Few people can even afford to try **because** an Everest expedition is very costly.

Which boldfaced word links two nouns? ____________
Which boldfaced word links two independent clauses? ____________
Which boldfaced word begins a dependent clause? ____________

Coordinating conjunctions (*and, but, or*) connect words or groups of words (including independent clauses) that are similar. **Subordinating conjunctions** such as *although, because, since, if,* and *before* show how one clause is related to another. Subordinating conjunctions are used at the beginning of adverb clauses.

See Handbook Section 22

Practice

Circle each coordinating conjunction. Draw a box around each subordinating conjunction. Then underline each adverb clause.

1. If you saw Erik Weihenmayer climb a mountain, you would never know he is blind.
2. He has been climbing since he was sixteen years old.
3. In 2001 he climbed Mount Everest, although he could not see the hazards along the route.
4. The summit of Everest stands at 29,035 feet, and it is covered in snow throughout the year.
5. Nearly ninety percent of climbers fail to reach the summit, but Weihenmayer believed he could.
6. He felt confident because he had already climbed four of the world's tallest mountains.
7. Since a climb takes teamwork, he assembled a team of experienced climbers.
8. They would work together, but the climbers ultimately had to look out for themselves.
9. Even a small mistake could cause serious injury, or worse, cost a life.
10. The entire trek took about two months because the climbers had to make back-and-forth trips to move supplies up the mountain.
11. They also had to spend several weeks at the base camp because they needed to acclimate their bodies to the high altitude.
12. Although the team experienced setbacks and weather delays, they successfully reached the summit on May 25, 2001.
13. Because a storm was approaching, Weihenmayer and his team had no time to celebrate.
14. They also knew that the climb wasn't over until they'd made it safely back down the mountain.

Erik Weihenmayer has climbed the Seven Summits, the tallest mountains on each of the seven continents.

Name ______________________________

Apply

Complete each sentence with a conjunction from the word bank. Write *C* if you used a coordinating conjunction or *S* if you used a subordinating conjunction.

because	but	although	as	and

15. Weihenmayer ________________ eighteen other team members summited Everest on May 25, 2001. _____
16. ________________ Weihenmayer reached his goal, he got a sudden burst of energy. _____
17. ________________ he could not see the view, he says he could hear the flapping of flags planted by earlier expeditions. _____
18. The team spent only a short time on the summit ________________ a storm was approaching. _____
19. It seemed that the trip down would be easier, ________________ it was just as dangerous. _____

Reinforce

Subordinating conjunctions are commonly used in proverbs, aphorisms, and other wise sayings. In many of these, the subordinating conjunction introduces a clause that tells the conditions under which something is true.

Underline the subordinate clause in each saying below; circle each subordinating conjunction.

Three may keep a Secret, if two of them are dead.

If you would be wealthy, think of saving, as well as of getting.

—Benjamin Franklin

Now try your hand at writing a proverb, aphorism, or wise saying of your own that includes a subordinating conjunction.

20. ____

____

____

____

____

____

Read and Analyze

For your history report, you can focus on either **the Underground Railroad** or **the Civil War.**

Circle the two words that link the boldfaced phrases.

Correlative conjunctions always appear in pairs. They connect words or groups of words and provide more emphasis than coordinating conjunctions. Some common correlative conjunctions are *both...and, either...or, neither...nor, not only...but (also),* and *whether...or.*

See Handbook Section 22

Practice

Circle the correlative conjunctions and coordinating conjunctions in these sentences. If a sentence contains correlative conjunctions, write *COR.* If the sentence does not contain correlative conjunctions, write *X.*

1. The Underground Railroad flourished between 1830 and 1860. ______
2. It was a network of secret routes and safe houses that slaves used to escape to freedom. ______
3. Routes led not only north but also south. ______
4. Many escaped slaves fled to either Canada or Mexico. ______
5. White abolitionists and free African Americans worked together to help the fugitives. ______
6. Abolitionists believed that slavery was wrong, but not all wanted to help fugitive slaves. ______
7. Sometimes it was hard for a fugitive to know whether to trust a person or to avoid him or her. ______
8. A fugitive seeking shelter might check to see whether a lantern outside a safe house was lit or unlit. ______
9. Harriet Tubman not only freed herself from slavery but also liberated scores of other enslaved people. ______
10. Neither Tubman nor any of her underground railroad "passengers" were ever captured. ______
11. It was both Tubman's clever techniques and her determination that helped her lead nearly 300 enslaved people to freedom. ______
12. The Harriet Tubman Home, located in Auburn, New York, preserves Tubman's legacy in the place where she lived and died in freedom. ______

During the Civil War, Harriet Tubman served as a nurse, scout, and spy for the Union Army.

Name ______________________________

Apply

Rewrite each sentence pair as one new, shorter sentence using the correlative conjunctions in parentheses.

13. The journey to freedom was long. The journey to freedom was dangerous. (not only/but also)

____

____

14. The Fugitive Slave Law meant freed slaves were in danger of capture. The Fugitive Slave Law meant free-born African Americans were in danger of capture. (both/and)

____

____

15. Fugitives often fled to Canada. Fugitives fled to Mexico. (either/or)

____

____

16. New York was not a slave state. Pennsylvania was not a slave state. (neither/nor)

____

____

Reinforce

Circle the correlative conjunctions in each clue. Then use the clues, along with information from the lesson, to fill in the blanks.

17. This term includes both whites and free African Americans who fought against slavery.

___ ___ ___ ___ ___ ___ ___ ___ ___ ___ ___ ___ ___

18. Fugitives went either north or south to seek this.

___ ___ ___ ___ ___ ___ ___

19. Neither New York nor Pennsylvania supported this.

___ ___ ___ ___ ___ ___ ___

20. "Conductors" not only hid escaped slaves but also taught them secret codes and phrases to help them find the next safe house along this.

___ ___ ___ ___ ___ ___ ___ ___ ___ ___ ___

___ ___ ___ ___ ___ ___ ___ ___

Verbs

Circle each linking verb. Underline each action verb. Then label each action verb as *transitive* (*T*) or *intransitive* (*I*).

1. A journey is a long trip, often into the unknown. _____
2. People take journeys for many different reasons. _____
3. Some individuals travel in the name of science. _____
4. Many people want adventure. _____
5. Others seek freedom or a new homeland. _____
6. Still others love the personal challenges of a journey. _____
7. Often, journeys are quite dangerous. _____
8. Earth has become very familiar. _____
9. We have explored almost every corner of our planet. _____
10. Many future journeys of exploration will be to distant worlds. _____

Verb Tenses and Forms

Circle the word or words in parentheses that identify the tense or form of each boldfaced verb.

11. We **are reading** about explorers in social studies. (present/present progressive)
12. I always **enjoy** books about Lewis and Clark. (present/present perfect)
13. They **saw** the American West unblemished by cities and freeways. (past/present)
14. By the end of the expedition, the two leaders **had met** many Native Americans. (past perfect/past)
15. The tribes **were living** as they had for thousands of years. (past perfect/past progressive)
16. If I **had lived** in the nineteenth century, I would have journeyed west. (past perfect/past progressive)
17. The country **has changed** greatly over the past two hundred years. (present/present perfect)
18. Next summer, my family **will travel** along part of the Oregon Trail. (future/future perfect)
19. I **will be counting** the days until then. (future/future progressive)

Verb Forms and Mood

Circle the word in parentheses that identifies the mood of each boldfaced verb.

20. If I **were** living in Alaska, I would learn to drive a dogsled. (indicative/subjunctive)

21. **Watch** this video of a dogsled race. (indicative/imperative)

22. The announcer recommends that each viewer **watch** the lead dog. (imperative/subjunctive)

23. The lead dog pushes forward, and the other dogs **follow.** (indicative/subjunctive)

Avoiding Shifts in Tense, Mood, and Voice

Write an *X* beside each sentence that includes an inappropriate tense shift.

24. Erie Weihenmayer made history on May 25, 2001, when he stands atop Mount Everest. _____

25. The ascent had been difficult and dangerous for every member of the team, but it had been especially difficult for Weihenmayer because of his lack of vision. _____

Write an *X* beside each sentence that includes an inappropriate mood shift.

26. "Uncle Steve recommends that my dad get in shape and then hikes the Appalachian Trail," said Marghi to Evan. _____

27. "Your dad plays soccer already, so he probably has good stamina," Evan said. _____

Write an *X* beside each sentence that includes an awkward voice shift.

28. My great-great-grandmother rode a train north to Chicago in 1942, and she was followed north by other family members soon after. _____

29. My great-great-grandmother quickly found a job in a factory, and she worked there for the next forty years. _____

Conjunctions

Circle each coordinating conjunction. Underline each subordinating conjunction. Draw boxes around the two parts of each correlative conjunction.

30. Mysteries remain not only in outer space, but also in the deepest oceans.

31. Because oceans are so deep, many unexplored regions lie beneath their depths.

32. Parts of the ocean are as deep as Mount Everest or K2 is high.

33. Ocean canyons are not only extremely deep but also totally dark.

34. We should support responsible sea exploration and use what we learn to protect the oceans.

Spelling Practice

Read and Analyze

The settlers traveling on the Oregon Trail had one main **objective**—to start a new, more prosperous life in a new land.

Circle the Latin root in the word in bold type. What does the word mean? ______________________________

Latin Roots: *act, port, dict, ject*

Many words in English contain Latin roots. The root ***act,*** as in *action,* means "to do." The root ***port,*** as in *export,* means "to carry." The root ***dict,*** as in *predict,* means "to say." The root ***ject,*** as in *project,* means "to throw." Knowing the meanings of common Latin roots will help you figure out the meanings of unfamiliar words you may encounter.

Word Sort

Use the words below to complete the word sort.

dictator	objective	activate	reject	transport	dejected
enact	reaction	portable	dictate	prediction	transportation

Latin root *act*	**Latin root *port***
Latin root *dict*	**Latin root *ject***

Name ______________________________

Pattern Practice

objective	portable	contradict	rejection	dejected	reaction
react	transaction	activate	unpredictable	dictate	export

Write the word from the word bank that is an antonym for each word.

1. agree ____________________
2. import ____________________
3. stationary ____________________
4. acceptance ____________________
5. happy ____________________
6. follow ____________________
7. ignore ____________________
8. reliable ____________________

Write the word from the word bank that best completes each sentence.

9. Using a credit card is a simple, easy ____________________.
10. These data ____________________ our earlier hypotheses.
11. The weather is so ____________________ in the spring.
12. My ____________________ for today is mowing the lawn.
13. Nate had a similar ____________________ to the bad news.
14. Lauren logged on to the website to ____________________ the account.
15. Juan's frown and slumped shoulders showed he felt ____________________.
16. Sometimes a writer faces much ____________________ before having his or her book published.
17. When camping we use a small ____________________ stove that is fueled by propane.

Use the Dictionary

Write *act, port, dict,* or *ject* to complete each word so that it matches the definition. Check your work in a print or an online dictionary.

18. __________**folio:** a large, flat case for carrying papers
19. **inter**__________**:** say something abruptly that interrupts
20. __________**ion:** the use of words in speaking and writing

(you) | Diagram | sentences

See Handbook Section 41

Diagramming Adverbs

You have learned how to diagram sentences containing adjectives (page 37). Like adjectives, adverbs are diagrammed on slanted lines. An adverb is connected to the verb, adjective, or adverb it modifies. This model shows how to diagram adverbs.

Some trappers **just barely** survived the very cold temperatures.

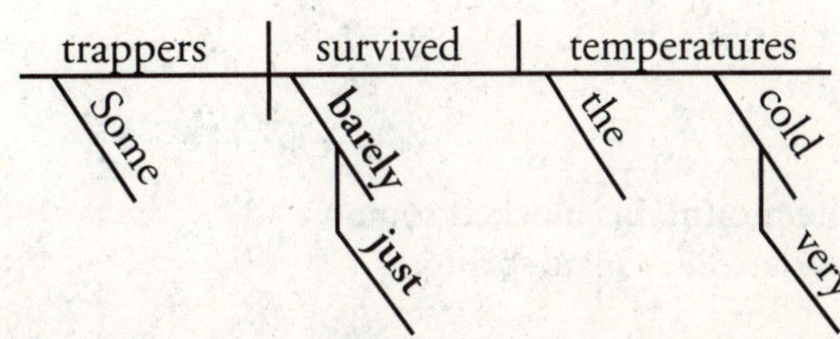

Diagram these sentences to show where the adverbs belong.

1. Beaver pelts brought very high prices then.

2. Trappers always guarded their pelts carefully.

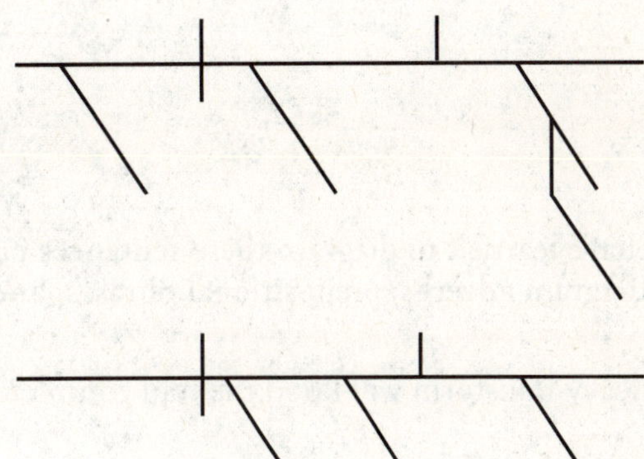

Diagramming Prepositions and Prepositional Phrases

You have learned that many adverbial prepositional phrases tell *how, when, where,* or *to what extent* about verbs. You have also learned that most adjectival prepositional phrases describe nouns. Note how the two types of prepositional phrases are diagrammed in the example.

Farmers **from the East** journeyed **along the Oregon Trail.**

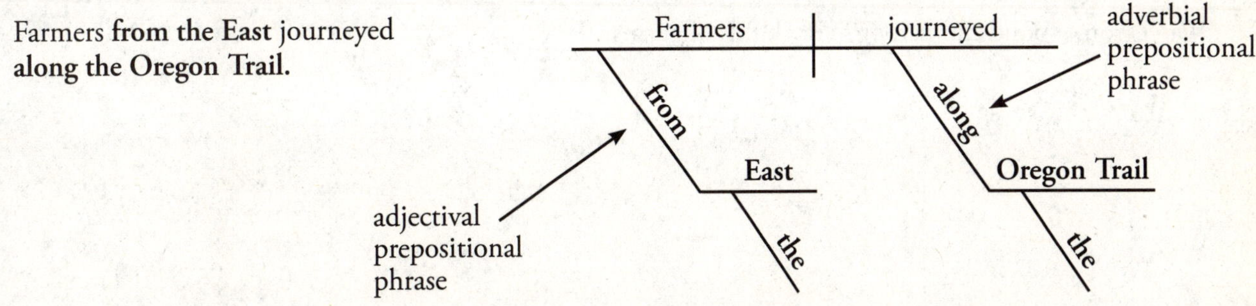

Name ______________________________

Diagram these sentences. Connect each adverbial prepositional phrase to the verb it tells about. Connect each adjectival prepositional phrase to the noun it tells about.

3. Families with livestock headed for the Willamette Valley.

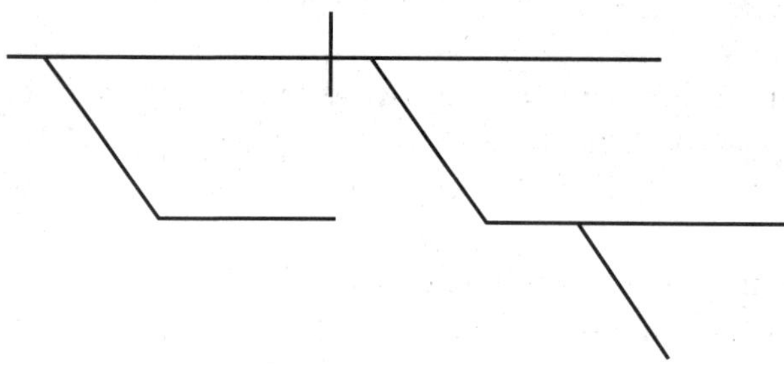

4. Snow in the mountains blocked some passes from late fall to late spring.

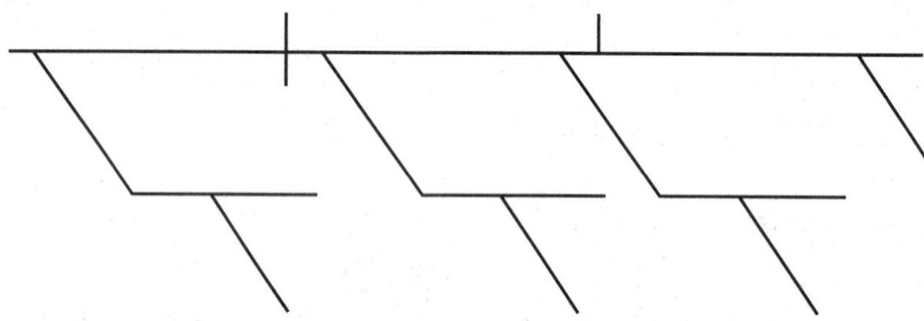

Use what you have learned to diagram these sentences on another piece of paper. Look back at the lesson to recall how to diagram adverbs, prepositional phrases, and correlative conjunctions.

5. A very heavy rainstorm will flood the trail completely.
6. A lack of rain slowly dries the grasses.
7. Clouds of dust billow behind wagons.
8. Riders often cover the lower part of their face with a bandana.
9. A very nervous horse may run away.
10. Then riders must chase it across the plains.
11. You absolutely must boil water from the pond.
12. Water from a pond can harbor many kinds of germs.

These sentences need help. Rewrite them so the verbs are in the proper tense.

1. I go to Guanajuato, Mexico, last summer because my grandmother lives there. ______________________

2. After Mom and I have flown to Mexico City, we took a bus to Guanajuato. ______________________

3. Guanajuato is having a beautiful tree-canopied square in the center of town. ______________________

4. In the evenings, we are listening to music in the square. ______________________

5. I am hoping to visit an old silver mine, but we did not have time. ______________________

6. I have gone to Guanajuato again soon. ______________________

When you write a paragraph, always include a topic sentence, two or more supporting sentences that add details about your topic, and a concluding sentence. Your reader will enjoy your paragraph more if you use time expressions, correct verb tenses, colorful adjectives, pronouns, possessives, and conjunctions appropriately. Notice how this model paragraph is written.

topic sentence

time expressions

verb tense

subordinating and coordinating conjunctions

concluding sentence

Every year my family takes a summer trip. We *have been* to San Antonio **and** New York. **Last year** we *visited* Washington, D.C. **Neither** my father **nor** my mother *had been* there **before**, **so** we *got lost* a few times. The Smithsonian *is* huge. It *is* **not** one museum **but** a collection of museums. In my opinion the best museum *is* the Smithsonian National Air **and** Space Museum **because** Charles Lindbergh's plane *is* there. He *flew* it across the Atlantic Ocean **in 1927**. The trip to Washington *has been* my favorite vacation, **and** I *hope* I *will visit* it again someday. *It is a wonderful place to learn about history.*

Name ___

Writing a Paragraph

The sentences you revised on page 147 can be used to write a paragraph. Decide whether the order of the sentences makes sense, and if it does not, change it. Write the paragraph on the lines below. Add other words and a concluding sentence, if necessary.

___

___

___

___

___

Write a personal narrative about a trip you have taken. You might write about a family vacation, a visit to a relative's, or another trip. Refer to the model paragraph on page 147 if you need help. Be sure to use the proper verb tenses to make the sequence of events clear. Use subordinating and coordinating conjunctions to make connections between ideas clear.

___

___

___

___

___

___

___

___

___

___

___

___

___

Read your paragraph again. Use this checklist to make sure it is complete and correct.

- ❑ My paragraph has a topic sentence.
- ❑ My paragraph has at least two supporting sentences.
- ❑ All my sentences are clear and make sense.
- ❑ I have used proper verb tenses.
- ❑ I have used conjunctions correctly.
- ❑ My paragraph has a concluding sentence.

Proofreading Practice

Read this passage about a great explorer. Use the proofreading marks to show how each mistake should be fixed. Use a dictionary to check and correct spellings.

Proofreading Marks

Mark	Means	Example
(delete mark)	delete	Trappers ~~they~~ sought beavers in mountain streams.
^	add	Trappers sought beavers in ^mountain streams.
≡	make into an uppercase letter	trappers sought beavers in mountain streams.
(sp)	fix spelling	Trappers saut beavers in mountain streams.
⊙	add a period	Trappers sought beavers in mountain streams⊙
/	make into a lowercase letter	Trappers sought beavers in Mountain streams.

Jedediah Smith, Western Trailblazer

Jedediah Smith ranks as one of America's greatest trailblazers. Not only did he help establish parts of the Oregon Trail and routes across the Great Basin, but he was also the first united states citizen to travel overland into California, and the first to cross the lofty Sierra Nevada.

One of Smith's remarkable journeys begins in August 1826. Smith had just attended the annual rendezvous of fur traders in Cache Valley, Utah. Accompanied by seventeen men, he will be heading south and then west. Searching for streams with beavers. Smith's party traveled over dry, sandy plains and rugged hills and then follow twisting creeks, but they found no beaver streams. With supplys exhausted, Smith decided to move his party westward to a California mission and seek provisions

Smith himself rode ahead of his group to Mission San Gabriel; from there he is sending a letter to the governor of California (then a part of mexico) asking permission to spend time in California. The governor orders Smith to San Diego. When Smith arrived, not only did the governor deny Smith's request, but he also accused him of being a spy. After much discussion.The governor agreed not to arrest Smith on condition that he and his party immediate leave California by the root they entered.

Smith returned to the mission, where his men had been treated well, and he did not obey the agreement. Instead, he led his party north to Californias' San Joaquin River valley to follow its course and trap beavers. A biography about Jedediah Smith had told you more about the subsequently adventures of he and his crew.

Name ______________________________

Proofreading Checklist

You can use the checklist below to help you find and fix mistakes in your own writing. Write the titles of your own stories or reports in the blanks at the top of the chart. Then use the questions to check your work. Make a check mark (✓) in each box after you have checked that item.

Proofreading Checklist for Unit 4

Titles				
Have I used colorful action verbs in sentences?				
Have I used the simple tense, the perfect tense, and the progressive tense correctly?				
Have I avoided inappropriate shifts in verb tense?				
Have I used correlative conjunctions correctly?				

Also Remember...

Have I written complete sentences?				
Does each sentence begin with an uppercase letter?				
Have I included correct end punctuation?				
Did I use a dictionary to check and correct spellings?				

Your Own List

Use this space to write your own list of things to check in your writing.

Community Connection

In Unit 4 of *Grammar, Usage, and Mechanics,* students learned about **forms, moods, and tenses of verbs and about conjunctions,** and they used what they learned to improve their own writing. The content of these lessons focuses on the theme **American Journeys.** As students completed the exercises, they learned about Americans' journeys through and beyond our lands. These pages offer a variety of activities that reinforce skills and concepts presented in the unit. They also provide opportunities for students to make connections between the materials in the lessons and the community at large.

Plan a Sightseeing Trip

Work with a group to identify five interesting places in the United States that you would all like to visit.

- Use a road map of the United States to plan an auto trip from your community to each of these places and then back home. Try to pick the shortest route possible. Make a map of your planned route.
- Next, use an Internet map site to get specific driving instructions for each leg of your journey. These should give mileage and time estimates. Add up the mileage and the estimated number of days needed to make the trip. (Remember to allow time for sleeping, eating, and enjoying each destination!)
- Write a paragraph telling about where you will go on your trip, what you hope to see, how far you will travel on each part, and how much time each segment of the trip will take. Use future tense verbs and future progressive verb forms.

Create a Postcard

Look online or in old magazines for a picture of someone traveling in an unusual way—for instance, by camel, by kayak, in a hot air balloon, on snowshoes, or in a submarine. Print out or cut out this image. Next, do some research on what it is like to travel in this way. Then imagine that you are the person in the picture; write four or five sentences about the journey you were on when the picture was taken. Use past forms of verbs in your sentences.

The Trade of Travel

Learn about job opportunities associated with journeys and travel, such as tour guide, travel agent, rafting guide, travel writer, hotel manager, helicopter pilot, cartographer (map maker), and flight attendant. Choose one occupation that interests you and learn more about it. Try to answer these questions:

- What skills are required to do this job?
- What preparation and training would I need for this job?
- Where is the training available?
- How long does it take to become proficient at this work?
- What is a typical working day like in this profession?

If possible, interview an adult who has a travel-related job you might be interested in. Take notes during the interview, and share the results of the interview with the class. Use the planning guide on the next page to help you plan the interview and organize your notes.

Name ______________________________

Interview Planner

Person I am interviewing:

Name ______________________________

Age ______________________________

Occupation ______________________________

Number of years employed in that field ______________________________

Date of interview: ______________________________

Questions to ask:

1. ______________________________
____
2. ______________________________
____
3. ______________________________
____
4. ______________________________
____
5. ______________________________
____
6. ______________________________
____
7. ______________________________
____
8. ______________________________
____

Notes:

____
____
____
____
____
____
____

Your and You're; Their, They're, and There

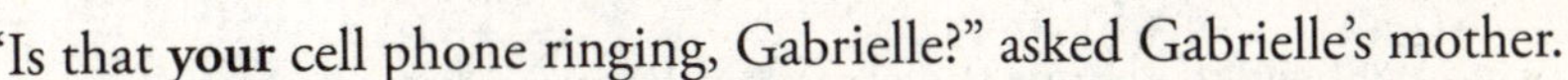

"Is that **your** cell phone ringing, Gabrielle?" asked Gabrielle's mother.

"**You're** right, it is." Gabrielle responded. "I forgot to turn it off."

"Please do that. **There** is no reason that your friends should be making **their** calls to you at dinnertime. **They're** in need of etiquette lessons," Gabrielle's mom continued.

Circle the boldfaced words that are contractions. Underline the boldfaced words that show ownership. Draw a box around the boldfaced word that is an introductory word.

Your is a possessive pronoun and shows ownership. ***You're*** is a contraction made from the words *you* and *are*. ***Their*** is a possessive pronoun that means "belonging to them." ***They're*** is a contraction that means "they are." ***There*** is an adverb and usually means "in that place." *There* may also be used as an introductory word.

See Handbook Section 33

Practice

Read the conversation below. Circle the word in parentheses that completes each sentence correctly. (1–15)

"(Your/You're) going to be happy to hear that we talked about cell phone etiquette today at school," Gabrielle said, switching off her cell phone.

"Well, I am glad. Did you also discuss how important it is to make sure that (your/ you're) polite in (your/ you're) e-mails?" her mother asked.

"Yes, our teacher said to begin each e-mail with an appropriate greeting and to proofread and spell check e-mails before (their/ they're /there) sent," said Gabrielle. "She told us to avoid typing words in all uppercase letters, because (their/ they're /there) like shouts. She also said, 'Including a subject line in (your /you're) e-mail is important.'"

"If you follow those rules," her mother said, "I'm sure (your/you're) e-mails will be received more favorably."

"(Their/They're/There) definitely going to be more polite from now on!" said Gabrielle. "My teacher also recommended that we avoid sarcastic remarks. She said that (their/they're/there) often misinterpreted in e-mail."

"(Your/You're) absolutely correct, Gabrielle," her mother said. "(Their/They're/There) have been many misunderstandings because of jokes sent via e-mail."

"Are Jesse and Dad getting home from (their/they're/there) trip tomorrow?" asked Gabrielle. "(Their/They're/There) e-mails should follow the same rules. Jesse is never polite in his e-mails to me!"

"Now that (your/you're) becoming an expert on e-mail etiquette, you can share what you know with your brother," said her mom. "(Their/They're/There) is no need for rudeness."

Name ______________________________

Apply

Rewrite each sentence, replacing the boldfaced words with *your, you're, their, they're,* or *there.* You may need to change the order of the words when you do this.

16. You may have to change **the** e-mail address **you have been using.** ______________________________

____

17. The e-mail provider **you are signed up with** is displaying more and more ads. ______________________________

____

18. **Those ads are** so annoying! ______________________________

____

19. Check out these providers; **the** features **that they offer** are better than what you currently have.

____

____

20. If you change e-mail providers, **you are** going to have to change your e-mail address. ______________________________

____

21. You'll have to notify people not to write you **at that address** anymore. ______________________________

____

INSTANOT
Internet Service Provider
GREAT PRICE!!!
- Simple to Use
- Hi-speed Connection
- Nationwide Network
- Junk Mail Filtering
- No Setup Fee
- No Banner Ads
- No Contracts
- No Problem

www.instanot.com
Sign Up Today!

Reinforce

Words like *your* and *you're* and *their, they're,* and *there* that sound alike but have different spellings and meanings are called *homophones.* Each sentence below uses one or more homophones incorrectly. Circle the misused word(s) in each one. Then write the correct word(s) on the line.

22. Check out our competitors' rates and features. We'll match what their offering. ______________

23. Stream you're favorite videos without interruptions! ______________

24. Quickly download games to you're PC. ______________

25. Compare Instanot to other Internet service providers. Find out what there doing to protect you're privacy.

____

26. Look for special offers in you're local area. ______________

27. Our support technicans take pride in they're work. ______________

28. Their aren't many ISP companies that are as reliable as Instanot. ______________

Read and Analyze

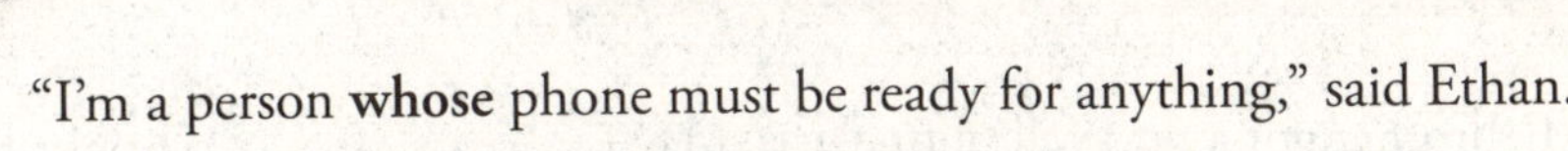

"I'm a person **whose** phone must be ready for anything," said Ethan.

"**It's** silly to watch a movie on such a tiny screen," Gina said.

"I like my phone because **its** battery lasts a long time," Corliss commented.

"**Who's** been using my phone to text message?" wailed Scott.

Underline the boldfaced words that are contractions. Circle the boldfaced words that show ownership.

Its is a possessive pronoun; it means "belonging to it." ***It's*** is a contraction that means "it is" or "it has." ***Whose*** shows ownership or possession. ***Who's*** is a contraction of "who is" or "who has."

See Handbook Section 33

Practice

Underline the correct word in parentheses. (1–15)

The cell phone has become more than just a phone, thanks to (its/it's) tiny but powerful computer hardware and advanced software. (Its/It's) capabilities include taking photos and making short films. If you're a person (who's/whose) interests are technology-related, you'll want a phone with these features.

But if you're someone (who's/whose) a frequent traveler, you may think (its/it's) really convenient to have a phone that can calculate the dollar value of prices in foreign currencies. Before you buy a phone for traveling, though, find out if (its/it's) usable in the countries you'll be visiting.

My sister is someone (who's/whose) easily bored. She says she bought her new phone because (its/it's) like an entertainment center. When she has to wait in line, she takes out her phone and watches video clips on (its/it's) screen.

Nowadays (its/it's) also common to see people listening to music on their cell phones. (Who's/Whose) your favorite group? Would you enjoy listening to (its/it's) greatest hits on your phone? Or would you be too busy using your phone's text messaging feature?

If you're someone (who's/whose) text messaging constantly, your cell phone could hurt you. (Its/It's) common for cell phone texters to have hand and wrist pain. Those (who's/whose) hands are already hurting should try a different use for their cell phone—use it to call people instead of texting them!

The first text message was sent on December 3, 1992.

Name ____

Apply

Write *its, it's, who's,* or *whose* to complete each sentence correctly. Remember to capitalize a word that begins a sentence.

16. My brother got a new cell phone yesterday. ____________ a bright blue phone.
17. With ____________ camera, he took a picture of a dog.
18. I don't know ____________ dog it is.
19. However, his phone displays that picture every time ____________ turned on.
20. I wonder ____________ the owner of the phone making that horrible sound.
21. ____________ my brother's phone; its ringtone is obnoxious.
22. When ____________ ringing, the phone sounds like a howler monkey.
23. I've heard howler monkeys ____________ cries are much more pleasant than that!

Reinforce

Write an ad for a cell phone that has many amazing features. Use *its, it's, who's,* and *whose* in your ad. Then draw a picture of your phone.

Read and Analyze

Two friends traveled **to** Louisiana for a visit with family. They visited Texas, **too**.

Which boldfaced word means "in the direction of"? _______ Which names a number? _______ Which means "also"? _______

To can be a preposition that means "in the direction of." *To* can also be used with a verb to form an *infinitive*, as in the sentence *We like to play computer games.* ***Too*** is an adverb and means "also" or "excessively." ***Two*** means the number 2.

See Handbook Section 33

Practice

Circle the word in parentheses that correctly completes each sentence.

1. For many people around the world, owning a computer has been (to/too /two) expensive.
2. Researchers have developed an affordable laptop so these people can access the Internet, (to/too/two).
3. This laptop's (to/too/two) components, the hardware and software, feature the bare essentials.
4. Encased in hard plastic, these laptops are designed (to/too/two) be sturdy and durable.
5. They can handle high temperatures, (to/too/two), unlike most computers marketed today.
6. Because these laptops use far less energy than the average laptop, they are more useful (to/too/two) people in areas where power is scarce or expensive.
7. In addition to a plug-in power cord, some of these laptops have (to/too/two) other energy sources: batteries and a wind-up crank.
8. The laptops allow students access (to/too/two) digital textbooks.
9. The laptops can do (to/too/two) other important things for students: they can function as word processors and provide access to the Internet.
10. Some villages in developing countries have purchased one or (to/too/two) laptops for sharing.

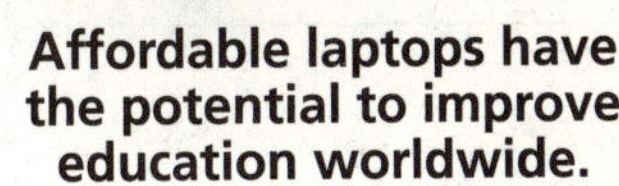

Affordable laptops have the potential to improve education worldwide.

11. The gap between how easily some people are able (to/too/two) access technology in developed countries and how hard it is for others to do so in developing countries is called the "digital divide."
12. However, a digital divide exists in developed nations, (to/too/two).
13. Perhaps affordable laptops can narrow the digital divide in prosperous nations, (to/too/two).

Name ____

Apply

Write *to, too,* or *two* to complete each sentence correctly.

14. "What are you going ________ do for the rest of the afternoon, Sumit?" asked Angie.
15. "I have to figure out how ________ get rid of my old computer," answered Sumit.
16. "I must finish my homework, ________," Sumit continued. "What about you?"
17. "I'm going to visit my ________ cousins," Angie said. "What are you thinking of doing with your computer?"
18. "I don't have any idea! My sister used it for three years, and I've used it for ________."
19. "What about donating it? I'm sure someone would be thrilled ________ own it," Angie suggested.
20. "That's a great idea. That way I can get rid of it and help someone, ________!" Sumit exclaimed.
21. "Exactly," Angie said. "New computers are ________ pricey for a lot of people."
22. "This afternoon I'll do research online ________ find an organization that accepts old computers," Sumit said.
23. "Let me know what you find out. I, ________, have an old computer at home," said Angie.

Reinforce

To, too, and *two* are *homophones*: they sound the same but are spelled differently. These riddles are based on other homophones.

Question: Why was she sore after the race?
Answer: The feat was hard on her feet.

Question: What do you call a sweet doe?
Answer: You call it a dear deer.

Choose three of the following sets of homophones to create your own riddles. Write them on the lines below. Use a dictionary to check the meaning of any word you don't know.

to/too/two	nose/knows	vain/vein	whale/wail	bored/board
bolder/boulder	peace/piece	pair/pear	heal/heel	see/sea

24. ____

____

25. ____

____

26. ____

____

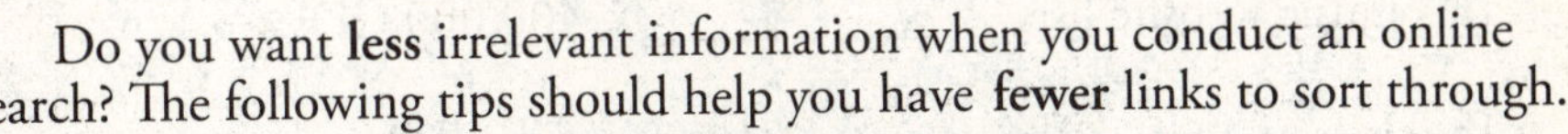

Read and Analyze

Do you want **less** irrelevant information when you conduct an online search? The following tips should help you have **fewer** links to sort through.

Circle the boldfaced word that is followed by a plural noun.

The words ***less*** and ***fewer*** have similar meanings but are used differently. *Less* can be used to refer to a **smaller amount** that is not a sum of items: *less gasoline; less anger. Fewer* is used to refer to a **smaller number** of items: *fewer cars; fewer arguments.*

The word ***over*** and the phrase ***more than*** also have similar meanings but are used differently. *Over* can be used to refer to a **larger amount** that is not a sum of items: *over 30 miles; over 200 pounds. More than* is used to describe a **larger number** of items: *more than 20 cars; more than 10 packages.*

See Handbook Section 32

Practice

Circle the word or phrase in parentheses that correctly completes each sentence.

1. Have you ever conducted an online search only to end up with (over/more than) the number of results you could handle?
2. Using quotation marks around search terms will help you get (less/fewer) fluff in your results.
3. You can also separate your search terms with *and* or *or* for (less/fewer) and better-targeted results.
4. It could take you (over/more than) an hour or two to research a topic if you do not set a time limit for your search.
5. It may also help to use (over/more than) one online database or search engine.
6. However, to obtain (less/fewer) useless information, you need to understand how a particular search engine ranks results.
7. Some rank results by how many times each listing has been viewed by users; the first listing is the result that has been viewed (over/more than) any other.
8. Other search engines figure out how many of your search terms exist in each result; the results with (less/fewer) terms appear toward the bottom of the list.
9. If you want to find (over/more than) the number of results your search turned up, try using a wildcard character.
10. The symbols ? and * are wildcard characters, but (over/more than) just two of these characters exist.
11. My friend says that using wildcard characters can make your search results (over/more than) 20 percent more effective.
12. For example, if you want your search to be (less/fewer) rigid and more productive, you can key in "swim*" for results that include *swimming, swimmers, swimsuit,* and even *swim team.*

Name ___________________________

Apply

Write *less, fewer, over,* or *more than* to complete each sentence correctly.

13. This music website lists ______________ 400,000 CDs.
14. The site says that ______________ 40% of the CDs are on sale.
15. It says that items will be shipped in ______________ than a week.
16. I have ______________ than 50 CDs.
17. It costs ______________ money to download songs from an online store than it does to buy CDs.
18. My personal music player weighs ______________ than ten ounces.
19. It has an extra output so that ______________ one person can listen at a time.
20. I biked ______________ ten miles to a retail store.
21. The store had ______________ than ten players to choose from.
22. But a trustworthy online store I visited had ______________ 50 players available!

Reinforce

See Handbook Section 35

Write an e-mail to a friend about an activity that you would like to do more often. In the body of your e-mail, use *less, fewer, over,* and *more than* correctly. Also, be sure to begin with the reason you are e-mailing. Use proper etiquette, such as typing a clear subject line; avoiding special type features, emoticons, or uppercase letters; and including a detailed salutation (full name and e-mail address). When you have finished your first draft, read your e-mail from beginning to end. Did you achieve your purpose for writing? Proofread for errors in capitalization, punctuation, and spelling. Then print a hard copy of your final draft.

Read and Analyze

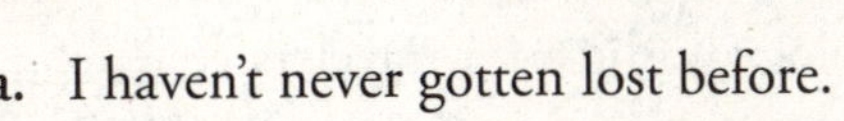

a. I haven't never gotten lost before.

b. I don't ever want to get lost, so I won't leave my house without a map.

Which sentence uses too many negative words? ___________ Which uses negatives correctly? _______

A **negative** is a word that means "no" or "not." The words *no, not, nothing, none, never, nowhere,* and *nobody* are negatives. The negative word *not* is found in contractions such as *don't* and *wasn't*. It is a convention of standard English to **use only one negative word to express a negative idea.** Use the contraction *doesn't* with singular subjects. Use the contraction *don't* with plural subjects and with *I* and *you*. Avoid the use of *ain't*. **Remember to use this information when you speak, too.**

See Handbook Section 26

Practice

Circle the correct expression in parentheses to complete each sentence.

1. Throughout the ages, there hasn't been (anything/nothing) more dependable for determining location than the position of the moon and stars.
2. However, the technology called Global Positioning System, or GPS, (isn't/ain't) dependent on visible objects; it uses satellites and software to give locations.
3. Although the system was developed by the U.S. Department of Defense and is maintained by the U.S. Air Force, users today (doesn't/don't) have to be in the military.
4. In fact, it's hard to think of (an/no) industry that doesn't benefit from GPS technology.
5. Although GPS devices are easy to use, GPS technology (isn't/ain't) easy to understand.
6. Almost nothing (never/ever) stops the GPS from working.
7. There are 24 satellites orbiting Earth, none of which (never/ever) switch themselves off.
8. A GPS device on Earth measures the time for its signal to travel from four of the satellites and calculates the distance to each satellite; nothing but a computer (can/can't) process data that fast.
9. It (don't/doesn't) take long for a GPS device to determine a user's location, even if the satellites aren't nearby.
10. While the GPS device (ain't/isn't) always perfectly accurate, it's seldom off by more than 33 feet.
11. You can use a GPS device night or day, in any weather, and in almost any place and not worry (none/at all) about getting lost.

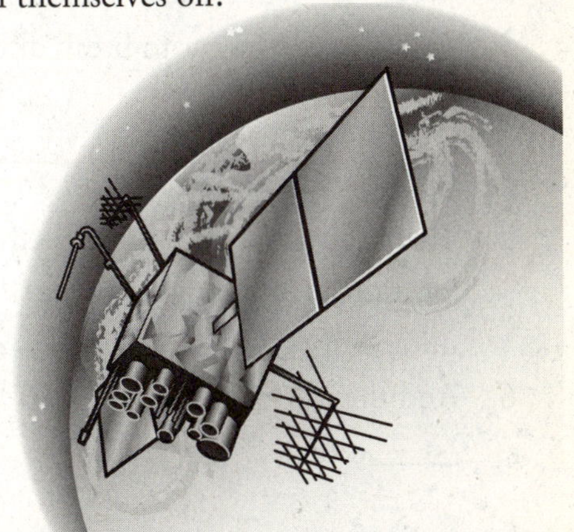

GPS technology relies on satellites to determine a user's location.

Name ______________________________

Apply

Rewrite each sentence so that it uses negatives correctly. Each sentence may be rewritten several ways.

12. Nobody never said that GPS technology was just for travelers. ______________________

13. "Geocaching" is a new game in which players hide prizes in places that ain't easy to locate. ______________________

14. The coordinates of the prize's location aren't no secret; they are posted on the Internet. ______________________

15. Players don't waste no time trying to locate the prize with their GPS devices. ______________________

16. The prize is inside a container called a cache; players don't never remove the cache itself. ______________________

17. If they did, there wouldn't be nothing for the next player to find. ______________________

18. Players take prizes from caches, but they don't leave no one disappointed. ______________________

19. They replace the prize inside the cache with one they have brought; ain't that a cool idea? ______________________

Reinforce

Fill in the crossword puzzle with negatives. Use the clues to help you.

Across

1. I _____ believe our car broke down!
2. We _____ had trouble with it before.
3. _____ expects a car to break down.

Down

4. It _____ an old car.
5. Thankfully the GPS pinpointed our location, even though we were in the middle of _____.
6. And the tow truck was there in _____ time.

1 5 4 3 2 6

Read and Analyze

Blogs **aren't** new, but **they're** still **way cool**. **Things** like blogs have changed the way people communicate.

Look at the boldfaced words. Circle each contraction. Underline the expression that is too informal for academic writing. Draw a box around the word that is vague or unspecific.

When you write essays, reports, and other types of compositions for classes, be sure to respect the conventions of standard English. **Avoid the use of shortened forms** of words (*gonna, gotta*); **do not use slang** or informal language (*super, cool, guys, whatever, lots of, okay*); and **replace vague words** (*thing, nice, good, bad*) with more precise terms. In addition, **do not use contractions.**

See Handbook Section 32

Practice

Underline each expression that should not be used in academic writing. These include contractions, shortened forms, slang, and vague words.

1. Can you imagine what the Internet was like before bloggers started doing their thing?
2. Jorn Barger was among the first dudes to write a blog.
3. He used the word *weblog* to describe the stuff he wrote; later the term was shortened to *blog*.
4. People write blogs about lots of topics.
5. Tons of people use blogs in the way that people have used personal journals in the past.
6. I've kept a handwritten journal, and that's okay, but keeping a blog is way better.
7. Other people use blogs to share opinions on things commonly discussed in letters to the editor of a newspaper.
8. More people seem totally comfortable writing blogs, though, perhaps because they don't feel so much pressure to be grammatically correct.
9. Blogs offer writers a nice way to connect with others interested in the same issues.
10. Blogs have lotsa different looks; some look totally amateurish, and others are quite sophisticated.
11. Bloggers post all kinds of awesome graphics.
12. The thing I like most about blogs is how varied they are.
13. All sorts of people from different backgrounds enjoy blogging.
14. You gotta view blogs with a critical eye, though, or you'll end up with false info.
15. One blogger spilled the beans: "I get my facts from others; if any facts in this blog are wrong, blame them."
16. According to one Internet tracking source, there are more than 100 million blogs. That's a bunch of blogs!

Name ____________________

Apply

Rewrite each sentence to eliminate contractions and informal or vague expressions. Each sentence may be rewritten several ways.

17. People write blogs about lots of topics. ____________________

18. I've kept a handwritten journal, and that's okay, but keeping a blog is way better. ____________________

19. Other people use blogs to share opinions on things commonly discussed in letters to the editor of a newspaper. ____________________

20. Bloggers post all kinds of awesome graphics. ____________________

Reinforce

See Handbook Section 33

Writers sometimes think that by using expressions such as *there is, there are,* and *it is* they can make their sentences sound formal and academic. In fact, using such expressions sometimes weakens sentences. Read the following examples and look at how the writer strengthened each sentence by using strong, active words.

Wordy sentences:	**Stronger sentences:**
There are two reasons why I enjoy blogs.	I enjoy blogs for two reasons.
It is unwise for students to reveal personal information in a blog.	Students should not reveal personal information in a blog.

Rewrite each sentence to eliminate the weak expression *there is, there are,* or *it is.* Each sentence may be rewritten several ways.

21. It is helpful to readers that each blog posting is dated. ____________________

22. There are many ways in which people can use blogs. ____________________

23. It is necessary for bloggers to keep up with developments in blogging software. ____________________

24. There is a strong possibility that people will continue to invent ways to express themselves on the Internet.

I will **sit** on that chair. You can **set** the computer on the floor. I will **raise** it later. I **laid** the instructions on my desk. You look tired; you should **lie** down. I will tell you when it's time to **rise**.

Which boldfaced word means "to move your body into a chair"? __________ Which means "to recline"? __________ Which boldfaced words mean "to place or put something somewhere"? __________ __________ Which boldfaced word means "to lift something"? __________ Which boldfaced word means "to move upward"? __________

Lie and ***lay*** are different verbs. *Lay* takes a direct object and *lie* does not. *Lie* means "to recline." *Lay* means "to put something down somewhere." ***Set*** and ***sit*** are different verbs. *Set* takes a direct object and *sit* does not. If you're about to use *set*, ask yourself, "Set what?" If you can't answer that question, use *sit*. Also, remember that you can't *sit* anything down—you must *set* it down. ***Rise*** and ***raise*** are different verbs. *Raise* takes a direct object and *rise* does not. *Rise* means "to move upward." *Raise* means "to lift something." **Remember to use this information when you speak, too.**

See Handbook Section 32

Practice

Underline the word in parentheses that correctly completes each sentence.

1. (Rise/Raise) your hand if you know what e-waste is.
2. *E-waste,* which stands for "electronic waste," has probably (laid/lain) in your garage for years.
3. Many people have (sat/set) old computers in their home, not knowing how to dispose of them.
4. After you (sit/set) down, I'll tell you about the impact of the improper disposal of e-waste.
5. Because a computer contains hazardous materials, it should not be (sat/set) in unmarked trash cans.
6. Components with heavy metals were (laid/lain) in place when the computer was assembled.
7. Once e-waste has (sat/set) in a landfill, those metals are likely to leak into the ground, contaminating soil and groundwater.
8. If e-waste is improperly incinerated, the fumes that (rise/raise) are likely to be hazardous.
9. The proper way to (lay/lie) your e-waste to rest is to have it recycled safely.
10. Plants have been (sat/set) up in other nations where the e-waste recycling process is less expensive.
11. Some recycling facilities have not (raised/risen) their safety standards high enough.
12. As standards (raise/rise), the health of workers should improve.
13. Recycling facilities need to make sure chemicals do not seep into the soil or (rise/raise) into the air.
14. So don't just (lay/lie) there on the couch.
15. (Rise/Raise) up, gather your e-waste together, and take it to a recycling facility!

Name ______________________________

Apply

Rewrite each sentence by replacing the underlined word(s) with a form of *lie, lay, set, sit, rise,* or *raise.*

16. Jessica had <u>stayed</u> in bed all morning instead of figuring out what to do with her old computer.

17. Finally, she <u>lifted</u> the blinds to let the sun stream in.

18. She noticed a brochure her mother had <u>placed</u> on her desk.

19. She wondered how long it had <u>rested</u> there.

20. Jessica <u>took a seat</u> at her new computer to research disposal options.

21. After locating a nearby recycling facility, she <u>got up</u> to ask her mother to take her there.

Reinforce

See Handbook Section 33

Raze and *raise* sound the same but have different meanings. *Raze* means "to destroy." The past tense form of *raze* is *razed,* and the past participle form is also *razed.*

Write two sentences about buildings. Use a form of *raise* in one sentence and a form of *raze* in the other.

22. ______________________________

23. ______________________________

Read and Analyze

Who **builded** that robot? How is it **held** together?

Cross out the boldfaced word that is an incorrect verb form.

Many verbs are **irregular;** they do not add *-ed* in the past tense. Here are some of those verbs:

Present	Past	With *has, have,* or *had*
go	went	gone
hold	held	held
build	built	built
make	made	made
find	found	found

Remember to use this information when you speak, too.

See Handbook Sections 18d, 18e

Practice

Circle the correct verb form in parentheses in each sentence.

1. You have (heard/heared) of robots vacuuming, but what about robots parking cars or weeding gardens?
2. Robots have been (builded/ built) for many different tasks.
3. A weeding robot pulled out weeds that had (taken/took) over our garden.
4. Our mowing robot (cut/cutted) our grass before we rose this morning.
5. A monitoring robot had (brought/bringed) polluted air to people's attention, but it was unable to smell the difference between mint and a banana.
6. Has anyone in your family (left/leaved) a car in a parking garage operated by a robot?
7. Robotic garages have (became/ become) more common because they can fit in more cars.
8. One parking area that had (holded/ held) only 24 cars was made into a robotic garage.
9. Thanks to a computer-controlled device that slides cars into vacant parking spots, the area's capacity has (rised/ risen) to 67.
10. To park our car, the robot (gone/ went) sideways.
11. Before our car was returned to us, it had been (spun/spinned) around on a turntable so that it faced the exit.
12. I wonder if the Robot Hall of Fame in Pittsburgh has (showed/ shown) a parking robot in a display.

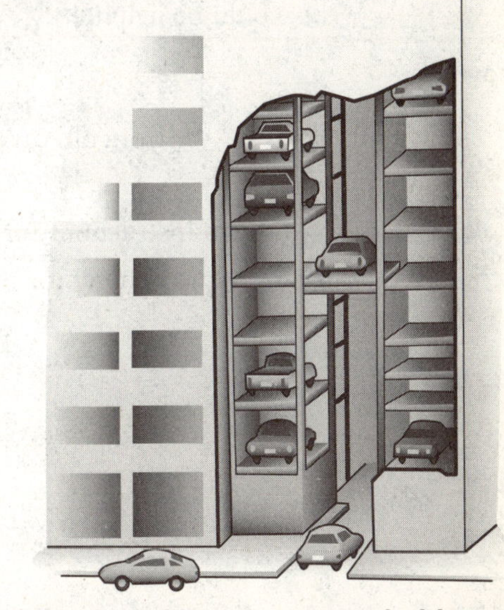

A robotic parking garage can hold more cars than an ordinary parking garage.

Name ______________________________

Apply

Fill in the blank with a past tense form of the verb in parentheses.

13. My family and I __________ to see an exhibit about robots. (go)
14. Not only have scientists built robots, but artists and others have __________ them, too. (build)
15. Some robots have been __________ of discarded electronic pieces. (make)
16. We __________ loud noises coming from a nearby room. (hear)
17. When we looked in, we __________ two robots in the middle of a battle. (see)
18. Competitors had __________ dozens of robots to this exhibit. (bring)
19. The sound of metal robots crashing into one another __________ our ears. (hurt)
20. At the show, I learned that Leonardo da Vinci had __________ plans for an armored humanoid machine in 1495. (draw)
21. The first humanoid robot, called Elektro, was __________ in 1939. (show)
22. The robot exhibit __________ me the idea to build my own robot. (give)
23. I have already __________ my research. (begin)

Reinforce

Use forms of the verbs in the word bank to complete the clues and solve the crossword puzzle.

know	bring	do	write	build	ring

Across

1. My dream robot had _____ the doorbell to be let inside.
2. He _____ me my slippers.
3. I _____ he would be helpful!

Down

2. My robot was _____ from old car and computer parts.
4. I had _____ down instructions for him.
5. He has just _____ my chores for me!

5 4 1 2 3

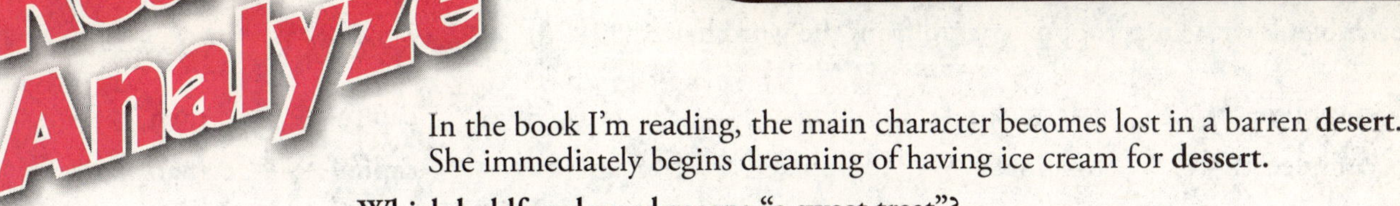

Read and Analyze

In the book I'm reading, the main character becomes lost in a barren **desert.** She immediately begins dreaming of having ice cream for **dessert.**

Which boldfaced word means "a sweet treat"? _______________

Which boldfaced word means "an extremely dry place"? _______________

People often confuse similar-sounding words. For example, they confuse ***than*** and ***then,*** which sound similar but are different words with different spellings and meanings. *Than* is a subordinating conjunction used to make comparisons, as in the sentence *Kendra is taller than Roger*. *Then* can be an adverb that tells about time. It can also mean "therefore." If you think you might be confusing one word with another, look up both words in a dictionary.

See Handbook Sections 32, 33

Practice

Circle the correct word in parentheses to complete each sentence.

1. A great library once existed in Alexandria, Egypt; it had many (aisles/isles) containing hundreds of thousands of documents.
2. That library was (razed/raised) one day, probably by fire, and the world lost all its documents.
3. Now a book's words can be (preserved/persevered) even if the book itself is destroyed.
4. With (currant/current) scanning technology, we can convert the text of books to digital files.
5. These files can then be (dispersed/disbursed) to secure computers.
6. Scanning every book in the world would be quite a (feat/feet)!
7. Preservation is only one reason to create digital books from (physical/fiscal) books.
8. Some people prefer to have (excess/access) to books in a digital format.
9. Reading books on a digital (device/devise) helps save paper.
10. Those who follow technology trends say we are not just going through a (phase/faze).
11. They believe that reading books online is the (weigh/way) of the future.
12. Still, many people (prefer/proffer) printed books.
13. Internet (sites/cites) are also being preserved digitally.
14. The CyberCemetery at the University of North Texas archives (officious/official) government websites and makes them permanently available to the public.
15. Another digital archive (perpetuates/perpetrates) patriotic images.
16. This (faculty/facility) stores and displays U.S. posters from the First and Second World Wars.

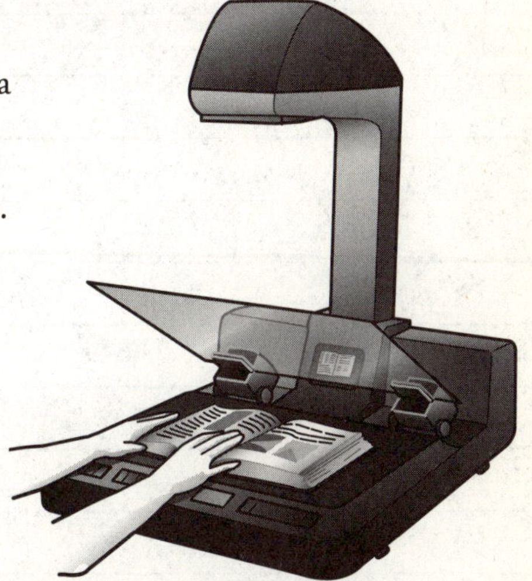

Book scanners help preserve text and save paper.

Lesson 57

Name ______________________________

Apply

Fill each blank with an appropriate word from the word bank. (17–26)

compliments	stationary	bazaar	fare	capitol	then
complements	stationery	bizarre	fair	capital	than

While she was away with her family, Amber used her favorite ______________ to write a letter to her best friend:

Today we explored the ______________ city. We took a boat ride along the river; the ______________ was reasonable. We also visited an Internet cafe. Later we went into a ______________ to do some shopping. A beautiful bedspread caught my eye. I purchased it because it ______________ the rug my sister and I have in our bedroom. The shopkeeper gave me a ______________ price.

______________ our family went to dinner, and the meal was so tasty that we gave ______________ to the chef. As we walked back to our hotel we noticed something ______________. A person painted silver was completely ______________. Then we saw a hat filled with coins and realized he was a street performer.

Reinforce

Write a paragraph about something you think should be preserved in a digital archive. Correctly use at least three easily confused words from this lesson.

____

____

____

____

____

____

____

____

____

____

____

____

____

____

I go, "We're learning about nanotechnology in science class."

Miguel is like, "What is that?"

So Tim goes, "It's technology on a tiny scale."

Has this conversation been written in formal language or informal language? ________________ Cross out the words that indicate that someone is speaking. Write *said* above the words you crossed out.

Go and ***went*** mean "move(d)." ***Is like*** means "resembles something." ***All*** means "the total of something." In your written work and in polite conversation, avoid using *goes, is all,* or *is like* to mean "said." Also be careful not to insert the word *like* where it doesn't belong, as in the sentence *This is, like, the fastest computer I have ever seen.* **Remember to use this information when you speak, too.**

See Handbook Section 32

Practice

Circle *go, went, all,* and *like* if these words are used incorrectly. (If the word *was* is part of the incorrect expression, circle it also.) (1–12)

Miguel went, "Sounds interesting. I like doing experiments. What have you learned?"

Tim was all, "Listen to this: An American physicist named Richard Feynman came up with the outrageous idea in 1959 that scientists would eventually be able to manipulate atoms and molecules. That's, like, happening today!"

"Wow! How tiny are these particles?" asked Miguel.

I go, "*Nano* means 'dwarf' in Greek. A nanometer is one billionth of one meter, which is like comparing the size of one marble to the size of Earth."

"And one strand of hair would be like a huge river," Tim added.

So then I went, "We're learning about how nanotechnology will soon be, like, everywhere."

And then Tim goes, "Scientists have used nanotechnology to help your clothes resist stains and spills."

I was like, "Nanotechnology may help us, like, cure cancer by sending tiny nano-missiles into the body to kill the cancerous cells while leaving the healthy ones untouched."

Tim was all, "Nanotechnology may help scientists create artificial human tissues."

Miguel went, "This is, like, making me want to be a scientist!"

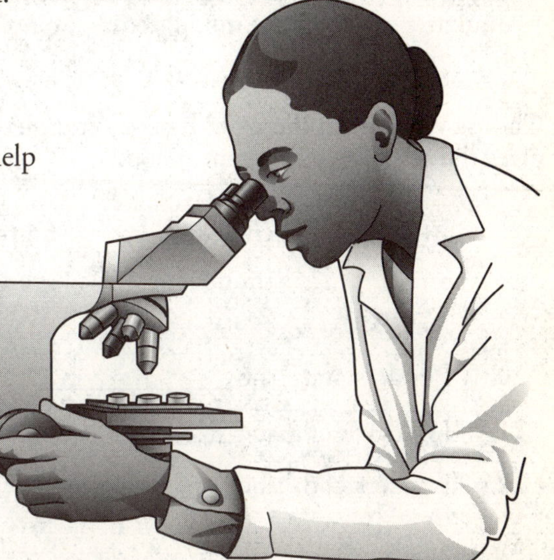

Name ______________________________

Apply

Rewrite each sentence to eliminate the incorrect expression. Each sentence may be rewritten several ways.

13. My little sister wants to be, like, a scientist.

____

14. Yesterday she goes, "Stay away! I'm conducting an experiment!"

____

15. I was all, "What are you doing?"

____

16. She was like, "I can't tell you, because it's top secret."

____

17. I went, "Now I know what to get you for your birthday!"

____

18. Intrigued, she went, "What are you going to get me?"

____

19. "I can't tell you. It's, like, top secret," I replied.

____

Reinforce

Many verbs, including *asked, answered, replied, added, exclaimed, remarked, suggested, began, continued, cried, whispered, grumbled,* and *yelled,* may be used to tell how a character is speaking. Using a variety of verbs for this purpose not only makes writing more interesting but also has a dramatic effect on the mood of direct quotations.

Choose verbs from the word bank to complete the sentence frame in six different ways. Notice how each verb gives the sentence a different mood.

muttered	chuckled	blurted	hissed	sighed	mumbled
sneered	thundered	grumbled	whispered	giggled	shrieked

20. "I understand," she ______________.
21. "I understand," she ______________.
22. "I understand," she ______________.
23. "I understand," she ______________.
24. "I understand," she ______________.
25. "I understand," she ______________.

a. The mouse it is one of the most widely used devices invented in the second half of the 20th century.

b. It enables people to give a computer a command just by rolling and clicking.

Which sentence makes sense if you take out the word *it*? ________

A **subject pronoun** takes the place of one or more nouns in the subject of a sentence or a subordinate clause. Follow the conventions of standard English in your writing: Do not use a subject pronoun right after the noun it stands for. **Remember this information when you speak, too.**

See Handbook Section 17b

Practice

Read each sentence. Draw a line through a subject pronoun if it is not needed.

1. In the 1950s, computers they were huge and slow.
2. Doug Engelbart he was an electrical engineer who worked with computers then.
3. In addition to understanding the properties of electricity, Engelbart was a great solver of mechanical problems.
4. He believed that computers they would become faster and more useful.
5. Computer users they would soon need a way of giving commands to the machine quickly and easily.
6. Engelbart he set up an experiment in his lab on the San Francisco Peninsula.
7. For several months he put volunteers in front of a computer screen.
8. The volunteers they were given different types of devices to use to control the cursor on the screen.
9. One device it was a knee pointer; another was a helmet with a pointer attached to it.
10. Volunteers moved the knee pointer with a knee and the helmet pointer with the head; the movements made the cursor move on the screen.
11. The best controlling device turned out to be a box on wheels that Engelbart himself built.
12. A volunteer she would roll it around the top of a desk, and the cursor would move around the screen in the same way.
13. This device it was connected to the computer by a wire.
14. Other researchers in Engelbart's lab began calling the device a mouse, because it was small and had a tail.
15. Engelbart he thought the name *mouse* sounded unprofessional; he called his device the "*x-y* position indicator for a display system."
16. The public has shown their strong preference for the engineers' name over the past fifty years.

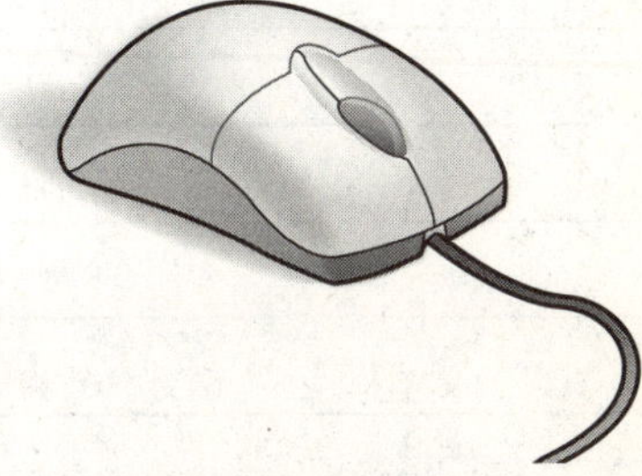

The computer mouse was invented by Doug Engelbart about 50 years ago.

Name ______________________________

Apply

Cross out the extra pronoun in each sentence. Then write the sentence correctly.

17. The trackball it was invented a decade before Doug Engelbart invented the mouse.

18. Two Canadian engineers they invented the trackball while working on improving a radar system.

19. This invention it is used as the controller in many laptops.

20. Touchscreen technology for mobile devices it was developed by Dr. Andrew Hsu.

Reinforce

New technology is continually being developed and brought to market by innovative companies. Do an Internet search to learn about a technology or a device that is of particular interest to you. Then on the lines below, write a paragraph that includes at least three facts you discovered about this technology or device. Use subject pronouns correctly in your paragraph.

a. Because of her ability to perform complex calculations in her head almost instantly, Shakuntala Devi became known as "the human computer."

b. Because of her amazing ability to perform complex mathematical calculations in her head without the use of a calculator or even pencil and paper almost instantly, Shakuntala Devi became known, not surprisingly, as "the human computer."

Which sentence above communicates information more effectively? ________
Why? ____

Effective writers **use the fewest words possible** to convey facts and ideas clearly. When you write, first decide what information you need to communicate, and then **state the information as simply and directly as you can**. When you edit, identify and **eliminate unnecessary words and repetitive ideas**.

See Handbook Section 14

Practice

Draw a line through unnecessary words in the sentences below.

1. Shakuntala Devi demonstrated an amazing and surprising ability to memorize numbers, an ability that young children almost never possess, when she was three.
2. By age five, Shakuntala Devi had learned to solve complex math problems that were very difficult.
3. A year later, her father, a lion tamer and trapeze artist, arranged for Shakuntala Devi to give public demonstrations of her skills in front of audiences throughout India.
4. When she was eleven, Shakuntala Devi toured the continent of Europe and demonstrated her computational skills.
5. At least twice she was told by math experts that an answer she had given was incorrect, only to have the math experts reverse themselves when they rechecked their calculations and discovered errors in their work.
6. In 1977, at Southern Methodist University in Texas, Ms. Devi competed against a computer in a contest to see whether she could solve a math problem faster than it could.
7. Ms. Devi extracted the 23rd root of a 201-digit number in 50 seconds; the computer needed 62 seconds to solve the problem, which meant that Ms. Devi had beaten it by 12 seconds.
8. Ms. Devi was so talented that she could use her math talents to multiply a 13-digit number by another 13-digit number almost instantly; this feat earned her a listing in the Guinness World Records.
9. If a person gave Ms. Devi any date in any week, month, or year in the twentieth century, she could tell that person what day of the week it fell on.
10. Ms. Devi wanted to simplify math for students, and she published several books on math skills for young audiences to help them solve math problems more easily.

Name ______________________________

Apply

Rewrite each sentence, eliminating the unnecessary words.

11. Shakuntala Devi was born in Bangalore, India; it is a city that has become an international center for information technology companies from all over the world.

____

____

12. Shakuntala Devi developed her math skills and learned to do complex calculations without ever attending school.

____

____

13. She discovered quick, effective shortcuts that enabled her to solve certain types of problems more quickly than she could have if she had used standard computational methods.

____

____

14. Ms. Devi helped many students conquer their fear of mathematics and gain confidence as they learned to solve challenging math problems successfully.

____

____

Reinforce

Look over an essay or a report you have written this year. Identify two sentences that have unnecessary words in them. Copy each sentence on the lines below, and rewrite each to be shorter and more effective.

15. Original sentence: ______________________________

New Sentence: ______________________________

16. Original sentence: ______________________________

New sentence: ______________________________

Usage

Circle the word in parentheses that correctly completes each sentence.

1. How many electronic devices are in (your /you're) home?
2. Many homes have one or (to/too/two) computers.
3. Do you know anyone (who's /whose) still without a cell phone?
4. Many people today depend greatly on (there/ their /they're) high-tech gadgets.
5. If (there/their/they're) in an area without cell phone reception, they become uneasy.
6. If (there/their /they're) Internet connection is down, they feel out-of-touch.
7. They cannot jog or ride the bus without listening (to /too/two) an MP3 player.
8. Are people (to/too /two) dependent on these high-tech devices?
9. It's true that technology has (its /it's) negative effects.
10. A person (who's /whose) at a computer all day may develop wrist pain.
11. A company (who's/whose) computer files are not properly backed up may lose data.
12. People using (there/their /they're) cell phones in public places may annoy others.
13. For all the disadvantages of technology, (its/it's) also brought many benefits.
14. Think of all the ways that technology has made (your /you're) life more convenient.
15. Can you imagine having (to /too/two) type a report on a typewriter?
16. If you're someone (who's /whose) often late, a cell phone is invaluable.

Circle the correct word or words to complete each sentence.

17. Not (everybody /nobody) in our class has an MP3 player.
18. However, (over/more than) fifteen students have them.
19. There are (less/fewer) students with CD players than with MP3 players.
20. I have purchased (less /fewer) music than my friend has.

Expressions to Avoid in Academic Writing

Circle the correct expression to complete each sentence.

21. Technology has provided students with (stuff/tools) they didn't have in earlier years.
22. Technology is (cool/motivating) for students because it allows them to learn independently.
23. They can (perform tasks /do things) and acquire information at their own pace.
24. The technical skills they learn are (going to /gonna) prepare them for joining the workforce.

Lie and *Lay; Set* and *Sit; Rise* and *Raise;* More Irregular Verbs; Easily Confused Words

Circle the correct word to complete each sentence.

25. There's a glare on my screen because someone (rised/raised) the blinds.

26. (Then /Than) why don't you lower them?

27. If you need more room, you can (sit/set) your laptop here.

28. (Wear/ Where) did I put the power cord?

29. Has someone (taken /took) it?

30. Oh, I think you're (sitting /setting) on it!

31. I need (current /currant) information on several topics.

32. Completing my research by Friday will be quite a (feet/feat).

33. How can I gain (access /excess) to this website?

34. Isn't the computer a marvelous (devise/device)?

Frequently Misused Words

Cross out each incorrect use of *go, went, like,* and *all.* (If the word *was* is part of the incorrect expression, cross that out also.) Write a correct word to replace the incorrect expression, if a replacement is needed. Try not to use the same word as a replacement more than once.

35. John was all, "Let's check out the new computer store." ______________

36. I went, "We don't even know if it's open on Sunday." ______________

37. John said, "It is, like, sure to be open on Sunday." ______________

38. Then I was like, "Why don't you check store hours online?" ______________

Eliminating Words

Read each sentence. Draw a line through any words that are not needed.

39. Deanna she is fascinated by online shopping.

40. Some shopping services they offer free delivery.

41. Because Deanna is on a tight budget and must carefully control her spending, she never makes a purchase the first time she visits a website she has not visited before.

42. She also waits at least one day before purchasing a product that is for sale.

Spelling Practice

Read and Analyze

Many adolescents today will undoubtedly choose to do their reading on a tablet instead of in a book.

Underline the two words in the sentence that have a silent consonant. Circle each silent consonant.

Spelling Patterns: Words With Silent Consonants

Some words have **silent consonants** that are not pronounced. For example, the *g* is silent in *gnarled* and *resign,* the *c* is silent in *fascinate* and *discipline,* and the *p* is silent in *raspberry* and *pneumonia.*

Word Sort

Use the words below to complete the word sort.

adjust	campaign	psychology	miscellaneous	subtle	acknowledgement
ascend	mortgage	undoubtedly	adjoin	raspberry	adjourn

Silent *c* or *k*	Silent *p* or *t*
Silent *d* in the first syllable	**Silent *b* or *g***

Name ______________________________

Pattern Practice

acquisition	undoubtedly	acknowledge	adjourn	psychology
adolescent	discipline	acquaintance	subtle	miscellaneous
raspberry	fascinate	pneumonia	adjust	

Write the word above that belongs in each group. Circle the silent consonant.

1. cranberry, blueberry, strawberry ______________________
2. positively, certainly, definitely ______________________
3. biology, geology, zoology ______________________
4. assorted, diverse, various ______________________
5. addition, purchase, possession ______________________
6. hypnotize, captivate, interest ______________________
7. juvenile, youth, minor ______________________
8. influenza, measles, mumps ______________________

Write the word above that best completes each sentence.

9. Sanjay is a new ______________________ I met at summer camp.
10. It takes a lot of time and ______________________ to learn a new language.
11. The lemon flavor is so ______________________ I can hardly taste it.
12. The class will ______________________ for the day at noon.
13. You can ______________________ the volume with this remote control.
14. Mr. Ito didn't ______________________ the whispering in the back of the room.
15. Two quarters, a gum wrapper, and a receipt are among the ______________________ items in my pocket.
16. A ______________________ is a type of fruit that grows on a bush.
17. It is important to go to the doctor right away if you think you have ______________________.

Use the Dictionary

Circle the word in each boldfaced pair that is spelled correctly. Check your work in a print or an online dictionary.

18. Trevor's **asma/asthma** keeps him from playing soccer.
19. We'll have to **hussle/hustle** to get to the movie on time.
20. Your blouse will go perfectly with my **khaki/kahki** pants.

Diagramming Indirect Objects

You have learned where to place a direct object in a sentence diagram. Here's how to diagram an indirect object. (The indirect object is in boldfaced type in this example.)

I gave my **sister** my old scanner.

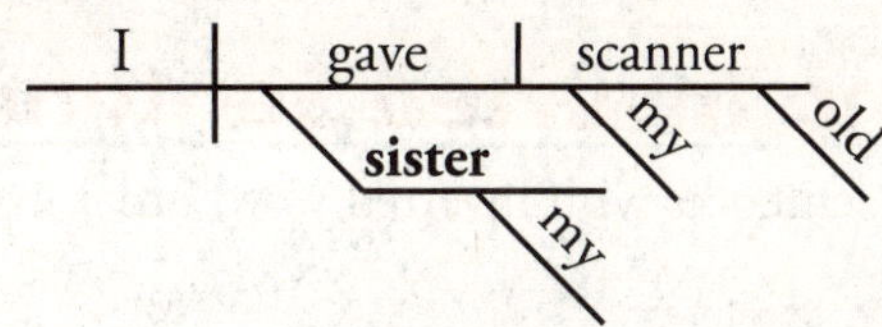

Try diagramming these sentences.

1. Uncle Leo bought me a new graphics program.

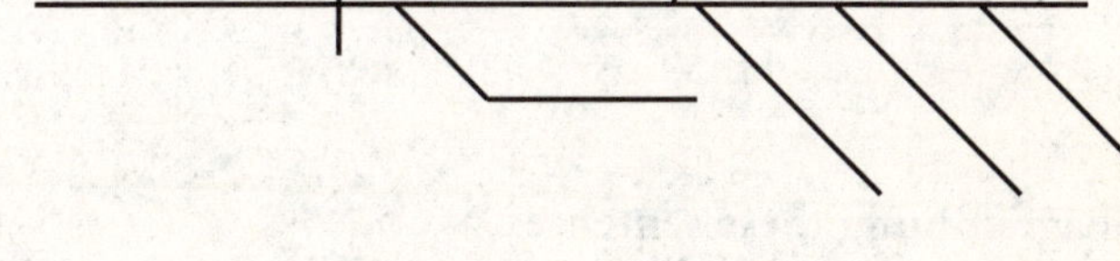

2. I lent Mom my new laptop.

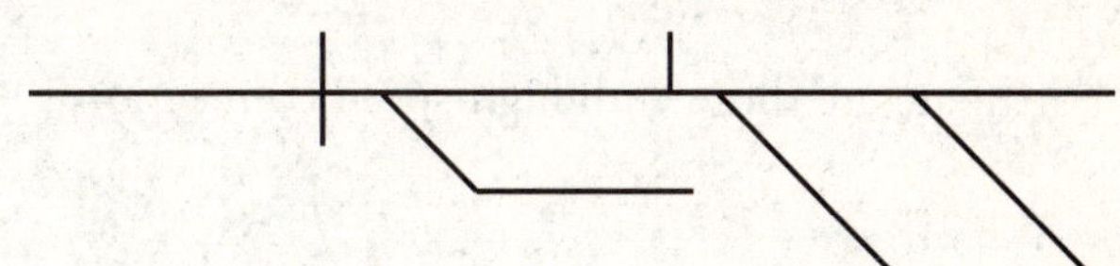

3. She bought us a faster modem.

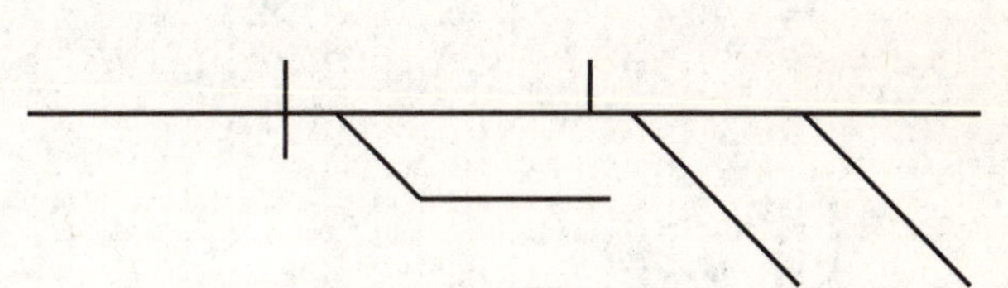

4. Viv gave Dixie the name of a consultant.

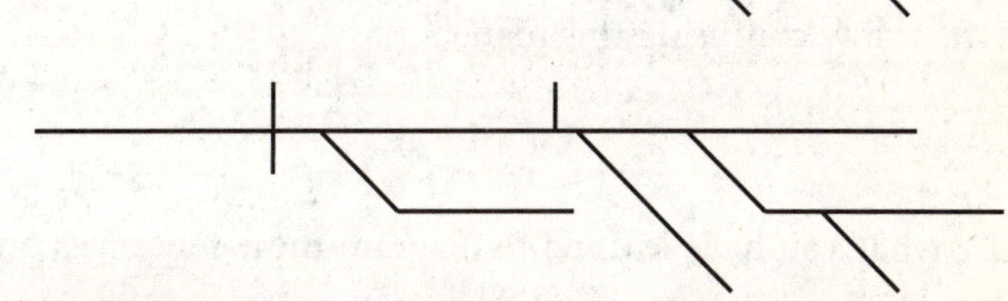

Diagramming Sentences with *There*

When the word *there* is used to begin a sentence, place it on a separate line above the subject.

There are blank disks in the drawer.

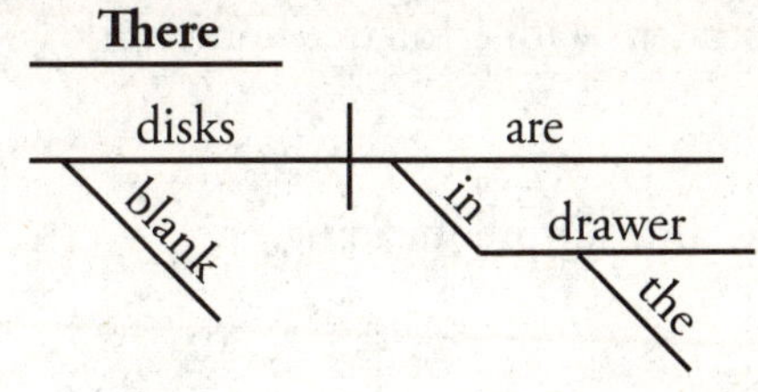

Diagram these sentences.

5. There is enough paper in the printer.

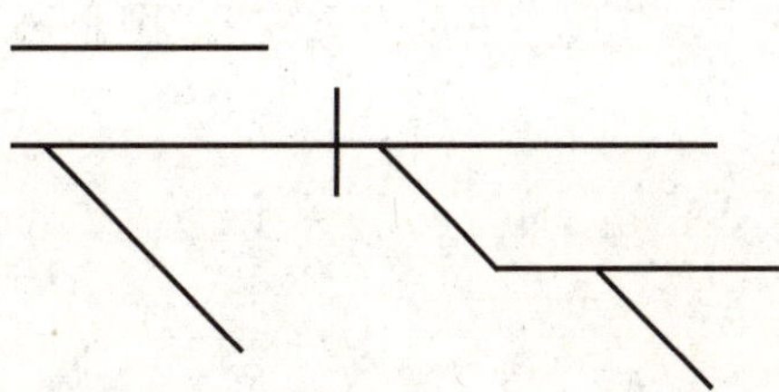

Name ____

6. There is an ant on your mouse!

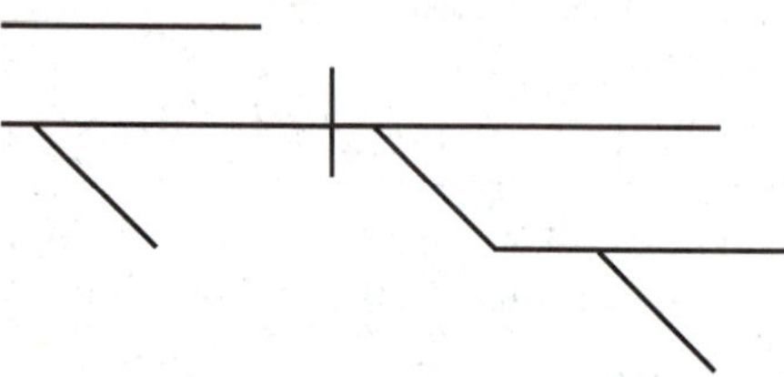

Diagramming Inverted Sentences

You learned about sentences with inverted word order in Unit 2. This model shows how to diagram an inverted sentence.

How wonderful my new flat-screen monitor is!

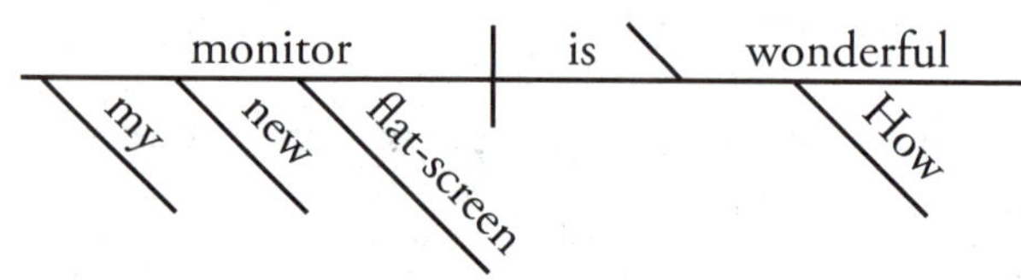

Try diagramming these sentences.

7. Fortunate are those with high-speed connections!

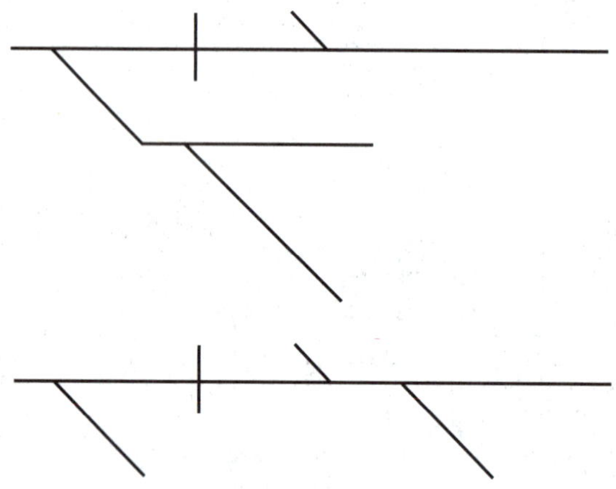

8. How confusing this manual is!

Use what you have learned to diagram these sentences on another sheet of paper.

9. How efficient I have been on my homework!

10. Happy is the student with error-free homework!

11. There is always time for proofreading.

12. My teacher will give me a high grade on this paper.

These sentences need your help. Rewrite each one so that homophones, problem words, and irregular verbs are used correctly.

1. Its important to evaluate the reliability of the information you find on the Internet. ____________________

____

2. First, you should think about whose written the website and what they're motives and qualifications are.

____

____

3. Try to find out if the sight has been updated in the passed year. ____________________

____

4. Notice the domain name of the website your exploring; .gov or .edu cites are usually more reliable then .com cites. ____________________

____

5. Look for footnotes and, like, links to other cites. ____________________

____

6. If possible, find out whether an author has wrote other articles on the same topic. ____________________

____

An informative paragraph's purpose is to inform readers. It should contain several important facts about a particular topic. The paragraph begins with an introductory sentence and ends with a concluding sentence. In between are sentences providing more information about the topic. Read this informative paragraph.

introductory sentence	**Computers have revolutionized the way students write reports.**
sentences that give more information about the topic	Students now do much of their research online. They read articles, locate primary sources, view videos, and access library databases all on the Internet. Drafting and publishing a report is much easier using a word processing program. Students have many options for formatting their reports. Most programs include automatic footnote and endnote features.
concluding sentence	**Computers aid students in many ways; still, a successful report requires original thinking and clear writing on the part of the student.**

Name ______________________________

Writing a Paragraph

The sentences you repaired on page 183 can be used to make an informative paragraph. Write the paragraph below. You will need to add your own concluding sentence.

Write an informative paragraph about how using a computer has helped you or someone you know accomplish a specific task. Use the paragraph at the bottom of page 183 as a model.

Reread your paragraph. Use this checklist to make sure it is complete and correct.

- ❑ My paragraph contains an introductory sentence and a concluding sentence.
- ❑ My paragraph provides several interesting facts about a topic.
- ❑ I have used homophones and problem words correctly.
- ❑ I have used irregular verbs correctly.
- ❑ I have used negatives correctly.

Proofreading Practice

Read this passage about how technology is helping to tackle environmental challenges, and find the mistakes. Use the proofreading marks below to show how each mistake should be fixed. Use a dictionary to check and correct spellings.

Proofreading Marks

Mark	Means	Example
(delete mark)	delete	Saving the planet is everyone's's responsibility.
^	add	Saving the planet ^is everyone's responsibility.
≡	make into an uppercase letter	saving the planet is everyone's responsibility.
/	make into a lowercase letter	Saving the Planet is everyone's responsibility.
⊙	add a period	Saving the planet is everyone's responsibility⊙
(apostrophe mark)	add an apostrophe	Saving the planet is everyones responsibility.
(sp)	fix spelling	Saving the planet is everyone's responsability.

Technology as Environmental Problem-Solver

Have you ever thought about how you're computer could help tackle environmental challenges the world is now facing? Although computers and other technological equipment can pollute soil and water when their not disposed of properly, these machines give us the means to solve difficult enviromental problems

For example, thanks too technology, sum people are now able to skip there commute to the office and work from home. Its called telecommuting, or teleworking, and it saves gassaline and cuts emissions. Many people who work from home are, like, more productive because of lesser distractions. Telephones, fax machines, and computers all help make working from a remote location simpel. Some who work at home use less paper then they would if they were working in an office. So, telecommuting can save trees, to.

Improvements on old tecnologies have also enabled americans to use fewer energy. Engineers have made standard car engines more efficient and have also developed the Hybrid engine, which gets better mileage. Over 100 people in our community now drive Hybrids, which means we're saving tons of gasoline. Its just a matter of time before researchers find even more ways to protect the environment.

Name ____________________

Proofreading Checklist

You can use the list below to help you find and fix mistakes in your own writing. Write the titles of your own stories or reports in the blanks at the top of the chart. Then use the questions to check your work. Make a check mark (✓) in each box after you have checked that item.

Proofreading Checklist for Unit 5

	Titles			
Have I used *your* and *you're* correctly?				
Have I used *their, they're,* and *there* correctly?				
Have I used *its* and *it's* correctly?				
Have I used *who's* and *whose* correctly?				
Have I used *to, too,* and *two* correctly?				
Have I used other easily confused words correctly?				
Have I used correct forms of irregular verbs?				
Have I used appropriate academic language?				
Have I used negatives correctly?				

Also Remember...

Does each sentence begin with an uppercase letter?				
Did I use a dictionary to check and correct spellings?				
Have I used commas correctly?				

Your Own List

Use this space to write your own list of things to check in your writing.

Community Connection

In Unit 5 of *Grammar, Usage, and Mechanics,* students learned how to use **easily confused words, quantity words, negatives,** and **irregular verbs** correctly. They also learned to avoid using **inappropriate expressions in academic writing.** The content of these lessons focuses on the theme **High-Tech Highlights.** As students completed the exercises, they learned about different types of technology, such as GPS devices and robots, and how new technologies have affected daily life. These pages offer a variety of activities that reinforce skills and concepts presented in the unit. They also provide opportunities for students to make connections between the material in the lessons and their community at large.

Your Town Online

Most communities have a presence in the virtual world of the Internet. Find out what your community's online profile is like by looking it up on the Internet. Type the name of your city and state into a browser's search engine and see what comes up. You may find that your town has its own website and that several other websites link to it.

Bird's Eye View

Have you ever wondered what your community looks like from the air? Type your city and state name into a search engine that links to satellite maps or street maps. Use the arrow buttons to zoom in on ten important places in the community, such as schools, shopping districts, parks, and hospitals. If possible, print out the map and label the places you located.

Tech Fair

Think about what you might include in a school technology fair, and make a plan for holding one. Answer these questions to help you plan the event.

- Where and when will you hold the tech fair?
- What kinds of devices and technologies do you want to include?
- Which tech companies would you invite to participate? What specific devices would you ask each company to bring?
- Will your tech fair include demonstrations? If so, what kinds of equipment and seating arrangements will you need?
- What kinds of furnishing will you need, such as tables, shelves, and movable walls for displays?
- How would you advertise the fair? Be specific.
- How much would you charge fair-goers in order to cover the cost of putting on the fair?

When you have finished working out your plan, develop a flier to advertise the event.

The Planning Stage

The planners of a school fair must make sure they follow school rules about holding events on school property. Talk with your teacher or principal about the rules you would need to comply with in order to hold a tech fair at your school. Use the Tech Fair Planner on the next page to help you organize what you learn.

Name ______________________________

Tech Fair Planner

When the fair will be held: ______________________________

Where it will be held: ______________________________

School rules the fair must comply with:

____

____

____

Other considerations (such as how many exhibits or people the space can hold):

____

____

____

Companies to Contact:	Contact Information:	Equipment/Furniture Needed:

Advertising Strategies:

____

____

____

Subject Pronouns and Object Pronouns

Unit 6: Lesson 61

a. Mr. Young taught our class about rivers.

b. He taught **us** about **them**.

Which boldfaced word replaces the word *rivers*? ________

Which boldfaced word replaces the phrase *Mr. Young*? ________

Which boldfaced word replaces the phrase *our class*? ________

Subject pronouns include *I, he, she, we,* and *they*. Subject pronouns can be the subject of a clause or sentence. **Object pronouns** can be used after an action verb or a preposition. Object pronouns include *me, him, her, us,* and *them*. The pronouns *it* and *you* can be either subjects or objects. **Remember to use this information when you speak, too.**

See Handbook Section 17b

Practice

Circle the correct pronoun in parentheses. Write *S* if you circled a subject pronoun. Write *O* if you circled an object pronoun.

1. (I/me) am reading about great rivers of the world in social studies. _____
2. Our teacher explained to (we/us) that many civilizations developed along rivers. _____
3. The cities of London, Paris, Moscow, and Tokyo all have rivers running through (they/them). _____
4. Our teacher wants (we/us) to create a guide for a major city on a river. _____
5. In the guide (we/us) must explain how the river has affected the city's development. _____
6. I'm writing about the Thames River because (us/we) visited London last year. _____
7. My friend Araceli is working with (I/me); she has been there, too. _____
8. (Her/She) and her family took a boat ride down the Thames. _____
9. Araceli has brought (I/me) maps and brochures about London. _____
10. London has a multitude of famous structures, and many of (they/them) are along the Thames. _____
11. On both sides of the Thames (we/us) saw historic buildings. _____
12. Our parents wanted us to see Shakespeare's Globe Theatre, so (they/them) took us across the river to visit it. _____
13. Then they treated (we/us) to a ride on the London Eye. _____
14. From atop the Eye, (we/us) could see the Thames snaking its way to the sea. _____

The London Eye is a giant slow-moving Ferris wheel on the bank of the Thames River.

Name ______________________________

Apply

Rewrite each sentence. Replace each boldfaced phrase with a pronoun. Circle each subject pronoun you write. Draw a box around each object pronoun.

15. **The Thames River** flows through London on its way to the English Channel. ______________________

____

16. **My friend Araceli** took a boat ride on the Thames. ______________________

____

17. I wish I could have gone with **Araceli and her family.** ______________________

____

18. **My classmates and I** have read about London's struggle to keep its river clean. ______________________

____

19. Heavy rainfall causes sewers to overflow into **the river.** ______________________

____

20. **London officials** monitor levels of contamination and keep the public informed. ______________________

____

Reinforce

Forms of personal pronouns in English have changed over the years. Until the sixteenth century the word *thou* was used as a subject pronoun to indicate the person being spoken to, and the word *thee* was used as the object form. Either *thy* or *thine* was used to show possession. Since that time, people have used the word *you* as both a subject and an object pronoun to indicate the person being spoken to; *your* has been used to show possession. Yet many writers continued to use *thou* and *thee* well into the nineteenth century.

Read the following quotations. Circle each pronoun that is no longer commonly used. Then write the modern English pronoun that would be used instead of each of these archaic pronouns.

This above all: to thine own self be true,
And it must follow, as the night the day,
Thou canst not then be false to any man.
— William Shakespeare

How do I love thee? Let me count the ways.
— Elizabeth Barrett Browning

21. __________

22. __________

23. __________

Read and Analyze

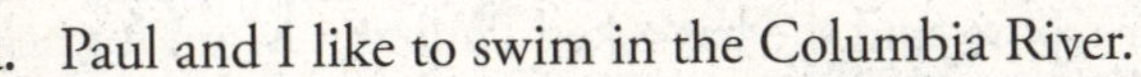

a. Paul and I like to swim in the Columbia River.

b. My father took Paul and I swimming last month.

If you delete "Paul and" from each sentence, which sentence sounds correct? _____

Use a **subject pronoun** in a compound subject. Use an **object pronoun** in a compound direct object, a compound indirect object, or a compound object of a preposition. If you are unsure which pronoun form to use, say the sentence with only the pronoun part of the compound: For example, *He told Carmen and I about his vacation* becomes *He told I about his vacation*. You can hear that *I* should be replaced with *me*. **Remember to use this information when you speak, too.**

See Handbook Section 17b

Practice

Circle the correct pronoun in each pair. Write *S* if you chose a subject pronoun and *O* if you chose an object pronoun.

1. My parents took Paul, Rosa, and (I/me) on a ride along the Columbia River Gorge. _____
2. Paul and (I/me) love hiking in the woods along the Gorge. _____
3. Rosa came along because (her/she), Paul, and I are writing reports on the Columbia River salmon run. _____
4. Mr. Tanaka had told Paul and (she/her) that salmon born in the Columbia River Basin migrate all the way to the Pacific Ocean. _____
5. (He/Him) and his aide showed a DVD of salmon swimming upstream to their birthplace. _____
6. When Paul asked why the salmon migrate, Mr. Tanaka told Rosa and (he/him) that the adult fish swim upstream to spawn, or lay eggs. _____
7. Mr. Tanaka told (she/her) and Paul that dams on the Columbia disturb this migration. _____
8. Dad said that (he/him) and Mom had seen the river churning with salmon. _____
9. My parents, my friends, and (I/me) visited Bonneville Dam, on the Columbia River. _____
10. Engineers there told Paul, Rosa, and (I/me) what they are doing to protect salmon. _____
11. Then (we/us) and my parents traveled to Multnomah Falls. _____
12. Paul, Dad, and (I/me) climbed to the top of the falls. _____
13. Rosa is afraid of heights, so (her/she) and Mom stayed below. _____
14. Dad took a photograph of Paul and (I/me) at the top of the falls. _____
15. I told (he/him) and Paul that the falls are 620 feet high. _____
16. Paul and (he/him) asked how I knew that, and I pointed to a sign. _____

Name ______________________________

Apply

Rewrite these sentences. Substitute a pronoun for each boldfaced noun or phrase. Circle each subject pronoun you write. Draw a box around each object pronoun.

17. Rosa is working on her report, and she has asked **Paul** and **Mom** for help. ______________________________

18. Years ago, **Mom** and **Dad** saw waters churning with salmon. ______________________________

19. Mr. Tanaka had told **Paul** and **other students** that many dams had been built along the Columbia for hydroelectric power. ______________________________

20. **Ms. Vu** and **Mr. Tanaka** have studied how dams disrupt the migratory patterns of salmon. ______________________________

21. According to **Ms. Vu** and **Mr. Tanaka**, salmon are better adapted to cold, fast-moving water than to lakes and reservoirs. ______________________________

22. **Mr. Johnson** and **other engineers** are seeking ways to save endangered salmon. ______________________________

23. A **fish slide** and **other devices** help juvenile fish slide over the dam spillway. ______________________________

24. **Mr. Johnson** and **the other engineers** explained that underwater screens guide fish away from the dam's dangerous turbines. ______________________________

Reinforce

When *I* or *me* is used in a pair with a noun or another pronoun, the pronoun *I* or *me* should come last (*Paul and me*, NOT *me and Paul*).

Circle the choice that completes each sentence correctly.

25. (I and Rosa/Rosa and I) presented what we knew about salmon migration to the class.
26. The class had many questions for (Rosa and me/me and Rosa).
27. The questions gave (Rosa and me/me and Rosa) a great idea.
28. (Paul, I, and Rosa/Paul, Rosa, and I) will plan a field trip to a salmon hatchery.

Read and Analyze

Pronoun-Antecedent Agreement

Unit 6: Lesson 63

The Nile is a river in Africa. **It** flows north through much of the continent.

Circle the proper noun that the boldfaced pronoun replaces. Draw an arrow from the pronoun to that name.

An **antecedent** is the word or words a pronoun refers to. When you write a pronoun, be sure its antecedent is clear. A pronoun must also **agree** with its antecedent. An antecedent and pronoun agree when they have the same number (singular or plural) and gender (male or female). **Remember to use this information when you speak, too.**

See Handbook Section 17c

Practice

Circle the antecedent of each boldfaced pronoun.

1. The Nile River flows over 4,100 miles through Africa. Near Alexandria, Egypt, **it** empties into the Mediterranean Sea.
2. The Nile River system is complex. **It** has many tributaries.
3. To find the source of a river, mapmakers search for the source of the longest tributary that feeds into **it**.
4. There are two major tributaries of the Nile. **They** are the White Nile and the Blue Nile.

The Nile River runs through the city of Cairo, Egypt.

5. The waters of the Blue Nile originate high in the mountains of Ethiopia. **They** are replenished each year by seasonal rains.
6. The White Nile flows from Lake Victoria and beyond. **It** supplies most of the Nile's water.
7. The two rivers flow together in Sudan. **They** meet near the capital city of Khartoum.
8. Later they are joined by a third major tributary. **It** is the Atbara River, which also flows out of Ethiopia.
9. For centuries, explorers searched for the source of the Nile. Many of **them** met with frustration.
10. A priest named Pedro Páez may have been the first European to reach the source of the Blue Nile. **He** traveled there in the early seventeenth century.
11. In 1858, John Hanning Speke saw a great lake. **It** fed the White Nile at Jinja, Uganda.
12. Speke named the lake after Queen Victoria. **She** ruled England at that time.
13. In 2004, members of the White Nile Expedition navigated the length of the Nile. The journey took **them** through remote parts of Africa.
14. Natalie McComb was part of that team. **She** was a tour guide based in Kampala, Uganda.
15. In recent years, other teams have navigated the Nile. **They** have braved many dangers to trace the course of this river.

Name ______________________________

Apply

Write a pronoun that relates to each boldfaced antecedent. Capitalize each word that begins a sentence.

16. Many **people** have explored the Nile. Mostly likely, __________ have been motivated by adventure as much as a search for knowledge.
17. In 2004, two **men** traveled the Blue Nile. No one before __________ had paddled its entire length.
18. Their **trip** was long and grueling. __________ took them 148 days.
19. Today, explorers still disagree over the true **source** of the White Nile. Some claim __________ lies in Burundi, and others claim __________ is in Rwanda.
20. In 2006, **Neil McGrigor** took a team with __________ to what he claimed was its true source.
21. McGrigor wanted to prove to **geographers** that the Nile was longer than __________ had believed.
22. Burundi is farther from Egypt than Rwanda is. However, the **tributary** in Rwanda twists back and forth, which makes __________ longer than the tributary in Burundi.
23. To measure the length precisely, the **explorers** took a GPS and a laptop computer with __________.
24. The "true **source** of the Nile" lay deep in the Nyungwe Forest. __________ was little more than a muddy hole.

Reinforce

The word part *ante* in *antecedent* means "before." A pronoun's antecedent should come before the pronoun so that the reader knows which word the pronoun replaces. Rewrite the paragraph below so that every pronoun has a clear antecedent. You will need to replace some pronouns with nouns, and some nouns with pronouns.

It lies on the west bank of the Nile. A necropolis is where pharaohs were buried. Around 1470 B.C. she erected a huge temple there. Queen Hatshepsut also erected four obelisks. On the wall of her temple there is a painting of how they were transported down the Nile on barges. Two obelisks were placed end to end on a barge. Each barge was towed by many boats rowed by them. It may have taken as many as 1,000 oarsmen to do the job.

____

____

____

____

____

____

____

____

____

Read and Analyze

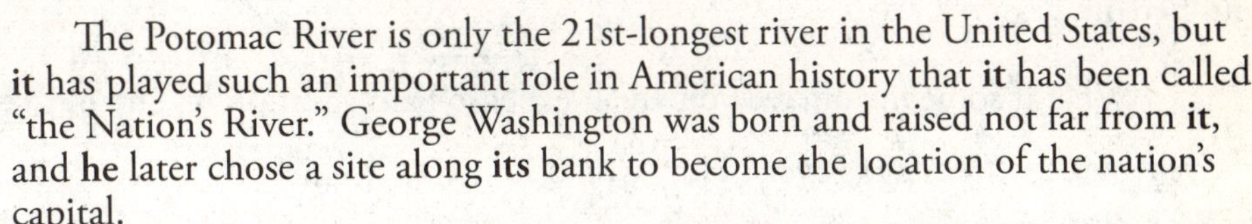

Correcting Shifts in Pronoun Number and Person

Unit 6: Lesson 64

The Potomac River is only the 21st-longest river in the United States, but **it** has played such an important role in American history that **it** has been called "the Nation's River." George Washington was born and raised not far from **it**, and **he** later chose a site along **its** bank to become the location of the nation's capital.

Circle the words that the pronouns *it* and *its* stand for in this paragraph. Draw a box around the words that the pronoun *he* stands for.

Pronouns must agree with their **antecedents** in number (singular or plural) and gender (male or female). When you use a pronoun to establish a point of view, be careful not to shift to a pronoun of a different number and person.

See Handbook Section 17c

Practice

In each item below, circle the pronoun form that agrees with its antecedent. Then underline the antecedent.

1. The Potomac River got its name from an Algonquian tribe that lived in its basin in colonial times. (He/It) had the name Patawomeck.
2. John Smith was the leader of the first successful colony in Virginia. (He/They) spelled the name "Patawomeke" on a map he drew.
3. On a map you can see that the Potomac has two sources, the North Branch and the South Branch. (You/They) converge near Green Spring in West Virginia.
4. George Washington's parents were plantation owners in the Potomac Basin. (His/Their) son George was born and grew up on that plantation in the 1730s.

People can take a boat ride on the Potomac in Washington, D.C.

5. Members of the United States Congress developed a plan for a new capital in 1790. (It/They) then decided to build this new city somewhere along the Potomac River on land that belonged to the federal government.
6. George Washington, who had just become America's first president, was asked to choose the precise location because (they/he) knew the Potomac region so well.
7. One of the most important events leading up to the Civil War took place where the Shenandoah River joins the Potomac. (It/They) involved the abolitionist John Brown, who led a raid on the United States arsenal there in the village of Harper's Ferry.
8. The Potomac River was a dividing line between the Union and the Confederacy in the Civil War; the Confederate General Robert E. Lee crossed (it/them) twice to invade Northern territory.
9. The Potomac has provided drinking water for residents of Washington, D.C., since the time of the Civil War. People in the region have used (it/them) for recreation activities for an even longer time.
10. President Bill Clinton named the Potomac an American Heritage River in 1998. (He/It) highlighted its great importance to our country by doing so.

Name ______________________________

Apply

The paragraph below includes several improper shifts of pronoun voice. Circle each improperly used pronoun. Then rewrite the paragraph, replacing the incorrect pronouns with pronouns that indicate the correct number and person.

What if someone offered you an all-expense-paid vacation on any of the fourteen waterways designated as American Heritage Rivers? How would someone decide which river to visit? We would probably begin by obtaining a list of these rivers. Many websites can provide you with this information. We might then give the list a quick look to see if any of the rivers are among your favorites. If not, the next step someone should take would be to decide which part of the United States you would most like to visit and see which rivers on the list are in that region. If they are an outdoor enthusiast, they might select the Far West for its verdant wild areas and mild weather. We would quickly notice that only one of the rivers on the list, the Willamette River, is in the Far West. Having identified this river as a possible destination, we would want to do research to learn about popular vacation areas and activities there. A few visits to Oregon websites would tell us that if we like fishing, swimming, boating, hiking, cycling, camping, or sightseeing, you are likely to have a great time on a Willamette River vacation!

____

____

____

____

____

____

____

____

____

____

____

____

Reinforce

On another sheet of paper, write a script for a 30-second TV commercial for a vacation area on a river located in or near your community. Use at least two personal pronouns in your commercial. Be careful not to shift pronoun voice in your script.

Correcting Vague Pronouns

Unit 6: Lesson 65

Read and Analyze

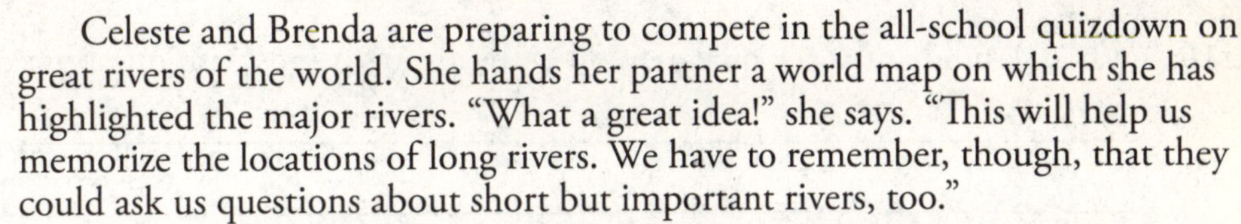

Celeste and Brenda are preparing to compete in the all-school quizdown on great rivers of the world. She hands her partner a world map on which she has highlighted the major rivers. "What a great idea!" she says. "This will help us memorize the locations of long rivers. We have to remember, though, that they could ask us questions about short but important rivers, too."

Can you tell from these sentences who highlighted the rivers on the world map? _______ Can you tell who talked about the need to study small but important rivers? _______ Does this speaker make clear who will ask the questions in the quizdown? _______ Mark an X through each pronoun that does not have a clear antecedent.

Each **personal pronoun** and each **demonstrative pronoun** you use should have a **clear antecedent**. If you see that you have written a sentence with a pronoun that does not refer clearly to an antecedent, you should rewrite the sentence.

See Handbook Sections 17a–c, 17i

Practice

Circle the antecedent for each boldfaced pronoun. If a boldfaced pronoun does not have a clear antecedent in the sentence, mark an X through it.

1. The library has many reference materials; Celeste wants to study **those** first.
2. Celeste and Brenda will also use the library's computers to find out more about **them**.
3. Arnold and Zack arrive at the library; **they** will be competing in **it**, too.
4. At first, **they** pretend **they** don't see **their** competitors.
5. Since all the students need to use the same books and maps, though, **they** eventually have to acknowledge **their** competitors' presence.
6. "Are you using **those**?" **he** asks.
7. Celeste and Brenda look at each other, and then **she** says, "We need **these**, but you can have **those**."
8. Arnold and Zack carry **them** to another table, but then **he** walks over to a computer and logs on.
9. "What have **you** learned about the Congo River?" **he** asks Brenda and Celeste.
10. "I know it's the most important river in West Africa." **he** responds.
11. "What about the Niger, the Gambia, and the Volta?" **she** adds.
12. "We are studying the Niger, the Gambia, and the Volta, too, but the Congo is far more important than **those**," **he** responds.
13. "Okay, I will test **you** with a question," Brenda says.
14. "What huge carnivorous fish lives in the Congo River?" **she** asks **him**.
15. At first neither Arnold nor Zack responds, but then Arnold smiles, raises **his** index finger, and says, "The answer to **your** question is the giant tigerfish!"

Name ______________________________

Apply

Each sentence below contains a pronoun that does not have a clear antecedent. Rewrite each sentence to correct the error.

16. When Arnold and Zack quiz each other, he always begins with questions about the Congo River.

17. "How did you find out that they would focus on that river at the quizdown?" his partner finally asks.

18. "Oh, I just made that up," he responds with a smile.

19. "I think the Congo is the most interesting river in the world," he continues.

20. "So you don't really care about winning the quizdown?" he asks him.

21. "Oh, I would like to win, but I also want to satisfy my curiosity about that great and mysterious river," he concludes.

Reinforce

Choose a river outside North America that you would like to visit and explore. Do some research to find five interesting facts about that river. Write the facts on the lines below. Then, on another sheet of paper, write a letter to a friend in which you try to convince her or him to join you on a trip to that river. Include the five facts you found, and make sure the personal pronouns and demonstrative pronouns you use have clear antecedents.

Fact 1: ______________________________

Fact 2: ______________________________

Fact 3: ______________________________

Fact 4: ______________________________

Fact 5: ______________________________

Read and Analyze

Using *Who* or *Whom*

Unit 6: Lesson 66

Are you the one **who** wrote this report? ___________

The people **whom** you described are quite colorful. ___________

Underline the clause in each sentence that includes *who* or *whom*. Which boldfaced word is the *subject* in its clause? ___________ Which boldfaced word is an *object* in its clause? ___________ After each sentence, write whether the boldfaced word is a subject or an object.

Use ***who*** as the **subject** of a sentence or a clause. Use ***whom*** as the **object** of a verb or of a preposition. **Remember to use this information when you speak, too.**

See Handbook Sections 17b, 17h

Practice

Underline the clause in each sentence that includes the words in parentheses. Decide whether the word in parentheses should be a subject or an object. Circle *who* or *whom* to complete each sentence correctly.

1. (Who/Whom) can point out the St. Lawrence River on the class map?
2. The first known European to travel up the St. Lawrence was Jacques Cartier, (who/whom) claimed the river's shores for the French crown in the early 1500s.
3. (Who/Whom) can point out Lake Ontario, where the St. Lawrence River originates?
4. The area from Lake Ontario to the sea was inhabited by Native Americans (who/whom) were members of the Iroquois nation.
5. The Mohawk, Seneca, and Oneida were Iroquois groups (who/whom) lived in North America then.
6. In 1608 Samuel de Champlain, (who/whom) wanted to establish French rights to the fur trade, founded Quebec City on the St. Lawrence.
7. Eventually control of the St. Lawrence passed to the British, (who/whom) defeated the French in 1763 in the French and Indian War.
8. The Canadians, (who/whom) wanted to open the Great Lakes to sea traffic, began building canals.
9. The U.S. Congress, (who/whom) formed a partnership with the Canadians, agreed to help construct the St. Lawrence Seaway.
10. In 1959 Queen Elizabeth II of Great Britain dedicated the seaway, along with Dwight Eisenhower, (who/whom) was president of the United States then.
11. The U.S. and Canada, (who/whom) oversee the waterway jointly, regulate traffic through it.
12. The two nations, for (who/whom) construction was costly, set tolls to help pay for the project.
13. A Canadian (who/whom) I spoke with said that sea traffic along the St. Lawrence amounts to about 50 million tons a year.

Name ___

Apply

Write a question to go with each statement. Include *who* or *whom* in your question. Be sure to end each sentence with a question mark. The first one is done for you.

14. I read a book about Jacques Cartier. **About whom did you read a book?**
15. I wrote a report about fur traders on the St. Lawrence. ___
16. Samuel de Champlain wanted to establish France's claims to the St. Lawrence.

    ___
17. The English took control of New France in 1763. ___
18. Canada worked with the United States to construct the St. Lawrence Seaway.

    ___
19. President Eisenhower dedicated the seaway with Queen Elizabeth II.

    ___
20. The U.S. government formed a partnership with the Canadians to run the seaway.

    ___

Reinforce

Read the descriptions below. Think of someone you know for whom each description is true. Write the person's name on the line.

Think of someone...

whom you admire ___

who is a great athlete ___

who lives near you ___

with whom you spend Saturdays ___

who has musical talent ___

Now, use your list to write five complete sentences using *who* or *whom*. (*Example: My grandmother is a person whom I admire.*)

21. ___
22. ___
23. ___
24. ___
25. ___

Subject-Verb Agreement

Unit 6: Lesson 67

Read and Analyze

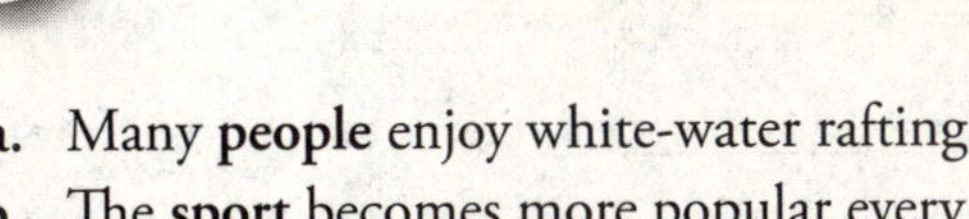

a. Many **people** enjoy white-water rafting.

b. The **sport** becomes more popular every year.

Underline the verb in each sentence. Then look at each boldfaced subject.

Which verb goes with a singular subject? ________________

Which verb goes with a plural subject? ________________

The **subject** and its **verb must agree**. Add *-s* or *-es* to a verb in the present tense when the subject is a singular noun or *he, she,* or *it*. Do not add *-s* or *-es* to a verb in the present tense when the subject is a plural noun or *I, you, we,* or *they*. Singular forms of the verb *be* are *is, am,* and *was*. Plural forms are *are* and *were*. Be sure the verb agrees with its subject and not with an object of a preposition that comes before the verb. **Remember to use this information when you speak, too.**

See Handbook Section 18f

Practice

Circle the correct expression in parentheses to complete each sentence.

1. White-water rafting trips (offer/offers) people an opportunity to enjoy wild areas in an exciting way.
2. With interest in extreme sports on the rise, individuals in the U.S. (want/wants) new challenges.
3. The International Scale of River Difficulty (rank/ranks) rivers by how difficult they are to paddle.
4. Six levels of difficulty (compose/composes) this scale.
5. Rivers with a Class I rating (is/are) the easiest to navigate.
6. Such a river (has/have) few obstructions, though it may have a swift current.
7. Rapids on a Class III river (require/requires) careful maneuvering.
8. Steep rapids, powerful and irregular waves, dangerous rocks, and whirlpools (is/are) features of Class IV and V rivers.
9. For Class IV through VI rivers, inspections of hazards from the riverbank (is/are) mandatory the first time the river is run.

The Gauley River in West Virginia is one of the most advanced white-water runs in the U.S.

10. Class VI rivers, the most difficult kind, (is/are) unrunnable, or runnable only by experts.
11. A run on any of these rivers (require/requires) taking extreme precautions.
12. A team of rafters never (run/runs) a Class VI river if water level or weather is unfavorable.
13. Rafting companies often (send/sends) experienced rafters to scout new rivers for rafting trips.
14. Scouts on a new river (note/notes) the types of hazards and the number of portages required.
15. Rafters on a portage (carry/carries) their raft or boat over land to a safer spot downriver.
16. If the number of hazards (is/are) too high, a company will not send rafters there.

Name ______________________

Apply

Circle the simple subject in each sentence. Then write the correct form of the verb in parentheses to complete the sentence.

17. Our team of expert rafters ______________ new rivers for commercial rafting. (scout)
18. The rafters in our company ______________ a river before recommending it to others. (paddle)
19. A group of experts ______________ on a classification for a river. (decide)
20. Many aspects of a river ______________ its relative safety. (affect)
21. The number of rapids, whirlpools, eddies, and boulders ______________ a river's rating. (increase)
22. Members of a classification team also ______________ the location of the river. (consider)
23. Any classification system that makes use of opinions ______________ imperfect. (be)
24. Sometimes people with similar qualifications ______________ different opinions about a river's difficulty. (have)
25. Risk factors such as the amount of water flow ______________ not constant. (be)

Reinforce

Imagine that you are watching a group of river rafters trying to run some difficult rapids. Write five sentences about what you see. Use present tense verbs in your sentences, and check subject-verb agreement.

26. ______________________________

27. ______________________________

28. ______________________________

29. ______________________________

30. ______________________________

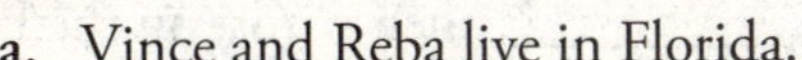

a. Vince and Reba live in Florida.

b. Neither Vince nor Reba visits the Everglades often.

Circle the compound subject in each sentence. Underline the verb in each sentence. Which sentence has a verb that goes with a singular subject? ________

A **compound subject** and its verb must agree. If a compound subject includes the conjunction *and,* the subject is plural and needs a plural verb. If a compound subject includes *or* or *nor*, the verb must agree with the last item in the subject. **Remember to use this information when you speak, too.**

See Handbook Sections 11, 18f

Practice

Look at the compound subject in each sentence. Draw a box around its conjunction. Then underline the correct verb in parentheses.

1. Each year Mr. White and Ms. Brooks (take/takes) their classes to Everglades National Park.
2. Either January or February (is/are) a good time to visit the park because many tours and programs are offered then.
3. The seventh grade class and the eighth grade class (learn/learns) about this distinctive wetland.
4. A ranger or a park administrator (explain/explains) that during the wet season, the Everglades is a wide, shallow, slow-moving river.
5. Sanje, Petra, and Anya (jot/jots) notes for a class report.
6. The Kissimmee River and smaller tributaries (feed/feeds) into Lake Okeechobee.
7. Rainwater and groundwater from Lake Okeechobee (supply/supplies) the water to the Everglades.
8. Ms. Brooks and the ranger (tell/tells) students how the "river of grass" drains into Florida Bay and the Gulf of Mexico.
9. Shallow water and sawgrass (cover/covers) much of the northern part of the Everglades.
10. Saltwater marshes and mangrove swamps (form/forms) the southern border of the Everglades.
11. A red mangrove or a white mangrove (thrive/thrives) in tidal water.
12. Live oak, mastic, and royal palm (grows/grow) on mounds of earth called tree islands.
13. Shark Valley, the Anhinga Trail, or Eco Pond (is/are) a good place for viewing alligators.
14. Look over there! A heron or an egret (is wading/are wading) in the water!

The blue heron is commonly found wading in the Everglades.

Name ______________________________

Apply

Write the correct present tense form of the verb in parentheses to complete each sentence.

15. Sanje, Petra, and Anya carefully ______________ their report on the Everglades. (research)
16. Plants and animals in this region ______________ interconnected in a fragile ecosystem. (be)
17. A young shrimp or bonefish ______________ the shelter offered by a mangrove swamp. (need)
18. Wading birds and alligators ______________ on fish and smaller animals. (snack)
19. Small animals and deer ______________ prey to Florida panthers. (be)
20. Agricultural runoff and other pollutants ______________ the water and threaten wildlife. (contaminate)
21. Neither the alligator nor the Florida panther ______________ in the Everglades as in the past. (thrive)
22. Disruption of water flow and invasion of non-native plant species ______________ the ecosystem in the Everglades. (damage)
23. Canals and levels ______________ water from the Everglades for agricultural and urban use. (divert)
24. Neither the Brazilian pepper tree nor the paperbark tree ______________ native to the Everglades; both have displaced native species there. (be)

Reinforce

Use the information in this lesson to fill in the puzzle. Some answers will be part of a compound subject. Then circle the correct verb in parentheses to complete each clue.

Across

2. Residents and visitors alike (enjoy/enjoys) the _____ Everglades.
4. Neither extreme cold nor sudden temperature change (characterize/characterizes) the climate of the _____.
6. Salt marshes and _____ forests (lie/lies) on the southern border of the Everglades.
7. The _____ River and other tributaries (feed/feeds) into Lake Okeechobee.

Down

1. Either a deer or a smaller animal (make/makes) a meal for a Florida _____.
3. Birds, fish, and _____ (thrive/thrives) in the wetlands.
5. Herons and _____ (is/are) wading birds.

Read and Analyze

Subject-Verb Agreement: Special Cases

Unit 6: Lesson 69

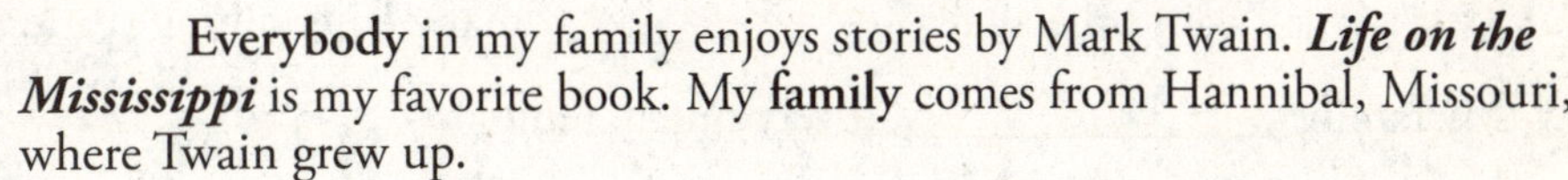

Everybody in my family enjoys stories by Mark Twain. ***Life on the Mississippi*** is my favorite book. My **family** comes from Hannibal, Missouri, where Twain grew up.

Look at the boldfaced subjects of these sentences. Circle the noun that refers to more than one person but is considered singular. Underline the book title. Draw a box around the indefinite pronoun. Are the verbs that follow these subjects used with singular subjects or with plural subjects?

____

The **subject** and its **verb must agree**. There are special rules for certain kinds of subjects. Titles of books, movies, stories, or songs are considered singular even if they end in *-s*. (The Borrowers *is my little brother's favorite book.*) A **collective noun,** such as *collection, group, team, country, kingdom, family, flock,* or *herd,* names more than one person or object acting together as one group. These nouns are almost always considered singular. (*Katie's team wins every game.*) Most **indefinite pronouns,** including *everyone, nobody, nothing, something,* and *anything*, are considered singular. (*Everybody likes pizza.*) A few indefinite pronouns, such as *many* and *several,* are considered plural. (*Many like spaghetti.*)

Remember to use this information when you speak, too.

See Handbook Sections 15, 17f, 18f

Practice

Underline the simple subject in each sentence. Circle the correct form of the verb in parentheses.

1. Everyone in my class (is/are) reading *The Adventures of Tom Sawyer.*
2. Many (is/are) aware that Samuel Clemens used the name *Mark Twain* as a pseudonym, or pen name.
3. Nobody in my class (know/knows) what that name means.
4. The phrase *mark twain* (refer/refers) to the second mark on a stick used by riverboat crews to measure the depth of the Mississippi River.
5. A shout of "mark twain" (mean/means) the river is deep enough for a steamboat to pass.
6. My favorite collection of Mark Twain's writings (is/are) the book *Life on the Mississippi.*
7. *Life on the Mississippi* (describe/describes) Twain's experiences learning to pilot a steamboat.
8. My family (has/have) copies of several of Twain's works.
9. Not everybody in my family (enjoy/enjoys) Twain's memoirs as much as I do.
10. Many of us (love/loves) his humorous stories, though.
11. "The Celebrated Jumping Frog of Calaveras County" (is/are) one of our favorites.
12. Right now my mother's book group (is/are) reading Twain's book about King Arthur.
13. *A Connecticut Yankee in King Arthur's Court* (tell/tells) the story of a young American who finds himself transported back to medieval England.
14. *The Prince and the Pauper* (is/are) a fun movie to watch.

Name ______________________________

Apply

Write the correct present tense form of the verb in parentheses to complete each sentence.

15. That Mark Twain collection ______________ many entertaining stories. (contain)
16. My family ______________ it very much. (enjoy)
17. *The Prince and the Pauper* ______________ my brother's favorite Mark Twain novel. (be)
18. My class at school ______________ *The Adventures of Tom Sawyer*. (like)
19. *The Adventures of Tom Sawyer* ______________ about a boy growing up on the Mississippi. (tell)
20. Joe Harper and Huckleberry Finn ______________ Tom's friends. (be)
21. Tom, Joe, and Huck ______________ pretending to be pirates. (enjoy)
22. Tom and his friends often ______________ into mischief. (get)
23. Nobody in my class ______________ how the story will end. (know)
24. Everyone ______________ if Tom will get out of trouble. (wonder)

Mark Twain published more than thirty books throughout his career.

Reinforce

Flock **and** ***herd*** **are not the only collective names that can refer to a group of animals. Groups of certain kinds of animals can be named by special collective nouns. Some of these nouns may be familiar to you, but others are used very rarely.**

Match the collective nouns below with the animal groups they refer to. Write the correct letter in the blank.

a. oxen
b. crocodiles
c. monkeys
d. owls
e. gorillas
f. wolves
g. bats
h. whales
i. crows
j. lions

25. colony _____
26. band _____
27. pride _____
28. team _____
29. pod _____
30. murder _____
31. parliament _____
32. bask _____
33. troop _____
34. pack _____

Now use one of these collective nouns in a sentence. Remember that a collective noun is almost always singular even when it is followed by a prepositional phrase *(Example: A pride of lions is sleeping near that tree.)*

35. ____

____

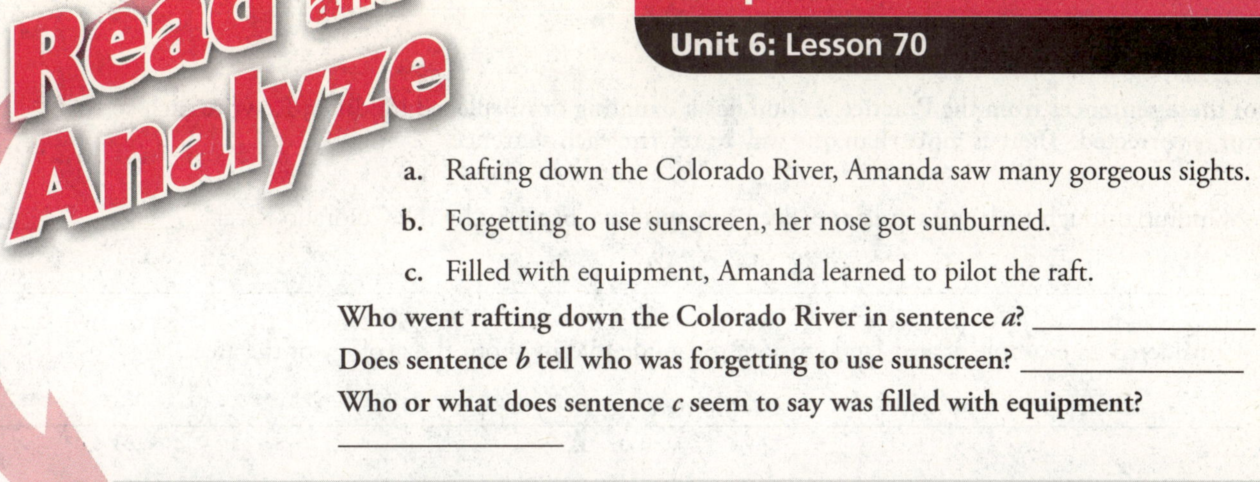

Avoiding Dangling and Misplaced Modifiers

a. Rafting down the Colorado River, Amanda saw many gorgeous sights.

b. Forgetting to use sunscreen, her nose got sunburned.

c. Filled with equipment, Amanda learned to pilot the raft.

Who went rafting down the Colorado River in sentence *a*? ________________

Does sentence *b* tell who was forgetting to use sunscreen? ________________

Who or what does sentence *c* seem to say was filled with equipment?

____

Verbal phrases must always refer to, or modify, a nearby noun or a pronoun in the main part of a sentence. **Dangling modifiers** are phrases that do not clearly refer to any particular word in a sentence. **Misplaced modifiers** are phrases that seem to refer to the wrong noun or pronoun in a sentence. When you begin a sentence with a verbal phrase such as "Traveling down the Colorado River," make sure that the question "Who is traveling?" is answered clearly in the first part of the rest of the sentence.

See Handbook Sections 25a, 25b, 31

Practice

Underline the verbal phrase that begins each sentence. Circle the simple subject or subjects of the clause it introduces. If the underlined phrase modifies the subject(s) you circled, write *C* on the line. If the phrase is a dangling modifier or a misplaced modifier, write *X* on the line.

1. Visiting Arizona last year, I rafted down part of the Colorado River. _____
2. Originating in the Rockies, the Colorado River flows 1,450 miles to the Gulf of California. _____
3. Winding through rock and sandstone, deep canyons have been cut by the Colorado River. _____
4. Stretching 277 miles, the Grand Canyon is the largest and most impressive of these. _____
5. Encompassing more than 1,200,000 acres, Grand Canyon National Park lies on the Colorado Plateau in northwestern Arizona. _____
6. Considered an example of arid-land erosion, the guide told us about the geology of the area. _____
7. Averaging 4,000 feet deep, the widest point is fifteen miles across. _____
8. Known for its geologic importance, we read why the Grand Canyon has been designated a World Heritage Site. _____
9. Blocked by dams, the guide said that the water flow of the Colorado has been reduced. _____
10. Needing water from the river, ranchers, farmers, and city-dwellers compete for water allocations. _____
11. Stopping the raft to point out petroglyphs, we learned about ancient cultures from our guide. _____
12. Wanting to capture their beauty, I took several photographs. _____
13. Leaning down to feel the cool water, my camera fell into the river. _____
14. Trying to grab the camera, my sister almost fell overboard! _____

Name ______________________________

Apply

Each of these sentences from the Practice section has a dangling or misplaced modifier. Rewrite each so that the error is corrected. There is more than one way to rewrite each sentence.

15. Winding through rock and sandstone, deep canyons have been cut by the Colorado River. ______________

16. Considered an example of arid-land erosion, the guide told us about the geology of the area.

17. Averaging 4,000 feet deep, the widest point is fifteen miles across. ______________

18. Known for its geologic importance, we read why the Grand Canyon has been designated a World Heritage Site. ______________

19. Blocked by dams, the guide said that the water flow of the Colorado has been reduced.

20. Stopping the raft to point out petroglyphs, we learned about ancient cultures from our guide.

21. Leaning down to feel the cool water, my camera fell into the river. ______________

Reinforce

Use your imagination to think of an independent clause to complete each sentence below. Write the clause on the line. Make sure the noun or pronoun that the verbal phrase modifies is near the introductory phrase.

22. Planning a trip to the river, ______________.

23. Swimming in the river, ______________.

24. Rafting down the river, ______________.

25. Leaving the river, ______________.

Read and Analyze

Comparative and Superlative Modifiers

Unit 6: Lesson 71

The Amazon River is **more powerful** than the Missouri River. The Amazon is the **most powerful** river in the world.

Circle the boldfaced words that compare the Amazon River with the Missouri River. Underline the boldfaced words that compare the Amazon River with more than one other river.

The **comparative form** of an **adjective** or **adverb** compares two people, places, things, or actions. Add *-er* to short adjectives and adverbs to create the comparative form. Use the word *more* before long adjectives and adverbs to create the comparative form (*more powerful*). The **superlative form** compares three or more people, places, things, or actions. Add *-est* to create the superlative form of short adjectives and adverbs. Use the word *most* before long adjectives and adverbs to create the superlative form (*most powerful*). Use *better* and *less* to compare two things. Use *best* and *least* to compare three or more things.
Remember to use this information when you speak, too.

See Handbook Section 27

Practice

Think about how many things are being compared in each sentence. Then underline the correct form of the adjective or adverb in parentheses.

1. For many years, geographers agreed that the Nile River was the (longer/longest) river in the world.
2. In 2007, some Brazilian scientists claimed that the Amazon River stretched slightly (farther/farthest).
3. Geographers have yet to agree on the Amazon's precise length, but they have proven that it carries (more water/most water) than any other river.
4. In fact, the volume of water flowing through the Amazon is (greater/greatest) than the volume of water in the Nile, the Mississippi, and the Yangtze rivers combined.
5. The Amazon begins in the Andes Mountains of Peru, at a site (higher/highest) than 17,000 feet in elevation.
6. As the Amazon wends its way toward the Atlantic Ocean, more than 200 (smaller/smallest) rivers flow into it.

About 20 species of piranha live in the Amazon.

7. Many unusual fish live in the Amazon; piranha are among the (fiercer/fiercest) fish on the planet.
8. One of the (larger/largest) freshwater fish of South America, the pirarucú, lives in the Amazon.
9. The rainforest that covers the Amazon River Basin is the world's (larger/largest) tropical rainforest.
10. Some of its birds are the (more colorful/most colorful) species ever seen.
11. Today, many scientists have called for the Amazon basin's resources to be guarded (more carefully/most carefully) than they have been in the past.

Name ________________________________

Apply

Write the correct form of the adjective or adverb in parentheses.

12. The Amazon may not be the ____________________ river in the world, but it is longer than the Mississippi. (long)
13. The volume of water flowing through the mouth of the Amazon is ____________________ than the volume that flows through the mouth of the Nile. (great)
14. The Amazon looks brown at times, but it's not the world's ____________________ river; that is probably the Yellow River in China. (muddy)
15. Plant and animal life in the Amazon basin is ____________________ than in any other area. (diverse)
16. What do you think is the ____________________ feature of the Amazon? (impressive)
17. Would you boat down the Amazon ____________________ than you would down the Nile? (eagerly)

Reinforce

Some adjectives are *absolute*: either they describe a thing or they do not. They cannot properly be put into the comparative form. For example, a plant is either dead or alive; it does not make sense to say "That plant is the *deadest* of all."

Read each of the sentences below. Think about each boldfaced adjective. Decide whether putting that adjective in the comparative or superlative form makes sense. If it does not, rewrite the sentence with an adjective or an adverb that does make sense in a comparative expression.

18. The Amazon River would be **more impossible** to swim than the Nile.

    ____

19. Rain gear is **more sensible** to take on an Amazon journey than on a Nile expedition.

    ____

20. The story you wrote about the Amazon was the **most unique** I have ever read.

    ____

21. I think the **most perfect** vacation would be to canoe down the Amazon.

    ____

I **have read** quite a bit about the Ganges River in India.

It **might be** the river I most want to visit.

Circle the main boldfaced verb in each sentence. Underline the boldfaced auxiliary verb that works with each main verb.

An **auxiliary verb,** or **helping verb,** works with a main verb. Auxiliary verbs have different purposes. Some auxiliary verbs, such as *do, are, have,* and *will,* help indicate the tense of the main verb. They can also be used to form negatives and questions. Other auxiliary verbs carry special meanings; these are called *modal auxiliaries. Could, should, would, might,* and *may* are used to refer to a possible action, or to tell how likely it is that something will happen. *May* is also used to express permission. *Can* expresses ability.

See Handbook Sections 18c, 18e

Practice

Circle the main verb or verbs in each sentence. Then underline each auxiliary verb. Not every main verb will have an auxiliary.

1. We are writing reports about India in my social studies class.
2. I will write a report about the Ganges River.
3. Do you know that the Ganges is considered the greatest river in India?
4. I can tell you why.
5. The Ganges has created a fertile river valley where many crops are grown.
6. Some of India's largest cities have been built along the banks of the Ganges.
7. The Ganges has been sacred to Hindus for thousands of years.
8. Every year pilgrims travel great distances so they can bathe in it.
9. Many believe that the river can cure ailments.
10. I will visit the Ganges as a tourist one day.
11. I may visit ancient sites along its banks.
12. I might even see a rare Ganges river dolphin.
13. My classmates did not know that some types of dolphins live in freshwater.
14. Today the Ganges river dolphin population may number only 2,000.
15. If conservation measures are taken soon, the species might be saved.

Many people travel to the city of Varanasi to bathe in the Ganges.

Lesson 72

Name ______________________________

Apply

Complete each sentence with an auxiliary verb. Some sentences have more than one correct answer.

16. I wish that I ______________ visit the Ganges River.
17. I ______________ imagine how exciting that would be!
18. I ______________ trace its course from high in the Himalayas all the way to the Bay of Bengal.
19. My family ______________ go to India next year to visit our relatives.
20. We ______________ not seen them in nearly five years.
21. We ______________ stay with my aunt and uncle in Kolkata, one of the biggest cities in the world.
22. You ______________ not know that Kolkata used to be known as Calcutta.
23. In that city, my sister and I ______________ visit the Indian Botanic Garden.
24. My family ______________ also visit Varanasi, the holiest Hindu city along the Ganges.
25. I ______________ not know how many people bathe in the Ganges at Varanasi.
26. It ______________ be more than 50,000 every day.
27. I ______________ research more sights along the Ganges.
28. Then I ______________ persuade my parents to take us there.

Reinforce

Find eight helping verbs in the puzzle and circle them.

O	M	R	I	C	A	N	Q
Z	I	B	S	R	D	L	X
W	G	U	K	F	H	C	M
I	H	A	V	E	P	U	G
K	T	I	H	M	O	X	I
J	N	M	V	U	Q	S	L
D	C	A	Q	W	V	E	D
O	V	Y	A	I	X	Z	V
E	P	X	S	L	G	Y	Y
S	H	O	U	L	D	K	K

Now imagine taking a trip along a famous river. Write two sentences about your trip, using helping verbs you found in the puzzle.

29. ____

30. ____

Spelling Practice

Read and Analyze

The river flows **continuously.**

The animals **continually** visit the river.

Circle the word in bold type that means "constantly." Underline the word in bold type that means "frequently."

Frequently Misspelled Words

Homophones, such as *assent* and *ascent,* and words that sound alike, such as *continually* and *continuously,* can cause confusion. One way to know which word to use is to consider the context of the sentence.

Words in Context

Write the word that best completes each sentence. Use a dictionary if you need help.

disburse	confidently	morale	canvas	moral	compliment
discrete	canvass	disperse	confidentially	complement	discreet

1. Politicians ______________________ our neighborhood during campaign season.
2. Do you have anything made of ______________________?
3. Is it ever ______________________ to borrow money and not return it?
4. Our team's ______________________ was low after we lost the game.
5. The police came to ______________________ the crowd.
6. The club treasurer will ______________________ the necessary funds.
7. My art teacher paid me a nice ______________________ on my painting today!
8. A speaker strode ______________________ on stage.
9. Speak to Dr. Kangas ______________________.
10. Are you ______________________ enough to keep a secret?
11. The new mechanism has six ______________________ parts.
12. *Sweet* and *salty* are flavors that ______________________ each other well.

Name ______________________________

Pattern Practice

ascent	affect	persecution	descent
immigrant	device	dissent	emigrant
assent	effect	prosecution	devise

Each of the boldfaced words in Sentences 13–18 has some letters missing. Finish the correct spelling of each word, using the word bank and a dictionary for help, as needed. Then correctly answer each question by circling *Yes* or *No*.

13. Would a climber make an **as**_________**t** up a mountain? (Yes/No)

14. Would you camp at the top of a mountain before starting your **d**_________**ent**? (Yes/No)

15. Do people ever **d**_________**ent** from others' opinions? (Yes/No)

16. Do disobedient children **as**_________**t** to their parents' requests? (Yes/No)

17. Does sunlight _______**fect** plant growth? (Yes/No)

18. Does studying usually have a negative _______**fect** on a student's grade? (Yes/No)

For Items 19–24, fill in each blank as directed, using a word from the word bank. Consult a dictionary if you need help.

19. Write a word that means "a person who migrates to." ______________________

20. Write a word that means "a person who migrates from." ______________________

21. Write a word that means "abuse." ______________________

22. Write a word that has to do with court proceedings. ______________________

23. Write a word that means "to imagine or plan." ______________________

24. Write a word that means "an instrument or a tool." ______________________

Use the Dictionary

Circle the word in each pair that best completes each sentence. Use a print dictionary or an online dictionary if you need help.

25. The color red has a (denotation/connotation) of danger.

26. Their arrival home is (imminent/eminent).

27. The gracious leader bowed (respectfully/respectively)

Diagramming Participial Phrases

You have learned that participial phrases function as adjectives. They are diagrammed as shown below.

The kayak **floating by the dock** is yours.

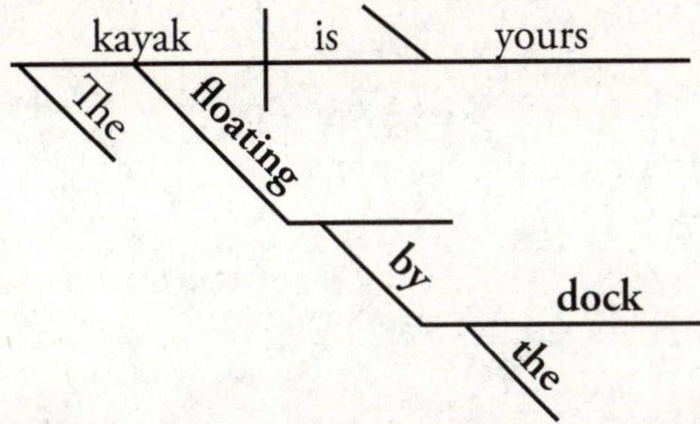

Diagram these sentences. Refer to the model if you need help.

1. The woman carrying paddles is our instructor.

2. We must avoid people behaving foolishly.

3. Rafters paddling together control their boat effectively.

Diagramming Infinitive Phrases

An infinitive phrase can function as a noun. The infinitive phrase in the sentence below functions as the direct object of the verb *wants*. Study how this type of phrase is diagrammed.

Kirk wants **to go faster.**

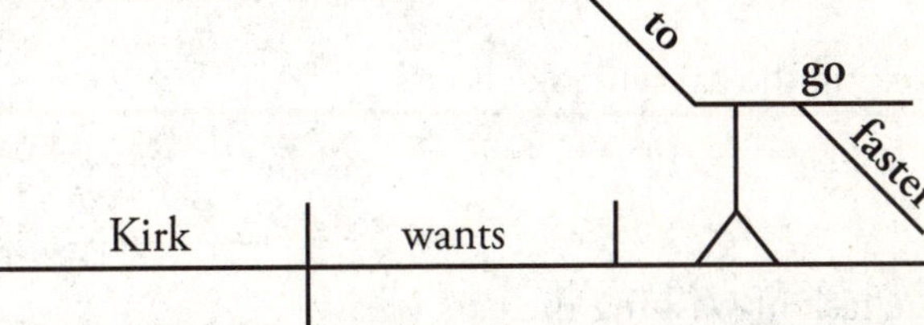

Diagram these sentences. Refer to the model if you need help.

4. The other rafters prefer to go slower.

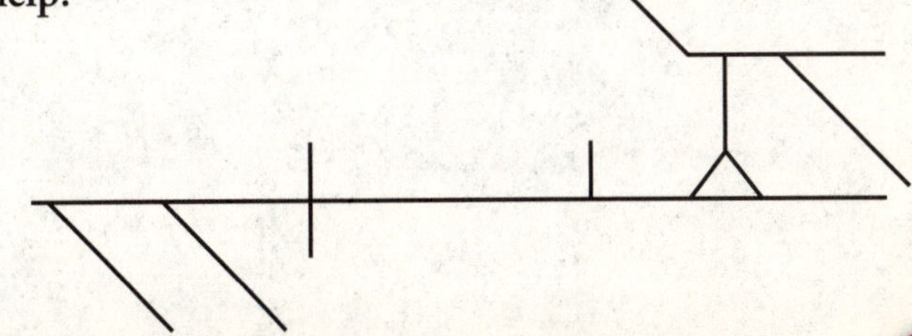

Name ____

5. I have to help my brother into the boat.

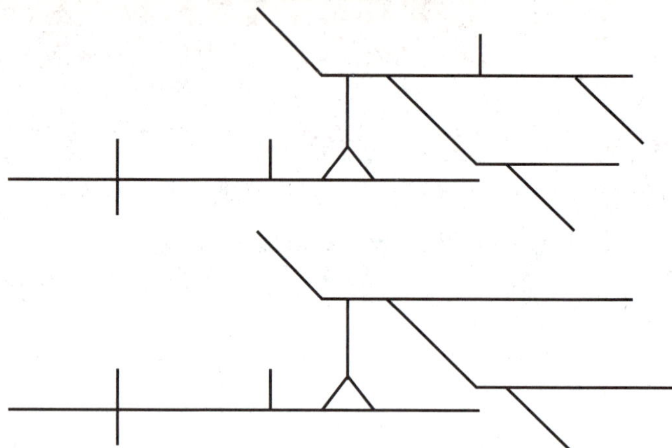

6. You will get to sing at the campfire.

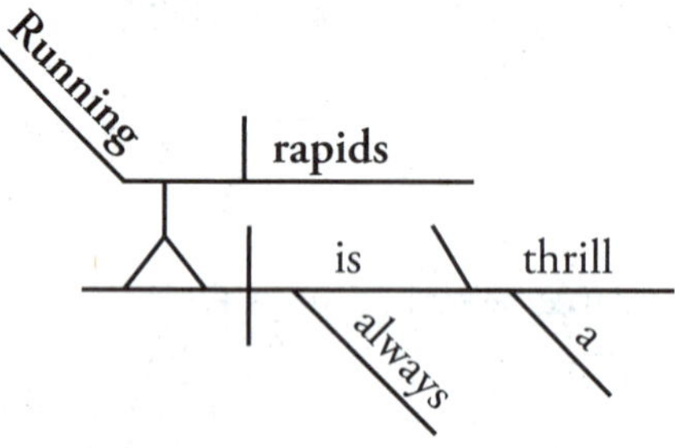

Diagramming Gerund Phrases

You have learned that gerund phrases function as nouns. The gerund phrase in the sentence below functions as the subject. Notice how it is diagrammed.

Running rapids is always a thrill.

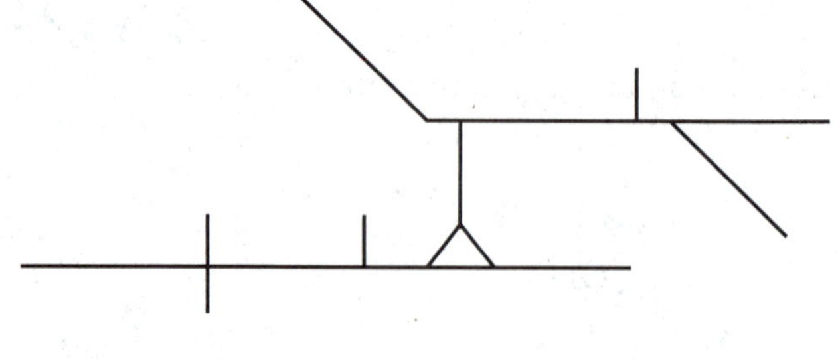

Diagram these sentences. Note that in one sentence the gerund phrase is the subject, in another it is a direct object, and in another it is the object of a preposition.

7. Bonnie loves building small boats.

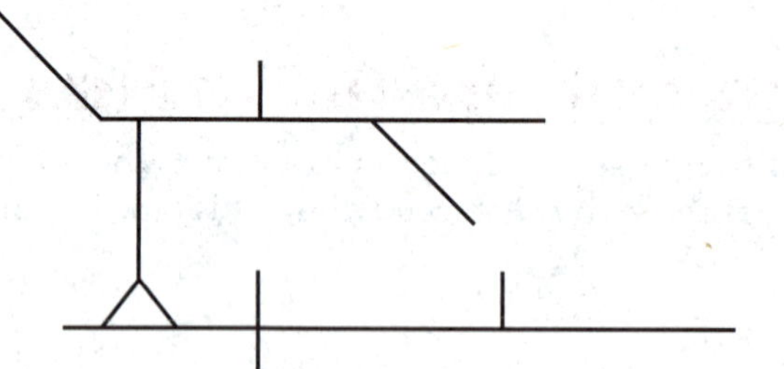

8. Packing the car will take hours.

9. The task of washing the oars is easy.

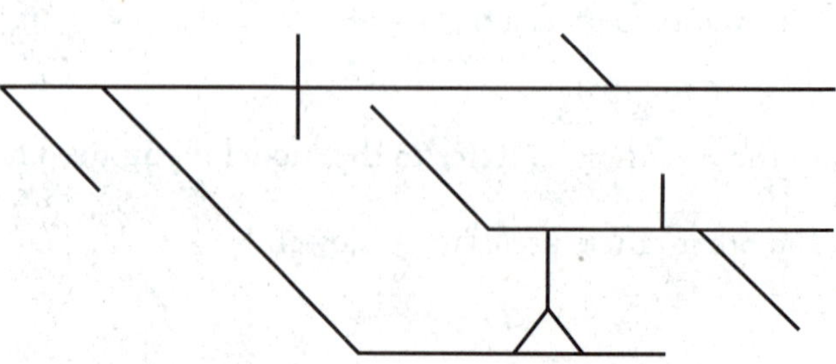

These sentences need your help. Rewrite each one so that the subject and verb agree.

1. The Nile and the Ganges has supported great civilizations for thousands of years. ______________________

____

2. Likewise, the Ganges and its many tributaries carries nutrient-laden soil from high in the Himalayas to the delta far below. ______________________

____

3. Each of the two rivers supply fertile soil in which to grow crops. ______________________

____

4. Floods along the Nile replenishes the soil with rich silt carried from high in the mountains.

____

5. Both the Ganges and the Nile is central to the cultural heritage of the surrounding regions.

____

____

6. The two rivers has long been important means of transportation through their respective continents.

____

7. The tombs of many Egyptian pharaohs is located near the Nile, and thousands of Hindus take their dead to the Ganges because they view the river as sacred. ______________________

____

A piece of writing that compares the characteristics of two people, places, or things may be divided into two paragraphs. The first paragraph may describe how the two things being compared are alike or how they are different. The second paragraph should describe the opposite. Each paragraph should have a topic sentence stating its main idea. Notice the structure of this model.

At first glance, the Colorado River and the Columbia River seem to be very different. The lower Columbia River flows through the lush green hills, fern-lined gorges, and evergreen forests of the Pacific Northwest on its way to the sea. The Colorado River winds through the desert valleys and immense rock and sandstone canyons of the Southwest. Each river supports distinct ecosystems.

A closer look reveals several important similarities between the two rivers. Each river has supported Native American populations for thousands of years. Both rivers serve as partial natural borders between states. The Columbia provides much of the border between Washington and Oregon. The Colorado River divides Arizona from the southeast corner of California. A number of dams have been constructed along both rivers to provide water and hydroelectric power to surrounding communities. Today, many people use these rivers for recreational activities, including rafting, fishing, and swimming.

Name ____________________

Writing a Paragraph

The sentences you repaired on page 219 can be reordered to make one paragraph describing similarities between the Nile and the Ganges rivers. Write a topic sentence to introduce the paragraph. Then reorder the supporting sentences, and write the paragraph on the lines below.

Write two paragraphs of your own in which you compare and contrast two rivers you have learned about or have visited. Be sure to use a topic sentence and supporting examples in each paragraph. Use the model paragraphs on page 219 as a guide. Continue writing on a separate sheet of paper if you need more room.

Reread your composition. Use this checklist to make sure it is complete and correct.

- ❑ My composition has a clear main idea.
- ❑ Each paragraph contains a topic sentence and supporting details.
- ❑ I have described both similarities and differences.
- ❑ The subject and verb in each sentence agree.
- ❑ I have included comparative adjectives and other words used to compare, such as *alike, different, both,* and *neither.*

Proofreading Practice

Read this passage about the Mackenzie River in Canada and find the mistakes. Use the proofreading marks below to show how each mistake should be fixed. Use a dictionary to check and correct spellings.

Proofreading Marks

Mark	Means	Example
℘	delete	The Mackenzie River flows through Alberta.
∧	add	The Mackenzie River flows through Alberta.
≡	make into an uppercase letter	The Mackenzie river flows through Alberta.
/	make into a lowercase letter	The MacKenzie River flows through Alberta.
⊙	add a period	The Mackenzie River flows through Alberta ⊙
(sp)	fix spelling	The Mackenzie River flows thru Alberta.

The Mackenzie River

Can you identify the most long river in Canada? Its the Mackenzie River, and it's 1,025 miles long. The river originates at Great Slave Lake, which are located in the Northwestern Territories of Canada, and flow north to the Arctic Ocean

Because it runs through some of the most remote parts of the country. The Mackenzie is known as canada's last truly wild river. Even so, the Mackenzie was been important to indigenous peoples, European explorers, fur traders, and miners. Alexander Mackenzie, the man after who the river was named, traveled to the river in 1789 as he is attempting to reach the Pacific Ocaen. Before Mackenzie arrived, native people refered to the river as *Deh Cho*, that means "big river."

In the summer, the river delta of the Mackenzie pruvides habitat for migrating snow geese and tundra swans. The estuary, or place wear the Mackenzie meets the ocean, are a calving area for Beluga whales. The river is only navigable for about five months of the year. The waters of the Mackenzie freezes over in October most years and remains frozen until May. During the winter, sections of the river is used as ice roads. Ice bridges are also constructed too carry truck traffic. In both summer and winter, the river serves as an important means of transportasion.

Name ________________________________

Proofreading Checklist

You can use the list below to help you find and fix mistakes in your own writing. Write the titles of your own stories or reports in the blanks at the top of the chart. Then use the questions to check your work. Make a check mark (✔) in each box after you have checked that item.

Proofreading Checklist for Unit 6

Titles				
Have I used the correct subject and object pronouns?				
Have I made sure that all pronouns agree with their antecedents in number and gender?				
Does every verb agree with its subject?				
Have I avoided dangling and misplaced modifiers?				

Also Remember…

Does each sentence begin with an uppercase letter?				
Did I use a dictionary to check and correct spellings?				
Have I used commas correctly?				

Your Own List

Use this space to write your own list of things to check in your writing.

Community Connection

In Unit 6 of *Grammar, Usage, and Mechanics,* students learned more about **grammar,** and they used what they learned to improve their own writing. The content of these lessons focuses on the theme **Rivers of the World**. As students completed the exercises, they learned about several of the world's major rivers. They also read about the importance of rivers for transportation, economic development, and recreation. These pages offer a variety of activities that reinforce skills and concepts presented in the unit. They also provide opportunities for students to make connections between the content of the lessons and the community at large.

Water Works

Invite an official from a local water agency to come to class. Have him or her speak about how that agency goes about providing water for residents, businesses, and farms in the area. Prior to the official's visit, prepare a list of questions to ask him or her. After the visit, write a summary of what you learned.

A River Profile

Choose a river that is important to people in your region. Do research in a library or on the Internet to find out as much as you can about the river. Try to answer these questions: Where is the river's source? How long is the river? How did it get its name? What cities and towns have been built along its course? How do people use its water? What dams have been built on it? How clean is its water? What types of wildlife depend on it? Create and present a display about this river. Use an electronic presentation program if possible. Be sure to include a map; also include photos and other graphics.

River Trivia

Work with a group to prepare 50 questions about rivers. Use facts from the lessons as well as facts from original research. Write each question and its answer on an index card or slip of paper. Rate each question as *easy, average,* or *difficult*. Then decide on rules for a trivia game. You can play just among the group; or you can play against other groups, mixing your questions with theirs.

River Sport Speech

Choose one of these river sports to learn more about:

- rowing
- windsurfing
- water skiing
- wakeboarding
- fishing
- kayaking
- canoeing
- rafting

Find out about this sport by conducting an Internet search, looking at books and magazines about this activity, or interviewing at least one local person involved with this activity. Then write a speech describing the activity and explaining what type of person would be likely to enjoy it. Use the speech planner on the following page to help you organize your ideas.

Name ____

River Sport Speech Planner

Sport to be profiled: ____

What the sport involves: ____

____

____

What equipment is required: ____

____

____

What skills must be learned: ____

____

____

What safety rules must be followed: ____

____

____

Where this activity can be done: ____

____

____

Why this activity is fun: ____

____

____

Why this activity can be healthful and educational: ____

____

____

What kind of person should choose this activity (for example, nature lover, adventurer, athlete, thrill seeker): ____

____

____

____

____

My mother volunteers with a **French** organization called **Doctors Without Borders**. She will spend two weeks in **Niger**, a **country** in western Africa.

Circle the boldfaced word that does not refer to a specific nation. Draw one line under the boldfaced word that names a specific nation. Draw two lines under the boldfaced phrase that names a specific organization. Draw a box around the boldfaced word that is an adjective.

Proper nouns are the names of particular people, places, or things. Capitalize each important word in the names of people, geographic locations, important events, holidays, periods of time, organizations, companies, and products. **Proper adjectives** are descriptive words formed from proper nouns. They must be capitalized. A **title of respect,** such as *Mr.* or *Judge,* is capitalized when it is used directly in front of a person's name.

See Handbook Sections 1, 2, 3, 15

Practice

Draw three lines (≡) under each lowercase letter that should be capitalized. (1–34) Then circle each proper noun and draw a box around each proper adjective.

Doctors without borders is an international humanitarian organization. Started in France in december of 1971, the organization now has offices in the united states, japan, canada, sweden, and many other countries. this organization's doctors are working to fight malnutrition in children under five years of age in Africa and Southeast asia. As dr. christophe fournier points out, young children who do not receive the right vitamins and nutrients are more susceptible to disease.

Fortunately a new food product called Plumpy'nut is helping in the fight against malnutrition. It was invented by french scientist dr. andré Briend. he got the idea from a european nut spread named Nutella. plumpy'nut, which is a combination of the words *plump* and *peanut,* is a mixture of peanut butter, powdered milk, and powdered sugar that is fortified with vitamins and minerals.

Foods such as plumpy'nut, which do not require refrigeration, are very useful in war-torn places such as Somalia and Sudan. Plumpy'nut costs less than milk formula, does not need to be mixed with anything, and has a shelf life of two years.

In october 2007 doctors without borders urged the united nations and the United States to contribute more money for the purchase of ready-to-use food. Currently one company, nutriset, is manufacturing Plumpy'nut. companies in malawi and in niamey, the capital of Niger, are making versions of the product as well. Chief nutritionist dr. Milton Tectonidis says that if the United states and the european union would spend more food aid on fortified foods, more companies would want to produce them.

Name ______________________________

Apply

Draw three lines (≡) under each lowercase letter that should be capitalized. Draw a line (/) through each capital letter that should be lowercase. (35–52)

On wednesday ms. lopez's social studies class learned about world hunger relief. Students created a map showing the three Regions where acute malnutrition is most prevalent: the Sahel, the Horn of africa, and southeast asia. The sahel is a vast dry region in Africa. It borders the atlantic ocean and extends east to the other side of the continent. Among the nations in this Region are senegal, mauritania, mali, Niger, Chad, and Sudan. The Horn of Africa refers to the large Peninsula of east africa that juts into the Arabian Sea. Countries in the Horn of Africa include ethiopia, eritrea, and Somalia.

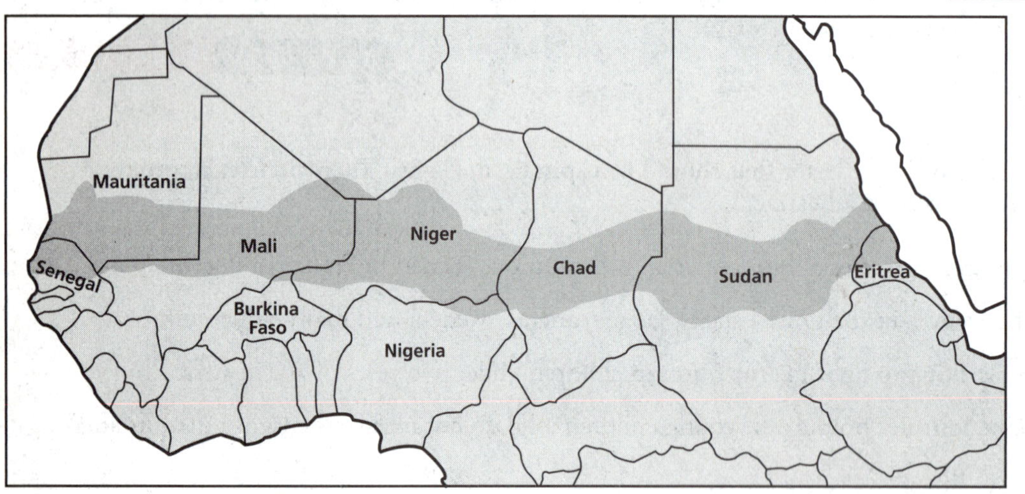

Reinforce

See Handbook Section 35

Today it is common for friends to exchange e-mails that do not include proper capitalization. Read this passage from a friendly e-mail. Then rewrite it with correct capitalization and punctuation. Afterward, discuss with a partner which version you prefer and why.

do you want to see the movie this saturday?? sam saw it and really liked it maybe we could catch the two o'clock show...i have to finish my report about africa first, but i should finish by noon let me know what you think...

Read and Analyze

"The Sinking of the Reuben James" is a song by Woody Guthrie. I saw a documentary film about Guthrie called American Masters: Woody Guthrie.

Circle the film title. Draw a box around the title of the song. How are they written differently?____

Underline the **titles** of **books, magazines, newspapers, movies, CDs,** and **DVDs**. These are written in italics in printed text. Use quotation marks around the titles of **songs, stories,** and **poems**. **Capitalize** the first word and the last word in titles. Capitalize all other words except articles, short prepositions, and coordinating conjunctions. Remember to capitalize short verbs, such as *is* and *are*.

See Handbook Section 3

Practice

Draw three lines (≡) under each lowercase letter that should be an uppercase letter. Underline or add quotation marks to titles.

1. I'm writing an essay called voices for social repairs, which focuses on writers and musicians who have used their compositions to highlight social injustice.
2. For example, Upton Sinclair's book the jungle exposed sanitation problems in the American meatpacking industry.
3. Woody Guthrie's song this land is your land was a reminder that America's wonders belong to all its people.
4. I read a biograpy about him called This land was made for you and me.
5. There is also a CD called bound for glory: songs and stories of woody guthrie.
6. Have you seen the movie the grapes of wrath? It was based on John Steinbeck's novel about refugees who came west from Oklahoma during the Great Depression.
7. to kill a mockingbird is a book that tells about injustice toward African Americans in the South during the 1930s.
8. Langston Hughes's poem mother to son encourages readers not to let life's burdens wear them down.
9. Many songs written in the 1960s protested the poor treatment of individuals and groups. A time magazine article from 1963 describes this phenomenon.
10. A TV show called bob dylan: live in newport 1963–1965 highlights several of his protest songs, which call for an end to prejudice, injustice, and aggression.
11. In 1972, Helen Reddy's song i am woman became an anthem of the women's movement to achieve equality.

Woody Guthrie wrote and sang songs that covered political topics and traditional themes.

Name ______________________________

Apply

Read the titles of the works on the library shelf. Look back at the titles of works mentioned in the Practice section. Then answer each question. Use correct capitalization and punctuation in each title.

12. Which book is probably a fiction book? ______________________________
13. Which DVD probably shows live music performances? ______________________________
14. Which DVD might contain information about Albert Einstein? ______________________________
15. Which book might you use to research a report on creative people? ______________________________
16. Write the title of one song you might hear on *Strong Voices of the 1970s*. ______________________________
17. Which CD presents a recorded version of a book? ______________________________
18. Which book might outline sources of air pollution? ______________________________
19. Which book would likely be a good source for help with algebra problems? ______________________________
20. Which book might have information about the American civil rights movement? ______________________________

Reinforce

A Hollywood film studio is interested in turning your book about a famous artist, musician, dancer, or athlete into a major motion picture. On another sheet of paper, write a paragraph to convince the company to do so. Include the title of the book, and create an exciting movie title. Use correct capitalization and punctuation.

Read and Analyze

Thurs., Oct. 10
9:00 — Report on Franklin D. Roosevelt due.
3:30 — Checkup at Dr. Turner's office, 220 Houston Blvd.

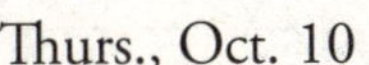

Underline a short way to write *Doctor*. Draw a square around a short way to write *Boulevard*. Circle short ways to write *Thursday* and *October*. Draw a star above a letter that stands for a name.

An **abbreviation** is a shortened form of a word. **Titles of respect** are usually abbreviated. So are words in **addresses,** such as *Street (St.), Avenue (Ave.),* and *Boulevard (Blvd.)*. The names of **days,** the names of some **months,** and certain words in the names of **businesses** are often abbreviated in informal notes. These abbreviations begin with a capital letter and end with a period. An **initial** can replace a person's or a place's name. It is written as an uppercase letter followed by a period.

See Handbook Section 2

Practice

Draw three lines (≡) under each lowercase letter that should be a capital letter. Draw a line (/) through each capital letter that should be a lowercase letter. Add periods where they are needed. (1–29)

World War II began in Sept 1939, but it wasn't until the Japanese attack on Pearl Harbor on Dec 7, 1941, that the U S finally joined the Allies in battle.

Two years later, on Dec 24, 1943, Pres Franklin D Roosevelt named Gen Dwight D Eisenhower as Supreme Commander of the Allied Expeditionary Force in Europe. The Allies' plan was to cross the English Channel and take control of France from the Germans. Gen Eisenhower's job was to see to it that the armies and navies of the U S, Great Britain, and the other Allies worked together as one force. Toward this end, he worked closely with Leaders such as British Prime Minister mr Winston Churchill, Admiral Bertram H Ramsay in charge of Allied naval forces, and Sir Trafford Leigh-Mallory in charge of air forces.

On the eve of the invasion, gen. Eisenhower faced a tough decision. Bad weather had already postponed the operation one day. To pursue the Assault in bad weather would put thousands of Troops in jeopardy, but delaying the landing could mean losing the element of surprise. Fortunately the weather cleared somewhat, and gen Eisenhower gave the go-ahead. Early the morning of Tues, June 6, 1944, the D-day invasion began. Some 130,000 troops stormed five beaches from about 3,500 landing craft, including ships designed for carrying tanks (LCTs) and those designed for carrying infantry (lcis). They were supported by some 11,000 planes.

The Germans fought fiercely, but by the time night fell, the Allies had a strong hold along sixty miles of Normandy coastline. D-day provided the foothold in France that the Allies needed. On Aug 25, Gen George S Patton Jr led the U S Third Army into Paris to reclaim the city. In less than a year, Germany was forced to surrender to the Allies.

Lesson 75

Name ___

Apply

Rewrite each item below, using abbreviations and initials for the underlined words.

30. President Franklin Delano Roosevelt ___
31. 1600 Pennsylvania Avenue ___
32. Mistress Mamie Geneva Eisenhower ___
33. Kaiser Shipbuilding Company ___
34. Tuesday, June 6, 1944 ___
35. Sergeant Edward Allen Carter Junior ___
36. General George Catlett Marshall ___
37. 10 Downing Street ___
38. August 25, 1945 ___
39. Army Navy Drive and Fern Street ___
40. September 2, 1945 ___
41. GenCorp Incorporated ___
42. Winston Leonard Churchill ___
43. Doctor Hattie Alexander ___
44. December 7, 1941 ___
45. General Motors Corporation ___

Reinforce

See Handbook Section 2

An acronym is formed from the first letters of a pair or group of words. Some acronyms, such as *NASA* (National Aeronautics and Space Administration), are written in all uppercase letters. Others, such as *scuba* (self-contained underwater breathing apparatus), are written as regular, lowercase words. Like an acronym, an initialism is also formed from the first letters of a pair or group of words. An initialism differs from an acronym in that it does not form a word; instead, each letter in the initalism is pronounced, as in *USA* (which stands for "United States of America") or *PDF* (which stands for "portable document format").

Read each phrase below and use its first letters to write a shortened form. Check a dictionary to make sure each acronym or initialism you write is correct.

46. light amplification by stimulated emission of radiation ___
47. frequently asked questions ___
48. radio detecting and ranging ___
49. North Atlantic Treaty Organization ___
50. digital video disk ___

Read and Analyze

Apostrophes in Possessives and Contractions

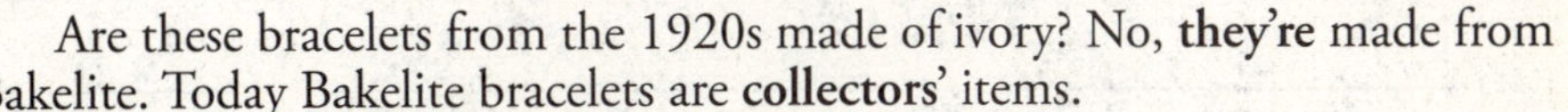

Are these bracelets from the 1920s made of ivory? No, **they're** made from Bakelite. Today Bakelite bracelets are **collectors'** items.

Which boldfaced word shows possession or ownership? ______________

Which boldfaced word is a combination of two words? ______________

To form the **possessive** of a singular noun, add an **apostrophe** and *-s* (*girl's shoe*). For plural nouns that end in *-s,* add an **apostrophe** (*birds' nests*) to form the possessive. For plural nouns that do not end in *-s,* add an **apostrophe** and *-s* (*children's boots*). **Apostrophes** are also used in **contractions,** two words that have been shortened and combined.

See Handbook Sections 7, 26, 28, 30

Practice

Circle the correct word in parentheses. If the answer is a possessive, write *possessive.* If the answer is a contraction, write the two words from which the contraction was made.

1. Some natural (resin's/resins') properties are similar to those of plastics. ______________
2. One (material's/materials') properties made it ideal for items such as brush handles. ______________
3. That material was called lac; (lac's/lacs') purified form was called shellac. ______________
4. Unfortunately, natural materials that could be molded (werent'/weren't) easy to find. ______________
5. Some (product's/products') compositions made them turn brittle over time. ______________
6. Many (researcher's/researchers') efforts focused on altering natural materials. ______________
7. One (man's/mans') efforts to create a more useful material produced a substance later called celluloid. ______________
8. The (substance's/substances) uses included products such as dentures and photographic films. ______________
9. (Celluloid's/Celluloids') advantages were that it was hard and it could be easily molded when hot. ______________
10. Unfortunately, it (wasn't/wasnt') stable around heat. ______________
11. One (chemist's/chemists') goal was to make a useful synthetic shellac. ______________
12. Leo Baekeland mixed two chemical compounds, but he (didn't/did'nt) come up with what he was after. ______________
13. Instead, he created the first pure plastic; this (product's/products') name became *Bakelite.* ______________
14. Soon many household items—from telephones to cooking (utensil's/utensils') handles—were made of Bakelite. ______________
15. (Baekeland's/Baekelands') discovery gave rise to the plastics industry. ______________

Name ______________________________

Apply

Rewrite these sentences. Replace boldfaced words with possessives or contractions.

16. Leo Baekeland **could not** have realized just how widespread plastics would become. ______________________________

17. **The homes of most people** are filled with plastic goods. ______________________________

18. **The adaptability of plastic** allows it to be shaped into almost any form. ______________________________

19. **The toughness or softness of a plastic product** can vary, depending on its chemical composition. ______________________________

20. Unfortunately, plastics **do not** decompose quickly. ______________________________

21. One of **the biggest environmental problems of today** is how to dispose of used plastic. ______________________________

Reinforce

Writers sometimes use contractions to reflect the way that words are pronounced in informal speech. These contractions sometimes look like possessives. Read the following examples. The first sentence contains a possessive noun. The second sentence contains a contraction.

1. My friend's bicycle has a flat.	**The bicycle of my friend has a flat.**
2. My friend's coming over.	**My friend is coming over.**

Read each sentence below. Then rewrite the sentence by replacing the possessive noun or contraction with an expression having the same meaning.

22. "This book's plot is quite gripping," said Ralph. ______________________________

23. "The heroine's trying to find a secret formula," he continued. ______________________________

24. "The mad scientist's a dangerous character," he added. ______________________________

25. Ralph concluded by saying, "The heroine's quick thinking saves her from the mad scientist's evil plan." ______________________________

Read and Analyze

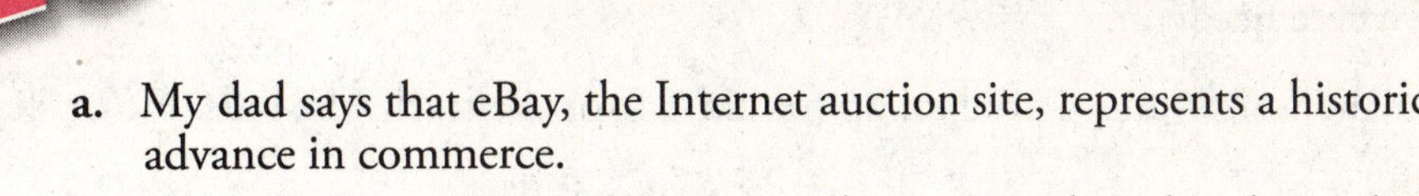

- **a.** My dad says that eBay, the Internet auction site, represents a historic advance in commerce.
- **b.** My uncle has sold items on eBay, and my cousin bought a lamp there.
- **c.** I would like to buy and sell comic books, posters, and baseball cards.

In which sentence do commas separate three items in a series? ________

In which sentence do commas set off words that rename a noun? ________

In which sentence does a comma help separate the clauses in a compound sentence? ________

Commas are used to **separate items in a series** of three or more words, phrases, or clauses. A comma is used to separate **coordinate adjectives**—pairs of similar adjectives. Commas are used to set off most **appositives,** as well as **nonrestrictive adjective clauses** and other nonrestrictive elements. A comma is used before a conjunction that joins the clauses in a **compound sentence.** A comma is also used after an **introductory element** in a sentence, such as a long prepositional or verbal phrase.

See Handbook Sections 8, 16, 24, 25a

Practice

Add the missing comma to each sentence.

1. Pierre Omidyar loves solving problems and he enjoys solving them in new ways.
2. In 1995 the young energetic computer scientist had a plan.
3. He wanted to use the Internet to help common ordinary individuals do business.
4. He didn't want business on the Internet to be dominated by wealthy powerful companies.
5. He envisioned a website for buying and selling items and he believed users would treat each other fairly.
6. He held another job but he spent weekends creating his auction website.
7. The new site, which was an immediate success grew very rapidly.
8. Omidyar knew he had created a thriving business so he quit his other job.
9. People use eBay to buy and sell antiques clothes, electronics, and much more.
10. After completing a transaction the buyer and the seller can post information about each other, which helps ensure honesty.
11. Omidyar who has made billions from his idea, is looking for worthwhile ways to spend his money.
12. Knowing that he has considerably more than he needs he wants to help others.
13. He has donated $100 million for microfinance the making of small loans to poor entrepreneurs.

Pierre Omidyar created the website that became the world's largest electronic marketplace.

Name ______________________________

Apply

Combine each group of sentences to form one sentence. Add, delete, or change words as necessary. Add commas where needed.

14. An auctioneer puts a product up for bid. He or she tracks the bids. He or she awards the item to the highest bidder. ______________________________

15. I watched an alert auctioneer at work last Saturday. The auctioneer was also quick-witted. ______________________________

16. In some ways eBay is like a live auction. In other ways it is different. ______________________________

17. You can buy antiques on eBay. You can buy collectibles on eBay, too. You can also buy other secondhand items there. ______________________________

18. Users can browse merchandise by categories. They can search by keyword. They can look up items of a particular seller. ______________________________

Reinforce

Think of an imaginary item you would like to sell. Write a description of this item that includes the following:

- an appositive that renames the item
- a pair of similar adjectives that describe the object
- three or more phrases in a series that tell what the item does

Be sure to use commas correctly.

____

a. Marilyn Hamilton is an amazing woman, she turned a tragedy into an opportunity.

b. Some people have that gift: they find a way to make the most of a bad situation.

c. They learn from their own misfortune; they use what they learn to benefit others.

In which sentence are two independent clauses separated incorrectly with only a comma and no conjunction? _______

What punctuation marks are used to separate the independent clauses in the other two sentences? _____ _____

A **semicolon** (;) can be used instead of a comma and conjunction to separate the independent clauses in a **compound sentence**. A **colon** (:) can be used to separate two independent clauses when the second explains the first. It can also be used to introduce a list at the end of a sentence, to separate parts of references in a bibliography, and to separate hours and minutes in an expression of time.

See Handbook Sections 8, 13

Practice

Write a colon or a semicolon to separate the clauses in each sentence.

1. Marilyn Hamilton was a very active young woman she enjoyed tennis and hang-gliding.
2. In 1978 an accident changed her life she crashed her glider into a mountain.
3. Hamilton became paraplegic she lost the use of her legs.
4. She confronted another problem her wheelchair was too bulky.
5. A standard wheelchair weighed about fifty pounds she wanted a lighter one.
6. She sought the aid of two friends both were weekend inventors.
7. The two men designed gliders Hamilton asked them to build a wheelchair out of hang-gliding material.
8. The new wheelchair was a vast improvement it weighed only twenty-six pounds.
9. It looked sleek and sporty it had a compact frame and an angled back.
10. Hamilton could return to sports she began competing in tournaments.
11. She became a national tennis champion she also joined the U.S. Disabled Ski Team.
12. Hamilton and her two friends went into business they began making wheelchairs.
13. Her partners focused on design and manufacturing Hamilton focused on marketing.
14. In response to customers' requests, she made another innovation she offered wheelchairs in bright colors.
15. Soon the sporty-looking chairs were not just for sports they were for everyday use.

Hamilton used a sports wheelchair to win the 1983 U.S. Women's Open Wheelchair Tennis Championships.

Name ______________________________

Apply

Draw a line from each item on the left to an item on the right to make a simple or compound sentence. Then rewrite each pair as one sentence. Use a semicolon or a colon to separate independent clauses. Use a colon to introduce a list.

The Paralympic Games are held every two years	she won a silver medal in skiing
Marilyn Hamilton competed in the 1984 Winter Paralympic Games	cycling, judo, swimming, and wheelchair basketball
The Summer Paralympic Games include the following sports	they take place in the same city as the Olympic Games

16. ______________________________

17. ______________________________

18. ______________________________

Reinforce

The colon has many uses in writing. Think about how the colon is used in these examples. Then draw a line from each example to the rule it matches. (19–23)

BEN: What sports do you play? GISELLE: Baseball and soccer.	Use a colon to separate hours and minutes in an expression of time.
The judo competition will begin at 3:30 P.M.	Use a colon after the speaker's name in a play.
Many cultures follow this basic rule: "Treat others the way you want them to treat you."	Use a colon to separate the place of publication and the name of publisher in a book reference in a bibliography.
Bailey, Steve. *Athlete First: A History of the Paralympic Movement.* West Sussex, Eng.: John Wiley & Sons, 2008.	Use a colon to introduce a list or series at the end of a sentence.
I enjoy four sports: football, soccer, basketball, and baseball.	Use a colon to introduce a quotation.

On another sheet of paper, write an example of your own to match each rule.

a. The first successful moon landing (the culmination of the *Apollo 11* mission) took place in 1969.

b. *Apollo 12,* the follow-up mission, was also a success.

In which sentence are parentheses ( ) used to enclose information that explains an idea? _____

In which sentence is a hyphen used to join a word pair that precedes a noun? _____

Hyphens and **parentheses** are used to make writing clearer. Use a **hyphen** to

- separate the syllables in a word when you must break a word at the end of a line of text.
- link the parts of some compound words, such as *behind-the-scenes.*
- link some word pairs or groups of words that precede a noun and act as an adjective, such as *best-selling novel.*
- link the parts of numbers (written as words) between twenty-one and ninety-nine.

Use **parentheses** to set off an explanation or example.

See Handbook Section 9

Practice

Write *C* beside each sentence or sentence pair in which hyphens and parentheses are used correctly. Cross out hyphens and parentheses that are used incorrectly. If you are not sure whether a hyphen should be used to link parts of a compound word or adjective phrase, check a dictionary.

1. (On April 15, 1970) Ed Smylie was at home watching television when he learned of an explosion on board *Apollo 13.* _____
2. Smylie knew he was needed (at the Houston Space Center) as soon as possible. _____
3. He oversaw a top-notch team of engineers in NASA's crew systems division. _____
4. He soon discovered that (the spacecraft) was losing oxygen, electricity, light, and water. _____
5. There was also a problem with the square lithium hydroxide canisters. (The canisters, which were used to cleanse carbon dioxide from the air, had square openings.) _____
6. Smylie and his staff had to find a way to make the square canisters compatible with the openings in the command module (which were round). _____
7. Also, they had to use only materials available on board the spacecraft to repair the problems. (If they did not succeed, the crew would perish within a day or two.) _____
8. The engineers devised a rough-and-ready contraption out of plastic bags, cardboard, and duct tape. _____
9. After testing their invention, they guided (the astronauts) to find the same materials on board-the-spacecraft. _____
10. Their around-the-clock efforts paid off: the astronauts made it home safely. _____

Name ______________________________

Apply

Add hyphens or parentheses where they belong.

11. Duct tape is not what comes to mind when you think of space age repair tools.
12. Still, duct tape has helped other astronauts besides those on board *Apollo 13.* In one instance, astronauts used it to do quick and dirty repairs to their air filtering system.
13. In 2006 the shuttle *Discovery* was on a 13 day mission to the International Space Station.
14. The latches on the jet-propelled backpack belonging to an astronaut Piers Sellers somehow came loose.
15. The backpack used only in emergency situations allows an astronaut to move backward or forward.
16. Mission Control guided the astronauts to make a quick fix repair that allowed Sellers to take the planned spacewalk.

Reinforce

See Handbook Section 9

A dash is a punctuation mark used to signal a pause. A dash is longer than a hyphen. Think about how dashes are used in the sentences in the left-hand column. Then draw a line from each sentence to the rule it matches.

This was the moment I had been waiting for—the spacewalk.	Use dashes to set off a phrase or an independent clause that interrupts an otherwise complete sentence.
I looked at the distant blue orb—Earth was 220 miles away—and wished my friends could see me.	Use a dash to mark an interrupted or unfinished sentence.
Then I recalled the incident at Mission Control. If only—	Use a dash to stress one or more words at the end of a sentence.

On the lines below, write your own example for each rule about the use of dashes.

17. ______________________________

____

18. ______________________________

____

19. ______________________________

____

a. The true men of action in our time, those who transform the world, are not the politicians and statesmen, but the scientists.

—W. H. Auden, *The Dyer's Hand*

b. The true men of action . . . are not the politicians and statesmen, but the scientists.

—W. H. Auden, *The Dyer's Hand*

How is sentence *b* different from sentence *a*? ______________________________ ______________________________ **What punctuation mark is used to signal this?** ______________________________

An **ellipsis**, a group of three spaced periods, is used to mark the omission of words from a quotation. An ellipsis can also be used to signal a pause. When you use an ellipsis after words that are not a complete sentence, leave a space before the first spaced period. When you use an ellipsis after a sentence, use the sentence's end mark, and leave a space between it and the first spaced period.

See Handbook Section 9

Practice

Read both versions of each quotation. Place an *X* by the one that has words left out. Circle the marks that indicate this. Then, in the full version of the quotation, underline the words that were replaced by the marks.

1. **a.** The reasons we know that we will discover things we can't describe now is that this has been the history of science. We do things to learn something we can define, and we wind up knowing things we never imagined asking about.

   b. . . . This has been the history of science. We do things to learn something we can define, and we wind up knowing things we never imagined asking about.

   —Maxine Singer, in *A World of Ideas*, by Bill Moyers

2. **a.** Not many appreciate the ultimate power and potential usefulness of basic knowledge accumulated by obscure, unseen investigators . . . who go on seeking answers to the unknown without thought of financial or practical gain.

   b. Not many appreciate the ultimate power and potential usefulness of basic knowledge accumulated by obscure, unseen investigators who, in a lifetime of intense study, may never see any practical use for their findings but who go on seeking answers to the unknown without thought of financial or practical gain.

   —Eugenie Clark, *The Lady and the Sharks*

 Name ___

Apply

Rewrite each quotation, replacing the boldfaced words with an ellipsis.

3. We live in a scientific age, yet we assume that knowledge of science is the prerogative of only a small number of human beings isolated and priestlike in their laboratories. **That is not true. The materials of science are the materials of life itself.** Science is part of the reality of living; it is the what, the how, and the why for everything in our experience.

—Rachel Carson, in *The House of Life,* by Paul Brooks

4. . . . Science is one of the grand human activities. **It uses the same kind of talent and creativity as painting pictures and making sculptures. It's not really very different except that you do it from a base of technical knowledge. Science is not an inhuman or superhuman activity.** It's something that humans invented, and it speaks to one of our great needs—to understand the world around us.

—Maxine Singer, in *A World of Ideas,* by Bill Moyers

Reinforce

Read the quotation below by American geneticist and Nobel Prize winner Barbara McClintock. Circle the ellipsis that signals a pause.

If you know you are on the right track, if you have this inner knowledge, then nobody can turn you off . . . no matter what they say.

On the lines below, write a paragraph telling how these words could inspire someone trying to solve a problem or make a discovery. Use the quotation in your paragraph.

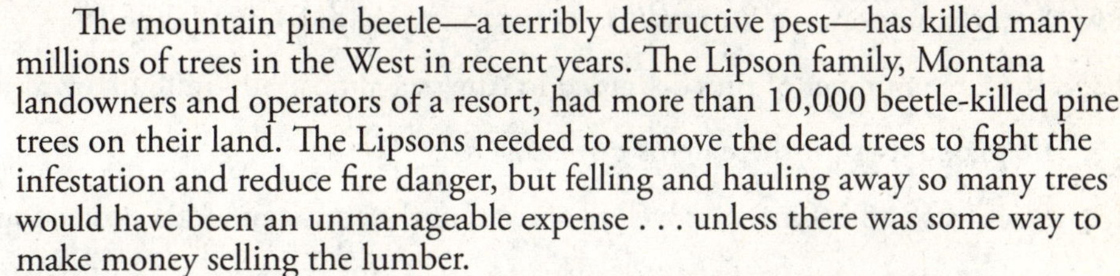

Read and Analyze

The mountain pine beetle—a terribly destructive pest—has killed many millions of trees in the West in recent years. The Lipson family, Montana landowners and operators of a resort, had more than 10,000 beetle-killed pine trees on their land. The Lipsons needed to remove the dead trees to fight the infestation and reduce fire danger, but felling and hauling away so many trees would have been an unmanageable expense . . . unless there was some way to make money selling the lumber.

What punctuation mark is used to signal pauses in the first sentence? _______________ What punctuation mark indicates pauses in the second sentence? _______________ What punctuation mark signals a long pause in the third sentence? _______________

Three types of punctuation marks can be used to signal pauses: **Long dashes** can signal pauses before and after an authorial comment or an explanatory phrase in a sentence. A long dash can also be used to signal a sudden interruption in a statement. **Commas** can be used to signal thoughtful pauses between groups of words. An **ellipsis** can be used in a sentence to indicate a long pause.

See Handbook Sections 8, 9

Practice

Read each sentence quietly to yourself. Circle each punctuation mark that indicates where you should pause.

1. The Lipsons first had to identify infested pines—an easy task, since their needles turned burnt red—and then cut and haul away both the damaged trees and the healthy ones growing near them.
2. This process stopped the infestation in their forest . . . but it left them with a huge amount of beetle-damaged timber.
3. Larry Lipson was determined to find a use—a use that would generate income—for these felled trees.
4. He learned that lumber from beetle-killed pine trees was as strong as any other pine lumber, as long as it had not begun to rot.
5. Larry Lipson sent a small amount of his timber to a sawmill to be cut into boards . . . and what came back certainly surprised him.
6. The wood had an almost-iridescent blue tinge to it which, he later learned, was produced by a fungus carried by the beetles.
7. The Lipson family decided to use this lovely lumber to make accessories for tablets and smartphones—primarily stands and backs.
8. They started a company called Bad Beetle—a name chosen to raise people's awareness of the beetle problem—and set up a website to sell their products.
9. Several other companies now produce a range of products, from kitchen cabinets to tree houses, using the blue-tinged wood.
10. You may have heard the saying, "If you're given lemons, make lemonade," and that is what Larry Lipson and other entrepreneurs are doing with timber formerly regarded as worthless.

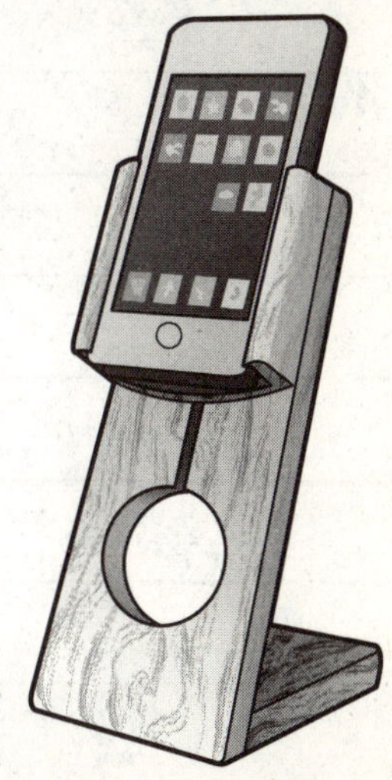

This smartphone stand is made out of lumber from trees killed by the mountain pine beetle.

Name ____________________

Apply

Add long dashes, commas, and ellipses where they are needed in these sentences.

11. Scrap tires too worn for road use were formerly thrown into landfills.
12. The large number of tires discarded in America almost 300 million a year at present makes it imperative that good uses for these items be discovered.
13. Scientists and engineers as well as officials in the Environmental Protection Agency's Office of Research and Development have developed a wide array of new uses.
14. Almost half of America's scrap tires are now burned as fuel a beneficial use, since tires produce more energy and fewer emissions than coal produces.
15. Tires are also used in civil engineering projects from erosion barriers for bridge piers to noise-absorbing walls alongside highways.
16. In addition, scrap tires are used to manufacture rubberized asphalt for paving roads roads that become remarkably smooth and quiet with their new surface.
17. One project now underway sponsored by the Department of Energy's Office of Energy Efficiency and Renewable Energy involves developing treatments for the rubber in scrap tires.
18. This rubber after being treated can be used to make gaskets, sealants, and adhesives.

Reinforce

Research some other ways that artists and communities have reused old tires. Write a paragraph about your findings. Use punctuation marks to signal pauses in your paragraph.

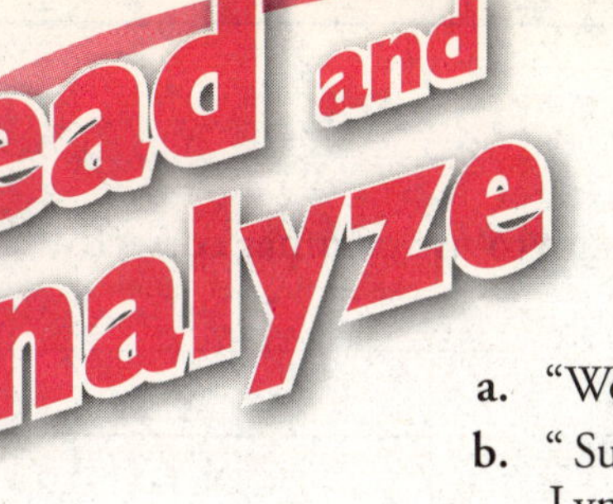

Punctuating Dialogue

Unit 7: Lesson 82

a. "Would you like to start your own Web-based organization?" asked Sid.

b. " Sure, but I don't know what type of organization I would start," answered Lyn.

Circle the marks that begin and end each quotation. Draw a box around the introductory word in the quotation in sentence *b*. Write the punctuation mark that follows that introductory word. _____ Write the punctuation mark that comes before the last quotation mark in sentence *b*. _____

A **direct quotation** is a speaker's exact words. Use **quotation marks** at the beginning and end of a direct quotation. Use a comma to separate direct speech, or a speaker's exact words, from the rest of the sentence. Begin a direct quotation with an uppercase letter. Add end punctuation (period, question mark, exclamation point, or comma in place of a period) before the last quotation mark. Use a comma to set off an introductory word such as *Yes*, a mild interjection such as *Oh*, a noun of direct address, or a tag question from the rest of a sentence.

See Handbook Sections 4, 8

Practice

Add quotation marks and commas to these sentences to make them correct.

1. Terry I heard about this great microfinance organization said Senko.
2. Microfinance is the process of giving small loans to people to start businesses isn't it? asked Terry.
3. Yes that's more or less what it means Senko agreed.
4. Well what is this organization you heard about? asked Terry.
5. It's called *Kiva,* which means "agreement" or "unity" in Swahili Senko explained.
6. Then Terry asked What impresses you about this organization?
7. It takes a slightly different approach to solving the problem of poverty answered Senko.
8. Aren't there other microfinance organizations? Terry asked skeptically.
9. Sure but Kiva arranges and manages its loans through a website said Senko.
10. Tell me more said Terry, who was now curious.
11. Kiva operates a person-to-person model Senko pointed out.
12. Local microfinance institutions post received loan applications on the Internet he continued.
13. Okay then what happens? asked Terry.
14. On the Kiva website, people read descriptions of the loan requests said Senko.
15. He added Then they decide which loan or loans to fund.
16. Lenders can ask questions of the borrowers can't they? Terry wondered aloud.
17. Yes they can replied Senko and borrowers send updates on how their businesses are progressing.
18. Hey that sounds like a great system! exclaimed Terry.

Name ______________________________

Apply

Rewrite the sentences, adding correct punctuation to the dialogue. Be sure to use commas correctly.

19. Fiona do you want to help finance a small business loan? asked Bobby. ______________________

20. Yes that sounds like a great idea Fiona replied. ______________________

21. We could ask friends in the neighborhood if they want to join us Bobby added. ______________________

22. Hey we could give a presentation to our parents and grandparents suggested Fiona. ______________________

23. Let's browse the microloan website and find a business to support said Bobby. ______________________

24. Why don't you come over after school so we can do online research together? Fiona suggested. ______________________

Reinforce

See Handbook Sections 23

An *interjection* is a word used to express strong or sudden feeling. Interjections are sometimes used as introductory words. If an interjection is said with force or strong feeling, it is followed by an exclamation mark; if a sentence follows this type of interjection, the first word of the sentence begins with a capital letter. If an interjection is not said with force or strong feeling, it is followed by a comma, and the word after the comma is not capitalized.

Choose an interjection from the word bank to complete each item. Add appropriate punctuation. Draw three lines (≡) under the first letter of any word that should be capitalized.

ugh	shh	bravo	alas	yikes	eureka

25. ______________ that was an amazing performance!
26. ______________ I've found just what I was looking for.
27. ______________ my new puppy is sleeping.
28. ______________ we didn't make the championships.
29. ______________ that's a snake!
30. ______________ we've got tons of chores to do.

Read and Analyze

Quotations From a Text

a. In an article published in the October 1928 issue of *Forum,* automobile manufacturing pioneer Henry Ford said, "The whole secret of a successful life is to find out what is one's destiny to do, and then do it."

b. Here is another great American's thought on individuality and success:

> **Why should we be in such desperate haste to succeed, and in such desperate enterprises? If a man does not keep pace with his companions, perhaps it is because he hears a different drummer. Let him step to the music which he hears, however measured or far away.**
>
> **—Henry David Thoreau, in *Walden***

Which quotation is longer? _______ **How is it presented?** ____________________
____
_____ **How is the other quotation presented?** ______________________________
____

Write a **short quotation** as you would the words of a speaker: Use **quotation marks** at the beginning and end of the quotation. Use a comma to separate the words of the quotation from the rest of the sentence. Write a **long quotation** as a block of text, indented and set off from the body of what you are writing by a line of space. Do not use quotation marks at the beginning or end of the quotation. Provide source information below the quotation.

See Handbook Section 4

Practice

Read each quotation below. Decide whether you would present it within a sentence or as a block of text if you were including it in a report or a composition. Circle your choice.

1. I must admit that I personally measure success in terms of the contributions an individual makes to her or his fellow beings.

   —Margaret Mead, in *Redbook,* November 1978

   in a sentence   **as a block of text**

2. I come to embrace the notion that I haven't done enough in my life; I heartily concur; I come to affirm that one's title, even a title like President of the United States, says very little about how well one's life has been led—that no matter how much you've done, or how successful you've been, there's always more to do, always more to learn, and always more to achieve.

   —Barack Obama, in "Arizona State University Commencement Address," May 2009

   in a sentence   **as a block of text**

3. Success is more a function of consistent common sense than it is of genius.

   —An Wang, in *Boston Magazine,* December 1986

   in a sentence   **as a block of text**

Name ______________________________

Apply

Rewrite each short quotation as part of a sentence. Rewrite each long quotation as a block of text. You may add words to introduce the quotation to the reader.

4. There is nothing mysterious about originality. Originality is merely the step beyond.

   —Louis Danz, *Dynamic Dissonances in Nature and the Arts*

5. Creativeness often consists merely of turning up what is already there. Did you know that right and left shoes were thought up only a little more than a century ago?

   —Bernice Fitz-gibbon, in *Peter's Quotations*, by Dr. Laurence J. Peter

6. We should be careful to get out of an experience only the wisdom that is in it—and stop there; lest we be like the cat that sits on a hot stove-lid. She will never sit on a hot stove-lid again—and that is well; but also she will never sit on a cold one anymore.

   —Mark Twain, *Following the Equator*

Reinforce

Select one of the quotations from this lesson, or find a quotation about success, creativity, or problem-solving in another source. On another sheet of paper, write a brief essay in which you present the quotation, explain what you think it means, and tell why you agree or disagree with it.

700 Franklin Drive
St. Louis, MO 63101
February 25, 20__

Dear Brenda,

Since we talked on the phone, I've been thinking about the trouble you're having making free throws. Here's my advice: Take a deep breath, bend your knees, and then straighten up and release the ball in one smooth motion.

As for your wanting to improve your defense, I think a coach will be able to give you the advice you need. Good luck!

Your friend,
Heather

There are five different parts of this letter. Two have already been circled. Circle the other three.

A **friendly letter** has five parts: the **heading,** the **greeting,** the **body,** the **closing,** and the **signature**. A friendly letter may include informal language. A **business letter** is a formal letter written to an employer or a business. It has the same parts as a friendly letter, but it also includes the address of the person to whom the letter will be sent. Use a colon after the greeting in a business letter. Omit paragraph indentations and align all letter parts along the left-hand margin. A formal **e-mail** is similar to a letter, but it usually has only four parts: a greeting, a body, a closing, and your name. An e-mail header contains your **e-mail address,** the e-mail address of the person you are writing to, the date, and a **subject line**.

See Handbook Sections 2, 8, 34, 35

Practice

Use the appropriate boldfaced words in the rule box above to label the five parts of this friendly letter.

253 Third Street
1. ______________________ Kansas City, KS 66101
March 3, 20__

Dear Heather, ______________________ 2.

I really appreciated your advice on how to perfect my free-throw style. It's helping! Also, I've asked the basketball coach at the community center to give me defensive pointers. He says that he can help me after practice on Tuesday.

How is your gymnastic routine coming along?

3. ______________________

4. ______________________ Your friend,

5. ______________________ Brenda

Name ____

Apply

Rewrite this business letter correctly on the lines below. (Hint: The sender's address and the date go first. The inside address goes second.)

Mr. Dan Kinney Fairview Community Center 2300 Baxter Avenue Kansas City, KS 66101 March 10, 20__ Dear Mr. Kinney I play on the Cougars basketball team in the C league. We have had a really great season. Would you consider moving our team to the B league next year? I think that playing better teams will push us to improve our skills. Thank you for considering this request. Sincerely Brenda Tyler 253 Third Street Kansas City, KS 66101

____

____

____

____

____

____

____

____

____

____

____

____

____

Reinforce

See Handbook Section 35

Think of an activity that you enjoy, such as playing a sport, practicing a hobby, or playing an instrument. Then think of someone you know who is more skilled than you are at that activity. Write that person an e-mail requesting advice about how to improve your skills. Be sure to begin with the reason you are e-mailing; type a clear subject line; avoid special type features, emoticons, or using all uppercase letters; and include a detailed salutation (full name and e-mail address). When you have finished your first draft, read your e-mail from beginning to end. Proofread for errors in capitalization, punctuation, and spelling. Then print out a copy of your final draft.

Capitalization

Draw three lines (≡) under each letter that should be capitalized.

1. people at the united nations are working to end world hunger.
2. The sahel and the Horn of africa are two regions of malnutrition.

Titles, Initials, Abbreviations, and Acronyms

Draw three lines (≡) under each letter that should be capitalized. Add underlines, quotation marks, and periods where they are needed.

3. A book called Children of the Depression has photos from the 1930s.
4. It includes photos by ms dorothea lange and mr walker evans.
5. The wpa (Works progress Administration) offered a solution.

Punctuation

Underline the correct word in each pair. Write *C* if the word is a contraction or *P* if the word is a possessive.

6. I (had'nt/hadn't) heard of the WPA before. _____
7. The (agency's/agencies') projects included bridges, parks, and airports. _____

Add commas, semicolons, and colons where they are needed. (Only one item requires a colon.)

8. WPA-sponsored artists created murals sculptures and paintings.
9. Writers compiled oral histories they also wrote books.
10. These are two famous WPA writers John Steinbeck and Studs Terkel.

Add hyphens, parentheses, and dashes where they are needed.

11. The National Youth Administration NYA sought to employ young people.
12. The NYA combined economic relief with on the job training.
13. Congress—by then focusing solely on winning World War II abolished the program in 1943.

Add dashes, commas, and ellipses where they are needed in these sentences.

14. Finding ways to recycle plastic containers millions of which now end up in landfills every year should be at the top of every environmental problem-solver's to-do list.
15. Tons of plastic and other trash now circulate in the middle of the Pacific Ocean a terrible overwhelming problem requiring a brilliant solution.

Punctuating Dialogue

Add quotation marks and other marks where they are needed. Draw three lines (≡) under each letter that should be capitalized.

16. Peggy asked Philip, do you have a summer job lined up?

17. yes, I'm going to mow lawns he answered.

Ellipses

Rewrite the quotation, replacing the boldfaced words with an ellipsis.

18. We know what a person thinks, **not when he tells us what he thinks, but** by his actions.

—Isaac Bashevis Singer, in *The New York Times Magazine,* November 26, 1978

____

Quotations From a Text

Rewrite each short quotation as part of a sentence. Rewrite each long quotation as a block of text. You may add words to introduce a quotation to the reader.

19. You cannot shake hands with a clenched fist.

—Indira Gandhi, in a press conference in New Delhi

____

20. Rhetoric is a poor substitute for action, and we have trusted only to rhetoric. If we are really to be a great nation, we must not merely talk, we must act big.

—Theodore Roosevelt, in the September 1917 issue of *The Metropolitan*

____

____

____

____

Letters and E-mails

Rewrite this business letter correctly on a separate sheet of paper.

21. 637 Lennox Street Fargo, ND 58102 April 17, 20__ Hank's Historical Poster Company 333 Douglas Avenue Little Rock, AR 72201 Dear Sir or Madam: I am enclosing a poster I received from you. It had a tiny tear when I received it. Would you please replace it? Sincerely yours, Paul Wingate

Spelling Practice

Read and Analyze

It must have been an **exhilarating** experience to be a part of the team that put the first person on the moon.

The word in bold type means "exciting and uplifting." Create a rule or mnemonic device to help you remember how to spell it.

Frequently Misspelled Words

Some words are more difficult to spell than others. For example, words that are commonly mispronounced, such as **irrelevant,** are often misspelled. Words with silent letters, such as **exhaust,** are also a challenge. And sometimes the sounds of words such as **jealousy** give no real clue to the spelling.

Words in Context

Write the word that best completes each sentence. Use a dictionary if you need help.

familiar	committee	minimum	forehead	luxury
prejudice	procedure	genuine	frivolous	postpone

1. Getting to know many different kinds of people prevents ___________.
2. I will need a ___________ of four correct answers to pass the test.
3. It is ___________ to buy two new dresses for the party.
4. Baking the scones is a fairly simple ___________.
5. Are you ___________ with this new young adult series?
6. Ordering dessert was a rare ___________ for us.
7. If this rain continues, they will ___________ the parade.
8. Dad has joined a ___________ that plans the annual block party.
9. Is this ___________ leather, or is it imitation?
10. The nurse felt my ___________ and determined I had a fever.

Name ______________________________

Pattern Practice

numerous	minimum	familiar	irrelevant	pursue	exhilarating
reliable	exhaust	genuine	maneuver	postpone	spontaneous

Replace the underlined word or phrase with a word from above that means the same thing. Use a dictionary if you need help.

11. Unfortunately, my feelings were unimportant. ____________
12. We took a sudden detour and got lost. ____________
13. There are many reasons why I've chosen to leave. ____________
14. This computer is a very trustworthy product. ____________
15. Cody practiced that skateboard move for hours. ____________
16. Molly will work toward a career in journalism. ____________
17. I will delay my doctor appointment until next week. ____________
18. Skydiving must be an exciting experience! ____________
19. This coin is a real artifact from the Civil War Era. ____________

Write the word from above that is an antonym of each word. Use a dictionary if you need help.

20. speed up ____________
21. fake ____________
22. foreign ____________
23. maximum ____________
24. depressing ____________
25. enliven ____________

Use the Dictionary

Circle the word in each pair that is correctly spelled. Check your work in a print or an online dictionary.

26.	courtesy	curtesy
27.	liaeson	liaison
28.	picnicing	picnicking
29.	cancellation	canselation

Diagramming Adjective Clauses

You have learned that an adjective clause is a dependent clause that describes a noun or pronoun and begins with a relative pronoun such as *who, that,* or *which.* Notice the way an adjective clause is diagrammed. In this sentence, the relative pronoun *who* is the subject of the adjective clause.

Dr. Charles Drew, **who was a surgeon,** did important research on blood transfusions.

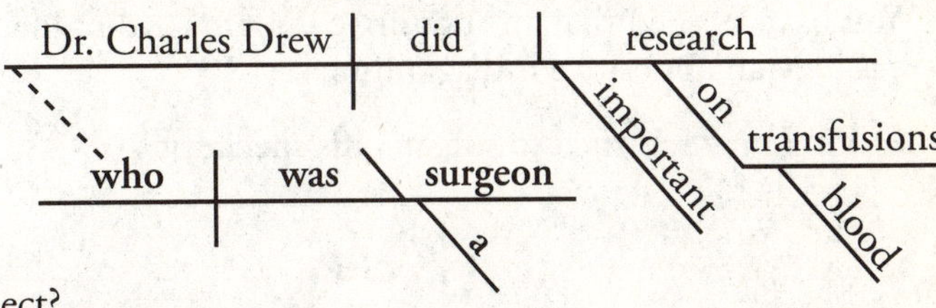

1. Which sentence elements does the dashed line connect? ________

   a. two nouns in the sentence

   b. the direct object and the relative pronoun *who*

   c. the relative pronoun *who* and the noun to which it refers

In the example to the right, the relative pronoun *which* refers to *blood,* the object of the preposition in the independent clause.

At the time, blood transfusions were done with whole blood, **which caused severe problems in some cases.**

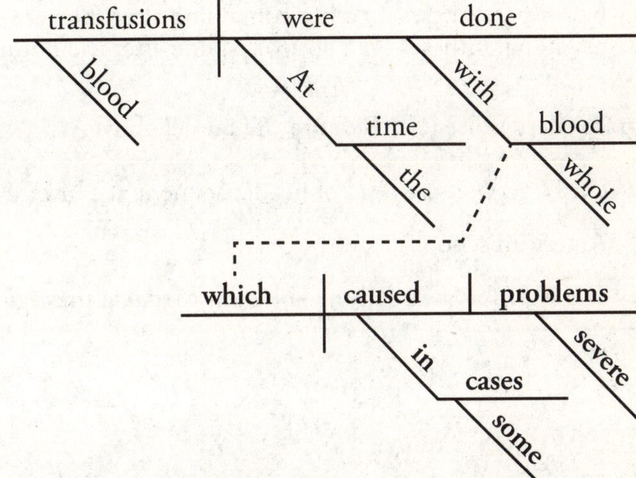

Try diagramming these sentences.

2. Dr. Drew, who served on an important committee, argued for the use of blood plasma.
3. Fewer problems occurred with transfusions that used blood plasma.

Diagramming Adverb Clauses

You have learned that an adverb clause is a dependent clause that tells about a verb, an adjective, or an adverb, and that an adverb clause often begins with a subordinating conjunction such as *although* or *because,* or with a relative adverb such as *when* or *where.*

When World War II began, the need for blood transfusions increased dramatically.

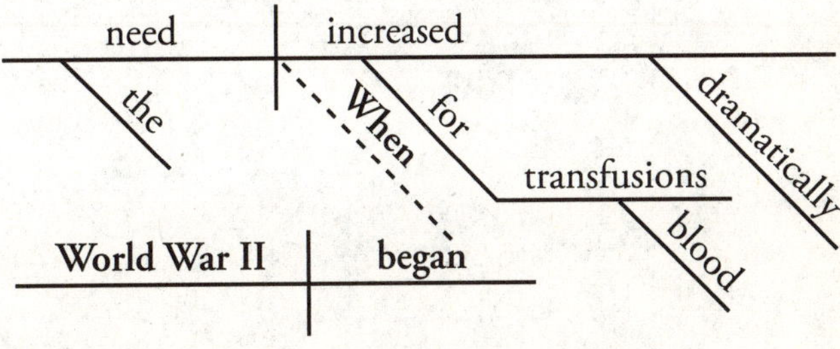

4. Where is the relative adverb *When* placed in this diagram? ________
   a. on a slanted line below the simple subject
   b. on a slanted dotted line connecting the verb in the clause to the word the clause modifies
   c. on a dotted line connecting two subjects

Name ______________________________

Diagram these sentences. Refer to the model on the previous page.

5. When a wounded soldier required a transfusion, fresh plasma was needed by the doctor.
6. After Dr. Drew instituted a system for the sanitary collection of blood, spoilage decreased significantly.

Diagramming Appositives

You have learned that an appositive is a phrase that identifies a noun. Here is how an appositive is diagrammed:

Dr. Drew returned to surgery, **his specialty,** in 1941.

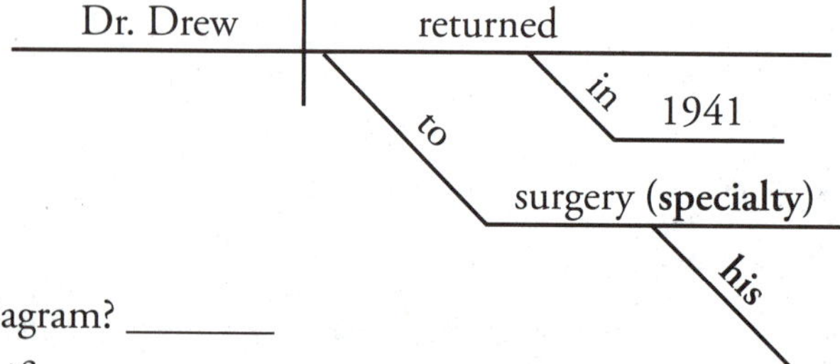

7. Where is the noun in the appositive placed in the diagram? ________
   a. on its own diagonal line below the noun it identifies
   b. in parentheses on a horizontal line after the verb
   c. in parentheses on a horizontal line after the noun it identifies

Diagram these sentences. Refer to the model above.

8. Dr. Drew became head of his department at Howard Medical School, a historically African American school.
9. The NAACP awarded the Spingarn Medal, a prestigious award, to Dr. Drew.

Writing Sentences

Rewrite each sentence so that it makes sense. Make each one easier to understand by using correct punctuation and capitalization.

1. I've decided to title my paper Carved in stone. ______________________________

____

2. I'm focusing on the reasons civic group's choose to erect statues. ______________

____

3. I'm sorry to take so long to write, but I've been working on a report for mr wongs class.

____

4. I'll leave you with two words before I sign off write soon! ____________________

____

5. When I told my dad the title, he said you're a regular chip off the old block! ________

____

6. The report is about civic art. Works of art installed in public spaces in cities and towns.

____

A friendly letter has a heading, greeting, body, closing, and signature. A well-written letter has a friendly tone, includes specific information, uses description to create pictures in the mind of its reader, and asks the reader questions to give him or her ideas for writing a letter in return. As you read the model letter below, notice the use of details and questions to the reader.

120 Fern Creek Avenue
Vancouver, WA 98660
March 7, 20__

Dear Wendy,

Your report sounds like it's going to be very interesting. I just saw the Sacagawea statue at Washington Park in Portland, Oregon, last weekend. As you know, Sacagawea was the Shoshone woman who accompanied her husband, Toussaint Charbonneau, on the Lewis and Clark Expedition. Along the way she acted as an interpreter, found plants to eat, and served as a symbol of peace—other tribes saw her and did not view the expedition as hostile.

Here's a fun fact for you: supposedly there are more statues of Sacagawea in the United States than of any other woman. Perhaps you can include information about her in your report.

Your friend,

Mimi

Name ___

Writing a Paragraph

The sentences you revised on page 255 can be used as the body of a friendly letter. Decide in what order the sentences should be. Write them on the lines below. Then add a heading, greeting, closing, and signature.

Think of an individual who has been commemorated in your community. Write a letter to a friend, telling him or her about this individual. Include facts and descriptions to make your letter interesting. Use the model on page 255 as your guide.

Reread your letter. Use this checklist to make sure it is complete and follows the friendly letter form.

- ❑ Does my letter have all five parts?
- ❑ Have I punctuated the greeting and closing correctly?
- ❑ Have I included specific information?
- ❑ Have I used abbreviations correctly?
- ❑ Have I capitalized proper nouns?
- ❑ Have I asked questions my reader will want to answer in a return letter?
- ❑ Have I used commas, semicolons, hyphens, parentheses, and dashes correctly?

Proofreading Practice

Read this passage about Florence Nightingale and find the mistakes. Use the proofreading marks to show how the mistakes should be fixed.

Proofreading Marks

Mark	Means	Example
ᓄ	delete	Florence Nightingalee was an English nurse.
∧	add	Florence Nightingale was ∧an English nurse.
≡	make into an uppercase letter	Florence Nightingale was an english nurse.
/	make into a lowercase letter	Florence Nightingale was an English Nurse.
⊙	add a period	Florence Nightingale was an English nurse⊙
(sp)	fix spelling	Florence Nightingale was an Inglish nurse.

Florence Nightingale, Originator of Modern Nursing

Florence Nightingale was born into a well to do english family in 1820. She was educated mostly by her father, William e. Nightingale. He taught her history philosophy and mathematics. He also taught her several world langauges Greek, Latin, french, German, and italian.

Young florence Nightingale developed an interest in nursing but there were no nursing programs in England at that time. In [illegible], she entered a nursing program in germany. When she returned to London in 1853, she was employed by the Institution For The Care Of Sick Gentlewomen. As superintendent at the institution, she made many posative changes. Still, she wanted to do more.

In 1854, war broke out on the Crimean peninsula—an area on the northern coast of the Black sea—between russia and Great Britain and it's allies. Nightingale was asked to take charge of the military hospitals in turkey. When she and a large party of nurses arrived there on nov 5, 1854, she was appalled by the poor conditions at the hospital great numbers of sick and wounded soldiers lay on filthy straw mattresses there was insufficient clean water and the place was infested with rats and fleas. Nightingale imediatly set people to work cleaning the place. She created a nursing schedule, and she wrote nummerous letters demanding supplies. She worked long hours and made nightly rounds in the wards thus earning the nickname "The Lady with the Lamp".

At the wars end two years later, Nightingale she returned to england, where she continued to work on behalf of the helth and welfare of british soldiers. In 1860, she established the Nightingale school for nurses at St thomas's Hospital, the first quality nursing program in the world.

Name ____________________

Proofreading Checklist

You can use the list below to help you find and fix mistakes in your own writing. Write the titles of your own stories or reports in the blanks at the top of the chart. Then use the questions to check your work. Make a check mark (✓) in each box after you have checked that item.

Proofreading Checklist for Unit 7

	Titles			
Have I capitalized proper nouns and proper adjectives?				
Have I capitalized and punctuated titles of works correctly?				
Have I used commas correctly?				
Have I used apostrophes correctly in possessives and contractions?				
Have I used colons and semicolons correctly?				
Have I used hyphens, dashes, and parentheses correctly?				
Have I punctuated direct and indirect quotations correctly?				

Also Remember...

Does each sentence begin with an uppercase letter?				
Did I use a dictionary to check and correct spellings?				
Have I used the right end marks at the end of sentences?				

Your Own List

Use this space to write your own list of things to check in your writing.

Community Connection

In Unit 7 of *Grammar, Usage, and Mechanics,* students learned about **capitalization, punctuation, and other aspects of writing mechanics,** and used what they learned to improve their writing. The content of these lessons focuses on the theme **Problem Solvers.** As students completed the exercises, they learned about individuals and groups of people who have solved problems to make life easier and more rewarding for others. These pages offer a variety of activities that reinforce skills and concepts presented in the unit. They also provide opportunities for the student to make connections between the materials in the lessons and the community at large.

Problems in the News

Read a print or online newspaper that serves your area. Find one article about a community problem that needs to be solved and one article about a problem that has already been solved. Discuss these articles with family members or classmates. Identify the people involved with the problem that has been solved, and decide whether they qualify as unforgettable folks. Then come up with a list of possible solutions for the unsolved problem.

Help the Problem Solvers

Choose one organization in your community that helps people with problems of a particular kind. This might be a group that helps people with disabilities, a group that provides free tutoring help to students, or a group that identifies and tries to solve environmental problems. Visit, call, or read about the group to find out more about the work it does. If possible, spend time volunteering for the organization. Then write an advertisement to convince others to become donors or volunteers for the organization.

Seekers of Solutions

It usually takes careful scientific research to find solutions to serious medical problems. Find out where in your area doctors and scientists do research to find vaccines, treatments, and cures for diseases. Browse that facility's website and read about one of the types of research it is doing. Write a letter or an e-mail to a friend, summarizing what you learn.

Family Report

Brainstorm with a relative about a problem affecting your family. Then work together to devise a solution to the problem. Answer each of these questions to help you formulate a plan of action.

- What is the problem?
- Which family member(s) are affected by it? Are there other relatives who could help solve the problem?
- What are some possible solutions? Could the problem be solved by developing a new process, such as planting a garden to save money; by creating an invention, such as a time-saving device; or by working to increase family communication?
- What are the advantages and disadvantages of each possible solution?

Choose the solution that you feel will work best, and write the details of your plan in a "family report." Then distribute the report to each family member.

Name ______________________________

Jobs for Problem Solvers

List some of the job opportunities available for people who want to solve problems in your community. Find out about employment in at least two fields such as product development, scientific research, medicine, environmental science, or social services. Then do research to learn more about careers in the field that interests you most. Find out what education and skills are needed in this field and what types of jobs you might someday quality for. Use the planner that follows to help organize the information you find.

I. First Field Researched: ______________________________

A. Types of Jobs Available:

1. ______________________________

2. ______________________________

3. ______________________________

B. Most Interesting Type: ______________________________

C. Kinds of Problems to Be Solved: ______________________________

____

____

D. Education and Skills Required: ______________________________

____

____

II. Second Field Researched: ______________________________

A. Types of Jobs Available:

1. ______________________________

2. ______________________________

3. ______________________________

B. Most Interesting Type: ______________________________

C. Kinds of Problems to Be Solved: ______________________________

____

____

D. Education and Skills Required: ______________________________

____

____

Appendix Table of Contents

TEST TIP: Be sure to read all four answer choices carefully before choosing and marking the answer you think is correct.

Read each item carefully. Fill in the circle next to the best answer.

1. Read this sentence.

A casual observer might mistake a red fox for a small furry dog.

Which of the following is the complete predicate of the sentence?

- (A) casual observer might mistake
- (B) mistake a red fox
- (C) might mistake a red fox for a small furry dog
- (D) mistake a red fox for a small furry dog

2. Read this sentence.

These members of the dog family can live in a variety of environments.

What are the simple subject and the simple predicate of the sentence?

- (A) family; can
- (B) family; can live
- (C) members; can live
- (D) family can; live

3. Read this sentence.

The Arctic fox and the fennec of the desert live and thrive in extreme environments.

Which of the following is a correct statement about the sentence?

- (A) It has a compound subject and a simple predicate.
- (B) It has a simple subject and a compound predicate.
- (C) It has a simple subject and a simple predicate.
- (D) It has a compound subject and a compound predicate.

4. Read this sentence.

A red fox can hear the peep of a chick from a distance of 90 feet.

Which word in the sentence is a direct object?

- (A) hear
- (B) peep
- (C) chick
- (D) distance

5. Read this sentence.

Unlike other canines, gray foxes are climbers of trees.

Which of the following is a predicate noun in the sentence?

- (A) canines
- (B) foxes
- (C) climbers
- (D) trees

6. Read this sentence.

A mated pair of foxes often hunt together and always protect each other.

Which of the following is a prepositional phrase in the sentence?

- (A) of foxes
- (B) often
- (C) always
- (D) each

Name ______________________________

Read each item carefully. Fill in the circle next to the best answer.

7. Read this sentence.

Wolves, coyotes, and foxes are all canines, members of the dog family, and have many similar characteristics.

Which group of words from the sentence is an appositive?

Ⓐ coyotes, and foxes
Ⓑ all canines
Ⓒ members of the dog family
Ⓓ many similar characteristics

8. Read this sentence.

Foxes raising pups live in family groups and stay in large dens.

Which group of words from the sentence is a participial phrase?

Ⓐ foxes raising pups
Ⓑ raising pups
Ⓒ live in family groups
Ⓓ stay in large dens

9. Read this sentence.

Quick reactions and incredibly sharp senses enable foxes to hunt effectively.

Which of the following is an infinitive phrase in the sentence?

Ⓐ quick reactions
Ⓑ incredibly sharp senses
Ⓒ enable foxes
Ⓓ to hunt effectively

10. Read this sentence.

A bat-eared fox running at top speed can change course suddenly.

What is the simple predicate of the sentence?

Ⓐ running
Ⓑ top speed
Ⓒ can change
Ⓓ change

11. Read each sentence. Which sentence provides the most useful information?

Ⓐ Llamas and alpacas are related to camels.
Ⓑ Llamas and alpacas live in South America.
Ⓒ The Incas, whose empire once stretched throughout the mountains and lowlands of western South America, domesticated the llama and the alpaca.
Ⓓ One was a pack animal, and the other provided wool.

12. Read this sentence.

What a soft coat the alpaca has!

What type of sentence is this?

Ⓐ declarative
Ⓑ interrogative
Ⓒ imperative
Ⓓ exclamatory

13. Read this sentence.

Neither the llama nor the alpaca is found in the wild, but their relatives the vicuña and the guanaco roam the slopes of the Andes.

What type of sentence is this?

Ⓐ declarative
Ⓑ interrogative
Ⓒ imperative
Ⓓ exclamatory

Read each item carefully. Fill in the circle next to the best answer.

14. Read this sentence.

Serious birdwatchers study the only creatures on Earth with feathers.

Which of the following is the complete predicate of the sentence?

Ⓐ serious birdwatchers
Ⓑ study the only creatures
Ⓒ study the only creatures on Earth with feathers
Ⓓ the only creatures on Earth

15. Read this sentence.

Nearly all birds outside Antarctica construct nests of twigs or mud.

What are the simple subject and the simple predicate of the sentence?

Ⓐ birds; nests
Ⓑ birds; construct
Ⓒ Antarctica; construct
Ⓓ construct; nests

16. Read this sentence.

The ostrich and the cassowary have wings but cannot fly.

Which of the following is a correct statement about the sentence?

Ⓐ It has a compound subject and a simple predicate.
Ⓑ It has a simple subject and a compound predicate.
Ⓒ It has a simple subject and a simple predicate.
Ⓓ It has a compound subject and a compound predicate.

17. Read this sentence.

Some birds waterproof their feathers with oil from a special gland.

Which word in the sentence is a direct object?

Ⓐ waterproof
Ⓑ feathers
Ⓒ oil
Ⓓ gland

18. Read this sentence.

An ancestor of modern chickens became an important domestic animal about 5,500 years ago.

Which of the following is a predicate noun in the sentence?

Ⓐ chickens
Ⓑ domestic
Ⓒ animal
Ⓓ years

19. Read this sentence.

All birds' offspring grow and develop inside hard-shelled eggs.

Which group of words from the sentence is a prepositional phrase?

Ⓐ all birds' offspring
Ⓑ grow and develop
Ⓒ and develop
Ⓓ inside hard-shelled eggs

Name ____________________

Read each item carefully. Fill in the circle next to the best answer.

20. Read this sentence.

Ornithologists, scientists who study birds, are interested in understanding more about how birds navigate.

Which group of words from the sentence is an appositive?

- Ⓐ scientists who study birds
- Ⓑ are interested
- Ⓒ understanding more
- Ⓓ birds navigate

21. Read this sentence.

Guided by the sun, stars, wind, and an internal compass, migratory birds can travel long distances to the same destination year after year.

Which group of words from the sentence is a participial phrase?

- Ⓐ guided by the sun, stars, wind, and an internal compass
- Ⓑ an internal compass
- Ⓒ travel long distances
- Ⓓ to the same destination year after year

22. Read this sentence.

A variety of birds, from colorful parrots to gray and white mockingbirds, have learned to imitate other birdcalls and noises.

Which of the following is an infinitive phrase in the sentence?

- Ⓐ a variety of birds
- Ⓑ to gray and white mockingbirds
- Ⓒ have learned to imitate
- Ⓓ to imitate other birdcalls and noises

23. Read this sentence.

Wearing a down coat, you are warmed by duck or goose feathers.

What is the simple predicate of the sentence?

- Ⓐ wearing
- Ⓑ warmed
- Ⓒ are warmed
- Ⓓ warmed by

24. Read each sentence. Which sentence provides the most useful information?

- Ⓐ Grebes are aquatic birds.
- Ⓑ Grebes are very capable swimmers but cannot move well on land; consequently, they seldom come ashore.
- Ⓒ Grebes build floating nests.
- Ⓓ They anchor their nests to plants.

25. Read this sentence.

Notice that the grebe by that small island has a baby on its back.

What type of sentence is this?

- Ⓐ declarative
- Ⓑ interrogative
- Ⓒ imperative
- Ⓓ exclamatory

TEST TIP: Don't spend too much time on one item.

Read each item carefully. Fill in the circle next to the best answer.

1. Which of the following sentences is a compound sentence?

Ⓐ Some processes build up Earth's surface, and others break it down.
Ⓑ Volcanism, or volcanic eruptions, builds up the surface of our planet.
Ⓒ Earth's surface is also built up when crustal movements cause warping or buckling.
Ⓓ If you place your hands flat on the edges of a sheet of paper and gently move them toward the middle, you will see a simple form of buckling.

2. Read this sentence.

After a volcano erupts, lava, ash, and cinders add to Earth's surface.

What types of clauses are in the sentence?

Ⓐ The first is an independent clause; the second is dependent.
Ⓑ The first is a dependent clause; the second is independent.
Ⓒ Both are dependent clauses.
Ⓓ Both are independent clauses.

3. Which of the following is a complex sentence?

Ⓐ Some volcanic eruptions are explosive, but others are not.
Ⓑ Cone-shaped volcanoes typically have explosive eruptions.
Ⓒ Mount Vesuvius, which is in Italy, erupted explosively in A.D. 79.
Ⓓ The eruption covered the surrounding lands with many feet of lava, ash, and cinders.

4. Which sentence has an adjective clause underlined?

Ⓐ Gravity is one process <u>that breaks down surface features</u>.
Ⓑ Gravity constantly <u>pulls on a rock overhang</u>.
Ⓒ At some point, the force of gravity will cause <u>the rock overhang to fall</u>.
Ⓓ Loose materials on mountainsides also move downward, <u>particularly after they are disturbed by wind or rain or animal movements</u>.

5. Which sentence has an adverb clause underlined?

Ⓐ Water is a <u>very important cause of change on Earth's surface</u>.
Ⓑ A hard rain can break <u>bits of rock off cliff sides</u>.
Ⓒ <u>After rainfall hits Earth</u>, it carries grains of rock with it.
Ⓓ These tiny bits of rock eventually are carried <u>all the way to the sea</u>.

6. Which of the following sentences has a restrictive clause underlined?

Ⓐ Wildfires, <u>which are becoming more frequent in the western United States</u>, cause changes to the landscape.
Ⓑ Many wild creatures flee; <u>some are unable to escape from the flames</u>.
Ⓒ Vegetation is obliterated, <u>which leaves hillsides barren</u>.
Ⓓ Hills <u>that are bare</u> usually suffer significant erosion during rainstorms.

Name ______________________________

Read each item carefully. Fill in the circle next to the best answer.

7. Which sentence has a gerund phrase underlined?

- Ⓐ Plant roots grow downward into cracks in rocks.
- Ⓑ As plants grow, roots expand and push against rocks.
- Ⓒ People are also contributing to the breakdown of surface materials.
- Ⓓ Hiking up a mountain breaks down rock on the trail.

8. Which of these sentences is in the passive voice?

- Ⓐ Boulders can be broken apart by frost action.
- Ⓑ First, water enters and fills a crack in a boulder.
- Ⓒ The water in the crack freezes and expands.
- Ⓓ The powerful force of that expansion can crack a huge boulder in two.

9. Read this sentence.

Ocean waves erode seaside cliffs over time.

What type of phrase or clause is underlined in this sentence?

- Ⓐ adjective phrase
- Ⓑ adverb phrase
- Ⓒ adjective clause
- Ⓓ adverb clause

10. Read this sentence.

If sea level rises throughout the world, coastal areas will flood more frequently.

What type of phrase or clause is underlined in this sentence?

- Ⓐ adjective phrase
- Ⓑ adverb phrase
- Ⓒ adjective clause
- Ⓓ adverb clause

11. Which of the following sentences shows the relationship between ideas most effectively?

- Ⓐ Wind is another force that causes changes in the landscape; strong winds can pick up loose soil particles and deposit them hundreds of miles away.
- Ⓑ Wind can change the landscape.
- Ⓒ Wind can move loose soil particles long distances.
- Ⓓ Wind can change the landscape by moving loose soil particles.

12. Which of the following sentences is written correctly?

- Ⓐ The study of processes that change Earth's surface.
- Ⓑ I want to learn more about forces that change our Earth's surface, I'm really interested in Earth processes.
- Ⓒ I would study physical geography I might also study geology.
- Ⓓ Physical geography is the study of the lands and waters of Earth; geology involves the study of Earth's structure and surface.

13. Read this sentence.

Powerful are the physical forces of change.

In what order are the words in the sentence?

- Ⓐ natural order
- Ⓑ inverted order
- Ⓒ interrupted order
- Ⓓ None of the above

14. Which of the following sentences is a compound sentence?

- Ⓐ Decomposers are living things that break down dead plants or animals for food.
- Ⓑ These organisms also break down waste produced by plants and animals.
- Ⓒ An earthworm is a decomposer, and so is a banana slug.
- Ⓓ Which are decomposers, algae or fungi?

Read each item carefully. Fill in the circle next to the best answer.

15. Read this sentence.

> Mushrooms are a type of fungi; many kinds of mushrooms grow on dead trees.

What types of clauses are in the sentence?

Ⓐ The first is an independent clause; the second is dependent.
Ⓑ The first is a dependent clause; the second is independent.
Ⓒ Both are dependent clauses.
Ⓓ Both are independent clauses.

16. Which of the following is a complex sentence?

Ⓐ Mushrooms get nourishment from dead trees, and they break it down into bits of organic material.
Ⓑ If fungi did not break down dead plant material, forest soil would likely be less fertile.
Ⓒ Worms also make soil fertile, but most do their work underground.
Ⓓ Most people do not appreciate the important work done by decomposers.

17. Which sentence has an adjective clause underlined?

Ⓐ The planet that we live on spins like a top.
Ⓑ Because Earth spins around once every 24 hours, that is the length of a day.
Ⓒ This spinning motion is called rotation; Earth rotates on its axis.
Ⓓ Earth's axis is an imaginary line running from the North Pole to the South Pole.

18. Which sentence has an adverb clause underlined?

Ⓐ Our planet moves in another way, too: it moves in a circle around the sun.
Ⓑ Planet Earth makes one complete circle every 365¼ days.
Ⓒ People define a year as 365 days, although this is not quite accurate.
Ⓓ To make up for this inaccuracy, we add one day to each fourth year.

19. Which of the following sentences has a nonrestrictive clause underlined?

Ⓐ We use a calendar that is based on the movement of Earth around the sun.
Ⓑ Other peoples have developed calendars that are based on the movement of the moon around Earth.
Ⓒ These calendars, which are known as lunar calendars, have months of 29 or 30 days.
Ⓓ The time from one new moon to the next is the time that a month lasts in the traditional Chinese calendar.

20. Which sentence has a gerund phrase underlined?

Ⓐ The sun appears to move across the sky each day.
Ⓑ The apparent movement of the sun across the sky is the result of Earth's rotation.
Ⓒ Seeing long shadows tells you that the sun is low in the sky.
Ⓓ The sun is low in the sky after dawn and before sunset.

Name ______________________________

Read each item carefully. Fill in the circle next to the best answer.

21. Which of these sentences is in the passive voice?

Ⓐ Most units of time relate to Earth's movements.
Ⓑ Seconds, minutes, and hours represent divisions of the length of one rotation.
Ⓒ Some cultures use the moon's movements to measure units of time.
Ⓓ A lunar calendar is used by several Asian cultures.

22. Read this sentence.

> A number of calendars that make use of lunar months are actually lunisolar calendars: extra months are added to some years to keep the calendar year aligned with the solar year and the seasons.

What type of phrase or clause is underlined in this sentence?

Ⓐ adjective phrase
Ⓑ adverb phrase
Ⓒ adjective clause
Ⓓ adverb clause

23. Which of the following sentences shows the relationship between ideas most effectively?

Ⓐ The Gregorian calendar, a solar calendar, is in use throughout the world today.
Ⓑ Although the Gregorian calendar, a solar calendar, is in use throughout the world today, the dates on which important holidays in many cultures are celebrated are dictated by those cultures' traditional lunar calendars.
Ⓒ The dates on which important holidays in many cultures are celebrated are not the same year after year, because even though those people use the Gregorian calendar, which is a solar calendar, they still use their traditional lunar calendar sometimes.
Ⓓ Important holidays in many cultures are celebrated according to their traditional lunar calendar.

24. Which of the following sentences is written correctly?

Ⓐ The change of seasons, probably the most easily recognizable cycle in nature.
Ⓑ Spring always follows winter, and spring always brings longer, warmer days.
Ⓒ When spring arrives seeds sprout, leaves begin to grow, many plants produce blossoms.
Ⓓ These changes happen every year at about the same time, how difficult life would be if we could not depend on the seasons!

25. Read this sentence.

> In the early days of spring, the hills turn green.

In what order are the words in the sentence?

Ⓐ natural order
Ⓑ inverted order
Ⓒ interrupted order
Ⓓ None of the above

TEST TIP: Eliminate answer choices that you know are incorrect.

Read each item carefully. Fill in the circle next to the best answer.

1. Read this sentence.

Many storytellers specialize in telling tales from a particular culture.

Which of these words is a singular noun in the sentence?

(A) many
(B) storytellers
(C) tales
(D) culture

2. Read this sentence.

Irina moved from Kiev to Oklahoma City; she tells tales from Ukraine.

Which of these words is a common noun in the sentence?

(A) Irina
(B) Kiev
(C) tales
(D) Ukraine

3. Read this sentence:

Our class has several skillful storytellers and comedians, but Irina is the most popular entertainer of all.

Which of these words from this sentence is a collective noun?

(A) class
(B) storytellers
(C) comedians
(D) entertainer

4. Read this sentence.

People of all ages love to listen to ______ tales.

Which of these words would correctly complete the sentence?

(A) Irinas
(B) Irina's
(C) Irinas'
(D) Irinases'

5. Read this sentence.

She is teaching <u>us</u> how to be better storytellers.

What kind of personal pronoun is underlined?

(A) first person
(B) second person
(C) third person singular
(D) third person plural

6. Read this sentence.

I myself practice telling tales in front of a mirror, to make my expressions and gestures more effective.

Which word from the sentence is an intensive pronoun?

(A) I
(B) myself
(C) to
(D) my

7. Read this sentence.

After I tell you my tale, you should tell me ______.

Which of these is the correct pronoun form to use to complete the sentence?

(A) your
(B) you're
(C) yours
(D) your's

Name ____________________

Read each item carefully. Fill in the circle next to the best answer.

8. Read this sentence.

> In my opinion, anyone who practices reading tales expressively can become an effective storyteller.

Which word from the sentence is an indefinite pronoun?

Ⓐ my
Ⓑ anyone
Ⓒ who
Ⓓ become

9. Read this sentence.

> What is the other skill necessary for a person who wants to become a storyteller?

What types of pronouns are *what* and *who* in the sentence?

Ⓐ **what**—interrogative pronoun; **who**—relative pronoun.
Ⓑ **what**—relative pronoun; **who**—interrogative pronoun.
Ⓒ Both **what** and **who** are interrogative pronouns.
Ⓓ Both **what** and **who** are relative pronouns.

10. Read this sentence. Look at the underlined words in it.

> A <u>good</u> storyteller <u>can</u> memorize details <u>quickly</u> and <u>accurately</u>.

Which underlined word in this sentence is an adjective?

Ⓐ good
Ⓑ can
Ⓒ quickly
Ⓓ accurately

11. Read this sentence. Look at the underlined words in it.

> A person <u>who</u> speaks <u>clearly</u> and has a <u>resonant</u> voice can gain the <u>attention</u> of an audience.

Which underlined word in this sentence is an adverb?

Ⓐ who
Ⓑ clearly
Ⓒ resonant
Ⓓ attention

12. Read this sentence.

> I have memorized the two tales in this book, but I haven't memorized any of ______ in that book.

Which of these words would correctly complete the sentence?

Ⓐ this
Ⓑ that
Ⓒ these
Ⓓ those

13. Read this sentence.

> If you were asked to name three, legendary heroes as your favorites, which brave clever characters would you choose?

How should this sentence be rewritten?

Ⓐ If you were asked to name legendary three heroes as your favorites, which clever brave characters would you choose?
Ⓑ If you were asked to name legendary, three heroes as your favorites, which brave clever characters would you choose?
Ⓒ If you were asked to name three legendary heroes as your favorites, which brave, clever characters would you choose?
Ⓓ The sentence should not be rewritten. It is correct as written.

Read each item carefully. Fill in the circle next to the best answer.

14. Read this sentence.

> Theater troupes in many parts of the world present plays based on timeless tales.

Which of these words is a singular noun in the sentence?

Ⓐ troupes
Ⓑ parts
Ⓒ world
Ⓓ plays

15. Read this sentence.

> Mario Lamo, who came from Colombia to California, writes delightful stories.

Which of these choices is a common noun in the sentence?

Ⓐ Mario Lamo
Ⓑ who
Ⓒ Colombia
Ⓓ stories

16. Read this sentence:

> Mario uses a book of folktales, a laptop, a keyboard, and his imagination to create puppet plays.

Which of these words from this sentence is an abstract noun?

Ⓐ book
Ⓑ laptop
Ⓒ keyboard
Ⓓ imagination

17. Read this sentence.

> Some theater troupes read many _______ published tales to find new material.

Which of these words would correctly complete the sentence?

Ⓐ storytellers
Ⓑ storyteller's
Ⓒ storytellers'
Ⓓ storytellerses'

18. Read this sentence.

> A member of a theater troupe read one of Mario's stories, loved it, and contacted <u>him</u>.

What kind of personal pronoun is underlined?

Ⓐ first person
Ⓑ second person
Ⓒ third person singular
Ⓓ third person plural

19. Read this sentence.

> Mario himself gave permission to have his story made into a play, and he gave the troupe suggestions on what changes to make.

Which word from the sentence is an intensive pronoun?

Ⓐ Mario
Ⓑ his
Ⓒ he
Ⓓ himself

Name ___________________________

Read each item carefully. Fill in the circle next to the best answer.

20. Read this sentence.

Mario was excited about the troupe's plan to present ______ story as a puppet play.

Which of these is the correct pronoun form to use to complete the sentence?

Ⓐ him
Ⓑ his
Ⓒ his's
Ⓓ he's

21. Read this sentence.

Not everyone who writes a story wants it performed by puppets.

Which word from the sentence is an indefinite pronoun?

Ⓐ everyone
Ⓑ who
Ⓒ story
Ⓓ it

22. Read this sentence.

Who among you has seen puppets that are ten feet tall?

What types of pronouns are *who* and *that* in the sentence?

Ⓐ **who**—interrogative pronoun; **that**—relative pronoun.
Ⓑ **who**—relative pronoun; **that**—interrogative pronoun.
Ⓒ Both **who** and **that** are interrogative pronouns.
Ⓓ Both **who** and **that** are relative pronouns.

23. Read this sentence. Look at the underlined words in it.

The puppet performance of Mario's story was a huge success: audiences and reviewers praised it enthusiastically.

Which underlined word in the sentence is an adjective?

Ⓐ performance
Ⓑ Mario's
Ⓒ huge
Ⓓ enthusiastically

24. Read this sentence.

______ puppets here are easy to move; those over there are more difficult.

Which of these words would correctly complete the sentence?

Ⓐ This
Ⓑ That
Ⓒ These
Ⓓ Those

25. Read this sentence.

The puppet wearing the bright green cloak is a wise, patient woman who saves her village from a monster.

How should this sentence be rewritten?

Ⓐ The puppet wearing the bright, green cloak is a wise, patient woman who saves her village from a monster.
Ⓑ The puppet wearing the bright green cloak is a wise patient woman who saves her village from a monster.
Ⓒ The puppet wearing the green, bright cloak is a patient wise woman who saves her village from a monster.
Ⓓ The sentence should not be rewritten. It is correct as written.

TEST TIP: Read every choice before deciding on an answer.

Read each item carefully. Fill in the circle next to the best answer.

1. Read these sentences.

> In 1916 the federal government passed the Federal Aid Road Act. Thanks to this law, money for new highways became available to states.

What kinds of verbs are in the sentences?

Ⓐ first sentence—action verb; second sentence—linking verb
Ⓑ first sentence—linking verb; second sentence—action verb
Ⓒ both sentences—action verbs
Ⓓ both sentences—linking verbs

2. Read each sentence. Which sentence has an intransitive verb?

Ⓐ In that era the use of automobiles grew rapidly.
Ⓑ Drivers throughout America wanted better roads.
Ⓒ Local and state officials chose routes for new roads.
Ⓓ Then, with federal money, the states built the new roads.

3. Read this sentence.

> A new form of transportation <u>changes</u> patterns of life.

In what tense is the underlined verb?

Ⓐ past
Ⓑ present
Ⓒ future
Ⓓ None of the above

4. Read this sentence.

> Before the advent of the automobile, most farmers <u>had lived</u> isolated lives.

In what tense is the underlined verb?

Ⓐ past perfect
Ⓑ present perfect
Ⓒ future perfect
Ⓓ None of the above

5. Read this sentence.

> By the 1920s some Americans <u>were commuting</u> from outlying communities to cities each day for work.

In what form is the underlined verb?

Ⓐ past progressive
Ⓑ present progressive
Ⓒ future progressive
Ⓓ None of the above

6. Which sentence has an inappropriate tense shift?

Ⓐ In 1920 less than 2% of America's highways had well-paved surfaces, so driving long distances was difficult.
Ⓑ As autos traveled on dirt roads, they created clouds of dust.
Ⓒ Sharp rocks punctured tires, and flying pebbles smash windshields.
Ⓓ Roads became impassable in rainstorms, when dirt turned to mud.

7. Read this sentence.

> Congress significantly **modified** the federal road law in 1921.

In what mood is the boldfaced verb?

Ⓐ indicative
Ⓑ imperative
Ⓒ subjunctive
Ⓓ It is not in any mood.

Name ______________________________

Read each item carefully. Fill in the circle next to the best answer.

8. Read this sentence.

> I recommend that a modern driver consider how difficult automobile travel was a century ago.

In what mood is the underlined verb?

Ⓐ indicative
Ⓑ imperative
Ⓒ subjunctive
Ⓓ It is not in any mood.

9. Which sentence has an inappropriate mood shift?

Ⓐ Our mechanic insists that my mom use one particular brand of gasoline and brings the car in for an oil change every 5,000 miles.
Ⓑ Our car runs well, and that is important to us.
Ⓒ My mom drives herself and several coworkers to their office every day; car trouble creates serious problems.
Ⓓ Put on an old shirt, grab a sponge, and help me wash this beautiful automobile!

10. Which sentence has an awkward voice shift?

Ⓐ Today America has an extensive network of highways, and that network facilitates the movement of goods.
Ⓑ Prior to the 1920s almost all freight in America was shipped by rail; freight could not be transported by truck efficiently because of the poor condition of most roads.
Ⓒ America needed better roads in 1921, and the new law required states to build them.
Ⓓ All across the country, workers widened, leveled, and smoothed roadbeds, and then the roadbeds were paved by them using huge machines.

11. Read this sentence.

> Although the law required construction of highways connecting states, it did not specify routes.

Which of these words is a subordinating conjunction in the sentence?

Ⓐ although
Ⓑ required
Ⓒ connecting
Ⓓ not

12. Read each sentence. Which sentence has a pair of correlative conjunctions?

Ⓐ Cy Avery of Tulsa, Oklahoma, emerged as a highway specialist.
Ⓑ Avery was not only a successful business owner but also a strong supporter of highway improvement.
Ⓒ Avery was given the task of mapping out what would become the United States Highway System.
Ⓓ He planned a highway route that would connect Chicago with Los Angeles.

13. Read these sentences.

> The first part of Avery's new route ran south from Chicago to St. Louis. That stretch of the route utilized part of an existing highway.

What kinds of verbs are in the sentences?

Ⓐ first sentence—action verb; second sentence—linking verb
Ⓑ first sentence—linking verb; second sentence—action verb
Ⓒ both sentences—action verbs
Ⓓ both sentences—linking verbs

Read each item carefully. Fill in the circle next to the best answer.

14. Read each sentence. Which sentence has an intransitive verb?

Ⓐ The route then ran in a southwestward direction to Oklahoma City.
Ⓑ Avery ran this stretch of the road right past his own service station near Tulsa, Oklahoma.
Ⓒ The next stretch crossed the Texas Panhandle.
Ⓓ It then ascended the mountains of New Mexico and Arizona.

15. Read this sentence.

> The final stretch of the route traversed desert lands in southern California.

In what tense is the underlined verb?

Ⓐ past
Ⓑ present
Ⓒ future
Ⓓ None of the above

16. Read this sentence.

> Some readers will have guessed the identity of this great American road by now.

In what tense is the underlined verb?

Ⓐ past perfect
Ⓑ present perfect
Ⓒ future perfect
Ⓓ None of the above

17. Read this sentence.

> This narrative is telling about Route 66.

In what form is the underlined verb?

Ⓐ past progressive
Ⓑ present progressive
Ⓒ future progressive
Ⓓ None of the above

18. Which sentence has an inappropriate tense shift?

Ⓐ On November 11, 1926, a committee of local and national highway officials met and approved Avery's plan for Route 66.
Ⓑ About 800 miles of the 2,500-mile route were already paved, and more are being prepared for paving at that time.
Ⓒ Cy Avery recommended "The Main Street of America" for the new road's nickname, and the representatives approved it.
Ⓓ Author John Steinbeck later called it "the Mother Road," and that nickname became popular, too.

19. Read this sentence.

> If I were a college student, I would study civil engineering.

In what mood is the underlined verb?

Ⓐ indicative
Ⓑ imperative
Ⓒ subjunctive
Ⓓ It is not in any mood.

20. Read this sentence.

> Imagine being part of a team that designs and constructs highways!

In what mood is the underlined verb?

Ⓐ indicative
Ⓑ imperative
Ⓒ subjunctive
Ⓓ It is not in any mood.

Name ______________________________

Read each item carefully. Fill in the circle next to the best answer.

21. Which sentence has an inappropriate mood shift?

   Ⓐ To prepare yourself for this career, develop your math skills, study hard in science classes, and you should talk with engineers.
   Ⓑ My next-door neighbor is an engineer; he recommends that an engineering student work on construction crews during summer breaks.
   Ⓒ Today's road-building machines are much more powerful than the machines of the 1920s were.
   Ⓓ Although they did not have sophisticated equipment, yesterday's engineers built roads through incredibly challenging terrain.

22. Which sentence has an awkward voice shift?

   Ⓐ Workers built and paved more roads, and drivers experienced fewer mishaps.
   Ⓑ Trucks could travel farther and faster, and so they began to haul more freight.
   Ⓒ More people purchased automobiles, and these autos were used by people for vacation travel as well as everyday transportation.
   Ⓓ Motels and drive-in restaurants sprang up along highways; travelers found them affordable and convenient.

23. Read this sentence.

Many of America's highways passed through scenic areas, but drivers were not always able to enjoy the natural beauty because newly constructed billboards blocked the view.

   Which of these words is a coordinating conjunction in the sentence?

   Ⓐ through
   Ⓑ but
   Ⓒ to
   Ⓓ because

24. Read this sentence.

As workers paved more stretches, representatives from the Route 66 states told the rest of America about the wonderful new highway.

   Which of these words is a subordinating conjunction in the sentence?

   Ⓐ as
   Ⓑ more
   Ⓒ from
   Ⓓ about

25. Read each sentence. Which sentence has a pair of correlative conjunctions?

   Ⓐ Traffic on the new national highway increased rapidly.
   Ⓑ Both business travelers and sightseers used Route 66.
   Ⓒ Singer Nat "King" Cole had a number one hit with a song about Route 66.
   Ⓓ For about 50 years "The Main Street of America" moved motorists back and forth across the West.

TEST TIP: Mark your answers neatly. If you erase, erase completely and clearly without smudging.

Read each item carefully. Fill in the circle next to the best answer.

1. **Which of the following sentences has *your* or *you're* used *incorrectly*?**

   Ⓐ Your new mobile phone is an amazing device!
   Ⓑ I'm surprised at the quality of you're photos.
   Ⓒ You're really good at typing messages on its little keyboard.
   Ⓓ When you're browsing the Internet with your phone, how hard is it to read the pages?

2. **Which of the following sentences has *its* or *it's* used *incorrectly*?**

   Ⓐ It's likely that future cell phones will have additional capabilities.
   Ⓑ I want a phone with GPS as one of its capabilities.
   Ⓒ It's possible that a future phone will have temperature sensors.
   Ⓓ Then it's screen could display the temperature as well as the time.

3. **Read each sentence. Look at the underlined word in it. Which sentence is written *incorrectly*?**

   Ⓐ Jelani thinks that fancy cell phones are <u>to</u> expensive.
   Ⓑ He places calls <u>to</u> family members and friends with his plain old cell phone.
   Ⓒ He says that phone screens are <u>too</u> small to display Web pages.
   Ⓓ He says he doesn't need his cell phone to be an MP3 player because his family already has <u>two</u> of those.

4. **Read this sentence.**

When I was young, our family would usually take _____ 25 pictures during a vacation.

   Which of these choices would correctly complete the sentence?

   Ⓐ less
   Ⓑ fewer
   Ⓒ less than
   Ⓓ fewer than

5. **Read each sentence. Which sentence is written *incorrectly*?**

   Ⓐ Nowadays it's not unusual for our family to take 1000 photos during a vacation.
   Ⓑ It's not difficult to delete the ones that aren't good.
   Ⓒ We don't never upload photos to an Internet photo storage site until we have deleted the bad ones.
   Ⓓ We haven't ever ordered more than 25 prints of any vacation.

6. **Read this sentence.**

In my report on technological gadgets, which I wrote for science class, I discussed several things.

   Which word or words in the sentence do *not* belong in academic writing?

   Ⓐ technological gadgets
   Ⓑ science class
   Ⓒ several
   Ⓓ things

Name ______________________________

Read each item carefully. Fill in the circle next to the best answer.

7. **Read each sentence. Look at the underlined word in it. Which sentence is written *incorrectly*?**

   Ⓐ Our new big-screen TV sets on a strong table.
   Ⓑ It took two of us to raise it from the floor.
   Ⓒ We set it carefully on the table.
   Ⓓ When I sit in the big blue chair, I can see the picture clearly.

8. **Read each sentence. Look at the underlined word in it. Which sentence is written *incorrectly*?**

   Ⓐ My grandfather built the table we are using for the big-screen TV.
   Ⓑ The table has always held heavy things well, because it's so sturdy.
   Ⓒ Grandfather maked a cabinet for the cable box, too.
   Ⓓ We have found that low-tech skills like his make living with high-tech equipment more pleasant.

9. **Read each sentence. Look at the underlined word in it. Which sentence is written *incorrectly*?**

   Ⓐ If you want to get a good job in a high-tech company, you should persevere in your math studies.
   Ⓑ Most people who devise high-tech methods use math in the process.
   Ⓒ Many high-tech jobs involve fiscal management; companies have to be careful with their money!
   Ⓓ Accounts payable departments disperse money only for invoices with purchase order numbers.

10. **Read each sentence. Look at the underlined word(s) in it. Which sentence is written *incorrectly*?**

   Ⓐ Meg and Heather went to a high-tech job fair.
   Ⓑ Meg was all, "I'm not leaving until I get a job offer!"
   Ⓒ Heather replied, "If I don't find a job that I think I will like, I'm not signing anything."
   Ⓓ "How do you know what a job will be like until you start it?" asked Meg.

11. **Read each sentence. Look at the underlined word in it. Which sentence is written *incorrectly*?**

   Ⓐ Jacob has discovered that he really enjoys physics.
   Ⓑ He has already taken the only physics course his high school offers.
   Ⓒ Jacob's counselor has suggested to Jacob that he take a free physics MOOC.
   Ⓓ Jacob he is very excited to take a course taught by a famous physicist.

12. **Read each sentence. Which sentence contains words that are unnecessary and should be eliminated?**

   Ⓐ For those of you who don't already know, MOOC stands for massive open online course.
   Ⓑ Many universities now offer MOOCs for free.
   Ⓒ Students typically do not receive academic credit.
   Ⓓ For students willing to work hard, MOOCs offer a chance to learn from top-level instructors.

13. **Which of the following sentences has *there, they're,* or *their* used *incorrectly*?**

   Ⓐ A list of upcoming physics MOOCs is posted over there.
   Ⓑ The courses are challenging, but their likely to be fascinating.
   Ⓒ Prospective astronomers may want to expand their knowledge by taking "Dark Matter in Galaxies."
   Ⓓ More and more professors are planning MOOCs; they're excited to be able to offer large numbers of people the opportunity to learn about important topics.

Read each item carefully. Fill in the circle next to the best answer.

14. Which of the following sentences has *your* or *you're* used *incorrectly*?

Ⓐ Your a big music fan, aren't you?
Ⓑ Would you like to play the solos your favorite guitarist plays?
Ⓒ If so, you're someone who might enjoy learning to play a real guitar.
Ⓓ You're also a prospective customer for a certain type of video game.

15. Which of the following sentences has *its* or *it's* used *incorrectly*?

Ⓐ It's amazingly easy to play great guitar solos using that video game.
Ⓑ That certainly explains its popularity.
Ⓒ Its not easy to train your brain and fingers to play a real guitar well.
Ⓓ If guitar games continue to improve, it's possible that fewer people will take time to learn to play the real instrument.

16. Read each sentence. Look at the underlined word in it. Which sentence is written *incorrectly*?

Ⓐ I am talking <u>to</u> my friend Miriam in Kenya.
Ⓑ She lives in a village that is <u>two</u> hundred miles from Nairobi.
Ⓒ You might think such a village would be <u>too</u> remote for the use of cell phones.
Ⓓ Many remote villages are linked <u>too</u> the rest of the world by cell phones.

17. Read this sentence.

> According to the electronic scale, the weight of my suitcases is ______ the limit.

Which of these choices would correctly complete the sentence?

Ⓐ over
Ⓑ more
Ⓒ more than
Ⓓ None of the above

18. Read each sentence. Which sentence is written *incorrectly*?

Ⓐ Cell phone use is not allowed during an airline flight.
Ⓑ My friend wasn't paying attention when the announcement about cell phones was made.
Ⓒ Although he didn't hear the announcement, I did.
Ⓓ I told him to turn off his phone, because I didn't want it to cause no problems.

19. Read this sentence.

> Modern automobiles have stuff that makes them safer and more efficient to drive.

Which word or words in the sentence do *not* belong in academic writing?

Ⓐ modern
Ⓑ stuff
Ⓒ safer
Ⓓ more efficient

Name ______________________________

Read each item carefully. Fill in the circle next to the best answer.

20. Read each sentence. Look at the underlined word in it. Which sentence is written *incorrectly*?

Ⓐ Computers rise the efficiency of automobile engines.
Ⓑ You can set a desired speed, and cruise control will maintain the speed automatically.
Ⓒ When you sit in a front seat, a computer senses your presence and warns you to buckle up via an alarm.
Ⓓ If you fasten your seat belt or rise from the seat, the alarm stops.

21. Read each sentence. Look at the underlined word in it. Which sentence is written *incorrectly*?

Ⓐ My parents took me with them to a new car dealership.
Ⓑ We seen a car with a rear-view camera.
Ⓒ It showed on a small screen what was behind the car.
Ⓓ Will this device cut the number of accidents that occur when drivers go in reverse?

22. Read each sentence. Look at the underlined word in it. Which sentence is written *incorrectly*?

Ⓐ Shopping on the Internet is like visiting a great bazaar.
Ⓑ You can find pillows that compliment the color of your couch.
Ⓒ You can design your own stationery and have it printed and sent to you very quickly.
Ⓓ You can find items cheaper on the Internet than at local stores.

23. Read each sentence. Look at the underlined word in it. Which sentence is written *incorrectly*?

Ⓐ Lily went, "The Internet is a great homework helper."
Ⓑ "My assignments are all posted on our school's website," she continued.
Ⓒ Estrella said that she goes to the library as often as she goes online for information.
Ⓓ "I like doing research in the library more than on the Internet," she added.

24. Read each sentence. Look at the underlined word in it. Which sentence is written *incorrectly*?

Ⓐ Rita and Jackie they love to visit travel websites.
Ⓑ Although they cannot afford to travel to far-off places now, they dream of doing so someday.
Ⓒ The travel sites let them see fascinating buildings and breathtaking landscapes.
Ⓓ Both of them have long lists of countries they hope to visit.

25. Read this sentence.

> Rita and Jackie have discovered websites that enable travelers to find the most economical airline flights at the lowest cost, discover reasonably priced hotels in good locations, and buy specially priced train and bus passes in advance.

Which words in this sentence are unnecessary and should be eliminated?

Ⓐ that enable travelers
Ⓑ at the lowest cost
Ⓒ in good locations
Ⓓ in advance

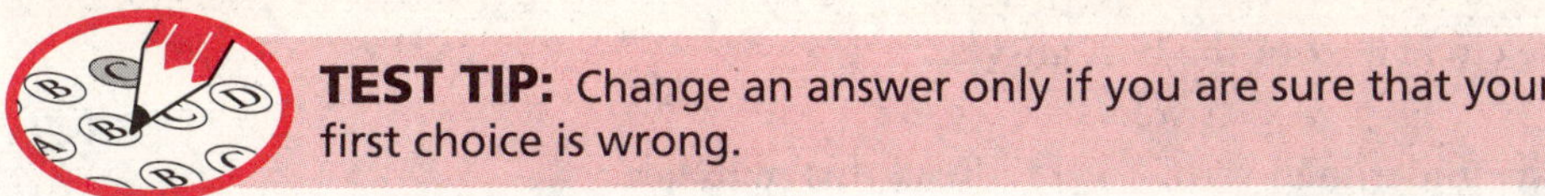

Read each item carefully. Fill in the circle next to the best answer.

1. Read this sentence.

Those of us who love fishing have learned to analyze rivers.

Which word in the sentence is an object pronoun?

Ⓐ those
Ⓑ us
Ⓒ who
Ⓓ None of the above

2. Read each sentence. Which sentence is written *incorrectly*?

Ⓐ My sister and me have learned to read rivers.
Ⓑ The ripples on a river's surface tell her and me about the location of the main channel.
Ⓒ When she and I are in a canoe on a river, we know where to steer.
Ⓓ We and our parents go fishing every year.

3. Read this sentence.

My dad caught a salmon and had to work hard to reel it into the boat.

Which is the antecedent for the underlined pronoun?

Ⓐ year
Ⓑ dad
Ⓒ salmon
Ⓓ boat

4. Each of these sentences is from the same paragraph. Read each sentence, and look at the underlined word. Which sentence is written *incorrectly*?

Ⓐ How does a stream biologist prepare herself to conduct a research project?
Ⓑ First, she selects a stream and uses what she knows about it to establish a hypothesis.
Ⓒ For example, she might hypothesize that a stream is polluted.
Ⓓ You would then spend time researching what is already known about the stream.

5. Read each sentence. Look at the underlined word. Which sentence has a pronoun that does *not* have a clear antecedent?

Ⓐ Robert's cousin, Dr. Robin Lynn, is a stream biologist; he invited her to speak at his school.
Ⓑ Robert and other interested students listened to Dr. Lynn talk about her stream studies, and they asked her some good questions.
Ⓒ After the talk, they walked to a nearby creek.
Ⓓ The students stood by the creek as Robert demonstrated techniques for collecting water samples from it.

6. Read each sentence. Look at the underlined word. Which sentence is *not* correct?

Ⓐ Who has observed a waterfall?
Ⓑ I met a photographer who has photographed more than 100 waterfalls.
Ⓒ To who is she sending that photo?
Ⓓ My aunt is the person with whom I traveled to Niagara Falls.

7. Read each sentence. Look at the underlined verb. Which sentence is *not* correct?

Ⓐ A river in the mountains runs swiftly.
Ⓑ The slope of its bed is generally fairly steep.
Ⓒ When a river flowing through mountains reach a cliff, a waterfall results.
Ⓓ A waterfall on the plains is a relatively rare sight.

Name ____________________

Read each item carefully. Fill in the circle next to the best answer.

8. Read each sentence. Look at the underlined verb. Which sentence is *not* correct?

Ⓐ Neither Kansas nor Nebraska have many waterfalls.
Ⓑ Washington and the other Pacific states have many dramatic waterfalls.
Ⓒ At the bottom of a waterfall, binoculars or a camera lens becomes wet from the mist.
Ⓓ Spray or bubbles are fascinating to watch.

9. Read each sentence. Look at the underlined verb. Which sentence is *not* correct?

Ⓐ Everyone in these canyons fear floods.
Ⓑ All of us know how high the river can get.
Ⓒ Anyone whose cabin has been flooded prepares for flood season.
Ⓓ "Tips for Avoiding Flood Damage" is a helpful pamphlet.

10. Read each sentence. Which sentence is *not* correct because of a dangling or misplaced modifier?

Ⓐ Fearing damage from spring floods, we remove items from our cabin in the fall.
Ⓑ Checking weather reports regularly, we know when floods are likely to occur.
Ⓒ Hearing a prediction of heavy rains last week, we drove to our cabin.
Ⓓ Loading up the car with furniture, the flood did little damage to our cabin.

11. Read this sentence.

What is the _____ river you have ever swum in?

Which choice would complete the sentence correctly?

Ⓐ colder
Ⓑ more cold
Ⓒ coldest
Ⓓ most cold

12. Read this sentence.

I actually have never swum in a really cold river.

Which word in the sentence is an auxiliary verb?

Ⓐ actually
Ⓑ have
Ⓒ never
Ⓓ swum

13. Read this sentence.

Ricardo has measured the temperature of this river, and now he must decide whether to swim in it.

Which word in this sentence is a modal auxiliary?

Ⓐ has
Ⓑ must
Ⓒ to
Ⓓ swim

Read each item carefully. Fill in the circle next to the best answer.

14. Read this sentence.

> My friend Lesley quizzed me about rivers, and I answered most questions correctly.

Which word in the sentence is an object pronoun?

Ⓐ my
Ⓑ me
Ⓒ I
Ⓓ most

15. Read each sentence. Which sentence is written *incorrectly*?

Ⓐ Then she and I switched roles, and I asked her questions.
Ⓑ She also did well, so her and me felt well prepared for the geography test.
Ⓒ Billy and she answered all the test questions correctly.
Ⓓ They were trailed closely by Njoki and me; we each missed only one question.

16. Read these sentences.

> What is the largest river in Africa that empties into the Atlantic Ocean? It is the Congo River, which drains the Congo Basin.

Which is the antecedent for the underlined pronoun?

Ⓐ river
Ⓑ Africa
Ⓒ Atlantic Ocean
Ⓓ Congo Basin

17. Each of these sentences is from the same paragraph. Read each sentence. Look at the underlined word in it. Which sentence is written *incorrectly*?

Ⓐ You can access satellite images to learn about rivers far from where you live.
Ⓑ Imagine that you want to learn about South America's Orinoco River.
Ⓒ We can find satellite images of it on websites such as zonu.com.
Ⓓ You will notice that NASA is the source of many satellite images of rivers.

18. Read each sentence. Look at the underlined word. Which sentence has a pronoun that does *not* have a clear antecedent?

Ⓐ Christopher Columbus made Europeans aware of the mouth of the Orinoco after he viewed it at the end of the 15th century.
Ⓑ The source of this long river was not identified until 1951, more than 450 years after Columbus visited it.
Ⓒ They found its origin at a spot along the border between Venezuela and Brazil.
Ⓓ From its origin, the Orinoco flows northward into the center of Venezuela, and then curves toward the east, eventually reaching the Atlantic near the Guyana border.

19. Read each sentence. Look at the underlined word. Which sentence is *not* correct?

Ⓐ Who can name a song about the Mississippi River?
Ⓑ To whom are you listening on your MP3 player?
Ⓒ I am listening to Johnny Cash; he's the singer from who I learned "Big River."
Ⓓ Was Jimmie Rodgers the musician who wrote "Miss the Mississippi and You"?

Name ________________________________

Read each item carefully. Fill in the circle next to the best answer.

20. Read each sentence. Look at the underlined verb. Which sentence is *not* correct?

Ⓐ Rivers in the Midwest <u>are</u> the subjects of many songs.
Ⓑ This song from pioneer days <u>has</u> the Ohio River as its setting.
Ⓒ Several songs by songwriters from Texas <u>mentions</u> rivers in the Lone Star State.
Ⓓ A song by Stephen Foster, one of America's best-loved songwriters, <u>celebrates</u> the Suwannee River, which flows through Georgia and Florida.

21. Read each sentence. Look at the underlined verb. Which sentence is *not* correct?

Ⓐ Neither the Colorado River nor the Rio Grande <u>is</u> as long as the Yukon River.
Ⓑ Canada's Yukon Territory and the state of Alaska <u>are</u> crossed by the mighty Yukon.
Ⓒ The Missouri River and the Mississippi River <u>are</u> each longer than the Yukon.
Ⓓ The Hudson River or the Delaware River <u>are</u> where my aunt will go to kayak this year.

22. Read each sentence. Look at the underlined verb. Which sentence is *not* correct?

Ⓐ Almost everyone in the United Kingdom <u>knows</u> the location of the Thames River.
Ⓑ Anyone who has visited the west coast of Ireland <u>has</u> an idea of where the river Shannon is.
Ⓒ *Great Rivers of the British Isles* <u>have</u> information about these and other major rivers.
Ⓓ Several of us <u>are</u> planning a summer trip to the U.K.

23. Read each sentence. Which sentence is *not* correct because of a dangling or misplaced modifier?

Ⓐ Seeking shade from the desert sun, we were hiking in a dry desert canyon.
Ⓑ Hearing thunder in the distance, we quickly climbed up to high ground.
Ⓒ Sitting in a safe place, a torrent of water flooded the canyon.
Ⓓ Watching the flash flood, we were very thankful that we had heeded the thunder's warning.

24. Read this sentence.

The great rivers in Siberia are ______ than those in almost any other region.

Which choice would complete the sentence correctly?

Ⓐ longer
Ⓑ more long
Ⓒ longest
Ⓓ most long

25. Read this sentence.

Have you ever heard of the Ob, the Yenisey, or the Lena?

Which word in the sentence is an auxiliary verb?

Ⓐ have
Ⓑ you
Ⓒ ever
Ⓓ heard

Lesson 1 **Circle the complete subject in each sentence. Underline the complete predicate.**

1. I am taking swimming classes.
2. Classes are held every Friday after school.
3. This class will make me a stronger swimmer.
4. My blue swimsuit has big white polka dots on it.
5. The temperature of the pool is usually very warm.
6. My goggles provide protection from the chemicals in the pool water.
7. My swimming teacher demonstrated the backstroke for the first time last Friday.
8. Most of that class time was spent on the mechanics of the stroke.
9. A new stroke can be challenging.
10. I noticed my improvement after each lap.
11. The other students in the class are developing their swimming skills, too.
12. A group of us calls ourselves "the sharks."
13. My teacher often uses a stopwatch to time us.
14. My muscles feel sore sometimes after a long class.
15. Hard work is making me a better swimmer.

Lesson 2 **Circle the simple subject in each sentence. If the subject is understood *you*, write *yo* on the line. Underline the simple predicate.**

1. A visit to the library is always an adventure. _____
2. The library is a great destination for after school. _____
3. Be quiet! _____
4. Tall shelves full of so many books can intimidate a visitor. _____
5. A patron can find mystery, science fiction, and nonfiction books. _____
6. Some libraries have DVDs and comic books, too. _____
7. A special section for teens exists at some libraries. _____
8. Ask a librarian for a book recommendation. _____
9. Tell the librarian about your favorite book. _____
10. Some of the most popular books might be temporarily unavailable. ____
11. Other patrons may have borrowed them. _____
12. Search the shelves for other interesting books. _____
13. Reference librarians can help with any research project. _____
14. A library card is a passport to the world of knowledge. _____
15. Enjoy your books! _____

Extra Practice

Name ______________________________

Lesson 3 Each sentence has a compound subject or a compound predicate. Circle the two or three simple subjects that make up each compound subject. Underline the two verbs that make up each compound predicate.

1. Brittany, Kevin, and I went ice-skating on Saturday.
2. The Polar Bears and the Walruses were finishing their hockey game.
3. We watched the end of the game and huddled together for warmth.
4. Then we laced our skates and stepped onto the ice.
5. I slipped on the ice and fell.
6. The ice was cold and soaked my clothes.
7. Kevin and Brittany helped me back onto my feet.
8. I gripped the ice rink wall and steadied myself.
9. My friends and I skated in large circles around the ice rink.
10. Kevin skated backward and impressed us with other fancy moves.
11. Brittany and Kevin suggested some hot chocolate as a treat.
12. I carefully hopped off the ice and followed my friends to the cafeteria.
13. The ice sweeper drove onto the ice and smoothed its surface.
14. Loud music blared from speakers and beckoned us back onto the ice.
15. We were tired but skated until closing time.

Lesson 4 Circle each direct object in each sentence. If the sentence contains an indirect object, underline it.

1. Hank wags his tail impatiently.
2. Roger walks him every day after school.
3. Today Roger is taking Hank to a park several blocks away.
4. Well-behaved Hank puts his leash in his mouth.
5. Scents along the way distract Hank.
6. He sniffs every shrub, tree, and rock enthusiastically.
7. A mother with a stroller approaches Hank and Roger cautiously.
8. Hank's large size intimidates most people and even other dogs.
9. Nobody has any reason for fear, in Roger's opinion.
10. Roger tells the mother stories about sweet Hank.
11. She finally allows her child out of his stroller.
12. The happy child pets Hank lovingly.
13. Hank thoroughly enjoys this attention from the child.
14. Roger has taught Hank some tricks.
15. Roger gives Hank a treat and a pat on the head after each trick.

Lesson 5 **Underline each predicate noun and predicate adjective in the sentences below. Write *PN* after each sentence with a predicate noun. Write *PA* after each sentence with a predicate adjective. Circle the linking verb in each sentence.**

1. Paul is late for a movie date on his birthday. __________
2. Paul's friends are worried about his late arrival. __________
3. Movie previews are a well-known interest of Paul's. __________
4. His friends are generous with praise for the previews. __________
5. He feels sad about his tardiness. __________
6. The audience for the evening's feature film is mostly teenagers. __________
7. A comic book superhero is the subject of the movie. __________
8. Suddenly the theater speakers become fountains of noise. __________
9. An enormous beetle becomes the center of attention on the screen. __________
10. The beetle becomes a black-caped superhero in the blink of an eye. __________
11. The superhero is beloved throughout the city. __________
12. The ending of the movie is a shock. __________
13. Paul and his friends are hungry for birthday cake after the movie. __________
14. The beetle-shaped chocolate cake is the best after-movie treat ever. __________
15. The birthday present from his friends is a superhero poster! __________

Lesson 6 **Underline each prepositional phrase. Circle the preposition that begins each phrase. Draw a box around the object of the preposition. There may be more than one prepositional phrase in a sentence.**

1. I ride my bike through a forest to my grandmother's house.
2. My grandmother lives in a small cottage with her dog.
3. The trees in the forest are very thick above my head.
4. The sun does not show through their branches.
5. Moss grows on the trees and hangs from the branches.
6. At the river, I must bike across a narrow bridge.
7. The fish in the river glide through the water.
8. The road runs along the river bank for almost a mile.
9. At the forest edge, I turn left on another road.
10. This new road takes me through an apple orchard and up a small hill.
11. After my bike ride, I will run with my grandmother's dog.
12. Finally my grandmother's house comes into view.
13. I pedal faster toward the gate and don't skid to a stop until the last second.
14. I lean against the heavy gate and then step into the garden.
15. My grandmother opens the front door and greets me with a big hug.

Name ____

Lesson 7 **Underline the appositive phrase in each sentence.**

1. Mike, a student who had a report due the next day, was panicking.
2. His computer, a usually dependable machine, had suddenly locked up.
3. Scary buzzing sounds, ones that made him fear a crash, were coming from the computer.
4. After Mike restarted it, the computer made reassuring noises, normal warm-up sounds.
5. However, Mike's report, a nearly finished assignment, had disappeared.
6. The research report, a ten-page paper on the pyramids of Egypt, had taken him all week to write.
7. What was Mike, a worrywart by nature, going to do now?
8. Ms. Spiker, his teacher, never accepted late homework.
9. Then the doorbell rang, and Mike saw Melissa, his neighbor, on the front stoop.
10. She had already finished her homework, a report on the Colosseum in Rome.
11. Mike told Melissa, a computer whiz, about his lost pyramid report.
12. She went to the computer table, a place messy beyond belief, and looked at the computer.
13. She spotted an earlier draft of the paper, a copy decorated with scribbled edits.
14. Mike, a hopelessly slow typist, was still frantic.
15. Melissa, a quick thinker, decided that the task would go faster if she read aloud while Mike typed.

Lesson 8 **Underline the participial phrase in each sentence. Circle the participle.**

1. Running through the house, Lucy grabbed her lunch and her backpack.
2. The front door slammed behind her, making a noise like a small explosion.
3. She glanced at her watch, knowing she would only see bad news.
4. Discovering she was disastrously late, Lucy picked up the pace.
5. Rounding the corner, she saw the taillights of her bus.
6. She ran with all her might, powered by fear of tardiness.
7. Called "Dasher" by her track coach, Lucy was a champion sprinter.
8. Seeing a green light change to yellow, Lucy slowed her pace.
9. Watching the same light, the bus driver accelerated.
10. The bus sailed through the intersection, leaving Lucy behind.
11. Frustrated by the experience, she nervously checked her watch again.
12. She waited impatiently for the next bus, breathing fast from her run.
13. Standing on her tiptoes, Lucy saw another bus on its way toward her.
14. Stepping off the bus in front of school, Lucy heard the clang of the warning bell.
15. Thrilled with her on-time arrival, Lucy gave herself a pat on the backpack.

Lesson 9 **Underline the infinitive phrase in each sentence.**

1. A gardener has just gone to the nursery to select new plants for her garden.
2. She puts on gardening gloves to protect her hands from thorns.
3. She has many thorny bushes to rip out.
4. The bushes were just thick enough to be home to small critters.
5. Some insects poke their heads out to see what is going on.
6. Certain insects are necessary to keep a garden healthy.
7. The gardener clears the garden of weeds to make room for her new plants.
8. She mixes fertilizer into the soil to add nutrients.
9. The gardener prepares to plant a small apple tree.
10. She uses a shovel to dig a hole.
11. To stabilize the tree in the hole, she puts earth back around the base.
12. The gardener brings the hose closer to water the newly planted tree.
13. Sunshine and water are needed to make the tree grow.
14. Someday the tree will provide shade to protect garden visitors from the sun.
15. In future years, the gardener will pick the tree's apples to make jams and pies.

Lesson 10 **Draw one line under the simple subject in each sentence. Draw two lines under the simple predicate. Circle each participial phrase. Draw a box around each infinitive phrase.**

1. My sisters traveled to the desert to see the stars.
2. Gazing at the night sky, they became silent.
3. Countless points of light twinkled, creating an unforgettable sight.
4. To get the best view, the girls had hiked to the highest point around.
5. In the city, we see far fewer stars twinkling above.
6. To stargaze properly, you must go to a place far from city lights.
7. The bright desert stars seemed to be out just for my sisters.
8. The temperature dropped dramatically, chilling the girls thoroughly.
9. Setting up camp earlier, they had been assaulted by the hot sun.
10. Desert nights tend to be quite cold.
11. The girls were happy to wrap themselves in more blankets.
12. The girls began to invent new constellations.
13. Soon they became too sleepy to continue the game.
14. Packed together for warmth inside the tent, all three girls soon were asleep.
15. Yipping mournfully, a coyote bid them good night.

Name ____

Lesson 11 **Combine the information in each group of sentences to write one sentence.**

1. The platypus is a mammal. It can be found in Australia. It also lives in Tasmania. It is a very strange-looking animal. ______________________________

2. The male platypus has a spur on its hind foot. This spur contains poison. This poison can hurt people and animals. Most people don't know this about the platypus. ______________________________

   ____

3. The platypus is covered in fur. The fur is dense and dark brown. The thick fur traps heat. This phenomenon keeps the platypus warm. ______________________________

   ____

4. The platypus is a good swimmer. It lives near streams. It is in the water most of the day swimming and looking for food. It eats worms, shrimp, and crayfish. ______________________________

   ____

5. People used to hunt the platypus. They wanted it for its fur. The platypus is now protected. There are laws that prohibit hunting the platypus. ______________________________

   ____

Lesson 12 **Add the correct punctuation mark to each sentence. Then label each sentence *declarative, interrogative, imperative,* or *exclamatory.***

1. Would you like to see a movie with me ______________
2. Yes, that would be fun ______________
3. Find out what is playing ______________
4. What kinds of movies do you like ______________
5. I like animated movies the best ______________
6. Animated movies are so childish ______________
7. Could we see a comedy instead ______________
8. Sure, I like comedies, too ______________
9. Let me use your computer to look up movie times ______________
10. Here's a good comedy that starts in 30 minutes ______________
11. Do you think we can make it ______________
12. We can if we leave right now ______________
13. Slow down or we'll be in an accident ______________
14. Wow, what a long line ______________
15. It has to be a good movie if so many people are waiting to see it ______________

Lesson 13 **Write *S* next to each simple sentence and *CD* next to each compound sentence. Circle the comma and conjunction or the semicolon in each compound sentence.**

1. Emily is enjoying a summer day at the beach. _______
2. Hearing waves crash onto the shore is soothing, and watching them is mesmerizing. _______
3. The sand is warm from the sun, and Emily feels warm, too. _______
4. She takes out her sandwich; she has also packed a book. _______
5. What a perfect lazy day it is! _______
6. A toddler waddles toward Emily, and she smiles at him. _______
7. He wobbles, but he catches himself. _______
8. He seems keenly interested in Emily. _______
9. She smiles and says hello. _______
10. The wobbly toddler is startled, and he runs toward his parents. _______
11. Emily waves good-bye, and then she turns back to watch the waves. _______
12. The beach is not always this sunny and pleasant. _______
13. Clouds block the sun, and a cold wind blows on many days. _______
14. The wind can kick up the sand, and a visitor can be freezing cold even with a parka on. _______
15. Emily finishes her sandwich and opens her book. _______

Lesson 14 **Draw one line under each independent clause and two lines under each dependent clause. Circle the subordinating conjunction that begins each dependent clause.**

1. After I pulled on my rain boots, I stepped outside.
2. I take long walks when it rains.
3. Although most people avoid the rain, it's wonderful to me.
4. Though I like the rain, I do not like water inside my shoes.
5. When that happens, my socks get wet and chill my feet.
6. I wear my rain boots because they prevent that.
7. The sky becomes dark before a rainstorm begins.
8. My town looks very different when rain pours down.
9. It looks different because not many people come out.
10. They stay indoors until the rain stops.
11. While I walk, my imagination takes me to a new town.
12. I explore it as I listen to the rain.
13. When I return home, I notice a slug on the front step.
14. Although some animals avoid the rain, others move about in it.
15. When I remove my boots, I find two warm and dry feet.

Extra Practice

Name ____________________

Lesson 15 **Write *CD* next to each compound sentence and *CX* next to each complex sentence. Write *CCX* next to each compound-complex sentence.**

1. When her parents announced a plan for a family camping trip, Gloria groaned. ________
2. Her parents and her younger brother were excited, but Gloria did not feel that way at all. ________
3. This year the family would camp for a whole week; they usually went for just a few days. ________
4. When they had camped in the hills last year, a bee had stung Gloria. ________
5. The sting had hurt, and the site had swelled up because she is allergic to bee stings. ________
6. It had been on her cheek, and it had itched and throbbed even though she put lotion on it. ________
7. When she thought about camping, Gloria could only think of that sting. ________
8. Her parents were sympathetic, but they wanted her with the family. ________
9. When they expressed their feelings to Gloria, she began to think of all the fun she had last year. ________
10. They had lounged in the sun, and they had told stories by candlelight while stars twinkled above. ________
11. She had ridden bikes with her brother, and they had explored all around the lake. ________
12. She had made s'mores with her favorite kind of chocolate, and she had swum in the creek. ________
13. Cooking outside had been fun, and she had enjoyed bird songs in the mornings. ________
14. As she thought about these events, Gloria had a change of heart; maybe camping wasn't so bad. ________
15. If there were morning birdsongs and s'mores ahead, Gloria was ready to go. ________

Lesson 16 **Underline the adjective clause in each sentence. Circle the noun it describes. Draw a box around the relative pronoun or the relative adverb that begins the clause.**

1. Larry, who is a strong, quick player, passed the ball to Mike.
2. Mike caught the pass right at the moment when it seemed it would zip past him.
3. The two were practicing for the championship tournament, which their school had never reached before.
4. The team had a great record during a season when other local teams had faltered.
5. Mike fired a shot that touched nothing but net.
6. The few students who were still sitting in the bleachers cheered loudly.
7. Larry and Mike had stayed after practice, which had ended at 5 p.m.
8. Their coach had given them permission; there was no reason why they shouldn't practice a bit more.
9. They had until 6 p.m., which was minutes away.
10. Mike lofted a jump shot, which swished through the net.
11. Suddenly the gym, which had been brightly lit, was plunged into darkness.
12. Larry, whose sense of humor was well known, complimented Mike on his "lights-out" shooting.
13. The students who were still in the stands groaned.
14. Suddenly a flashlight beam appeared in the corner where the coach had his office.
15. The coach walked the students out to a bus stop where they could catch a ride home.

Lesson 17 **Underline the adverb clause in each sentence. Draw a box around the subordinating conjunction that begins the clause.**

1. Because Clarissa hopes to become an elite gymnast, she works hard in her gymnastic classes.
2. She goes to class three times a week after she finishes school.
3. When the final bell rings, she always feels a surge of energy.
4. Clarissa stretches before she practices any of her moves.
5. Her favorite event is the balance beam, while her least favorite is the horse.
6. Before the gymnasts begin the rings, the coach describes the workout for the day.
7. The rings are hard for many gymnasts because they require much strength.
8. Although the rings are still difficult for her, Clarissa feels stronger as a result of so much practice.
9. After everyone has had a turn on the rings, the gymnasts move to the uneven bars.
10. As Clarissa twirls around the high bar, she mentally prepares for the dismount.
11. Now Clarissa is excited because it is time for the balance beam.
12. When it is her turn, she executes two perfect somersaults on the balance beam.
13. Something terrible happens when Clarissa begins her work on the horse.
14. When she runs and leaps, she overshoots the horse and falls onto the mat.
15. Although she is a bit sore and embarrassed, she quickly lines up for another try.

Lesson 18 **Read each sentence. Draw a line under the dependent clause and circle the noun it modifies. Write *RC* if it is a restrictive clause and *NC* if it is a nonrestrictive clause.**

1. The woman who runs this tennis camp is my mother's oldest friend. _______
2. She coaches tennis at the local college, which is known for its excellent team. _______
3. There was a time when she played professionally all over the world. _______
4. But playing competitive tennis, which can be grueling, was not for her. _______
5. She hopes this camp will instill in students the love for tennis that she has always had. _______
6. My mother, who also plays tennis, signed me up immediately. _______
7. I'll likely enjoy playing this sport, which I have watched on television for years. _______
8. Do you have any relatives who have played tennis in the past? _______
9. My mother will probably give me some tips that will help me improve as well. _______
10. The camp used to be held on the courts where the college students play. _______
11. Now we will meet at the city courts, which are not kept up as well. _______
12. I will be using an older racquet that my mother loaned to me. _______
13. I will purchase my own racquet at a time when I have more money. _______
14. The coach, who can seem rather strict at times, is a very caring teacher. _______
15. This camp will be a great experience that we won't soon forget. _______

Name ____

Lesson 19 **Underline each gerund phrase. Draw a box around the gerund.**

1. Building a gingerbread house is a lot of work.
2. Mixing all the ingredients of the gingerbread batter is the first step.
3. Next comes pouring the batter into large, flat pans.
4. Baking the gingerbread is the easiest part of the process.
5. Smelling the delicious scent of the spices is a treat.
6. While the gingerbread cools, sneaking a piece is not allowed!
7. The walls and roof of the house are made by cutting the hard, flat bread into rectangles.
8. A special icing is used for gluing the walls and candy pieces together.
9. Spreading icing along the edges of the walls and roof is the next step.
10. The job of putting the house together requires skill and patience.
11. Collecting all the candy pieces is the best part.
12. Attaching the candy pieces onto the gingerbread house is also a lot of fun.
13. The hardest part is making all the candy pieces stick.
14. Standing back for a better view of the finished house is a satisfying experience.
15. Creating something from scratch can be very rewarding.

Lesson 20 **Write *A* if the verb in the sentence is in the active voice. Write *P* if the verb in the sentence is in the passive voice.**

1. Alex was being followed. _______
2. He sensed it. _______
3. He swiftly turned around. _______
4. A dog stopped in its tracks. _______
5. The dog was surprised by Alex's sudden movement. _______
6. Alex and the dog stared at each other. _______
7. Neither of them moved. _______
8. Then the dog cocked its head in a quizzical gesture. _______
9. Why was Alex being followed by this dog? _______
10. A friendly little whine was produced by the dog. _______
11. Alex interpreted the sound as a plea for food. _______
12. The next day a dog treat was packed in Alex's backpack by his mother. _______
13. The treat would be given to the dog by Alex. _______
14. On his walk home from school, Alex saw the dog up ahead. _______
15. This time the dog was being followed by Alex. _______

Lesson 21 **Look at the boldfaced group of words in each sentence. Underline the word or words it modifies. Then write *PH* if it is a phrase or *CL* if it is a clause.**

1. Mr. Irwin has volunteered to help me build a bookcase **for my books.** ________
2. My old bookcase, **which I have had for years**, has become too small. ________
3. The shelves, **sagging under the weight of many books**, are no longer sound. ________
4. I asked Mr. Irwin to help me **because he has all the tools we'll need.** ________
5. He is also a skilled woodworker **who has made all kinds of furniture.** ________
6. Mr. Irwin thinks it would be best to build the bookcase **with oak.** ________
7. Furniture **made of a solid wood** will last for many years. ________
8. **Because I lack experience**, I warned Mr. Irwin that I couldn't offer much help. ________
9. He said there were probably many things **that I could do to assist him.** ________
10. For example, I can hold the ends of the boards **while he saws them.** ________
11. I can also keep the shelves in place **until Mr. Irwin has tightened the screws.** ________
12. We will paint the bookcase **with a dark stain** before we are finished. ________
13. I selected the color myself **when we went to the hardware store.** ________
14. **Hoping to start as soon as possible**, Mr. Irwin has suggested that we meet tomorrow. ________
15. His workshop is **next to my school**, so I will just walk there. ________

Lesson 22 **Read each pair of sentences. Mark a star beside the one that more effectively expresses the idea and shows relationships. Then label the sentences *S* for simple, *CD* for compound, *CX* for complex, or *CCX* for compound-complex.**

1. We consider Europeans such as Columbus and Captain Cook to be great navigators; the ancient Polynesians were perhaps even more impressive. __________

   Though Europeans such as Columbus and Captain Cook are considered great navigators, the ancient Polynesians of the South Pacific were even more impressive. __________
2. Because they lived on islands surrounded by water, the Polynesians had much experience with water travel. __________

   The island-dwelling Polynesians had much experience with water travel. __________
3. The Polynesians' islands became overpopulated; when there was no more room on their islands, they sailed far away in search of new island homes. __________

   When their islands became overpopulated, the Polynesians sailed far away in search of new island homes. __________
4. The Polynesians had a knack for navigation, but they were also smart inventors who developed a special double canoe. __________

   The Polynesians were good navigators and smart inventors. __________

Extra Practice

Name ____________________

Lesson 23 **Label each item *F* (fragment), *RO* (run-on), *CS* (comma splice), or *RA* (ramble-on).**

1. It was a beautiful day, Damian was going to take advantage of it. ___
2. Damian decided it was perfect for a bike rally he invited some friends to the park. ___
3. His friends, Marcus, Jennifer, and Martin, thought a bike rally was a great idea when Damian told them about it over the phone, and they talked about what they would wear and eat. ___
4. The neighborhood park not far from Damian's house. ___
5. Martin wore his new baseball cap he bought some raisins on his way to the park. ___
6. Jennifer baked brownies, she wrapped them carefully in foil. ___
7. Marcus wearing his lime green biking shirt. ___
8. Damian planned the route, it was going to be challenging! ___
9. The four friends met up at one o'clock in a sunny area by the large rock near the playground in between the maple grove and the tennis courts. ___
10. A quick snack before hitting the road. ___
11. Some curious squirrels and pigeons approached they were looking for leftovers. ___
12. Jennifer threw some sunflower seeds to a pigeon soon there were pigeons everywhere. ___
13. Marcus led the way on the first part of the rally, it was an easy ride along shady streets. ___
14. Jennifer the leader on the steep ride up to the lookout point. ___
15. The group then followed Marcus, they rode back to the park. ___

Lesson 24 **Write *N* after each sentence with natural order. Write *IV* after each sentence with inverted order. Write *IT* after each sentence with interrupted order.**

1. Dorothy, Vikash, and Patrick had a decision to make. ___
2. The friends, who had planned a pizza party, could not agree on toppings. ___
3. Empty were their stomachs! ___
4. Sharp were their arguments! ___
5. Patrick, who hated olives, wanted pepperoni and mushrooms. ___
6. Vikash liked pepperoni but despised mushrooms. ___
7. How ill Dorothy became at the suggestion of anchovies! ___
8. On and on went the debate, with rejection after rejection. ___
9. Suddenly Dorothy snapped her fingers and suggested pineapple and ham. ___
10. This combination, which was called "Hawaiian pizza" on the menu, won unanimous approval. ___
11. That pizza the friends ordered. ___
12. Patrick felt relieved that everyone seemed happy. ___
13. The pizza, which looked absolutely delicious, was cut into six pieces. ___
14. Tangy was the sauce! ___
15. Tasty was the topping! ___

Lesson 25 **Write each noun in parentheses in its correct plural form.**

1. Two (week) ago my (parent), my sister, and I went camping. ____________________
2. Our little car was stuffed with our tent, sleeping (bag), and (box) of food. ____________________
3. We took our two (dog) along, which turned out to be a bit of a mistake. ____________________
4. They kept jumping around and wagging their (tail) in our (face). ____________________
5. Dusty chased the (bird) away, and Red scared the (deer) with his barking. ____________________
6. We had a lot of fun, though, especially with some (child) at the next campsite. ____________________
7. At night, we all played (game) and sang (song) by the fire. ____________________
8. We found (stick) and used them to roast (marshmallow) over the coals. ____________________
9. We were not bothered by (fly) or (mouse) on the trip. ____________________
10. Mom taught us the (name) of many of the (tree) and (plant) in the area. ____________________
11. We walked through (valley) and (canyon) and listened for (echo). ____________________
12. Dad taught us to use (compass), but we still got lost a couple of (time). ____________________
13. I've got lots of (photograph) that we took during the trip. ____________________
14. My family will be telling (story) about this trip and enjoying (memory) of it for years.

____

Lesson 26 **Underline each proper noun. Circle each common noun.**

1. William H. Johnson was born in Florence, South Carolina.
2. Johnson received a lot of encouragement from teachers in high school.
3. When he was still a teenager, he moved to New York City to study art.
4. He studied at the National Academy of Design, and his works received many awards.
5. Johnson then went to France, where he studied the works of great artists such as Cezanne and Gauguin.
6. He visited museums all over Europe.
7. Johnson was considered an expressionist.
8. Over the years, Johnson deliberately chose to paint in a style known as "primitive."
9. He painted objects and people in a colorful, two-dimensional way.
10. His subjects were often African Americans.
11. One of his most famous paintings is titled *Going to Church*.
12. During the Great Depression and World War II, Johnson worked for the Works Progress Administration.
13. That was a program that gave many artists and writers employment.
14. Johnson sold few of his paintings, but he exhibited his works often and received much critical acclaim.
15. Johnson donated his works to the National Museum of Art, which is a part of the Smithsonian Museum in Washington, D.C.

Extra Practice

Name ______________________________

Lesson 27 **Read each sentence. Circle the boldfaced word that is the type of noun listed in parentheses.**

1. My merry **band** of friends and I went to the Renaissance festival in the **fairgrounds**. (collective)
2. To our **amazement**, the **fairgrounds** had been transformed into an English village from the 1500s. (concrete)
3. **Troupes** of actors roamed the **grounds** dressed as lords and ladies. (collective)
4. The **hilarity** of the **skits** was rewarded with laughter. (abstract)
5. We really admired the **knights** for their wit—and their **bravery**. (abstract)
6. In the main field, **knights** were jousting with long wooden poles for the **victory**. (concrete)
7. The **knights** were dressed from head to toe in an **array** of armored gear. (collective)
8. We smiled with **amusement** as we watched them try to mount their **horses**. (abstract)
9. The field was decorated with a **variety** of colorful **flags** featuring various coats of arms. (concrete)
10. These elaborate **pictures** were **symbols** of the famous families of England. (abstract)
11. The **festival** also featured **carts** selling authentic foods. (concrete)
12. My stomach rumbled with **hunger** as I smelled the roasting **turkey**. (abstract)
13. A small **crowd** had gathered around the artisans selling **crafts**. (collective)
14. I was attracted by **thoughts** of purchasing the lovely **necklaces** for sale. (concrete)
15. The **artistry** displayed by these beautiful **pieces** was impressive. (abstract)

Lesson 28 **Write the possessive form of each noun in parentheses. Circle each plural possessive noun you write.**

1. Airplanes are one of (humankind) greatest inventions. ________________
2. I enjoy sailing through the clouds thousands of miles above (Earth) surface. ________________
3. I really like looking out through the (cabin) windows. ________________
4. Houses and cars look like little toys, and fields resemble a patchwork (quilt) squares. ________________
5. I love to see a (city) outline from the air. ________________
6. Most (travelers) minds wander as they look out the window. ________________
7. The hum of the (aircraft) engines is oddly soothing. ________________
8. Sometimes (people) conversations can make it hard to sleep, though. ________________
9. (Airlines) food offerings are limited, so it's wise to carry snacks onboard. ________________
10. I've noticed that (passengers) responses to rough weather are very different. ________________
11. Once we flew through a storm, and the (wings) vibrations made me a little nervous. ________________
12. Another time, the (brakes) squeals made me slightly uneasy. ________________
13. Fortunately, the (attendants) calm words helped reassure me. ________________
14. At the (journey) end, I'm usually a little tired, but excited to be in a new place. ________________
15. Hopefully, next (year) vacation will involve flying someplace. ________________

Lesson 29 **Circle each personal pronoun. Write *1* if it is a first person pronoun, *2* if it is a second person pronoun, and *3* if it is a third person pronoun.**

1. Marty and I played chess on Saturday. _______
2. He is a pretty good player. _______
3. Do you agree? _______
4. You are better, though. _______
5. Mai beat him last month. _______
6. She is an incredible player. _______
7. Did Marty challenge her? _______
8. Yes, they played after school. _______
9. She won in fewer than 30 minutes. _______
10. Am I as good as Mai? _______
11. You are good, but Mai seems unbeatable. _______
12. We should watch more of Mai's matches. _______
13. Maybe I could learn something. _______
14. Marty told me that Mai is playing Tony soon. _______
15. Do you want to watch that match? _______

Lesson 30 **Read each sentence. Underline each compound personal pronoun that is a reflexive pronoun. Circle each compound personal pronoun that is an intensive pronoun.**

1. Seth tried to teach himself to make raviolis, but the venture was a disaster.
2. He admitted to himself that he needed help from a master—his grandma.
3. "I myself was a novice once," Nana said with a chuckle.
4. "First we need to clear ourselves a large space on the counter," she said.
5. Seth himself organized the kitchen clutter and wiped the marble surface.
6. Nana wrapped herself in a giant apron and got down to work.
7. "When making raviolis, the dough itself often presents a challenge," she said.
8. "Remind yourself to always keep the dough as cold as possible," she suggested.
9. Seth himself had found rolling the dough difficult, so this advice was perfect.
10. Soon Nana was expertly wielding the rolling pin and covering herself in flour.
11. Seth himself was coated in the white stuff after rolling his dough.
12. "Clean yourself off and start cooking mushrooms in the skillet," Nana said.
13. "Add some cheese, and we will have ourselves a tasty filling," she added.
14. Seth and Nana both cut and filled their own raviolis by themselves.
15. When they were finished, Nana herself couldn't tell which ones were hers!

Name ____

Lesson 31 **Circle each possessive pronoun.**

1. Ray's bike is newer than mine.
2. His is red and black.
3. I don't like it as well as yours.
4. Tammy's bike is blue, and its handlebars are flecked with gold.
5. I wish my bike had thicker tires.
6. Ray's bike has twenty speeds, but mine has only ten.
7. Your bike is just fine!
8. Its brakes are squeaking a bit.
9. Have you checked their pads?
10. If you fix your brakes, do you want to join us on Saturday?
11. What's your plan?
12. Sam and Ngoc want to train for their race, so we're all biking a 20K.
13. Should I meet you at your house or at theirs?
14. Why don't you come over to my place?
15. Then we'll head over to their house together.

Lesson 32 **Circle each indefinite pronoun.**

1. Everyone in my family loves chili.
2. Nobody uses the same recipe as anyone else uses.
3. My uncle thinks his chili is the best that anyone has ever tasted.
4. Most of us prefer my aunt Ruth's chili.
5. I am glad to be served either.
6. Both are very delicious.
7. Everyone in my family enjoys spicy food.
8. Few can eat chili as hot as my dad makes it, though.
9. All of us are afraid to ask him to make it milder.
10. None of us wants to hurt Dad's feelings.
11. I wish someone had the courage to tell him, though.
12. Now, everybody just takes a gulp of water after every spoonful.
13. There's nothing else we can do.
14. Maybe somebody should hide the peppers next time Dad cooks.
15. That way everyone can enjoy Dad's chili.

Lesson 33 **Circle each relative pronoun and underline the noun it refers to. Draw a box around each interrogative pronoun.**

1. What is a hybrid?
2. It is a type of car that runs on two kinds of power.
3. The hybrid has an engine that uses fuel such as gasoline.
4. It also has a motor that uses electricity.
5. Each hybrid has a generator that powers the motor.
6. Who has ridden in a hybrid?
7. One thing that you will notice is the silence.
8. What is the reason for this?
9. The energy that is produced in the generator is stored in a battery.
10. The gasoline engine, which is the noisiest part of the car, shuts off at lower speeds.
11. The only thing propelling the car at these speeds is the quiet electric motor, which draws power stored in the battery.
12. People who drive hybrids should watch carefully for pedestrians.
13. Visually impaired people, who rely on noise to know when a car is near, may not hear a hybrid coming.
14. Which of the hybrids gets good gas mileage?
15. Hybrids emit less pollution than do most other cars, which makes hybrids easier on the environment.

Lesson 34 **Underline each adjective, including each article. Circle each adverb.**

1. Fiji is an island nation in the southern Pacific Ocean.
2. It is a popular destination for tourists who dearly love the tropics.
3. People flock to Fiji to enjoy the white, sandy beaches and sparkling waters.
4. They enthusiastically soak up the warm sunshine, which persists year-round.
5. Tourists often rent scuba gear and go for dives in the clear water.
6. Divers can easily see colorful coral reefs and schools of exotic fish.
7. Fiji also features dense tropical forests and volcanic mountains.
8. It consists of hundreds of islands, but the main ones are Viti Levu and Vanua Levu.
9. Fiji has 860,000 residents who live permanently on the major islands.
10. The many tourists add to this population throughout the year.
11. Fiji mostly depends on tourism to support its economy.
12. Fijian farmers also grow sugar to export to other countries.
13. Popular Fijian foods include seafood and cassava, an edible, starchy root.
14. Because residents are constantly surrounded by water, fishing is common.
15. Fiji's mix of native, European, Indian, and Chinese cultures makes the country an interesting place to live.

Extra Practice

Name ________________________________

Lesson 35 **Circle each demonstrative adjective. Underline each demonstrative pronoun.**

1. This is a photo album I made in my art class.
2. I decorated it with these shells I found on the beach.
3. I wish I had some shells like those!
4. Where did you find this one?
5. I found that one at Stinson Beach.
6. These others my sister gave to me.
7. How did you get those shells to stick to your album cover?
8. They sell this special glue at the craft store.
9. I'm really impressed with all the work you've put into this album.
10. Will you show me those pictures?
11. Who is that?
12. This is my Aunt Lupe.
13. These are my cousins.
14. That looks like a fun game they're playing.
15. I'll teach you how to play after I show you these pictures.

Lesson 36 **Underline the adjectives in parentheses that are written correctly.**

1. It was (an autumn gorgeous/a gorgeous autumn) day in mid-October.
2. We decided to explore the (Vermont scenic/scenic Vermont) countryside.
3. Everyone hopped in the (reliable blue/reliable, blue) minivan, and we were off.
4. The (bright afternoon/afternoon bright) sun shone in our faces.
5. The (cool, crisp/cool crisp) air made us shiver, so we rolled up the windows.
6. There are many (narrow winding/narrow, winding) roads outside of town.
7. We took one that leads to (several small/small several) lakes.
8. The birch trees lining the road had (yellow large/large yellow) leaves.
9. Their (delicate white/white, delicate) branches quivered in the breeze.
10. A flock of (honking twenty/twenty honking) geese flew overhead.
11. They were heading south to escape the (harsh Canadian/Canadian harsh) winter.
12. The trees surrounding the lakes were an (intense fiery/intense, fiery) red.
13. We could see their reflections in the (clear, calm/clear calm) water.
14. A (steep, tree-covered/steep tree-covered) hill rose behind the lake.
15. With its many colors, it looked like my (patchwork old/old patchwork) quilt.

Lesson 37 **Underline each action verb. Circle each linking verb.**

1. *Pathfinder* was a Mars mission.
2. It launched in 1996.
3. The craft had a lander and a rover.
4. The lander communicated information to NASA.
5. The name of the rover was *Sojourner*.
6. The six-wheeled rover looked like a toy.
7. It was about the size of a microwave oven.
8. The machine was able to move over small boulders.
9. After landing, *Pathfinder* had modem trouble.
10. Scientists at NASA corrected the problem.
11. *Pathfinder* sent many images back to NASA.
12. Possibly, Mars was once a wet planet.
13. At some point, it became a cold, dry desert.
14. The *Pathfinder* mission was very successful.
15. Like *Viking 1* and *Viking 2, Pathfinder* outlasted its design life.

Lesson 38 **Underline each transitive verb and draw a box around its direct object. Draw a circle around each intransitive verb.**

1. I love the ocean.
2. In the summer, my family often goes to the beach.
3. Mom naps under an umbrella.
4. My little sister and I wade in the water.
5. Then we gather seashells.
6. Last summer, I found a sea star.
7. It lay near a piece of driftwood.
8. I keep the sea star on my dresser at home.
9. Sometimes we stay at the beach until dark.
10. Once we built a bonfire.
11. On rare occasions, a pod of whales swims by.
12. One day, I will take a long voyage.
13. I will go diving far beneath the waves.
14. I may see strange fish and amazing plants.
15. Perhaps I will discover a wrecked ship!

Name ______________________________

Lesson 39 **Circle each present tense verb. Underline each past tense verb. Draw a box around each future tense verb.**

1. Last month my community center group took a trip to Maine.
2. I almost stayed home.
3. Many bears wander around the woods there.
4. My best friend laughed at my fears.
5. That journey was my first camping trip.
6. The Maine wilderness is very beautiful.
7. We hiked through meadows and forests.
8. Fortunately, I had no encounters with bears.
9. We saw many of them, but from a safe distance.
10. The community center group will go again next year.
11. Next time, I will take a camera.
12. I forgot it this time.
13. The gift shops sell a lot of postcards.
14. I bought some as souvenirs.
15. I want my own pictures for my blog, though.

Lesson 40 **Circle the boldfaced verbs in present perfect tense. Underline the boldfaced verbs in past perfect tense. Draw a box around the boldfaced verbs in future perfect tense.**

1. Recently, I **have started** a scrapbook of great journeys.
2. I never **had enjoyed** scrapbooks before.
3. Back in sixth grade I **had made** a scrapbook of a trip I took.
4. The project **had bored** me thoroughly.
5. Something about the journey's topic **has made** me think differently.
6. The scrapbook **has grown** quite thick since I started it.
7. After I add details about Lewis and Clark, I **will have included** more than twenty journeys.
8. I **have found** a really great map of their expedition.
9. I **have added** many pages to my scrapbook, but I need to add more.
10. Soon I **will have used** all the available space.
11. By the time I finish this project, I **will have learned** a great deal about different journeys.
12. I **have enjoyed** all the research I've done about explorers' lives.
13. I **had heard** of only a few of the explorers before I began my report.
14. My teacher **has asked** to see the scrapbook.
15. None of her students **has created** a scrapbook like mine before.

Lesson 41 **Circle each boldfaced verb that is a progressive form. Cross out each boldfaced verb that is not a progressive form.**

1. I **am writing** a science-fiction story.
2. This **is** a summary of the story so far.
3. Vin **was flying** over the equator when suddenly he had engine trouble.
4. He **saw** a stretch of deserted beach.
5. Vin **was attempting** an emergency landing there when his radio died.
6. Just before that, Vin **had heard** shouts and strange crackling sounds.
7. What Vin did not know was that Martians **were attacking** Earth.
8. The second chapter of the story **is giving** me some problems.
9. I am not sure what **will happen** next.
10. My writing group **will be discussing** the story tomorrow.
11. The story **is taking** me a long time to write.
12. I **have made** many revisions to it already.
13. I **am looking** forward to the group's feedback.
14. They **have given** me sound advice in the past.
15. They gave me a good deal of support while I **was writing** my last story.

Lesson 42 **Read each sentence. If a verb in the sentence creates a time shift that doesn't make sense, mark an X through the verb. Write the correct tense of the verb on the line.**

1. Brandon was trying to study when he hears a tap on his window. ______________
2. He saw his friend Max peering in from the bushes outside his room. ______________
3. He sighed as he abandoned the books on his desk and goes to open the window. ______________
4. "What's up, Max?" he says. "Why aren't you home studying for the science exam?" ______________
5. Though he got very good grades, Max never seemed to study much at all. ______________
6. He has an annoying habit of distracting Brandon right before a test. ______________
7. Brandon did well in school too, but his success requires more time and effort. ______________
8. "Martin and I are going to a movie," Max said. "Are you in?" ______________
9. Brandon rolled his eyes in frustration and will point to the books on his desk. ______________
10. "You know I have to study, Max," he says. "Why do you always do this?" ______________
11. "Oh, that test will be easy. You can study later," Max replied with a grin. ______________
12. "It's almost six, and we'd be out until at least eight or nine," Brandon said. ______________
13. "Go and ask your mom," Max will plead. "You know you want to go." ______________
14. Brandon protested again and promptly shuts the window on his friend. ______________
15. Max shrugged his shoulders and went to join Martin. ______________

Name ______________________________

Lesson 43 **Read each sentence. Write whether the mood of the boldfaced verb is *indicative* or *imperative*.**

1. The Mount Rushmore National Memorial **is** near the town of Keystone, South Dakota. ____________
2. Its sixty-foot carvings of four presidents **compose** an iconic national image. ____________
3. The memorial **was built** to bring tourists to the American West. ____________
4. **Consider** its popularity and you will agree the project was a success. ____________
5. The sculptor, Gutzon Borglum, **chose** the men to be represented: Washington, Jefferson, Roosevelt, and Lincoln. ____________
6. In 1927, he and 400 workers **began** carving the faces into the granite cliffs. ____________
7. **Imagine** how much work it took to create such gigantic sculptures. ____________
8. Originally, the face of Jefferson **was supposed** to be to the right of Washington's. ____________
9. But the rock **was** not stable enough to support the carving. ____________
10. **Look** carefully at the memorial and **picture** what Jefferson would have looked like in a different position. ____________
11. The first face, that of Washington, **was completed** in 1934. ____________
12. The three other faces **were finished** by 1939. ____________
13. Original plans to also carve the presidents' bodies **were abandoned** because of a lack of funds. ____________
14. **Visit** this spectacular sight as soon as you have an opportunity. ____________
15. **Leave** plenty of time to tour the museum and visitors' center as well. ____________

Lesson 44 **Read each sentence. Write whether the mood of the boldfaced verb is *indicative* or *subjunctive*.**

1. "If I **were** you, I would definitely go," Ella said to her friend Cara. ____________
2. The girls **were discussing** Cara's invitation to visit her aunt in Spain. ____________
3. Cara **was** not sure whether she wanted to spend the summer in a strange country. ____________
4. "But I **am** totally unfamiliar with the language and the customs," Cara protested. ____________
5. "If I **were** fluent in Spanish, things would be different," she added. ____________
6. "I suggest that you **stop** thinking about reasons you can't go," Ella said. ____________
7. "This **is** a wonderful opportunity that you can't pass up," Ella asserted. ____________
8. Ella **was** shocked that Cara could consider staying home. ____________
9. "A little preparation **will help** you feel more comfortable," she said. ____________
10. Then Ella proposed that they **meet** every weekend to learn some Spanish together. ____________
11. She suggested that they also **find** some books about Spanish culture and cuisine. ____________
12. "If there **were** a Spanish restaurant in town, we could go there too," Ella concluded. ____________
13. Cara **was changing** her mind about this possible adventure. ____________
14. "If I **were** more knowledgeable, I think I could overcome my fear," she said. ____________
15. "Bueno," Ella replied. "See? I **am teaching** you already." ____________

Lesson 45 **Underline each boldfaced verb that is in the indicative mood. Circle each boldfaced verb that is in the imperative mood. Draw a box around each boldfaced verb that is in the subjunctive mood. If a sentence contains an inappropriate mood shift, mark an *X* beside it.**

1. I suggest that you **drive** to the orchard and **pick** apples. _____
2. It **is** a beautiful day, and the place **is bursting** with fruit. _____
3. If I **were** available, I **will love** to go with you. _____
4. **Take** the freeway south, **exit** onto Wyatt Road, and then I suggest that you **turn** right. _____
5. The orchard **sits** at the top of the hill; its driveway **is** on the left. _____
6. I recommend that you **arrive** early and **park** in the grass near the farmhouse. _____
7. **Find** the owner, Mr. Kay, and then I recommend that you **ask** him for a bushel basket. _____
8. The basket **looks** really big, but you **will have** no trouble filling it. _____
9. If I **were** you, I **will start** by picking a few Granny Smith apples. _____
10. This tart green fruit **is** perfect for making pies and **tastes** good, too. _____
11. **Gather** some Honeycrisp apples, and then you **will grab** some Red Delicious as well. _____
12. **Take** your basket back to the farmhouse and **pay** Mr. Kay promptly. _____
13. I also suggest that you **talk** with Mr. Kay and **ask** him to show you around the farm. _____
14. He **raises** goats and **grow** acres of pumpkins as well. _____
15. **Enjoy** your day and **tell** me all about it when you get back! _____

Lesson 46 **Underline each boldfaced verb that is in the active voice. Circle each boldfaced verb that is in the passive voice. If a sentence contains a voice shift, mark an *X* beside it.**

1. Like many young Victorian women, Mary Kingsley **stayed** home, and her parents **were nursed** by her. _____
2. But Mary **loved** to read about nature, and she **yearned** to travel around the world. _____
3. By 1892, fate **granted** her wish, and a boat to Africa **was boarded** by this brave woman. _____
4. Mary **explored** Africa's rivers in canoes, and she often **traveled** by herself. _____
5. Her trip **was funded** by trading; she **exchanged** cloth for rubber and ivory. _____
6. English merchants **clamored** for these rare goods, and she **sold** them at a good price. _____
7. Mary **befriended** many Africans, and their unfamiliar ways **were understood** by her. _____
8. She **wrote** a respectful book about their culture, but people back in England **reacted** with disapproval. _____
9. In 1894, Mary **was hired** by the British Museum; she **collected** African plants and animals for them. _____
10. Mary **found** a new species of fish, and the fish **was named** after Mary by scientists. _____
11. Mary also **encountered** some dangerous situations, for she **refused** to let anything hold her back. _____
12. She once **met** a dangerous hippo, but the creature **was** somehow **tamed** by her. _____
13. She **was** also **surprised** by an angry gorilla, but she **survived** to tell the tale. _____
14. Mary **climbed** Mt. Cameroon before any European woman, and she **lived** with the Fang people. _____
15. She **spoke** to the British about Africa, and much **was learned** about this place because of her. _____

Name ____

Lesson 47 **Underline each coordinating conjunction. Circle each subordinating conjunction.**

1. I auditioned for the school play, and I was shocked to get a part.
2. Although I was trying for a small role, I got the lead.
3. Everyone told me I would be great, but I was absolutely terrified.
4. The director gave us scripts on Friday, and I read the entire play.
5. That put me into a panic because my character had more than fifty lines!
6. When my father saw my nervousness, he read through the play with me.
7. He coached me all weekend, although I said he didn't have to.
8. He cued me when I had trouble remembering a line.
9. That helped me, and I began to feel more confident.
10. After we had our first practice, I discovered the value of my hard work.
11. Because I had read the play so many times, I knew other actors' lines, too.
12. I could whisper a line to them if they forgot it in rehearsal.
13. We will perform the play on Saturday, after we have a dress rehearsal.
14. I'm still nervous, but I'm nervous in a good way.
15. If I don't trip on stage, I'll do just fine!

Lesson 48 **Circle each conjunction. If a sentence contains correlative conjunctions, write *CC* on the line.**

1. I don't know whether to write my essay about my summer trip or about my winter trip. ________
2. My summer trip was to the Maryland shore, and my winter trip was to Atlanta. ________
3. Either the Maryland shore or Atlanta would be interesting to write about. ________
4. We stayed with Grandma in Maryland, and we stayed in a motel in Atlanta. ________
5. Both staying with Grandma and visiting a big city were fun. ________
6. Because the motel in Atlanta had a heated pool, we swam a lot. ________
7. We drove through North Carolina and South Carolina on our way to Atlanta. ________
8. At the Maryland shore, we hiked on the beach or went shopping each day. ________
9. We not only hiked but also played miniature golf. ________
10. Neither I nor my sister made a hole-in-one. ________
11. I took only a few pictures at the beach, but they turned out great! ________
12. Both Nina and Wing have asked me about my trips. ________
13. Neither Nina nor Wing has been to Maryland or Georgia. ________
14. I like to learn and have fun on a vacation. ________
15. After I write my essay, I will print a copy with digital photographs. ________

Lesson 49 Circle the correct word in parentheses.

1. Where are you and (your/you're) family going this weekend?
2. Will you visit (your/you're) grandparents?
3. I'm sure (there/their/they're) going to be delighted to see you.
4. (There/Their/They're) eyes will surely light up.
5. (Your/You're) going to take the train, aren't you?
6. I hope you enjoy the trip (there/their/they're).
7. Be sure to take (your/you're) camera.
8. I'm sure (your/you're) going to get some great shots.
9. (There/Their/They're) may be snow along the way.
10. The trees will have lost (there/their/they're) leaves in that area.
11. Do (your/you're) grandparents have many animals on their farm?
12. (There/Their/They're) really lucky to live in such a great place.
13. Could we visit (there/their/they're) place someday?
14. I will ask them for (there/their/they're) permission.
15. Maybe I can go with you and (your/you're) parents next time you visit.

Lesson 50 Circle the correct word in parentheses.

1. (Who's/Whose) bike is parked outside?
2. It looks like (its/it's) front tire is flat.
3. Oh, you're the one (who's/whose) got the flat?
4. If you want to borrow my pump, (its/it's) in the garage.
5. (Its/It's) a good idea to carry extra tire patches around with you.
6. A tire can lose (its/it's) tread quickly on these rough roads.
7. I think (its/it's) helpful to learn basic bike repair.
8. (Who's/Whose) going to fix your bike for you out in the middle of nowhere?
9. (Its/It's) not that hard to fix a flat tire.
10. If the chain falls off (its/it's) track, that's an easy repair, too.
11. If you're someone (who's/whose) bike often has flats, you should learn to fix them.
12. A person (who's/whose) prepared to make minor repairs can feel more secure.
13. (Its/It's) a shame that basic bike repair isn't taught at our school.
14. Your tire looks like (its/it's) fixed for the time being.
15. (Its/It's) inner tube doesn't appear to be leaking.

Extra Practice

Name ______________________________

Lesson 51 **Circle the word in parentheses that correctly completes each sentence.**

1. Do you like (to/too/two) do research on the Internet?
2. I think articles are (to/too/two) difficult to read online.
3. I know several tricks (to/too/two) use to make Internet research more efficient.
4. Can you tell me how (to/too/two) use a search engine?
5. Use at least (to/too/two) keywords together to narrow your search.
6. Do you use quotation marks (to/too/two) narrow your search even further?
7. That helps, (to/too/two).
8. I never know how (to/too/two) recognize the most reliable information.
9. There are (to/too/two) kinds of sites that are particularly reliable.
10. What are the (to/too/two) you recommend?
11. Government sites are very useful, and educational sites can be, (to/too/two).
12. Are sites ending in **.com** good ones (to/too/two) use for research?
13. They may be unreliable, or they may be (to/too/two) biased.
14. Wow, there's a lot (to/too/two) know about using the Internet!
15. Yes, sometimes I think there's (to/too/two) much to learn.

Lesson 52 **Circle the word or phrase in parentheses that correctly completes each sentence.**

1. (Over/More than) a dozen kids in our class are collecting state coins.
2. That's (over/more than) 40% of the entire class.
3. (Less/Fewer) students are collecting stamps.
4. You have (over/more than) 30 United States quarters in your collection.
5. That's well (over/more than) the number that Ted Brown has.
6. I have (less/fewer) quarters than either of you.
7. It will probably take me (over/more than) a year to complete my collection.
8. I am still hunting for (over/more than) 20 state quarters.
9. I have spent (less/fewer) time collecting coins than you have.
10. You have been gathering coins for (over/more than) a year now.
11. Did you know that there were (over/more than) six billion quarters minted in 2000?
12. That's two billion (over/more than) the number of quarters our nation minted in 1999.
13. (Less/Fewer) state quarters were minted in subsequent years.
14. The U.S. Mint produces (less/fewer) coinage for some states than for others.
15. For example, Delaware has (less/fewer) state quarters in circulation than Connecticut has.

Lesson 53 **Circle the correct expression in parentheses to complete each sentence.**

1. Our basketball team has not lost (any/no) games this year.
2. We haven't (ever/never) had such a good year before.
3. Last year, our team did not play well (anywhere/nowhere) except at home.
4. This year, the team has not lost (any/no) confidence while on the road.
5. Our team (ain't/isn't) afraid of any other team.
6. I've never seen (anyone/nobody) better than our center, Jerome Lee.
7. He never shoots (no/any) air balls.
8. No opposing player has been able to block (any/none) of his shots.
9. There isn't (anyone/no one) else on our team who shoots as well as Jerome.
10. He isn't a bad rebounder, (either/neither).
11. None of our players lets (no one/anyone) on the other team have an easy shot.
12. Last Saturday, the other team didn't score (any/no) points in the second quarter.
13. I didn't see (anybody/nobody) on the other team who was thrilled about it.
14. No one wants to miss (none/any) of the action in Saturday's play-off game.
15. There's not going to be (anywhere/nowhere) to sit if we don't get there early.

Lesson 54 **Circle the expression in parentheses that is appropriate to use in academic writing.**

1. This report explains why computers are such (awesome/valuable) inventions.
2. Before we had computers, we (could not/couldn't) do many of the activities we do today.
3. Today (we're/we are) able to communicate with friends through the use of computers.
4. Most (folks/people) I know use e-mail to stay in touch with friends and family.
5. People can buy various (stuff/items) for their computers over the Internet.
6. The Internet makes it (quite/way) easy to find information.
7. Some sites provide (abundant/tons of) information.
8. You can (check out/look up) when the next bus is coming.
9. You can (gripe about/critique) movies and restaurants.
10. I like to (read/check out) the statistics about my favorite sports teams.
11. More and more books are (gonna/going to) be available online in the next ten years.
12. My friends and I listen to some very (cool/innovative) music on the Internet.
13. The Internet has (a whole lot of/800 million) users.
14. Can you imagine how your life (would have/would've) been without the Internet?
15. I wonder what new (things/features) the Internet will offer in the next ten years.

Name ____

Lesson 55 **Circle the word in parentheses that correctly completes each sentence.**

1. Where did I (sit/set) my yoga mat?
2. Oh, I (lied/laid) it over there near the door.
3. Are you going to (lie/lay) there, or are you going to do yoga with me?
4. All right, (sit/set) your mat next to mine.
5. You can (rise/raise) the blinds if it seems too dark in here.
6. Stand up and (rise/raise) your arms above your head.
7. When you (rise/raise) from this forward lunge, your leg muscles might be tired.
8. Now let's (sit/set) quietly and take deep breaths.
9. Slowly (rise/raise) your left leg and then your right.
10. You may want to (lie/lay) a pillow under your neck for this next pose.
11. My favorite pose is the one where we (lie/lay) still and close our eyes.
12. Once I (lie/lay) down and fell asleep!
13. The person (sitting/setting) next to me woke me when I started snoring.
14. Even if I'm tired before stretching, I always (rise/raise) afterward feeling refreshed.
15. Some enthusiasts do stretches as soon as they (rise/raise) in the morning.

Lesson 56 **Write the correct past tense form of the verb in parentheses to complete each sentence.**

1. Everyone ______________ the school musical was a huge success. (say)
2. The Art Club had ______________ amazing sets. (build)
3. The music director had ______________ plenty of rehearsals. (hold)
4. This year, all of the performers ______________ to practice on time. (come)
5. Everyone ______________ their scripts along with them. (bring)
6. As a result, no one ______________ his or her lines. (forget)
7. The rehearsals all ______________ very smoothly. (go)
8. That ______________ everyone confidence. (give)
9. We all ______________ our stage fright. (overcome)
10. My mother had never ______________ such a strong lead singer. (hear)
11. The band had ______________ pains to learn each song. (take)
12. No one ______________ during the intermission. (left)
13. Everyone ______________ that the musical was the best in years. (think)
14. At the closing curtain, the audience ______________ us a standing ovation. (give)
15. The local music critic ______________ a glowing review of the musical. (write)

Lesson 57 Circle the word in parentheses that correctly completes each sentence.

1. This (past/passed) summer I began helping out at my parents' grocery store.
2. It's at the end of the colorful downtown (bizarre/bazaar).
3. Like my parents, I (wear/ware) a smock when I'm at work.
4. I help my parents keep the (isles/aisles) stocked with groceries.
5. It's quite a (feet/feat) to maintain the proper inventory.
6. My parents don't want the store shelves to be (bear/bare).
7. They arrange merchandise so that customers can (access/assess) it easily.
8. My parents pride themselves on the freshness of their (wears/wares).
9. Sometimes my parents let me (wring/ring) up groceries.
10. Working the cash register is harder (then/than) it seems.
11. You have to quickly count the change people (pour/poor) into your hand.
12. You need to (way/weigh) all of the produce and punch in the right prices.
13. I bagged a senior's groceries and (then/than) helped her to her car.
14. She gave me (compliments/complements) on my good work.
15. The next day she wrote a thank-you note on her personal (stationary/stationery).

Lesson 58 Cross out each incorrect usage of *go, went, all,* and *like*. (If the word *was* is part of the incorrect expression, cross that out also.) Write correct words to replace the crossed out words if a replacement is needed.

1. Lily was all, "How can we raise money for new softball uniforms?" ______________
2. Ty went, "I don't have a single good idea." ______________
3. "We could have a raffle," Miriam went. ______________
4. I was all, "Then we've got to offer really good prizes." ______________
5. Ty went, "Selling raffle tickets is no fun!" ______________
6. Then Miriam was like, "Why don't we have a car wash?" ______________
7. I went, "That's an excellent idea!" ______________
8. Lily was, like, skeptical at first, but she finally agreed. ______________
9. Then Ty went, "Where will we have it?" ______________
10. Miriam was all, "At the school, of course!" ______________
11. Then I said I was, like, willing to make the signs. ______________
12. At first Ty thought supplies would be, like, too expensive. ______________
13. Then Miriam said she could, like, borrow buckets from her parents' nursery. ______________
14. I was like, "We can all bring a few rags and sponges from home." ______________
15. Finally, Lily was like, "This is going to be fun!" ______________

Name ___

Lesson 59 **Draw a line through each unneeded pronoun. Note: Some sentences are correctly written.**

1. The painting *Washington Crossing the Delaware* it is a famous work of art.
2. It depicts General Washington and his troops crossing the Delaware River during the Revolutionary War.
3. Washington he hoped to surprise the enemy with an attack in the winter of 1776.
4. Surprisingly, this painting it was not completed until 1851.
5. It was painted by a German American artist named Emanuel Gottlieb Leutze.
6. Leutze he was actually in Germany when he began work on the first version.
7. Europeans fighting in the revolutions of 1848 they inspired him.
8. The first version was destroyed in a World War II air raid on a German museum.
9. Luckily, Leutze he had painted a second copy.
10. Visitors they can still see the painting today.
11. Critics have noted a number of inaccuracies in *Washington Crossing the Delaware.*
12. The American flag shown it had not yet been designed in 1776.
13. And all the men depicted in the boat they would have easily sunk such a small vessel.
14. The real crossing actually took place at night and in the rain.
15. However, Leutze he painted Washington's face lit up by the rising sun of dawn.

Lesson 60 **Draw a line through unnecessary words in each sentence.**

1. One of the most impressive World's Fairs in history was held in Chicago in 1893, well over 100 years ago.
2. The fair's official name, or the name it is called in important records, was the World's Columbian Exposition.
3. It marked the 400th anniversary of Columbus's arrival in the Americas after his ocean journey.
4. People came from almost 50 countries to share aspects of and things about their culture with visitors.
5. Organizers and people in charge oversaw the building of an entire city on the fairgrounds.
6. Most of the structures were designed and conceived in a neoclassical style that recalled ancient Greek buildings.
7. The display was called the White City because the buildings were white, not dark and dreary.
8. They were also lit up by many electric lights, so they were really bright.
9. The structures, which were not meant to last forever, were intended to be only temporary.
10. They were composed and made of plaster instead of brick and stone, harder substances.
11. There were many other celebrated attractions at the fair that drew people to it.
12. The first Ferris wheel took riders 264 feet into the air above the fair below.
13. Early electric companies that were the first ones in America demonstrated their technologies.
14. And many artists and inventors showed off their creations, the things they made.
15. The fair ran from the month of May through October and had 26 million visitors.

Lesson 61 **Circle each boldfaced word that is a subject pronoun. Underline each boldfaced word that is an object pronoun.**

1. What did **you** do last weekend?
2. **I** took my little brother to see a movie.
3. I told **him** to keep quiet.
4. **He** often talks to **me** during the most suspenseful part of the movie.
5. People shush **us** if **we** make too much noise.
6. That embarrasses **me**, so **I** try to be as quiet as possible.
7. Do **you** eat popcorn when **you** see a movie?
8. If **I** see people with popcorn, **I** try not to sit by **them**.
9. The crunching drives **me** crazy.
10. To **me**, crunching is worse than my little brother's whispers.
11. **I** will give **you** a piece of advice.
12. If **you** eat candy in a movie, take **it** out of the wrapper before the movie starts.
13. My mom says **she** finds the rustling of candy wrappers distracting.
14. A family sat behind **me** once, and all of **them** were eating.
15. **They** crunched, rustled, and slurped their way through the whole film.

Lesson 62 **Circle the correct pronoun in each pair. Write *S* if you chose a subject pronoun and *O* if you chose an object pronoun.**

1. Rob and (I/me) wanted to go hiking last Saturday. ________
2. (He/Him) and I asked Mom if we could go. ________
3. (She/Her) and my dad were cleaning the garage. ________
4. Dad said that (he/him) and Mom were almost finished. ________
5. Mom asked Rob and (I/me) if she could hike with us. ________
6. (Rob and I/Me and Rob) told her she could. ________
7. Dad told (Mom and me/Mom and I) that we should phone Uncle Tim and my cousin. ________
8. Cousin Mara said that (her/she) and her dad would love to come. ________
9. So they joined Mom, Rob, and (I/me) at Pine Ridge Park. ________
10. Uncle Tim and Mara hadn't eaten, so we gave (him/he) and her lunch. ________
11. Then Mom and (I/me) led everyone on our favorite trail. ________
12. Uncle Tim said that (he and Mara/Mara and him) had never gone that way. ________
13. Rob, Mara, and (me/I) raced to the top of a hill. ________
14. Rob said that (him and Mara/Mara and he) had tied for first. ________
15. Mara said that (her/she) had beaten him by a nose. ________

Extra Practice

Name ______________________________

Lesson 63 **Circle the antecedent or antecedents of each boldfaced pronoun.**

1. Kay and her friend Liam got lost as **they** were going to the mall.
2. They missed their bus stop although the driver called **it** out.
3. Liam was talking on his cell phone, so **he** didn't hear the driver.
4. Kay was daydreaming, so **she** didn't hear the driver either.
5. Once the two friends realized their error, **they** asked the driver what to do.
6. He gave them directions, but they forgot **them** as soon as they got off the bus.
7. They boarded another bus, but **it** had a different number.
8. The bus took a different route; **it** was longer than the way they had come.
9. Finally Kay spotted River Park Mall; the bus dropped them off in front of **it**.
10. As soon as Kay and Liam got off the bus, **they** hurried inside the mall.
11. Kay wanted to buy her father a present because **he** had a birthday coming.
12. Kay was drawing a blank, so **she** asked Liam to help her.
13. Liam led her into a department store; **it** was having a sale.
14. Liam fell behind a crowd of shoppers, and Kay worried that she had lost **him**.
15. Kay found a fishing hat on sale; she decided **it** was just what her dad needed.

Lesson 64 **Circle the pronoun that agrees with the antecedent in each pair of sentences.**

1. Liz and Eric went to a hockey game downtown. (They/It) was the last game of the season.
2. Thousands of fans streamed into the arena. (They/It) wore jerseys and sweatshirts with the team colors.
3. Eric insisted on buying a program. (It/He) wanted to read about all the players.
4. Liz's and Eric's seats were in the top level of the arena. (It/They) had to climb many steps to get to them.
5. Liz got a little dizzy looking down at the ice. (She/It) was so far below them!
6. "The Star-Spangled Banner" was sung by two local music students. (They/We) sounded like professional singers.
7. Everyone applauded when the students finished. The team will likely ask (him/them) to sing again next year.
8. The crowd cheered when the players took the ice. (They/It) spent a few minutes warming up.
9. Both teams took their positions when the buzzer sounded. (She/It) was so loud it startled Eric.
10. Liz was impressed with the players' skills. (They/She) knew how difficult skating was.
11. Liz had taken skating lessons before. After falling repeatedly, she had learned that the sport was not for (her/it).
12. Eric admired the players, too. While watching (him/them), he dreamed of playing himself.
13. After ten minutes, the home team scored. Eric and Liz jumped out of (its/their) seats.
14. The noise from the crowd was louder than ever. In fact, (it/they) was deafening.
15. The whole arena seemed to shake. Eric had to cover (his/their) ears.

Lesson 65 **Read each boldfaced pronoun. If the pronoun does not have a clear antecedent, mark an *X* through it.**

1. There is a farmers' market in our town every Saturday. **They** hold it in the town square.
2. At least two dozen farmers sell their fruits and vegetables. **They** are always nice to see.
3. Dad and I try to arrive early at the market each week. **We** want to have the best selection possible.
4. Dad chats with Mr. Ruiz and buys some of his eggs. **It** is his first priority.
5. Dad knows Mr. Ruiz from high school when **he** was on the wrestling team.
6. Though he is a farmer and Dad can't even grow a houseplant, **they** are still friends.
7. Mr. Ruiz's children help him sell beans and tomatoes as well. **They** are always fun to see.
8. If the tomatoes seem ripe enough, Dad and I will buy **them** for making salsa.
9. The woman in the stall next door sells berries. **She** always smiles and waves us over.
10. She tells Dad how pretty I am and gives me a raspberry. **It** is the highlight of my day.
11. "**She** is the loveliest person," Dad always says with a grin.
12. Next we usually fill our bags with melons and potatoes. **They** are always so heavy!
13. Our last stop is the Mexican food truck where **they** make the best tamales.
14. There is always a long line of people waiting for this treat. **It** is pretty impressive!
15. Dad and I appreciate the market because **we** love buying from local farmers.

Lesson 66 **Circle the pronoun in parentheses that completes each sentence correctly.**

1. (Who/Whom) is that sitting over there on the grass?
2. To (who/whom) are you pointing?
3. I am pointing to the man (who/whom) is talking to Mr. Chen.
4. Do you mean the one (who/whom) is wearing the blue baseball cap?
5. Yes, that is the person to (who/whom) I'm referring.
6. Isn't he the guy (who/whom) plays his saxophone here on weekends?
7. No, I think the man (who/whom) plays sax is taller and has darker hair.
8. That person looks familiar, though; to (who/whom) is he talking now?
9. He is talking to a woman (who/whom) comes to the park often.
10. Yes, she's someone (who/whom) I've seen here many times before.
11. She's the one (who/whom) sits at the other end of the park.
12. Is she the one (who/whom) paints portraits for twenty dollars?
13. Yes! Maybe the man to (who/whom) I was pointing wants his portrait painted.
14. We are the ones (who/whom) should have our portrait painted.
15. Then we could give it to Mom, (who/whom) has always wanted to have a portrait of us.

Extra Practice

Name ____

Lesson 67 **Circle the simple subject in each sentence. Then underline the correct form of each verb in parentheses.**

1. This can of clams (smell/smells) fishy!
2. Clams (is/are) supposed to smell fishy.
3. Fresh clams from New England (taste/tastes) great in chowder.
4. When fresh clams aren't available, chowder made with canned clams (is/are) just fine.
5. The students in my cooking class (make/makes) chowder with fresh fish.
6. Clam juice from bottles (enhance/enhances) the chowder's flavor.
7. Too much liquid in chowder (make/makes) the broth watery.
8. Chunks of potato (help/helps) to thicken the broth.
9. The broth in these bowls (seem/seems) too thin.
10. But thick and lumpy soup (do/does) not appeal to me, either.
11. The pot full of vegetables (is/are) bubbling vigorously.
12. Cooks with experience (stir/stirs) chowder to keep solid ingredients from sticking.
13. Chowder without salt and pepper (taste/tastes) bland.
14. A package of oyster crackers (is/are) served with each bowl of chowder.
15. The ingredients in this soup (was/were) the freshest the cook could find.

Lesson 68 **Look at the compound subject in each sentence. Circle the conjunction(s). Then underline the correct verb.**

1. Ben and his sister Veronica (is/are) very active on weekends.
2. A bike ride, a swim, or a hike (is/are) likely to be their choice this weekend.
3. Sometimes Rene and Jaime (go/goes) biking or swimming with them.
4. Neither Rene nor Jaime (enjoy/enjoys) hiking, though.
5. Veronica, Ben, Jaime, and Rene often (bike/bikes) to the neighborhood park.
6. Bike lanes and paths (make/makes) their rides at the park safe and pleasant.
7. On occasion, either Ben or Jaime (bring/brings) along a soccer ball.
8. Veronica and her brother also (like/likes) rainy days.
9. On those days, either Veronica or Ben (bake/bakes) cookies.
10. Peanut butter or oatmeal (is/are) the kind Veronica usually makes.
11. Shortbread or ginger snaps (is/are) more to Ben's liking.
12. Sometimes Veronica, Ben, and their little brother Freddy (watch/watches) TV.
13. Ben or Freddy usually (pick/picks) the show.
14. Veronica and her two brothers (prefer/prefers) classic cartoons to new ones.
15. Now and then, Freddy or Ben (choose/chooses) a nature show.

Lesson 69 **Circle the simple subject in each clause. Then underline the correct form of each verb in parentheses.**

1. The Lincoln Pool Rays (is/are) the name of our water polo team.
2. Our team (is/are) the best one that Lincoln High School has had in years.
3. Almost no one ever (defeat/defeats) us.
4. Nothing (stop/stops) us once we start scoring.
5. All of the players (follow/follows) the rules in a book our coach recommended.
6. *Water Polo for Winners* (describe/describes) how to raise the level of your game.
7. Everything about offensive and defensive plays (is/are) clearly explained.
8. Many of our competitors (use/uses) this book, too.
9. Few of them (succeed/succeeds) the way we do, though.
10. At the dinner table, our family (talk/talks) about our matches.
11. The whole group (travel/travels) to tournaments to cheer for our team.
12. Sometimes the school's band (play/plays) at our matches.
13. Not all of the members (come/comes), though.
14. The group (perform/performs) between periods.
15. The horn section (play/plays) loudly to encourage us.

Lesson 70 **Underline the verbal phrase that begins each sentence. If the phrase is a dangling or misplaced modifier, write *X* on the line. If the phrase is used correctly, circle the word it modifies and write *C* on the line.**

1. Having forgotten to set his alarm, Ed overslept. _______
2. Worried about being late for school, Ed sprang out of bed. _______
3. Getting dressed quickly, his socks were mismatched. _______
4. Tying his shoes, Ed's shoelaces broke. _______
5. Forgetting the bread in the toaster, the toast was burned. _______
6. Dropping his cereal bowl, Ed splashed milk and cereal everywhere. _______
7. Darting under his feet, Ed tripped over the new puppy. _______
8. Hurrying out the door, the sack lunch was left on the counter by Ed. _______
9. Running for the bus, Ed's hat fell off his head. _______
10. Bending to pick it up, Ed dropped all of his books. _______
11. Stopping to retrieve everything, the bus left without Ed. _______
12. Determined to get Ed to school on time, a shortcut was taken by Ed's mother. _______
13. Sitting in heavy traffic, Ed and his mother felt anxious. _______
14. Pulling into the parking lot, Ed thanked his mother and leaped from the car. _______
15. Beating the final bell, class started with Ed in his seat. _______

Extra Practice

Name ____________________

Lesson 71 Think about how many things are being compared in each sentence. Then underline the correct form of the adjective or adverb in parentheses.

1. Thuy is a (better/best) pitcher than Leah is.
2. Leah's pitches are a bit (slower/slowest) than Thuy's.
3. I am a (worse/worst) pitcher than either of them.
4. Both of them pitch (more accurately/most accurately) than I do.
5. I'm not a great pitcher, but I am the (better/best) catcher on the team.
6. I can keep the (faster/fastest) runners from stealing bases.
7. Marina has a (stronger/strongest) arm than Fia has.
8. Paula steals bases (more often/most often) than Thuy does.
9. Anne is the (more powerful/most powerful) hitter in our league.
10. She is a (better/best) bunter than anyone else, too.
11. There is no player who is (more committed/most committed) to winning than Rhea.
12. She is also the (more conscientious/most conscientious) about showing up for practice.
13. Tanya is the (more relaxed/most relaxed) player on the team.
14. Even in the (trickier/trickiest) situations, she never loses her cool.
15. We are definitely (better/best) prepared than we were last year!

Lesson 72 Underline the correct auxiliary verb in each sentence.

1. (Have/Could) you tried the new Thai restaurant on Grove Street?
2. If you enjoy Thai food, you (have/might) be interested in trying it.
3. I don't think I (have/might) ever tasted better Thai food.
4. You (would/have) enjoy it, too, I'm sure.
5. Your family (had/should) take you there some time.
6. The reviews of the restaurant (might/have) all been exceptionally good.
7. We (can/must) have ordered six dishes!
8. All of the dishes (have/were) made with the freshest ingredients.
9. The Thai noodles (may/should) be the best I have ever eaten.
10. My mother (could/had) never tasted such delicious coconut soup.
11. If you go there on a Saturday, you (have/might) need a reservation.
12. I (can/do) not know whether it is open on Sundays.
13. There (should/might) have been people eating there last Sunday.
14. My mom has said that I (do/may) invite a friend next time we go.
15. (Would/Can) you enjoy joining us for dinner there on Saturday?

Lesson 73 **Draw three lines (≡) under each lowercase letter that should be capitalized. Draw a line (/) through each uppercase letter that should be lowercase.**

1. I would like to visit several Countries in africa one day.
2. One country I would visit is the Republic of senegal.
3. Senegal lies on the coast of the atlantic ocean.
4. Some of its neighboring countries are Guinea-Bissau, guinea, mauritania, and mali.
5. The senegal river runs along the northern Border of senegal.
6. Like many other countries in africa, Senegal is a former french colony.
7. Its people celebrate Independence Day on april 4.
8. President abdoulaye wade took office on April 1, 2000, and was reelected in march 2007.
9. the capital city of dakar lies on the Cape Verde Peninsula.
10. Senegal is slightly smaller than the State of south dakota.
11. This tropical land experiences a rainy season from may through november.
12. The dry season lasts from december through april.
13. The official language of Senegal is french, but several other languages are spoken, including wolof.
14. About 350 miles off the Coast of the country lie the Cape verde Islands.
15. People in this island Nation speak cape Verde Creole and portuguese.

Lesson 74 **Draw three lines (≡) under the letters that should be capitalized. Underline or add quotation marks where they are needed in titles.**

1. My little brother just read the book The Great Broccoli Mystery by Edna Gernert.
2. Another great book by Edna Gernert is Streets Paved With Chocolate.
3. The movie version was called Fantastic Chocolate March.
4. Better Brush Your Teeth was a popular song from the movie.
5. I wrote a funny short story titled Orville and the Organic Farm.
6. If it's ever made into a movie, the theme song will be the veggie Guy.
7. The song at the end will be Lettuce all be friends.
8. Someday I will publish all my writing in a book titled Selected works of Matt Thompson.
9. My mother, who's a chef, wrote the cookbook artichoke artistry.
10. She was inspired to write it by the Pablo Neruda poem Ode to an Artichoke.
11. My mother says I eat wholesome foods because she read the methods of healthful cooking to me as a baby.
12. Dad says it's because he read me the poem It Mighta Been a Vitamin.
13. Maybe it's because I watched reruns of Julia Child and Company with my grandma.
14. My grandpa was fond of the movie Sylvester Graham and His Amazing Crackers.
15. I think that the next movie I watch will be attack of the brutal zucchini.

Extra Practice

Name ______________________________

Lesson 75 **Rewrite each item below. Use initials and abbreviations where you can.**

1. Doctor Judith Anne Green ______________
2. Mister Tristan Scott Reese ______________
3. Lindbergh Drive ______________
4. Mount Whitney ______________
5. Courtland Street ______________
6. Mistress Melissa Eve Choy ______________
7. Rotund Rock Corporation ______________
8. General Lloyd Henry MacIntyre ______________
9. Oak Glen Boulevard ______________
10. Mister Alberto Jose Lopez ______________
11. Green Meadow Road ______________
12. Doctor Elija Bergman ______________
13. Spiffy Sports Shoes Incorporated ______________
14. Sixteenth Avenue ______________
15. Parent Teacher Association ______________

Lesson 76 **Underline the correct word in parentheses. If the word is a possessive, write *P*. If the word is a contraction, write the two words it was made from.**

1. My (brother's/brothers') teacher wants him to enter the science fair. ______________
2. The (fair's/fairs') application deadline is next Tuesday. ______________
3. Wade (didn't/did'nt) know what to create. ______________
4. We had looked in books but (hadn't/had'nt) come up with a project idea. ______________
5. My (dad's/dads') suggestion was to make a robot. ______________
6. I told him that (wasn't/was'nt) a very realistic suggestion. ______________
7. My mother said that Wade could simulate a (volcano's/volcanos') eruption. ______________
8. That idea, while achievable, certainly (isn't/is'nt) an original one. ______________
9. (There's/Theres') always at least one erupting volcano at every science fair. ______________
10. Then I had the idea of using the (Internet's/Internets') resources. ______________
11. Wade and I went online, and within one (hours'/hour's) time, we had a great idea. ______________
12. Wade will determine which is cleaner, (dog's/dogs') mouths or the mouths of people. ______________
13. First, he will get cotton swab samples of several (people's/peoples') mouths. ______________
14. Then, he'll swab our dog (Red's/Reds') mouth. ______________
15. Finally, he will examine each (sample's/samples') bacteria under a microscope. ______________

Lesson 77 **Add commas where they belong. Remember that a comma is needed to separate pairs of similar adjectives.**

1. I went to the flea market with my mom and we found some great stuff.
2. She bought a used blender a stew pot, and a set of cups.
3. I found some tools, a pair of in-line skates and an old camera.
4. It was fun to walk around and look at all the affordable low-priced goods.
5. There was such a bright colorful array of kitchen items.
6. Despite the gray weather there were many buyers and sellers.
7. We saw antiques used clothing cookware, and a lot more.
8. I looked at vintage posters, old photographs postcards and sheet music.
9. The colorful treasure-laden stalls were packed with goods.
10. Food vendors were there as well so we sampled their wares.
11. We ate hot pretzels, corn on the cob and hot dogs.
12. A few raindrops fell in the afternoon but it was not enough to slow things down.
13. My sweet soft-spoken mother is quite a shrewd bargainer.
14. Thanks to her skills we got everything for less than the asking price.
15. There was a lively energetic feel to the place.

Lesson 78 **Add a colon or a semicolon to punctuate each sentence correctly.**

1. Joe helped his parents paint the living room it really needed it.
2. First, they moved out the furniture they stored it in the garage.
3. Next, they removed the light fixtures they also took the covers off the light switches.
4. They bought supplies paint, drop cloths, brushes, rollers, and so on.
5. Joe's parents had trouble deciding on the paint color his father wanted white, and his mother wanted color.
6. Joe considered the options he chose a soft blue.
7. The prep-work was tedious the family members had to mask all the windows with tape.
8. They washed the walls then they sanded them.
9. They did what's called "cutting in" that is the process of carefully painting the places where walls meet.
10. Joe liked the roller work it went more quickly than the brush work.
11. At the end of the day, they surveyed their work the room needed a second coat.
12. On day two, Joe had to paint the window frames and trim he didn't enjoy that.
13. His spirits lifted when his parents ordered the best pizza ever mushroom and pepperoni.
14. The family members were finished painting by 630, just in time to watch the football game.
15. Joe looked at the windows he'd painted he was proud of his handiwork.

Extra Practice

Name ______________________________

Lesson 79 **Cross out hyphens, parentheses, and dashes that are used incorrectly. Add hyphens, parentheses, and dashes where they belong.**

1. The word *astronaut* is derived from the Greek words *astron* ("star" and *nautes* "sailor").
2. Becoming an astronaut a dream for many young people is not easy to do.
3. Astronauts need to be physically fit. Much stamina is required for space travel.)
4. Astronauts also need to be highly qualified, self motivated individuals.
5. A background in the sciences (either biological or physical is highly desirable.
6. Math (and engineering) are two other valuable fields of study.
7. Candidates must exhibit a "can do" attitude.
8. Space exploration is a multinational endeavor astronauts from several nations often fly together so it's desirable for astronauts to be bilingual.
9. Finalists undergo a week long interview and orientation process.
10. Those selected for the program report to the Lyndon B. Johnson Space Center NASA headquarters.
11. They embark on a two year training and evaluation program.
12. Astronauts accumulate a number of flight hours in high performance jet aircraft.
13. To experience the zero gravity sensation of outer space, astronauts ride in a special four engine jet.
14. A series of steep climbs and dives forces passengers to float in mid air for up to 30 seconds at a time!
15. Do you think you have what it takes (to be) an astronaut?

Lesson 80 **Read each pair of quotations below. The first one is complete. The second one features an ellipsis that replaces a part of the first one. Mark an *X* if the ellipsis is used incorrectly.**

1. "A visit to Niagara Falls during any season of the year is a pure pleasure," says travel writer Ned Minor in *Best American Vacations.*

   "A visit to Niagara Falls . . . is a pure pleasure," says travel writer Ned Minor in *Best American Vacations.*

   _____

2. "Make time to ride the *Maid of the Mist*, a boat that takes tourists along the bottom of the falls, if you want to feel their power up close," he suggests.

   "Make time to ride the *Maid of the Mist* . . . a boat that takes tourists along the bottom of the falls . . . if you want to feel their power up close," he suggests. _____

3. "There are also parks and observation towers on both sides of the border that offer stunning views of the falls from all angles," Minor adds.

   "There are also parks and observation towers . . . that offer stunning views of the falls from all angles," Minor adds. _____

4. Minor warns, "This is a very popular destination, especially in the summer. Make sure you book your hotel early."

   Minor warns, "This is a very popular destination, especially in the summer. Make sure you. . . ." _____

Lesson 81 **Each sentence below is missing one or two punctuation marks. Rewrite the sentence. Insert the punctuation mark in parentheses to correctly indicate a pause. You may use the mark more than once.**

1. Last weekend, we saw an excellent new film *Beyond the Night* at the local theater. (,)

___

2. I found the movie very entertaining and it made me want to be an astronaut. (. . .)

___

3. The first scene surely one of the best in history shows two NASA crew members in space. (—)

___

4. The two women young astronauts on their first mission are repairing a satellite. (,)

___

5. It could be just a routine day or it could be a day that will change their lives forever. (. . .)

___

6. Ominous music I think it was also composed by the director rises in the background. (—)

___

7. Sensing some horrible accident would befall them I felt my heart racing and my palms sweating. (,)

___

8. I won't reveal anything more about the film that would be cruel of me until you've seen it. (—)

___

Lesson 82 **Add the missing quotation marks and/or commas to each sentence.**

1. Have you seen that new kung fu movie Juan? Lee asked.
2. "You mean the one that takes place at the space station don't you?" asked Juan.
3. Yes I've heard that the special effects are amazing, Lee replied.
4. I haven't seen it, but I read good reviews of it, Juan answered.
5. "Slow motion takes on new meaning in outer space doesn't it?" Lee said.
6. Juan answered with a laugh I guess there's faster action inside the station.
7. Let's see the movie this weekend, Lee suggested.
8. "Hey our social studies reports are due Monday" Juan reminded him.
9. "Ugh you're right!" groaned Lee as he slumped in his chair.
10. "You haven't started writing yours yet have you?" Juan inquired.
11. I've only done the outline, answered Lee, a worried frown on his face.
12. Let's work together on Saturday Juan suggested.
13. If we finish, he continued, maybe we can see the movie Sunday.
14. "Wow that's a great idea!" exclaimed Lee.
15. The thought of seeing the movie will motivate us to work efficiently, said Juan.

Extra Practice

Name ______________________________

Lesson 83 **Read each direct and indirect quotation from a text and add the correct punctuation. (Hint: Not all sentences need punctuation added.)**

1. The author of *Spotlight* makes his theme clear when he writes Lacey would find that friendship was the most important thing.
2. When he introduces his heroine, she has just told her best friend Meg that she is on the verge of realizing her dream of becoming a movie star.
3. Soon everyone in the world will know me, and I'll have a million friends she announces to Meg.
4. Meg is skeptical and a little jealous when she replies Yes, but only your true friends will be there when you need them.
5. The author hints that Lacey will learn this lesson the hard way when he later says As her name grew bigger, Lacey's old friends played a smaller part in her life. She couldn't believe it, but she was lonely.
6. He wants the reader to understand that there is a difference between people in our lives and real friends we can count on.
7. Luckily, Lacey shows she realizes this too when she says I took friendship for granted. I need it more than fame.
8. Lacey later apologizes to Meg and tries to explain that she let fame get the better of her.
9. Meg has trouble forgiving Lacey, and says I warned you not to leave your old friends behind.
10. In the end, however, the author writes Lacey finally learned how to live in the spotlight and keep the people she loved in her life.

Lesson 84 **Rewrite this business letter in correct letter form. Add in missing punctuation marks.**
Made Swift Sports Uniforms 9800 Settler Boulevard Denver, CO 80002 Dear Sir or Madam My soccer team is interested in purchasing new uniforms. Will you please send me a copy of your latest catalog? Sincerely yours Diana Hughes 253 Sunrise Avenue Greenville, SC 29602 May 12, 20__

____

____

____

____

____

____

____

____

____

____

____

Read this text and answer the questions on the next page.

China's Mighty Ships

The *Niña*, the *Pinta*, and the *Santa María* Columbus's legendary ships may be world-famous, but they were neither the first nor the largest vessels to explore the unknown. For thousands of years, Chinese sailors had been commanding ships called junks, which were massive enough to carry hundreds of people and many tons of cargo. In particular, the junks using in the 1405 expedition of Zheng He overshadowed any Western boat of that time. Some are thought to have been over 400 feet long and almost 200 feet wide. Putting this size in perspective, Columbus's *Pinta* was only about 56 feet long.

Nearly 100 years before the Italian's voyage, Zheng He and his fleet began a series of journeys that would take them to Africa, India, and other parts of Asia. The fleet included over 300 ships and nearly 30,000 men. It must have been quite an extraordinary sight, even at the vast ocean. There were boats for carrying supplies, boats for horses, boats for soldiers, warships, and boats that transported only fresh water for drinking.

Zheng He traded China's silk and fine pottery for African and Middle Eastern spices, ivory, wood, and gems? He brought novel items back to his native land to the delight and wonder of the emperor and his court. During a trip to Africa, he collected lions, zebras, and a giraffe. Zheng He not only oversaw the exchange of goods and ideas between China and the world and he also spread the influence of his empire far and wide.

After Zheng He died in 1433, China began a period of isolation that would last for centuries! The mighty expeditions of Chinese explorers were forgotten.

Name ______________________________

Read each item carefully. Fill in the circle next to the best answer.

1. What change, if any, should be made to the underlined words in lines 1–3?

Ⓐ NO CHANGE
Ⓑ Columbus's legendary ships,
Ⓒ , Columbus's legendary ships
Ⓓ , Columbus's legendary ships,

2. What change, if any, should be made to the underlined words in lines 3–5?

Ⓐ NO CHANGE
Ⓑ junks, which, were
Ⓒ junks which, were
Ⓓ junks which were

3. What change, if any, should be made to the underlined words in lines 5–6?

Ⓐ NO CHANGE
Ⓑ used in the
Ⓒ were used in the
Ⓓ to use in the

4. What change, if any, should be made to the underlined words in lines 7–8?

Ⓐ NO CHANGE
Ⓑ Put this size
Ⓒ After putting this size
Ⓓ To put this size

5. What change, if any, should be made to the underlined words in lines 11–12?

Ⓐ NO CHANGE
Ⓑ under the vast ocean
Ⓒ on the vast ocean
Ⓓ through the vast ocean

6. What change, if any, should be made to the underlined words in lines 15–16?

Ⓐ NO CHANGE
Ⓑ and gems;
Ⓒ and gems.
Ⓓ and gems!

7. What change, if any, should be made to the underlined words in lines 18–20?

Ⓐ NO CHANGE
Ⓑ world, or he
Ⓒ world but he
Ⓓ world, but he

8. What change, if any, should be made to the underlined words in lines 21–22?

Ⓐ NO CHANGE
Ⓑ for centuries.
Ⓒ for centuries?
Ⓓ for centuries:

Read each item carefully. Fill in the circle next to the best answer.

9. Read the following sentences.

> Observed under a microscope, snowflakes look like works of art. Each crystal is a unique six-sided marvel.

What part of the first sentence is underlined?

Ⓐ complete subject
Ⓑ complete predicate
Ⓒ simple subject
Ⓓ simple predicate

10. Read the following sentences.

> Loons are aquatic birds found in North America. These black-and-white swimmers dive underwater to catch fish.

What part of the first sentence is underlined?

Ⓐ direct object
Ⓑ indirect object
Ⓒ predicate noun
Ⓓ predicate adjective

11. Read the following sentences.

> I'm going to loan you my umbrella for the afternoon. Those dark clouds look threatening.

What part of the first sentence is underlined?

Ⓐ direct object
Ⓑ indirect object
Ⓒ predicate noun
Ⓓ predicate adjective

12. Read the following sentences.

> The magnolia, a flowering tree, is common throughout the South. With its large waxy leaves and even larger blossoms, it is hard to miss.

What part of the first sentence is underlined?

Ⓐ appositive
Ⓑ prepositional phrase
Ⓒ compound subject
Ⓓ simple subject

13. Read the following sentences.

> Sparky grabbed the bone and ran to the back of the yard. She immediately started burying her treat in the soft earth.

What part of the second sentence is underlined?

Ⓐ appositive
Ⓑ prepositional phrase
Ⓒ compound predicate
Ⓓ simple predicate

14. Read the following paragraph.

> [1] Joe and Mario want to earn money this summer. [2] They racked their brains to think of jobs they could do. [3] Mario's dad suggested that they do yard work for neighbors. [4] Now Mario and Joe are mowing grass and watering flowers for Mrs. Tran.

Which sentence has a compound predicate?

Ⓐ sentence 1
Ⓑ sentence 2
Ⓒ sentence 3
Ⓓ sentence 4

Name ______________________________

Read each item carefully. Fill in the circle next to the best answer.

15. Read the following sentences.

> The students <u>playing in the orchestra</u> are all excellent musicians. They were chosen after several rigorous auditions.

What part of the first sentence is underlined?

Ⓐ participial phrase
Ⓑ prepositional phrase
Ⓒ appositive
Ⓓ infinitive phrase

16. Read the following sentences.

> Many birds migrate, or relocate to a different area, for a certain season. Some fly thousands of miles <u>to reach their destinations</u>.

What part of the second sentence is underlined?

Ⓐ participial phrase
Ⓑ prepositional phrase
Ⓒ appositive
Ⓓ infinitive phrase

17. Read the following sentences.

> Althea has sent a care package <u>to her sister</u> in college. It is her first year away from home, and Althea misses her terribly.

What part of the first sentence is underlined?

Ⓐ participial phrase
Ⓑ prepositional phrase
Ⓒ appositive
Ⓓ infinitive phrase

18. Read the following paragraph.

> [1] Congratulations, you have been voted student of the month! [2] Come to the principal's office this afternoon to receive your prize. [3] There will be a photographer from the local paper there as well.

Where is the best place to add the following sentence?

> Do you mind if she takes your picture?

Ⓐ Before sentence 1
Ⓑ After sentence 1
Ⓒ After sentence 2
Ⓓ After sentence 3

19. Read the following sentences.

> [1] Wilson must choose an activity for next fall. [2] He might play lacrosse. [3] He might play the drums in the marching band. [4] No matter which activity he chooses, he will be busy.

What is the best way to combine sentences 2 and 3?

Ⓐ He might play lacrosse and play drums in the marching band.
Ⓑ He might play lacrosse or he might play the drums in the marching band.
Ⓒ He might play lacrosse, or he might play the drums in the marching band.
Ⓓ He might play lacrosse or, he might play the drums in the marching band.

20. Read the following sentences.

> I smell something cooking in the kitchen. <u>Did you start making dinner already?</u>

Which kind of sentence is underlined?

Ⓐ exclamatory
Ⓑ interrogative
Ⓒ declarative
Ⓓ imperative

Read this text and answer the questions on the next page.

Not Just a Falling Apple

Sir Isaac Newton, famed victim of that falling apple, gave much more to science than a funny story about observing gravity. Though his many ideas and theories greatly advanced our understanding of how the world works, he is mostly remembered for, watching a piece of fruit drop from a nearby tree. Some versions of the tale even describe the apple hitting him on the head!

Newton did tell others about this experience, but it is not likely, that he developed his theory of gravitation in an instant. The apple anecdote has lived on; because it is amusing. It also helps us hold on to a myth we enjoy about scientists: they come upon their ideas in a sudden moment of inspiration. In reality, scientific discovery takes a lot of thought and work. It involves trial and error, which takes time. Newton carefully formed his theory over many hours. He stated that all bodies with mass have a certain force that attracts them to each other, it is this force that causes an apple to always fall to the earth.

Newton thought of other laws that describe how and why objects move. Although they aren't linked to a legend about fruit, they are very important. These basic ideas are still considered in scientific study and still taught to every student in science class. Are the three universal laws of motion. The first law states that an object will continue moving or resting unless it is acted upon by an outside force. The second law describes how a moving object accelerates, or changes its speed. The third law says that when an object exerts a force on another object, the second object pushes back with an equal force. Remember these laws when you think of Newton next to them, that apple means nothing.

 Name ____________________

Read each item carefully. Fill in the circle next to the best answer.

1. What change, if any, should be made to the underlined words in lines 2–4?

   Ⓐ NO CHANGE
   Ⓑ remembered, for watching
   Ⓒ remembered for watching
   Ⓓ remembered; for watching

2. What change, if any, should be made to the underlined words in lines 6–7?

   Ⓐ NO CHANGE
   Ⓑ likely; that he
   Ⓒ likely. That he
   Ⓓ likely that he

3. What change, if any, should be made to the underlined words in lines 7–8?

   Ⓐ NO CHANGE
   Ⓑ lived on, because
   Ⓒ lived on: because
   Ⓓ lived on because

4. What change, if any, should be made to the underlined words in lines 10–11?

   Ⓐ NO CHANGE
   Ⓑ error. Which takes
   Ⓒ error; which takes
   Ⓓ error which takes

5. What change, if any, should be made to the underlined words in lines 12–13?

   Ⓐ NO CHANGE
   Ⓑ other. It is
   Ⓒ other it is
   Ⓓ other; is

6. What change, if any, should be made to the underlined words in line 15?

   Ⓐ NO CHANGE
   Ⓑ fruit they are
   Ⓒ fruit; they are
   Ⓓ fruit. They are

7. What change, if any, should be made to the underlined words in line 17?

   Ⓐ NO CHANGE
   Ⓑ Are three
   Ⓒ The three
   Ⓓ They are the three

8. What change, if any, should be made to the underlined words in lines 21–22?

   Ⓐ NO CHANGE
   Ⓑ Newton, next to
   Ⓒ Newton, Next to
   Ⓓ Newton. Next to

Read each item carefully. Fill in the circle next to the best answer.

9. Read the following sentences.

> Jane Austen wrote several novels, but she is most remembered for *Pride and Prejudice*. It is the story of five sisters living in England at the turn of the nineteenth century.

What kind of sentence is underlined?

Ⓐ simple
Ⓑ compound
Ⓒ complex
Ⓓ compound-complex

10. Read the following sentences.

> Although darkness will come sooner tomorrow, I am glad that daylight saving time is ending. We will gain an extra hour of sleep tonight.

Which part of the first sentence is underlined?

Ⓐ prepositional phrase
Ⓑ participial phrase
Ⓒ dependent clause
Ⓓ independent clause

11. Read the following sentences.

> [1] The flowers are perennials. [2] They grow in front of Sasha's house. [3] They bloom every year at the beginning of June.

What is the best way to combine sentences 1 and 2?

Ⓐ The flowers, they grow in front of Sasha's house.
Ⓑ The flowers that grow in front of Sasha's house are perennials.
Ⓒ The flowers that grow, in front of Sasha's house are perennials.
Ⓓ The flowers are growing perennials in front of Sasha's house.

12. Read the following sentences.

> Set up your tents and gather some kindling. We'll build the campfire after the sun has gone down.

Which part of the second sentence is underlined?

Ⓐ independent clause
Ⓑ adjective clause
Ⓒ adverb clause
Ⓓ nonrestrictive clause

13. Read the following sentences.

> The counselor who works at our school is my aunt, Fiona. She has an advanced degree in psychology.

Which part of the first sentence is underlined?

Ⓐ nonrestrictive clause
Ⓑ restrictive clause
Ⓒ adverb clause
Ⓓ independent clause

14. Read the following paragraph.

> [1] It is true that Orville and Wilbur were in the Kitty Hawk area on that day in 1903. [2] The famous flight, however, took place closer to Kill Devil Hills. [3] This lesser-known town is several miles south of Kitty Hawk.

Where is the best place to add the following sentence?

> Kitty Hawk, North Carolina, is often cited as the place where the Wright brothers first flew their plane.

Ⓐ Before sentence 1
Ⓑ After sentence 1
Ⓒ After sentence 2
Ⓓ After sentence 3

Name ______________________________

Read each item carefully. Fill in the circle next to the best answer.

15. Read the following sentences.

> Writing words with suffixes can be quite challenging. The spelling of the base word is often changed.

What kind of phrase is underlined?

- (A) appositive
- (B) infinitive
- (C) gerund
- (D) participial

16. Read the following sentences.

> Springtime, when tree branches are still bare, is the perfect time for birding. Birds are more easily spotted, and great numbers of them are on the move.

Which part of the first sentence is underlined?

- (A) independent clause
- (B) nonrestrictive clause
- (C) prepositional phrase
- (D) appositive

17. Read the following sentences.

> I agree with the moral of this folktale. Wise is the person who chooses happiness over material wealth.

Which kind of order is represented by the underlined sentence?

- (A) natural
- (B) inverted
- (C) chronological
- (D) interrupted

18. Read the following sentences.

> Mosquitoes, which can carry a disease called malaria, are a danger in tropical areas. Make sure you use repellent and sleep inside protective netting.

Which kind of order is represented by the underlined sentence?

- (A) natural
- (B) inverted
- (C) chronological
- (D) interrupted

19. Read the following sentences.

> The first federal United States postage stamp was issued on July 1, 1847. Before the national government _____ could be bought only from private printers.

Which words and punctuation best complete the second sentence?

- (A) sold stamps, they
- (B) sold stamps they
- (C) sold stamps; they
- (D) sold stamps: they

20. Read the following paragraph.

> [1] The art show features many of the artists in our class. [2] Devon sculpted that figure out of clay. [3] The giant mural was painted by Tonya and Wang Li. [4] Tim took those photographs of the old factory downtown.

Which sentence is written in the passive voice?

- (A) sentence 1
- (B) sentence 2
- (C) sentence 3
- (D) sentence 4

Read this text and answer the questions on the next page.

Lost!

The sun was sinking lower in the sky, and Charlotte was worried. "How could I have let myself get separated from the group?" she said out loud. The dense thicket of conifers in front of her will not respond. Charlotte had wandered in what seemed like circles for three hours, and now she had to admit that she was lost, darkness was coming, and her only companions were these trees. As these realizations washes over her, worry quickly turned to panic.

"Get a grip, Lottie." She again speaks to herself, this time in a whisper. She sat down on a nearby log, took a few deep breaths, and looked carefully at the surrounding forest. She tried to remember the moment when she will have first found herself alone and cut off from her friends. She had stopped, for only a moment, to investigate an unusual wildflower a few yards off the trail. She had taken several pictures of the blossom so she could identify it later. And then, suddenly, she had noticed the silence around her.

"I should have just retraced my steps back to camp," Charlotte thought, "but instead I ran blindly through the woods after my friends. I wish I could see just one familiar landmark that would help me get on the right track. These trees all look exactly alike!" More shadows gathered. The light was fading.

Frantically, Charlotte thought of her older brother, an Eagle Scout. "If I was Drew, what would I do?" she asked. Then it hit her. The sun was setting in the west, and the camp was on the western edge of the park. "I'll walk toward the sun!" she said, her feet already blazing a trail through the underbrush. A half hour later, she is relieved to see the camp lights twinkling in the dusk.

Unit 4 Posttest

Name ______________________________

Read each item carefully. Fill in the circle next to the best answer.

1. What change, if any, should be made to the underlined words in line 1?

   Ⓐ NO CHANGE
   Ⓑ The sun is sinking
   Ⓒ The sun were sinking
   Ⓓ The sun will have sunk

2. What change, if any, should be made to the underlined words in lines 2–3?

   Ⓐ NO CHANGE
   Ⓑ is not responding
   Ⓒ does not respond
   Ⓓ did not respond

3. What change, if any, should be made to the underlined words in line 6?

   Ⓐ NO CHANGE
   Ⓑ washed over her
   Ⓒ wash over her
   Ⓓ will wash over her

4. What change, if any, should be made to the underlined words in line 7?

   Ⓐ NO CHANGE
   Ⓑ She again has spoken
   Ⓒ She again spoke
   Ⓓ She again is speaking

5. What change, if any, should be made to the underlined words in lines 9–10?

   Ⓐ NO CHANGE
   Ⓑ when she had first
   Ⓒ when she has first
   Ⓓ when she was first

6. What change, if any, should be made to the underlined words in line 12?

   Ⓐ NO CHANGE
   Ⓑ She has taken
   Ⓒ She is taken
   Ⓓ She will have taken

7. What change, if any, should be made to the underlined words in lines 18–19?

   Ⓐ NO CHANGE
   Ⓑ If I will be Drew
   Ⓒ If I were Drew
   Ⓓ If I am Drew

8. What change, if any, should be made to the underlined words in lines 21–22?

   Ⓐ NO CHANGE
   Ⓑ she has been relieved
   Ⓒ she will be relieved
   Ⓓ she was relieved

Read each item carefully. Fill in the circle next to the best answer.

9. Read the following sentences.

> Ellen could not sleep because she was anxious about her track meet. She tossed and turned all night.

Which underlined word is a linking verb?

- (A) could
- (B) sleep
- (C) was
- (D) tossed

10. Read the following sentences.

> Kudzu is an invasive vine that grows mainly in the southeastern United States. It has become an undesirable plant because it strangles the surrounding flora.

Which underlined word is a transitive verb?

- (A) is
- (B) grows
- (C) has become
- (D) strangles

11. Read the following sentences.

> The Farmville Humane Society _____ popcorn and hot dogs at tomorrow's carnival. All money raised will go toward building a new animal shelter.

Which verb best completes the first sentence?

- (A) was selling
- (B) will be selling
- (C) has sold
- (D) had sold

12. Read the following sentences.

> Marco's teacher suggested that he interview a geologist before writing his research paper. Professional scientists can be great resources with up-to-date information.

Which mood is expressed by the underlined verb?

- (A) indicative
- (B) interrogative
- (C) imperative
- (D) subjunctive

13. Read the following sentences.

> "Read this book if you like mysteries," Xavier said. "I couldn't put it down."

Which mood is expressed by the underlined verb?

- (A) indicative
- (B) interrogative
- (C) imperative
- (D) subjunctive

14. Read the following paragraph.

> [1] In 1588, Philip II of Spain attempted to invade England and overthrow Queen Elizabeth. [2] He hoped the Spanish Armada would be the invincible weapon that achieved this goal. [3] The Spanish Armada was so large. [4] This caused it to take two days to leave the port in Lisbon.

What is the best way to combine sentences 3 and 4?

- (A) The Spanish Armada took two days to leave the port in Lisbon and it was so large.
- (B) The Spanish Armada was so large because it took two days to leave the port in Lisbon.
- (C) The Spanish Armada took two days to leave the port in Lisbon because it was so large.
- (D) Because it was so large the Spanish Armada took two days to leave the port in Lisbon.

Name ______________________________

Read each item carefully. Fill in the circle next to the best answer.

15. Read the following sentences.

> Brainstorm a topic for your report, and then look for appropriate resources at the library. Write important facts on note cards, and you should remember to include bibliographical information as well.

Which underlined verb represents a shift in mood?

- Ⓐ Brainstorm
- Ⓑ look
- Ⓒ Write
- Ⓓ should remember

16. Read the following sentences.

> "If I were you, I'd _____ French," Aunt Susan said. "It's such a beautiful language."

Which verb best completes the first sentence?

- Ⓐ take
- Ⓑ takes
- Ⓒ took
- Ⓓ taken

17. Read the following sentences.

> "Chocolate is my favorite flavor, _____ I think I'll try strawberry today," Jill said as she peered into the ice cream case. She was in the mood for something different.

Which word is a coordinating conjunction that correctly completes the first sentence?

- Ⓐ though
- Ⓑ but
- Ⓒ and
- Ⓓ since

18. Read the following sentences.

> When a storm forms in the warm waters near the equator, it can become a hurricane. The heat fuels the storm, and wind patterns cause the air to swirl.

Which underlined word is a subordinating conjunction?

- Ⓐ When
- Ⓑ near
- Ⓒ can
- Ⓓ and

19. Read the following sentences.

> _____ you ride the subway or take the bus, you will still arrive in plenty of time. The concert doesn't start for several hours.

Which correlative conjunction best completes the first sentence?

- Ⓐ Either
- Ⓑ Neither
- Ⓒ Not only
- Ⓓ Whether

20. Read the following paragraph.

> [1] Several local bands marched in the Independence Day parade. [2] Carriages and floats were pulled by beautiful draft horses. [3] The grand marshal, the town's mayor, rode in a shiny convertible. [4] She waved and threw candy to the spectators.

Which sentence contains a shift to passive voice?

- Ⓐ sentence 1
- Ⓑ sentence 2
- Ⓒ sentence 3
- Ⓓ sentence 4

Read this text and answer the questions on the next page.

Facing a Fear

Mrs. Jones paused outside her daughter's room and listened to the high, sweet voice raising and falling on the other side of the door. "That girl can really sing," she thought to herself with a sad smile. "I wish she had the courage to let the world hear it."

Keisha Jones she was known as the quietest girl in her class. She might have even been the biggest wallflower in all of James Madison Middle School. Speaking in class made her tremble, and talking to strangers made her blush. Shy Keisha thought and felt many things she could not bring herself to say out loud. She was an avid reader and a history buff. She loved jazz music, and, when she was alone, she could belt out a tune like a professional singer. Few people known, of course, about her amazing vocal talent.

Mrs. Jones wrapped softly on Keisha's door and entered the room. "Are you practicing something special, honey?" she asked. "It sounds wonderful."

"Oh, I'm just imagining what it would be like to try out for the school musical," Keisha replied. "I'd never get the part, but it's fun to dream, right?"

Mrs. Jones was all, "What makes you think you wouldn't get the part?"

"Well, there are over a dozen girls trying out for one thing," Keisha replied. "And then there's the fact that singing in public is terrifying."

"I know expressing yourself is scary, Keisha, but maybe it's time you faced that fear. It's a shame that nobody can't ever hear that lovely voice."

"You think my voice is lovely?" Keisha reddened a little, but then she looked determined. "I'll think about trying out." It was definitely a start.

Unit 5 Posttest

Name ______________________________

Read each item carefully. Fill in the circle next to the best answer.

1. What change, if any, should be made to the underlined words in lines 1–2?

   Ⓐ NO CHANGE
   Ⓑ sweet voice razing
   Ⓒ sweet voice rising
   Ⓓ sweet voice risen

2. What change, if any, should be made to the underlined words in line 5?

   Ⓐ NO CHANGE
   Ⓑ Keisha she was
   Ⓒ Keisha Jones was
   Ⓓ Keisha Jones her was

3. What change, if any, should be made to the underlined words in lines 8–9?

   Ⓐ NO CHANGE
   Ⓑ bring herself too say
   Ⓒ bring herself two say
   Ⓓ bring her to say

4. What change, if any, should be made to the underlined words in lines 10–11?

   Ⓐ NO CHANGE
   Ⓑ Few people knowed
   Ⓒ Few people knewed
   Ⓓ Few people knew

5. What change, if any, should be made to the underlined words in line 12?

   Ⓐ NO CHANGE
   Ⓑ rapt softly
   Ⓒ rapped softly
   Ⓓ wraps softly

6. What change, if any, should be made to the underlined words in line 16?

   Ⓐ NO CHANGE
   Ⓑ Mrs. Jones asked
   Ⓒ Mrs. Jones went
   Ⓓ Mrs. Jones was like

7. What change, if any, should be made to the underlined words in lines 17–18?

   Ⓐ NO CHANGE
   Ⓑ more then a dozen girls
   Ⓒ higher than a dozen girls
   Ⓓ more than a dozen girls

8. What change, if any, should be made to the underlined words in line 20?

   Ⓐ NO CHANGE
   Ⓑ nobody can never hear
   Ⓒ nobody can ever hear
   Ⓓ anybody can't never hear

Read each item carefully. Fill in the circle next to the best answer.

9. Read the following sentences.

> "This essay has _____ mistakes than your last one did," said Mr. Travers. "Your writing is really improving."

Which word best completes the first sentence?

Ⓐ less
Ⓑ littler
Ⓒ fewer
Ⓓ smaller than

10. Read the following sentences.

> I have no idea _____ going to win the top prize at the science fair. There are so many excellent projects this year.

Which word best completes the first sentence?

Ⓐ whose
Ⓑ whom
Ⓒ who's
Ⓓ whom's

11. Read the following sentences.

> The little tabby's kittens just opened _____ eyes yesterday. They sleep together in a fuzzy ball.

Which word best completes the first sentence?

Ⓐ it's
Ⓑ its
Ⓒ their
Ⓓ they're

12. Read the following sentences.

> Dad and I spent the afternoon sketching the natural scenes around us. "It's nice to see _____ artistic side," he said.

Which word best completes the second sentence?

Ⓐ you
Ⓑ you's
Ⓒ you're
Ⓓ your

13. Read the following sentences.

> Kevin was nervous about his job interview scheduled for the following day. He _____ out his clothes, résumé, and bus fare so he would be ready in the morning.

Which word best completes the second sentence?

Ⓐ lay
Ⓑ laid
Ⓒ lain
Ⓓ lied

14. Read the following paragraph.

> [1] Mahatma Gandhi was a leader of the early twentieth-century movement to end British rule of India. [2] He organized large demonstrations to protest taxes and other injustices imposed on his people. [3] This guy believed that much could be accomplished through nonviolent actions. [4] He was often imprisoned, however, for challenging the government.

Which sentence contains a word or words that should be avoided in academic writing?

Ⓐ sentence 1
Ⓑ sentence 2
Ⓒ sentence 3
Ⓓ sentence 4

Name ______________________________

Read each item carefully. Fill in the circle next to the best answer.

15. Read the following sentences.

> Lamar had so much nervous energy that he could not _____ still. He stood up and began pacing back and forth.

Which word best completes the first sentence?

- Ⓐ sit
- Ⓑ sat
- Ⓒ set
- Ⓓ sets

16. Read the following sentences.

> Elizabeth Blackwell _____ to study medicine at a time when only men were accepted as physicians. In 1849, she became the first woman in the United States to earn a medical degree.

Which word best completes the first sentence?

- Ⓐ choose
- Ⓑ chose
- Ⓒ chosen
- Ⓓ choosed

17. Read the following sentences.

> [1] Jeff pulled his laundry out of the dryer. [2] He had a look of horror on his face. [3] His favorite sweater had shrunk to half its original size!

What is the best way to combine sentences 1 and 2?

- Ⓐ Jeff pulled his laundry out of the dryer, he had a look of horror on his face.
- Ⓑ When Jeff pulled his laundry out of the dryer he, had a look of horror on his face.
- Ⓒ Jeff pulled his laundry out of the dryer, because he had a look of horror on his face.
- Ⓓ When Jeff pulled his laundry out of the dryer, he had a look of horror on his face.

18. Read the following sentences.

> Langston Hughes saw his first book of poetry, *The Weary Blues*, published in 1926. He went on to _____ plays, novels, short stories, and more poems.

Which word best completes the second sentence?

- Ⓐ right
- Ⓑ rite
- Ⓒ wright
- Ⓓ write

19. Read the following paragraph.

> [1] She loves tromping through the snow and feeling the icy breeze on her face. [2] Rhett, on the other hand, prefers the summer months. [3] He spends as much time as he can out in the sun.

Where is the best place to add the following sentence?

> Karen is always happiest during the winter.

- Ⓐ Before sentence 1
- Ⓑ After sentence 1
- Ⓒ After sentence 2
- Ⓓ After sentence 3

20. Read the following sentences.

> Mount Kilimanjaro, in Tanzania, is the tallest mountain in the continent of Africa. With a peak 19,341 feet above sea level, it is also the tallest free-standing mountain in the world.

Which underlined words are unnecessary?

- Ⓐ in Tanzania
- Ⓑ the continent of
- Ⓒ above sea level
- Ⓓ in the world

Read this text and answer the questions on the next page.

Little Italy, 1905

It has been two years since we arrived here in New York City, but it is still difficult to call it home. Papa assures me that we had to leave our friends and family in Italy. He says that life here is not perfect, but there are many more opportunities. This optimism has never wavered, despite the fact that Papa lost his job at the shoe factory several months ago. Mama has tried to support us by sewing shirts and petticoats at home, but I can tell by the anxious look he always wears that our situation is becoming desperate.

The air in our small flat are very oppressive, both literally and figuratively. We share one floor of a ten-story building with three other families. Our two rooms consist of a kitchen and a bedroom where Papa, Mama, Luciana, Natalia, Ernesto, and I sleep. The single window provides little breeze, and the flat is often hot and smoky. Just outside, the smells of garbage and manure from the streetcar horses assaults me as soon as I leave the building.

My one refuge is school, where I am learning English, mathematics, and science. It is my favorite subject, and my teacher thinks I have a natural talent for it. The school is also kind enough to provide a free hot lunch. Ernesto and me are so grateful for the meal because it ensures that we will not take food from the mouths of our sisters and parents.

I am afraid, however, that the time has come to put aside my education. I am almost fifteen and perfectly capable of finding work. I love my studies, but my family need me. Maybe things will begin looking up for us, as Papa says, and he will be able to open his store. Until then, hope is all we have.

Unit 6 Posttest

Name ______________________________

Read each item carefully. Fill in the circle next to the best answer.

1. What change, if any, should be made to the underlined words in lines 3–4?

   Ⓐ NO CHANGE
   Ⓑ You say that
   Ⓒ It says that
   Ⓓ She says that

2. What change, if any, should be made to the underlined words in lines 4–5?

   Ⓐ NO CHANGE
   Ⓑ had never wavered
   Ⓒ have never wavered
   Ⓓ was never wavered

3. What change, if any, should be made to the underlined words in lines 5–7?

   Ⓐ NO CHANGE
   Ⓑ she always wears
   Ⓒ they always wear
   Ⓓ it always wears

4. What change, if any, should be made to the underlined words in line 8?

   Ⓐ NO CHANGE
   Ⓑ were very oppressive
   Ⓒ is very oppressive
   Ⓓ was very oppressive

5. What change, if any, should be made to the underlined words in lines 12–13?

   Ⓐ NO CHANGE
   Ⓑ was assaulting me
   Ⓒ has assaulted me
   Ⓓ assault me

6. What change, if any, should be made to the underlined words in lines 15–16?

   Ⓐ NO CHANGE
   Ⓑ Mathematics is my
   Ⓒ They are my
   Ⓓ School is my

7. What change, if any, should be made to the underlined words in lines 16–18?

   Ⓐ NO CHANGE
   Ⓑ Me and Ernesto
   Ⓒ Ernesto and I
   Ⓓ I and Ernesto

8. What change, if any, should be made to the underlined words in lines 20–21?

   Ⓐ NO CHANGE
   Ⓑ family have needed me
   Ⓒ family needs me
   Ⓓ family are needing me

Read each item carefully. Fill in the circle next to the best answer.

9. Read the following sentences.

> Louisa May Alcott, _____ wrote the classic *Little Women*, was born in 1832. The novel is based on her life with her three sisters.

Which word best completes the first sentence?

Ⓐ that
Ⓑ whose
Ⓒ who
Ⓓ whom

10. Read the following sentences.

> Avery told her friend Warren that she was moving to another state. He looked devastated after she broke the news to him.

Which underlined word is an object pronoun?

Ⓐ her
Ⓑ she
Ⓒ He
Ⓓ him

11. Read the following sentences.

> Neither Talia nor Akira _____ action movies. Maybe we should think of something else to see.

Which verb best completes the first sentence?

Ⓐ like
Ⓑ likes
Ⓒ are going to like
Ⓓ have liked

12. Read the following sentences.

> [1] Nobody admires a sore loser. [2] Smile at your opponent. [3] Give him or her a handshake.

What is the best way to combine sentences 2 and 3?

Ⓐ Smile at your opponent, give him or her a handshake.
Ⓑ Smile at your opponent and, give him or her a handshake.
Ⓒ Smile at your opponent, and give him or her a handshake.
Ⓓ Smile at your opponent but give him or her a handshake.

13. Read the following paragraph.

> [1] They look like icicles, but they are actually made of minerals. [2] Stalactites are often found in caves made of limestone. [3] Water drips from the ceiling and leaves long tubular deposits of calcite.

Where is the best place to add the following sentence?

> Stalactites are formations that hang from the ceilings of caves.

Ⓐ Before sentence 1
Ⓑ After sentence 1
Ⓒ After sentence 2
Ⓓ After sentence 3

14. Read the following sentences.

> I promised my brother that I would take _____ to the park later. I couldn't tell who was more excited—little boy or dog.

Which words best complete the first sentence?

Ⓐ he and Scruffy
Ⓑ him and Scruffy
Ⓒ his and Scruffy
Ⓓ himself and Scruffy

 Name ______________________

Read each item carefully. Fill in the circle next to the best answer.

15. Read the following sentences.

> *Romeo and Juliet* _____ one of today's most popular Shakespearean plays. The tragic story of star-crossed lovers is read and performed in high schools everywhere.

Which verb best completes the first sentence?

- Ⓐ were
- Ⓑ was
- Ⓒ are
- Ⓓ is

16. Read the following sentences.

> Thanks, Julie, for the wool socks you knitted for me. _____ will keep my feet toasty all winter.

Which pronoun best completes the second sentence?

- Ⓐ You
- Ⓑ She
- Ⓒ They
- Ⓓ We

17. Read the following sentences.

> Violet clasped her hands together and gave Dad her most pleading look. "_____ I go to the concert?" she asked.

Which auxiliary verb best completes the second sentence?

- Ⓐ Can
- Ⓑ May
- Ⓒ Must
- Ⓓ Could

18. Read the following paragraph.

> [1] The sights and sounds of the rain forest were almost overwhelming. [2] The loud squawking of exotic birds filled the air. [3] Swinging from tree to tree, we saw the cutest monkeys. [4] And when we listened closely, we could hear the roar of a distant waterfall.

Which sentence contains a misplaced modifier?

- Ⓐ sentence 1
- Ⓑ sentence 2
- Ⓒ sentence 3
- Ⓓ sentence 4

19. Read the following sentences.

> The Charleston was the _____ dance of the 1920s. It involved twisting the feet and kicking them forward and backward.

Which word or words best complete the first sentence?

- Ⓐ popularest
- Ⓑ most popular
- Ⓒ more popular
- Ⓓ popularer

20. Read the following sentences.

> Marisol is clearly the more conscientious twin. She checked her homework <u>more carefully</u> than Miranda did.

What part of the second sentence is underlined?

- Ⓐ comparative adverb
- Ⓑ comparative adjective
- Ⓒ superlative adverb
- Ⓓ superlative adjective

Grammar, Usage, and Mechanics Handbook Table of Contents

Mechanics

Sentence Structure and Parts of Speech

(Continued on page 362)

(Continued from page 361)

Usage

Letters and E-mails

Research

Guidelines for Listening and Speaking

(you) | Diagram | sentences

Mechanics

Section 1 Capitalization

- **Capitalize the first word in a sentence.** The kangaroo rat is an amazing animal.
- **Capitalize all *proper nouns,* including people's names and the names of particular places.**
  Gregory Gordon   Washington Monument
- **Capitalize titles of respect.** Mr. Alvarez   Dr. Chin   Ms. Murphy
- **Capitalize family titles used just before people's names and titles of respect that are part of names.**
  Uncle Frank   Aunt Mary   Governor Adamson
- **Capitalize initials of names.**
  Thomas Paul Gerard (T. P. Gerard)
- **Capitalize place names.** France   Utah   China   Baltimore
- **Capitalize *proper adjectives,* adjectives that are made from proper nouns.**
  Chinese   Icelandic   French   Latin American
- **Capitalize the months of the year and the days of the week.**
  February   April   Monday   Tuesday
- **Capitalize important words in the names of products and companies.**
  Blue Brook Cheese Spread   Heart of Gold Applesauce
  Little Hills Bakery   Anderson and Mumford, Inc.
- **Capitalize important words in the names of organizations.**
  American Lung Association   Veterans of Foreign Wars
- **Capitalize important words in the names of holidays.**
  Veterans Day   Fourth of July
- **Capitalize the first word in the greeting or closing of a letter.**
  Dear Edmundo,   Yours truly,
- **Capitalize the word *I.*** Frances and I watched the movie together.
- **Capitalize the first, last, and most important words in a title. Be sure to capitalize all verbs, including *is* and *was.***
  Island of the Blue Dolphins   *Away Is a Strange Place to Be*
- **Capitalize the first word in a direct quotation.**
  Aunt Rose said, "Please pass the clam dip."

Section 2 Abbreviations and Initials

***Abbreviations* are shortened forms of words. Many abbreviations begin with an uppercase letter and end with a period.**

- **You can abbreviate words used in addresses when you write.**
  Street (**St.**)   Avenue (**Ave.**)   Route (**Rte.**)   Boulevard (**Blvd.**)   Road (**Rd.**)   Drive (**Dr.**)
- **Use postal abbreviations for names of states in addresses.**

Note: State names are abbreviated as two uppercase letters, with no periods.

Alabama (AL)
Alaska (AK)
Arizona (AZ)
Arkansas (AR)
California (CA)
Colorado (CO)
Connecticut (CT)
Delaware (DE)
District of Columbia (DC)
Florida (FL)
Georgia (GA)
Hawaii (HI)
Idaho (ID)
Illinois (IL)
Indiana (IN)
Iowa (IA)
Kansas (KS)
Kentucky (KY)
Louisiana (LA)
Maine (ME)
Maryland (MD)
Massachusetts (MA)
Michigan (MI)
Minnesota (MN)
Mississippi (MS)
Missouri (MO)
Montana (MT)
Nebraska (NE)
Nevada (NV)
New Hampshire (NH)
New Jersey (NJ)
New Mexico (NM)
New York (NY)
North Carolina (NC)
North Dakota (ND)
Ohio (OH)
Oklahoma (OK)
Oregon (OR)
Pennsylvania (PA)
Rhode Island (RI)
South Carolina (SC)
South Dakota (SD)
Tennessee (TN)
Texas (TX)
Utah (UT)
Vermont (VT)
Virginia (VA)
Washington (WA)
West Virginia (WV)
Wisconsin (WI)
Wyoming (WY)

- **You can abbreviate titles of address and titles of respect when you write.**
  Mister (**Mr.** Brian Davis) Mistress (**Miss** *or* **Mrs.** Maria Rosario) General (**Gen.** Robert E. Lee)
  Doctor (**Dr.** Emily Chu) Junior (Everett Castle **Jr.**) Saint (**St.** Andrew)

Note: *Ms.* is a title of address used for women. It is not an abbreviation, but it requires a period (**Ms.** Anita Brown).

- **You can abbreviate certain words in the names of businesses when you write.**
  Pet Helpers, Incorporated (Pet Helpers, **Inc.**) Zykar Corporation (Zykar **Corp.**)
- **You can abbreviate days of the week when you take notes.**
  Sunday (**Sun.**) Wednesday (**Wed.**) Friday (**Fri.**)
  Monday (**Mon.**) Thursday (**Thurs.**) Saturday (**Sat.**)
  Tuesday (**Tues.**)
- **You can abbreviate months of the year when you take notes.**
  January (**Jan.**) April (**Apr.**) October (**Oct.**)
  February (**Feb.**) August (**Aug.**) November (**Nov.**)
  March (**Mar.**) September (**Sept.**) December (**Dec.**)
  (May, June, and July do not have abbreviated forms.)
- **You can abbreviate directions when you take notes.**
  North (N) East (E) South (S) West (W)

An *initial* is the first letter of a name. An initial is written as an uppercase letter and a period. Sometimes initials are used in the names of countries or other places.

Michael Paul Sanders (**M. P.** Sanders) United States of America (**U. S. A.**)
Washington, District of Columbia (Washington, **D. C.**)

An *acronym* is a special type of abbreviation that is formed from the first letters of a group of words. Some acronyms, such as *NASA* (National Aeronautics and Space Administration), are written in all capitals. Others, such as *scuba* (self-contained underwater breathing apparatus), are written as regular words, in all-lowercase letters.

Section 3 Titles

- **Underline titles of books, newspapers, TV series, movies, and magazines.**
  Island of the Blue Dolphins Miami Herald I Love Lucy

Note: These titles are written in italics in printed text.

- **Use quotation marks around articles in magazines, short stories, chapters in books, songs, and poems.**
  "This Land Is Your Land" "The Gift" "Eletelephony"
- **Capitalize the first, last, and most important words in titles. Articles, short prepositions, and conjunctions are usually not capitalized. Be sure to capitalize all verbs, including forms of the verb *be* (*am, is, are, was, were, been*).**
  A Knight in the Attic *My Brother Sam Is Dead*

Section 4 Quotations and Quotation Marks

- **Put quotation marks (" ") around the titles of articles, short stories, book chapters, songs, and poems.**
  My favorite short story is "Revenge of the Reptiles."
- **Put quotation marks around a *direct quotation*, a speaker's exact words or direct speech.**
  "Did you see that alligator?" Max asked.
- **Do not put quotation marks around an *indirect quotation*, a person's words retold by another speaker. An indirect quotation is often signaled by *whether* or *that*.**
  Max asked Rory whether he had seen an alligator.

Writing a Conversation

- **Put quotation marks around the speaker's words. Begin a direct quotation with an uppercase letter. Use a comma to separate the quotation from the rest of the sentence.**
  Rory said, "There are no alligators in this area."
- **When a direct quotation comes at the end of a sentence, put the end mark inside the last quotation mark.**
  Max cried, "Look out!"
- **When writing a conversation, begin a new paragraph with each change of speaker.**
  Max panted, "I swear I saw a huge scaly tail and a flat snout in the water!"

  "Relax," Rory said. "I told you there are no alligators around here."

- **Put quotation marks around a quotation from a text. Include information on the source of the quotation.**
  In his letter from the Birmingham jail, which was reprinted in the *Atlantic Monthly* (August 1963), the great civil rights leader Martin Luther King Jr. wrote, "Injustice anywhere is a threat to justice everywhere."

Writing a Long Quotation From a Text

- **Set off a lengthy quotation from the rest of an essay or a report, either by indenting the whole block of text or by printing it in smaller type. Do not use quotation marks at the beginning and end of the quotation.**
- **Give source information either in the sentence that precedes the quotation or in indented lines below the quotation.**
  And then as the little plane climbed higher and Olive saw spread out below them fields of bright and tender green in this morning sun, farther out the coastline, the ocean shiny and almost flat, tiny white wakes behind a few lobster boats—then Olive felt something she had not expected to feel again: a sudden surging greediness for life. She leaned forward, peering out the window: sweet pale clouds, the sky as blue as your hat, the new green of the fields, the broad expanse of water—seen from up here it all appeared wondrous, amazing. She remembered what hope was, and this was it. That inner churning that moves you forward, plows you through life the way the boats plowed the shiny water, the way the plane was plowing forward to a place new, and where she was needed.

  —Elizabeth Strout,
  Olive Kitteridge

Section 5 Spelling

Use these tips if you are not sure how to spell a word you want to write:

- **Say the word aloud and break it into syllables. Try spelling each syllable. Put the syllables together to spell the whole word.**
- **Write the word. Make sure there is a vowel in every syllable. If the word looks wrong to you, try spelling it other ways.**
- **Think of a related word. Parts of related words are often spelled the same.**
  Decide is related to *decision*.

Correct spelling helps readers understand what you write. Use a dictionary when you need help. When you use the word-processing function of a computer to write something, you can use the spell-check feature. It will identify possible spelling errors in your writing. A spell checker will not catch errors with homophones, though. For example, if you type *break* instead of *brake*, the spell checker will not catch the mistake, because the word is spelled correctly.

Section 6 End Marks

Every sentence must end with a period, an exclamation point, or a question mark.

- **Use a *period* at the end of a statement (declarative sentence) or a command (imperative sentence).**
  Dad and I look alike. (*declarative*) Step back very slowly. (*imperative*)
- **Use an *exclamation point* at the end of a firm command (imperative sentence) or at the end of a sentence that shows great feeling or excitement (exclamatory sentence).**
  Get away from the cliff! (*imperative*) That is an incredible sight! (*exclamatory*)
- **Use a *question mark* at the end of an asking sentence (interrogative sentence).**
  How many miles is it to Tucson? (*interrogative*)

Section 7 Apostrophes

An apostrophe (') is used to form the possessive of a noun or to join words in a contraction.

- **Possessives show ownership. To make a singular noun possessive, add *'s*.**
  The bike belongs to Carmen. It is Carmen's bike.
- **To form a possessive from a plural noun that ends in *-s*, add only an apostrophe.**
  Those books belong to my sisters. They are my sisters' books.
- **Some plural nouns do not end in *-s*. To form possessives with these nouns, add *'s*.**
  The children left their boots here. The children's boots are wet.
- **Use an apostrophe to replace the dropped letter(s) in a contraction.**
  it's (it is) hasn't (has not)

Section 8 Commas, Semicolons, and Colons

Commas in Sentences

- **Use a comma after an introductory word in a sentence.**
  Yes, I'd love to go to the movies. Actually, we had a great time.
- **Use a comma after a mild interjection at the beginning of a sentence.**
  Oh, it has started raining. Hey, just grab an umbrella!
- **Use a comma to separate items in a series. A series is a list of three or more items. Put the last comma before *and* or *or*. A comma is not needed to separate two items.**
  Shall we eat cheese, bread, or fruit? Let's eat cheese and fruit.
- **Use a comma to separate a noun of direct address from the rest of a sentence.**
  Akila, will you please stand up? We would like you to sing, Akila.
- **Use a comma to separate a tag question from the rest of a sentence.**
  "It's a hot day, isn't it?" remarked Jill.
- **Use a comma to separate a direct quotation, or direct speech, from the rest of a sentence.**
  Joe asked, "How long must I sit here?" "You must sit there for one hour," Vic said.
- **Use a comma with the conjunction *and, or,* or *but* when combining independent clauses in a compound sentence.**
  Lisa liked the reptiles best, but Lyle preferred the amphibians.
- **Use a comma to separate a dependent clause at the beginning of a sentence from the rest of the sentence.**
  Because Lisa likes reptiles, she is considering a career as a herpetologist.
- **Use a comma to separate coordinate adjectives—a pair of adjectives of a similar kind. To decide whether to put a comma between adjectives, try reading the sentence with the word *and* inserted between the adjectives. If the word *and* sounds natural there, you should use a comma.**
  Reptiles have dry, scaly skin. (*needs a comma*)
  Look at that big green lizard! (*does not need a comma*)
- **Use commas to set off a clause or phrase that presents information that is not necessary for understanding the main idea of a sentence.**
  Alaska, the largest state in the Union, offers summer visitors the opportunity to see the midnight sun.

- **Use commas to set off a nonrestrictive adjective clause. A nonrestrictive clause is one that adds information about the word it modifies but is not essential to the meaning of the sentence.**
  Walt Jackson, who sold me a turtle last year, has a new pet gecko. (*The adjective clause just tells more about the noun it modifies. Because the information in the clause is not essential, the clause is nonrestrictive. Commas are needed.*)

  The woman who runs the pet store offered me a job. (*The adjective clause tells which woman is being talked about. Because the information in the clause is essential, no commas are used.*)

Semicolons and Colons in Sentences

- **You may use a semicolon in place of a comma and a conjunction when combining independent clauses.**
  Lisa likes reptiles; Lyle prefers amphibians.
- **A colon can be used when the second clause states a direct result of the first or explains the first.**
  Lisa owns reptiles: she has two pet snakes.
- **Use a colon to introduce a list or series.**
  I like three kinds of cheese: cheddar, Swiss, and colby.
- **Use a colon to introduce a quotation.**
  Cory always follows this motto: "A penny saved is a penny earned."
- **Use a colon after the speaker's name in a play.**
  LOGAN: Where were you on the night of October 5th, when the gold bullion was stolen?

  BLAKE: I was attending the opening night of *Carmen* at the opera house.
- **Use a colon to separate hours and minutes in an expression of time.**
  8:15 P.M. 11:45 A.M.
- **Use a colon between the city of publication and the publisher in a bibliographic entry.**
  O'Dell, Scott. *The Cruise of the Arctic Star*. Boston: Houghton Mifflin, 1973.

Commas With Dates and Place Names

- **Use a comma to separate the day from the date and the date from the year.**
  We clinched the division championship on Saturday, September 20, 20__.
- **Use a comma to separate the name of a city or town from the name of a state.**
  I visited Memphis, Tennessee.

Commas and Colons in Letters

- **Use a comma after the greeting and the closing of a friendly letter.**
  Dear Reginald, Your friend, Deke
- **Use a colon after the greeting of a business letter. Use a comma after the closing.**
  Dear Ms. Brocklehurst: Sincerely,

Section 9 Hyphens, Parentheses, Dashes, and Ellipses

Hyphens in Sentences

- **When you break a word at the end of a line, use a hyphen to separate the syllables.**
  There is no single "perfect food." Milk, for example, contains most of the nutrients needed by the human body, but it lacks enough iron.
- **Use hyphens to link the parts of some compound words.**
  son-in-law city-state
- **Use hyphens to link some pairs or groups of words that precede a noun and act as an adjective.**
  a family-style meal a horse-drawn carriage an up-to-date schedule
- **Use hyphens to link the parts of numbers between twenty-one and ninety-nine.**
  eighty-two fifty-seven seventy-six thirty-five

Parentheses in Sentences

- **Use parentheses to set off an explanation.**
  I interviewed my uncle **(he raises goats for a living)** for my report on animal husbandry.
  Rolf and Dana's farm is 100 miles **(160 km)** outside of Chicago.
- **Use parentheses to set off an example.**
  Many types of cheese **(chèvre, for example)** are made with goats' milk.

Dashes in Sentences

- **Use a long dash to signal a pause.**
- **Use long dashes to set off some types of nonessential information from the other parts of a sentence. An authorial comment may be set off with long dashes.**
  Tall sunflowers—my personal favorite among American wildflowers—grow on prairies across much of the United States.
- **Use a long dash to mark an unfinished sentence.**
  The door slowly opened, and—
- **Use a long dash to stress a word or phrase at the end of a sentence.**
  Only one thing can make me happy—a victory.

Ellipses in Sentences

- **An ellipsis is a series of three spaced periods.**
- **Use an ellipsis to mark the omission of words from a quotation.**
  No man can always be right. So the struggle is to do one's best; to keep the brain and conscience clear; never to be swayed by unworthy motives or inconsequential reasons, but to strive to unearth the basic factors involved and then do one's duty.

  —Dwight D. Eisenhower,
  in a letter to Mamie Eisenhower

  No man can always be right. So the struggle is to do one's best; to keep the brain and conscience clear . . . to strive to unearth the basic factors involved and then do one's duty.

  —Dwight D. Eisenhower,
  in a letter to Mamie Eisenhower
- **Use an ellipsis to signal a pause.**
  We were told that the speaker would step onto the stage momentarily. We waited . . . and waited . . . and waited.
- **When you use an ellipsis after words that are not a complete sentence, leave a space before the first spaced period.**
  Our conservation must be . . . a creative conservation of restoration and innovation.

  —Lyndon B. Johnson,
  in a message to Congress,
  February 8, 1965
- **When you use an ellipsis after a sentence, use the sentence's end mark, and leave a space between it and the first spaced period.**
  Vigorous writing is concise. . . . This requires not that the writer make all his sentences short, or that he avoid all detail and treat his subjects only in outline, but that every word tell.

  —William Strunk Jr.
  The Elements of Style

Sentence Structure and Parts of Speech

Section 10 The Sentence

A *sentence* is a group of words that tells a complete thought. A sentence has two parts: a *subject* and a *predicate*.

- **The subject tells *whom* or *what* the sentence is about.** The swimmers race.
- **The predicate tells what the subject *is* or *does*.** The judges watch carefully.

There are four kinds of sentences: *declarative, interrogative, imperative,* and *exclamatory*.

- **A *declarative sentence* makes a statement and ends with a period.**
  Jake swam faster than anyone.
- **An *interrogative sentence* asks a question and ends with a question mark.**
  Did Sammy qualify for the finals?
- **An *imperative sentence* gives a command and usually ends with a period; a firm command can end with an exclamation point.**
  Keep your eyes on the finish line. Watch out for that bee!
- **An *exclamatory sentence* ends with an exclamation point.** Jake has won the race!

Section 11 Subjects

The *subject* of a sentence tells whom or what the sentence is about.

- **A sentence can have one subject.** Mary wrote a book.
- **A sentence can have a *compound subject,* two or more subjects that are joined by a conjunction (*and, or*) and that share the same predicate.**
  Alex and Mark have already read the book.
- **Imperative sentences have an unnamed *understood subject,* the person being spoken to. This subject is referred to as "understood *you*."** Give me the book, please.
- **The *complete subject* includes all the words that name and tell about the subject.**
  Many students have borrowed the book.
- **The *simple subject* is the most important noun or pronoun in the complete subject.**
  Many students have borrowed the book. They discussed the book yesterday.

  Note: Sometimes the simple subject and the complete subject are the same.

  Ricardo is writing a book.

Section 12 Predicates

The *predicate* of a sentence tells what happened. The *complete predicate* includes a verb and all the words that tell what happened or tell more about the subject.

- **A complete predicate can include an action verb to tell what the subject of the sentence did.**
  Mary ***won* an award.**
- **A complete predicate can include a linking verb to tell more about the subject.**
  Mary ***is* a talented writer.**

The *simple predicate* is the verb that goes with the subject. It generally tells what the subject did, does, or will do.

Celia won an award for her performance.

She will receive a trophy next week.

A *compound predicate* is two or more predicates that share the same subject. Compound predicates are often joined by the conjunction *and* or *or*.

Ramon sang and danced in the play.

Mary wrote the play and directed it.

A *predicate noun* follows a linking verb and renames the subject.

Mary is a writer. Ramon is a singer.

A *predicate adjective* follows a linking verb and describes the subject.

Mary is talented. Ramon is clever.

Section 13 Clauses and Sentence Types

A *simple sentence* tells one complete thought.

Arthur has a rock collection.

A *compound sentence* is made up of two simple sentences (or *independent clauses*) whose ideas are related. The clauses can be joined by a comma and a conjunction (*and, or, but*).

Arthur has a rock collection, and Mary collects shells.

The two independent clauses in a compound sentence can also be joined by a semicolon.

Arthur collects rocks; Mary collects shells.

Two clauses in a compound sentence can be separated by a colon when the second clause is a direct result of the first clause.

Arthur enjoys visiting new places: he can hunt for rocks to add to his collection.

A *complex sentence* is made up of one independent clause and at least one dependent clause. A *dependent clause* is a group of words that has a subject and a predicate, but it cannot stand on its own.

Dependent Clause:	when Arthur visited Arizona
Independent Clause:	He learned a lot about desert plants.
Complex Sentence:	When Arthur visited Arizona, he learned a lot about desert plants.

A *compound-complex sentence* includes two or more independent clauses and at least one dependent clause.

Independent Clauses:	Arizona is proud of its saguaro cactus. The saguaro cactus can grow up to sixty feet tall.
Dependent Clause:	which is also called the giant cactus.
Compound-complex Sentence:	Arizona is proud of its saguaro cactus; the saguaro, which is also called the giant cactus, can grow up to sixty feet tall.

An *adjective clause* is a dependent clause that describes a noun or pronoun. An adjective clause always follows the word it describes and begins with a relative pronoun such as *who, whom, whose, which,* or *that.*

My cousin Arthur, **who has a rock collection,** visited the Arizona desert. (*describes* Arthur)

He studied the interesting rock formations **that rise above the desert floor**. (*describes* formations)

An *adverb clause* is a dependent clause that tells more about a verb, an adjective, or an adverb. Adverb clauses tell *where, when, why,* or *how much*. They often begin with a subordinating conjunction such as *after, since, where, than, although, because, if, as, as if, while, when,* or *whenever*.

Whenever Arthur came across an unfamiliar rock, he took a photograph of it.

(*tells* when *Arthur took a photograph*)

Arthur didn't take any rocks away **because the desert environment is fragile**.

(*tells* why *Arthur didn't take rocks away*)

A *noun clause* is a dependent clause that functions as the subject of a sentence or the object of a verb. A noun clause begins with a relative pronoun.

She said **that the floor was slippery**. (*The noun clause* that the floor was slippery *is the direct object of the verb* said.)

Most simple sentences and independent clauses follow what is called the *natural order* of sentence elements: first the subject; then the verb; then the direct object, predicate noun, or predicate adjective.

S V DO S V DO

I will take the turkey with me; I will leave the yams behind.

S LV PA

The leaves are green.

In some simple sentences and independent clauses, a verb, direct object, predicate noun, or predicate adjective comes before the subject. A sentence with this order of elements is said to have *inverted order*.

DO S V DO S V

The turkey I will take with me; the yams I will leave behind.

PA LV S

Green are the leaves.

A sentence in which a dependent clause appears between the subject and the verb is said to have *interrupted order*.

S DC LV PN

Thanksgiving, which came early this year, is my favorite holiday.

Section 14 Fragments, Run-ons, Comma Splices, and Ramble-ons

A *fragment* is an incomplete sentence that does not tell a complete thought.

Sumi and Ali. (*missing a predicate that tells what happened*)

Went hiking in the woods. (*missing a subject that tells who went hiking*)

A *run-on sentence* is two complete sentences that are run together. To fix a run-on sentence, use a comma and a conjunction (*and, or, but*) to join the two sentences. (You may also join the sentences with a semicolon.)

Incorrect: Sumi went hiking Ali went swimming.

Correct: Sumi went hiking, **but** Ali went swimming.

A *comma splice* is two complete sentences that have a comma between them but are missing a conjunction (*and, or, but*). To fix a comma splice, add *and, or,* or *but* after the comma.

Incorrect: Sumi went hiking yesterday, Ali went swimming.

Correct: Sumi went hiking yesterday, **and** Ali went swimming.

A *ramble-on sentence* is grammatically correct but contains extra words that don't add to its meaning.

Incorrect: Hiking through the wilderness to enjoy nature is my favorite outdoor sports activity, probably because it is so enjoyable and such good exercise, and because I enjoy observing wild animals in the wilderness in their natural environment.

Correct: Hiking through the wilderness to enjoy nature is my favorite outdoor sports activity. I enjoy observing wild animals in their natural environment.

Try not to string too many short sentences together when you write. Instead, combine sentences and take out unnecessary information.

Incorrect: I stared at him and he stared at me and I told him to go away and he wouldn't so then I called my big sister.

Correct: We stared at each other. I told him to go away, but he wouldn't. Then I called my big sister.

Section 15 Nouns

A *common noun* names any person, place, thing, or idea.

Ira visited an auto **museum** with his **friends**. Ira has always had an **interest** in **cars**.

He likes that blue **convertible**.

A *proper noun* names a certain person, place, thing, or idea. Proper nouns begin with an uppercase letter. A proper noun that is made up of two or more words is considered one noun.

Ira wants to visit the **Sonoran Desert** in **Mexico** in **April**.

He is reading a guidebook about the region entitled ***The Undiscovered Desert***.

A *collective noun* names a group of people or things that act as one unit.

jury **family** **committee** **audience** **crowd**

- **Most often, a collective noun is treated as a singular subject.**
  The track **team is** the strongest one we've had in years.
- **Sometimes, if a writer wants to emphasize the different members of a group, he or she may treat the noun as a plural subject.**
  The track **team are** congratulating one another on their fine performances.
- **A noun can also be used to describe another noun:**
  freeway exit
  eye chart
  ocean current

A *concrete noun* names something you can see, touch, hear, smell, or taste.

dog **meadow** **pebble** **stove**

An *abstract noun* names an idea, a quality, or a characteristic.

freedom **bravery** **freshness** **excellence**

Section 16 Adjectives

An *adjective* is a word that tells more about a noun or a pronoun.

- **Some adjectives tell what kind.**
  Jim observed the huge elephant. The enormous beast towered above him.
- **Some adjectives tell how many.**
  The elephant was twelve feet tall. It weighed several tons.
- **A *predicate adjective* follows a linking verb and describes the subject.**
  Jim was careful not to anger the elephant. He was happy when the trainer led it away.
- ***A, an,* and *the* are special kinds of adjectives called *articles*. Use *a* and *an* to refer to any person, place, thing, or idea. Use *the* to refer to a specific person, place, thing, or idea. Use *a* before a singular noun that begins with a consonant sound. Use *an* before a singular noun that begins with a vowel sound.**
  An elephant is heavier than a rhino. The elephant in this picture is six weeks old.
- **A *demonstrative adjective* tells which one. *This, that, these,* and *those* can be used as demonstrative adjectives. Use *this* and *these* to talk about things that are nearby. Use *that* and *those* to talk about things that are farther away.**
  This book is about rhinos. These rhinos just came to the zoo.
  That rhino is enormous! Those funny-looking creatures are wildebeests.

  Note: Never use *here* or *there* after the adjectives *this, that, these,* and *those.*
- **A *proper adjective* is made from a proper noun. Capitalize proper adjectives.**
  Italian cooking Democratic convention Apache legend
- **Two or more adjectives can be used to describe a noun. When you use two or more adjectives to describe a noun, put the adjectives in an order that sounds natural. This chart can help you.**

how many	what quality	how big	how old	what shape	what color	what material	→ noun
three	*beautiful*	*small*	*new*	*round*	*pink*	*silken*	→ *petals*

Section 17 Pronouns

A *pronoun* can replace a noun.

17a Personal Pronouns

***Personal pronouns* include *I, me, you, we, us, he, him, she, her, it, they,* and *them*. Personal pronouns can be used to stand for the person speaking, the person spoken to, or the person spoken about.**

- ***First-person pronouns* refer to the speaker (*I, me*) or include the speaker (*we, us*).**
  Let me know when I am next at bat. It took us hours, but we managed to get to the stadium.
- ***Second-person pronouns* refer to the person or people being spoken to (*you*).**
  Are you going to the game? I asked Marisa to give the bases to you.
- ***Third-person pronouns* refer to the person, people, or thing(s) being spoken about (*he, him, she, her, it, they, them*).**
  They played well. Pass the ball to him. Kick it to her.
- **The third-person pronoun *he* (with *him* and *his*) was once accepted as a universal pronoun that could refer to anyone, male or female, if a generalization about people was being made. Now most writers try to avoid the use of universal *he*.**
  One solution to this pronoun problem is to make the pronoun and the word it refers to plural.
  When a chef cooks, he displays creativity. **becomes:** When chefs cook, they display creativity.
  Each player should bring his own racket. **becomes:** Players should bring their own rackets.
  Another solution is to replace *he* with *he or she,* or replace *his* with *his or her*.
  Each player should bring his own racket. **becomes:** Each player should bring his or her own racket.

17b Subject and Object Pronouns

A *subject pronoun* takes the place of the subject of a sentence. Subject pronouns are said to be in the *nominative case*. Subject pronouns include *I, you, he, she, it, we,* and *they*.

Rita is an excellent soccer player. She never lets the other team score.

Note: Do not use both the pronoun and the noun it replaces together.

Incorrect: Rita she made the team.

Correct: Rita made the team. OR She made the team.

An *object pronoun* replaces a noun that is the object of a verb or a preposition. Object pronouns are said to be in the *objective case*. Object pronouns include *me, him, her, us,* and *them*.

Rita's team played the Bobcats. Rita's team beat them.

The pronouns *it* and *you* can be either subjects or objects.

It was a close game. (*subject pronoun*) The Bobcats almost won it. (*object pronoun*)

- **Use a subject pronoun as part of a compound subject. Use an object pronoun as part of a compound object. To test whether a pronoun is correct, say the sentence without the other part of a compound subject or object.**

  Incorrect: Rita told Ellen and I it was a close game. (Rita told I it was a close game.)

  Correct: Rita told Ellen and me it was a close game. (Rita told me it was a close game.)

- **When the pronouns *I* and *me* are used in a compound with a noun or another pronoun, *I* or *me* always comes second in a pair or last in a series of three or more.**

  Incorrect: The coach gave the Most Improved Players awards to me and Carlos.

  Correct: The coach gave the Most Improved Players awards to Carlos and me.

17c Pronoun Antecedents

An *antecedent* is the word or words a pronoun refers to. The antecedent is almost always a noun.

The Bobcats are excellent players. They won every game last season.

- **A pronoun must agree with its antecedent. An antecedent and a pronoun agree when they have the same *number* (singular or plural) and *gender* (male or female).**

  Nick's mother cheered. She was very excited.

17d Possessive Pronouns

***Possessive pronouns* show ownership.**

- **The possessive pronouns *my, your, his, her, its, their,* and *our* replace possessive nouns.**

  Those skates belong to my brother Jorge.

  Those are his kneepads, too. (*The pronoun* his *replaces the possessive noun* Jorge's.)

- **The possessive pronouns *mine, ours, yours, hers, his, its,* and *theirs* replace both a possessive noun and the noun that is possessed.**

  Alisha's kneepads are blue. Mine are red and hers are blue.

  (*The possessive pronoun* hers *replaces both the possessive noun* Alisha's *and the noun* kneepads.)

- ***Whose* is the possessive form of the relative pronoun *who*. It is also used as the possessive form of the relative pronoun *which*.**

  The skaters whose parents cannot pick them up at 6 P.M. must wait inside the office.

  (Whose *indicates that the parents belong to the skaters.*)

17e Compound Personal Pronouns

***Compound personal pronouns* can be used as *reflexive pronouns* or *intensive pronouns*.**

- **A *reflexive pronoun* refers back to the subject of a sentence.**

  My brother bought himself a new puck. We cheered for ourselves.

- **An *intensive pronoun* emphasizes the identity of the sentence subject.**

  I myself am not a hockey fan.

17f Indefinite Pronouns

Indefinite pronouns* refer to persons or things that are not identified as individuals. These pronouns include *all, anybody, both, anything, few, most, no one, either, nothing, everyone, one, several, none, everybody, nobody, someone, everything, something, anyone,* and *somebody.

Somebody lost the ball. We can't play anything until we find it.

17g Relative Pronouns

When the pronouns *who, whom, whose, which,* and *that* are used to introduce an adjective clause, they are called *relative pronouns.* A relative pronoun always follows the noun it refers to.

The player who brought the volleyball can serve first.

I joined the team that chose me.

This net, which I found in my closet, will be perfect for our volleyball game.

Note: For more information on using *who, whom, which,* and *that,* see Section 32, Problem Words.

17h Interrogative Pronouns

When the pronouns *who, whom, which,* and *what* are used to begin a question, they are called *interrogative pronouns.*

Who has brought the volleyball?

Which is the net for volleyball?

What is a wicket used for?

To whom did you hit the ball?

17i Demonstrative Pronouns

This, that, these,* and *those* can be used as *demonstrative pronouns.

- **Use *this* and *these* to talk about one or more things that are nearby.**

  This is a soft rug.

  These are sweeter than those over there.

- **Use *that* and *those* to talk about one or more things that are far away.**

  That is where I sat yesterday.

  Those are new chairs.

Section 18 Verbs

18a Action and Linking Verbs

An *action verb* shows action.

Scientists study the natural world.

They learn how the laws of nature work.

A *linking verb* does not show action. It connects the subject of a sentence to a word or words in the predicate that tell about the subject. Linking verbs include *am, is, are, was, been,* and *were. Seem, appear,* and *become* can be used as linking verbs, too.

Explorers are brave.

That route seems long and dangerous.

Some verbs, such as *appear, look, smell, feel, grow, sound,* and *taste,* can be either action verbs or linking verbs, depending on how they are used. You can test whether a verb is a linking verb by substituting a form of the verb *be* (*am, is, are, was,* or *were*) in its place. If the form of *be* makes sense, the verb probably is a linking verb.

I looked at the bear. (*"I was at the bear" does not make sense:* looked *is an action verb.*)

The bear looked hungry. (*"The bear was hungry" makes sense:* looked *is a linking verb.*)

18b Transitive and Intransitive Verbs

A *transitive verb* is an action verb that transfers its action to a direct object.

The polar bear watched a seal's air hole in the ice.

The polar bear caught the seal.

An *intransitive verb* does not have a direct object. An intransitive verb shows action that the subject does alone.

The bear waited patiently.

Suddenly the bear struck.

Many verbs can be either transitive or intransitive, depending on whether or not there is a direct object.

The bear ate the seal. (*Seal* is the direct object: *ate* is a transitive verb.)

The bear ate hungrily. (*Hungrily* is an adverb, and there is no direct object: *ate* is an intransitive verb.)

18c Main Verbs and Auxiliary Verbs

A *main verb* is the most important verb in a sentence. An *auxiliary verb,* or helping verb, comes before the main verb to help it show action. Auxiliary verbs such as *had, are,* and *will* indicate the tense of the main verb. Others, such as *could, might,* and *may,* show how likely it is that something will happen.

Certain auxiliary verbs have special functions. The auxiliary verbs *may* and *might* can be used to ask or give permission. The auxiliary verbs *can* and *could* can be used to indicate ability. The auxiliary verbs *should* and *must* can be used to communicate a duty or an obligation. The auxiliary verbs *may, might, could, should,* and *will* can be used to indicate possibility—how likely something is to happen. Auxiliary verbs that have these special functions are called *modal auxiliaries.*

Scientists ***are* studying** glaciers. The studies ***may* help** us learn more about Earth.

18d The Principal Parts of a Verb

Each verb has three *principal parts:* its *present form,* its *past form,* and its *past participle form.*

- Most verbs add *-ed* to the present form to create both the past form and the past participle form. These verbs are called *regular verbs.*
- *Irregular verbs* form their past and past participle forms in other ways. The chart below shows the principal parts of several common irregular verbs.

Present	Past	Past Participle
arise	arose	arisen
(be) is	was	been
blow	blew	blown
bring	brought	brought
build	built	built
cut	cut	cut
drive	drove	driven
eat	ate	eaten
fall	fell	fallen
fly	flew	flown
give	gave	given
go	went	gone
grow	grew	grown
have	had	had
hear	heard	heard
hide	hid	hidden
hold	held	held
know	knew	known
lay	laid	laid
leave	left	left
lie	lay	lain
light	lit	lit
make	made	made
ring	rang	rung
run	ran	run
say	said	said
see	saw	seen
shake	shook	shaken
sing	sang	sung
swim	swam	swum
take	took	taken
tell	told	told

(Continued on page 376)

(Continued from page 375)

Present	Past	Past Participle
think	thought	thought
throw	threw	thrown
wear	wore	worn
write	wrote	written

- **Almost all verbs add *-ing* to the present form to create the *present participle* form: *sing/singing; talk/talking.***

18e Verb Tense

Verb tense places an action in time.

- **The *present tense* is used to show that something happens regularly or is true now.**
  Squirrels <u>bury</u> nuts each fall.
- **Add *-s* to most verbs to show present tense when the subject is *he, she, it,* or a singular noun. Add *-es* to verbs ending in *-s, -ch, -sh, -x,* or *-z.* Do not add *-s* or *-es* if the subject is a plural noun or *I, you, we,* or *they.***

add *-s*	add *-es*	change *y* to *i*
speak/speak<u>s</u>	reach/reach<u>es</u>	carry/carr<u>ies</u>

- **The *past tense* shows past action. Add *-ed* to most verbs to form the past tense. Verbs that do not add *-ed* are called *irregular verbs.***
  reach/reach<u>ed</u> (regular) speak/<u>spoke</u> (irregular)
  Note: You can find the past and past participle forms of an irregular verb in a dictionary.
- **The *future tense* shows future action. Use the verb *will* to form the future tense.**
  Mom <u>will visit</u> Antarctica next year. She <u>will photograph</u> penguins.
- **The *present perfect tense* shows action that began in the past and may still be happening. To form the present perfect tense, add the helping verb *has* or *have* to the past participle of a verb.**
  Mom <u>has studied</u> Antarctica for years. Her articles <u>have appeared</u> in science journals.
- **The *past perfect tense* shows action that was completed by a certain time in the past. To form the past perfect tense, add the helping verb *had* to the past participle of a verb.**
  Before she visited Antarctica, Mom <u>had imagined</u> it as a wasteland.
- **The *future perfect tense* shows action that will be complete by a certain time in the future. To form the future perfect tense, add the helping verbs *will have* to the past participle form of a verb.**
  By the end of next year, Mom <u>will have published</u> a book on Antarctic wildlife.
- ***Progressive forms* of verbs show continuing action. To form a *present progressive* verb, add *am, is,* or *are* to the *present participle* of a verb (usually the present form + *-ing*). To form the *past progressive* verb, add *was* or *were* to the present participle. To form a *future progressive* verb, add *will be* to the present participle.**
  Scientists <u>are learning</u> new facts about Antarctica every day. (*present progressive*)
  When Mom <u>was traveling</u> in Antarctica, she saw its beauty. (*past progressive*)
  Someday soon I <u>will be visiting</u> Antarctica with Mom. (*future progressive*)
- **Choose verb tenses carefully so that the verb forms you use work together to indicate time accurately and consistently. When you describe events that happen in the same time frame, do not shift tenses. When you describe events that happen at different times, use verbs in different tenses to indicate the order in which the events happened.**
  Malcolm wanted to stay dry on the hike, so he <u>packed</u> a poncho. (not <u>packs</u>)
  The doves begin their calls early in the morning, and they <u>continue</u> them past noon. (not <u>continued</u>)

18f Subject and Verb Agreement

The subject and its verb must agree in number. Be sure that the verb agrees with its subject and not with the object of a preposition that comes before the verb.

An Antarctic explorer needs special equipment.

(*singular subject:* **An Antarctic explorer;** *singular verb* [*verb* + -s *or* -es]: **needs**)

Explorers in Antarctica carry climbing tools and survival gear.

(*plural subject:* **Explorers;** *plural verb* [*verb without* -s *or* -es]: **carry**)

A *compound subject* and its verb must agree.

- **Compound subjects joined by *and* are usually plural.**
  Snow and ice make exploration difficult.
- **If a compound subject is joined by *or* or *nor,* the verb must agree with the last item in the subject.**
  Either the helpers or the leader checks the weather report.

There are special rules for agreement with certain kinds of subjects.

- **Titles of books, movies, magazines, newspapers, stories, and songs are always considered singular, even if they end in *-s.***
  The Secret Life of Penguins is the title of Mom's book.
  "**Ice and Darkness**" is the name of a poem I wrote.
- **Collective nouns, such as *collection, group, team, country, kingdom, family, flock,* and *herd,* name more than one person or object acting as a group. These nouns are usually considered singular.**
  My family lives in southern Australia. A flock of seagulls is flying overhead.
- **Most indefinite pronouns, including *everyone, nobody, nothing, everything, something,* and *anything,* are considered singular.**
  Somebody has left the tent flap open. Is anything missing? Everything is fine.
- **Some indefinite pronouns that clearly refer to more than one, such as *many, most, few,* and *both,* are considered plural.**
  Many are interested in Antarctica, but few are able to make the journey there.

18g Active and Passive Voice

A verb is in *active voice* if its subject performs an action. A verb is in *passive voice* if its subject is acted upon by something else. Many sentences in the passive voice have a prepositional phrase that begins with the word *by* and follows the verb.

Explorers plan trips months in advance. (*active voice*)

Trips are planned by explorers months in advance. (*passive voice*)

The active voice can communicate action briefly and powerfully. In most cases, the active voice is stronger and clearer than the passive voice. Try to write most of your sentences in the active voice.

Strong active voice: The penguin snapped up the fish.

Weak passive voice: The fish was snapped up by the penguin.

Some writers believe that the passive voice should be used only when an action is done by an unknown or unimportant agent.

The tent flap was left open. (*The agent who left the tent flap open is unknown.*)

18h Mood of Verbs

Mood as an aspect of grammar has to do with the way different forms of verbs reflect a speaker's attitude toward the information he or she is conveying in a sentence.

- **The *indicative mood* is the most common mood in English. Verbs in the indicative mood represent actions or situations the speaker believes to be factual or at least close to reality.**
  Kathryn Sullivan **was** the first American woman to walk in space.
  As a scientist, she **has studied** the lands and the ocean here on Earth.

- **Verbs in questions that seek real information are usually considered to be in the indicative mood.**
  Which President **appointed** Dr. Sullivan Chief Scientist of the National Oceanic and Atmospheric Administration (NOAA)?
  Note: Some grammarians consider verbs in questions to be in another mood, the interrogative mood.
- **The *imperative mood* is another common mood in English. Commands, requests, warnings, and other directives have verbs in the imperative mood.**
  Go to the NOAA website.
- **The *subjunctive mood* is the other mood in English. Verbs in the subjunctive mood (sometimes called the *conditional mood*) are used to express conditions contrary to fact.**
  If I **were** you, I would join the Science Club. (*Were* expresses a condition contrary to fact: I can never be you.)
- **Verbs in the subjunctive mood are also used after verbs of suggesting, representing, or commanding.**
  I recommend that Rob **join** the Science Club, too.
- **Only the third-person present tense has special subjunctive forms. (The verb *be* is an exception.)**
  Sue **joins** many clubs. (indicative)
  I recommend that Sue **join** the Science Club. (subjunctive)
- **Verbs in other tenses that are in the subjunctive mood have the same form as verbs in the indicative mood.**
  The twins **join** many clubs. (indicative)
  I recommend that the twins **join** the Science Club. (subjunctive)
- **The verb *be* has special present tense and past tense forms for the subjunctive mood. The form *be* is used with first, second, and third person pronouns in the present tense.**
  The coach insisted that I **be** ready to play. (first person)
  She insisted that they **be** ready, too. (third person)
- **The form *were* is used with first, second, and third person pronouns in the past tense.**
  If I **were** the coach, I would tell everyone to be ready. (first person)
  If she **were** the coach, she would tell everyone to be ready. (third person)
- **The modal auxiliaries *should, could, might,* and *may* can be joined with main verbs to create a form of the subjunctive that suggests rather than tells someone what to do.**
  You **might check** with the custodian to see if he found your backpack in the gym.
- **Be careful to keep the mood of verbs consistent in clauses that have a similar structure. Do not shift from imperative to subjunctive when you are giving instructions.**
  Incorrect: Unlock the door, turn on the light, and you should open a window.
  Correct: Unlock the door, turn on the light, and open a window.
  Do not shift from subjunctive to indicative mood in a compound structure.
  Incorrect: I suggest that a passenger read a book or listens to music.
  Correct: I suggest that a passenger read a book or listen to music.

Section 19 Adverbs

An *adverb* describes a verb, an adjective, or another adverb. Adverbs tell how, when, where, or to what extent.

- **Many adverbs end in *-ly*. Some adverbs do not end in *-ly*. These include *now, then, very, too, often, always, again, sometimes, soon, later, first, far, now,* and *fast*.**
  Andrew approached the snake cage <u>slowly</u>. He knew that snakes can move <u>fast</u>.
- **Some adverbs tell *how*.**
  She spoke <u>confidently</u>. He <u>eagerly</u> bit into the sandwich.
- **Some adverbs tell *when*.**
  <u>Then</u> the bell rang. School ended <u>yesterday</u>. I eat pizza <u>only</u> on Friday.

- **Some adverbs tell *where.***
  We went inside. They built a house there. Come here.
- **Some adverbs tell *to what extent.***
  It is very quiet. I am almost finished.
- **When the word *when, where,* or *why* begins a dependent clause that tells about a place, a time, or a reason, it is called a *relative adverb.***
  Tucker Avenue is a street where many accidents happen. (place)
  Friday is the day when my report is due. (time)
  This article gives five reasons why you should drink water instead of soda. (reason)

  Note: A word that is a relative adverb can also be classified as a subordinating conjunction.

Section 20 Prepositions

A *preposition* shows a relationship between a word in a sentence and a noun or pronoun that follows the preposition. Prepositions tell when, where, what kind, how, or how much.

- **Prepositions include the words *after, in front of, without, above, down, among, with, of, from, for, about, such as, throughout, into, onto, inside, in, at, under, over, on, through, to, across, around, by, beside, during, off,* and *before.***
  Jeff left the milk on the table. He knew it belonged in the refrigerator.
- **A *prepositional phrase* is a group of words that begins with a preposition and ends with its object. The object of a preposition is a noun or a pronoun. A prepositional phrase can be at the beginning, middle, or end of a sentence.**
  Jeff's mom would be home in five minutes. Within three minutes he had put it away.
- **Prepositional phrases that modify (or tell more about) nouns or pronouns are called *adjectival prepositional phrases.* An adjectival prepositional phrase usually comes after the noun or pronoun it modifies. Adjectival prepositional phrases often tell *which.***
  The milk in the refrigerator is spoiled. (*modifies the noun* milk *and tells* which milk)
  I can't stand the odor of spoiled milk! (*modifies the noun* odor *and tells* which odor)
- ***Adverbial prepositional phrases* modify a verb, an adverb, or an adjective. Many adverbial prepositional phrases tell *when, where, how,* or *how long* something was done.**
  Jeff usually drinks orange juice before breakfast. (*modifies the verb* drinks *and tells* when)
  He says his mom's fresh-squeezed orange juice is the best in the world. (*modifies the adjective* best *and tells* where)
  Late in the evening I heard a knock at my door. (*modifies the adverb* late *and tells* when)

Section 21 Direct Objects and Indirect Objects

A *direct object* is the noun or pronoun that receives the action of the verb. Direct objects follow action verbs. To find the direct object, say the verb and then "Whom?" or "What?"
Jacques painted a picture. (Painted whom or what? Picture. *Picture* is the direct object.)

- **A *compound direct object* occurs when more than one noun or pronoun receives the action of the verb.**
  He used a brush and oil paints. (*Brush* and *paints* compose the compound direct object.)
- **A sentence with a direct object may also have an *indirect object.* An indirect object is a noun or pronoun and usually tells to whom something is given, told, or taught.**
  Jacques gave his mom the painting.
- **A direct object may be modified by an *object complement.* An object complement is a noun, pronoun, or adjective that follows a direct object and identifies or describes it. Object complements are often used with verbs such as *make, name, elect, paint,* and *call.***
  The new grass turned the hills green. (*Green* describes what color the hills turned.)
  The officer called Javier a hero. (*Hero* identifies what Javier was called.)

Section 22 Conjunctions

The words *and, or,* and *but* are *coordinating conjunctions.*

- Coordinating conjunctions may be used to join words within a sentence.
  My favorite reptiles are snakes and lizards. Najim doesn't like snakes or lizards.
- A comma and a coordinating conjunction can be used to join two or more simple sentences. (The conjunction *and* does not need a comma if both sentences are short.)
  I like snakes, but he says they're creepy. We can get a snake, or we can get a lizard.

A *subordinating conjunction* relates one clause to another. Dependent clauses begin with a subordinating conjunction. Subordinating conjunctions include *because, if, although, when, where, as, while, though, than, as if, whenever, since, wherever, after, often, over,* and *before.*

Before his mom left, Bo cleaned his room. Because he had a favor to ask, he vacuumed, too.

Correlative conjunctions always appear in pairs. They connect words or groups of words and provide more emphasis than coordinating conjunctions. Some common correlative conjunctions are *both . . . and, either . . . or, neither . . . nor, not only . . . but (also),* and *whether. . . or.*

She is not only a good singer but also an excellent athlete.

Neither Raj nor Chris came to the concert.

Section 23 Interjections

An *interjection* expresses emotion and is not part of any independent or dependent clause.

Wow! This bread is delicious. Mmmm, this bread tastes good!

Section 24 Appositives

An *appositive* is a phrase that identifies a noun or pronoun.

My favorite snack, cornbread with honey, is easy to make.

- Most appositives are separated from the rest of a sentence by commas. These appositives, called *nonrestrictive appositives,* just give more information about the nouns or pronouns they describe.
  Tara, my friend who figure skates, is traveling to Dallas for a competition.
- Some appositives should not be set off by commas. A *restrictive appositive* is an appositive that is vital to the meaning of a sentence; therefore, it should not be set off by commas.
  His book ***The Basics of Automobile Maintenance*** tells how to take care of a car.

  My sister Katie likes to read on the porch.

Section 25 Verbals and Absolutes

25a Verbals

Sometimes a verb does not act as a predicate. *Verbals* are forms of verbs that play other roles in sentences.

- One type of verbal, a *participle,* acts as an adjective. A participle may be the present participle or the past participle form of a verb. (See Handbook Section 18d.)
  George heard the bell ringing. (*acts as an adjective describing the noun* bell)

  A shivering child stood at the door. (*acts as an adjective describing the noun* child)

  A *participial phrase* is made up of a participle and other words that complete its meaning.
  Filled with pride, Angela accepted her medal. (*acts as an adjective modifying the noun* Angela)

  Matt noticed a skunk waddling through the bushes. (*acts as an adjective modifying the noun* skunk)
- An *infinitive* is a phrase made up of the word *to* followed by the present form of a verb (*to defend*). Infinitives may act as adjectives, adverbs, or nouns. An *infinitive phrase* is made up of an infinitive and other words that complete its meaning.
  I like to walk in the woods. (*acts as a noun; the direct object of the verb* like)

  This is a good way to appreciate nature. (*acts as an adjective modifying the noun* way)

  I listen carefully to hear the sounds of woodland creatures. (*acts as an adverb modifying the verb* listen)

- **A *gerund* is a verbal that acts as a noun. All gerunds are present participles. (See Handbook Section 18d.)**

  My brother enjoys **swimming**. (*acts as a noun; the direct object of the verb* enjoys)

  A *gerund phrase* is made up of a gerund and the other words that complete its meaning.

  Riding the waves on a surfboard is his great ambition. (*acts as the subject of the sentence*)

- **A sentence may contain more than one participial or infinitive phrase. Using two verbals of the same type to express similar ideas is using *parallel structure*.**

  Warmed by the sun and **cooled by sea breezes,** Smith Beach is the perfect place for a vacation. (two participial phrases)

  Mac wants **to paddle a kayak,** but Ruthann wants **to swim**. (two infinitive phrases)

25b Absolutes

An *absolute phrase* consists of a noun or noun phrase followed by a descriptive word or phrase.

- **An absolute phrase may contain a present or past participle.**

  Her face **glowing,** Sue looked as happy as she felt. (*noun phrase plus a present participle*)

  The general, his army **defeated**, prepared to surrender. (*noun phrase plus a past participle*)

- **An absolute phrase may also contain an adjective, a noun, or a prepositional phrase.**

  Teri woke from a deep sleep, her mind and body **alert**. (*noun phrase plus an adjective*)

  Melissa, good grades **her prime objective,** never went out on a school night. (*noun phrase plus a noun phrase*)

  Teri rode home, her guitar **across her back**. (*noun phrase plus a prepositional phrase*)

Usage

Section 26 Negatives

A *negative word* means "no" or "not."

- **The words *no, not, nothing, none, never, nowhere,* and *nobody* are negatives.**
  The notebook was nowhere to be found. Nobody wanted to miss the party.
- **Often negatives are in the form of contractions.**
  Do not enter that room. Don't even go near the door.
- **In most sentences it is not correct to use two negatives.**

Incorrect	Correct
We can't see nothing.	We can't see anything.
We haven't got no solution.	We haven't got a solution.

- **Some sentences express ideas that require the use of two negative words.**
  No one will work for you for nothing. (*In other words, anyone who works will expect to be paid.*)
  I couldn't ***not*** say hello to her. (*In other words, the speaker had to say hello, even if the speaker might not have wanted to.*)
- **Do not use the word *ain't*.**

Section 27 Comparisons

- **The *comparative form* of an adjective or an adverb compares two people, places, or things. The comparative form is often followed by "than." To compare two people, places, or things, add *-er* to short adjectives and adverbs.**
  An elephant is tall. A **giraffe** is taller than an **elephant**. (Giraffe *is compared with* elephant.)
  A lion runs fast. A **cheetah** runs faster than **any other animal**. (Cheetah *is compared with* any other animal.)
- **The *superlative form* of an adjective or an adverb compares three or more people, places, or things. The article *the* usually comes before the superlative form. To compare three or more items, add *-est* to short adjectives and adverbs.**
  The giraffe is the tallest land animal. The cheetah runs the fastest of any animal on land.
- **When comparing two or more persons, places, or things using the ending *-er* or *-est,* never use the word *more*.**

Incorrect	Correct
She is more faster than he is.	She is faster than he is.

- **The word *more* is used with longer adjectives to compare two persons, places, or things. Use the word *most* to compare three or more persons, places, or things.**
  Mario is excited about the field trip.
  Duane is more excited than Mario.
  Kiki is the most excited student of all.
- **Sometimes the words *good* and *bad* are used to compare. These words change forms in comparisons.**

Mario is a good athlete.	The basketball court is in bad shape.
Kiki is a better athlete.	The tennis court is in worse shape than the basketball court.
Bill is the best athlete of all.	The ice rink is in the worst shape of all.

Note: Use *better* or *worse* to compare two things. Use *best* or *worst* to compare three or more things.

Section 28 Contractions

When two or more words are combined to form one word, one or more letters are dropped and replaced by an apostrophe. These words are called *contractions.* For example, when *he will* becomes the contraction *he'll,* the apostrophe replaces *wi.*

- Here are some other common contractions.

can't (cannot)	haven't (have not)	she'd (she would)
couldn't (could not)	I'll (I will)	they've (they have)
doesn't (does not)	it's (it is, it has)	we're (we are)

Section 29 Plural Nouns

- A *singular noun* names one person, place, thing, or idea.
  girl pond arrow freedom
- A *plural noun* names more than one person, place, thing, or idea. To make most singular nouns plural, add *-s.*
  girls ponds arrows freedoms
- For nouns ending in *-sh, -ch, -x,* or *-z,* add *-es* to make the word plural.
  bush/bushes lunch/lunches quiz/quizzes box/boxes
  For nouns ending in a consonant and *-y,* change the *y* to *i* and add *-es.*
  penny/pennies army/armies
- For some nouns that end in *-f* or *-fe,* replace *-f* or *-fe* with *-ves* to make the noun plural.
  shelf/shelves wife/wives (Exceptions: cliff/cliffs; reef/reefs; cafe/cafes)
- Some words change spelling when the plural is formed. These plurals are called *irregular plurals.*
  man/men woman/women mouse/mice goose/geese
- Some words have the same singular and plural form. These plurals are also called *irregular plurals.*
  deer sheep offspring scissors

Section 30 Possessive Nouns

A *possessive* shows ownership.

- To make a singular noun possessive, add an apostrophe and *s.*
  John's bat the girl's bike
- When a singular noun ends in *-s,* add an apostrophe and *s.*
  Ross's project James's glasses
- To make a plural noun that ends in *-s* possessive, add an apostrophe.
  the soldiers' songs the girls' bikes
- When a plural noun does not end in *-s,* add an apostrophe and *s* to show possession.
  the men's ideas the children's shoes

Section 31 Dangling Modifiers and Misplaced Modifiers

A verbal phrase acting as an adjective must modify, or refer to, a specific word in the main part of a sentence. A *dangling modifier* is a phrase that does not refer to any particular word in the sentence. A *misplaced modifier* is a phrase that seems to refer to the wrong word in a sentence.

Incorrect: Walking down the street, deep thoughts come to mind.

(*Are deep thoughts walking down the street? No. This verbal phrase does not refer to any particular word in the main part of the sentence: it is a dangling modifier.*)

Dangling and misplaced modifiers make your writing unclear, so avoid them. When you begin a sentence with a verbal phrase such as "Walking down the street," make sure that the question "Who is walking down the street?" is answered clearly in the first part of the rest of the sentence.

Correct: Walking down the street, I often think deep thoughts.

(*Who is walking down the street? I am. This verbal phrase clearly relates to the pronoun* I.)

When you proofread your work, check to make sure you have not written any sentences with dangling or misplaced modifiers. If you have, rewrite those sentences so modifiers appear near the words they describe.

Section 32 Problem Words

These words are often misused. Be sure to use them correctly when you speak and when you write.

sit	***Sit* means "rest or stay in one place."** Sit down and relax for a while.
sat	***Sat* is the past tense of *sit*.** I sat in that chair yesterday.
set	***Set* is a verb meaning "put."** Set the chair here.
lay	***Lay* means "to put something down somewhere." It takes a direct object. The past tense form of *lay* is *laid*, and the past participle form of *lay* is also *laid*.** Each day I lay a tablecloth on the table. Yesterday I laid the yellow tablecloth. I had never laid that one on the table before.
lie	***Lie* means "to recline." It does not take a direct object. The past tense form of *lie* is *lay*, and the past participle form of *lie* is *lain*.** Most mornings I lie half awake just before the alarm rings. Early this morning I lay with my eyes open, waiting for the alarm. I had lain there for a few minutes before I realized that it was Saturday.
may	***May* is used to ask permission or to express a possibility.** May I have another hot dog? I may borrow that book someday.
can	***Can* shows that someone is able to do something.** I can easily eat three hot dogs.
learn	***Learn* means "to get knowledge."** Who will help you learn Spanish?
teach	***Teach* means "to give knowledge." Never use *learn* in place of *teach*.** **Incorrect:** My sister will learn me to speak Spanish. **Correct:** My sister will teach me to speak Spanish.
is	**Use *is* to tell about one person, place, or thing.** Alabama is warm during the summer.
are	**Use *are* to tell about more than one person, place, or thing. Also use *are* with the word *you*.** Seattle and San Francisco are cool during the summer. You are welcome to visit me anytime.
doesn't	**The contraction *doesn't* is used with the singular pronouns *he, she,* and *it*.** He doesn't like sauerkraut. It doesn't agree with him.
don't	**The contraction *don't* is used with the plural pronouns *we* and *they*. *Don't* is also used with *I* and *you*.** They don't like Swiss cheese. I don't care for it, either.
I	**Use the pronoun *I* as the subject of a sentence. When using *I* or *me* with another noun or pronoun, always name yourself last.** I am going to basketball camp. Renée and I will ride together.
me	**Use the pronoun *me* after action verbs.** Renée will call me this evening. **Also use *me* after a preposition, such as *to, at,* and *with*.** Pass the ball to me. Come to the game with Renée and me.
good well	***Good* is an adjective.** ***Well* is an adverb. These words are often used incorrectly.** **Incorrect:** Renée plays good. **Correct:** Renée is a good basketball player. She plays well.

raise	***Raise* must be followed by a direct object.** I raise the flag every morning.
rise	***Rise* is not used with a direct object.** I rise at dawn every morning.
like	***Like* means "similar to" or "have a fondness for." Do not use *like* to indicate a pause or to mean "says."** **Incorrect:** I enjoy, like, all kinds of water sports. He was like, "Swimming is fun." **Correct:** I like swimming and water polo. He said, "I like the water."
go	***Go* means "move from place to place." Don't use *go* or *went* to mean "says" or "said."** **Incorrect:** She went, "The swim meet was yesterday." **Correct:** She said, "I went to the swim meet."
all	***All* means "the total of something." Avoid using *was all* to mean "said."** **Incorrect:** He was all, "Everyone likes swimming." **Correct:** He said, "Everyone likes swimming."
you know	**Use the phrase *you know* only when it helps a sentence make sense. Try not to use it in places where it does not belong.** **Incorrect:** We can, you know, go canoeing. **Correct:** Did you know that my family has a canoe?
let	***Let* is a verb that means "allow."** Please let me go to the mall with you.
leave	***Leave* is a verb that means "go away from" or "let stay."** We will leave at noon. Leave your sweater here.
was	***Was* is a past tense form of *be*. Use *was* to tell about one person or thing.** Hana was sad yesterday.
were	***Were* is also a past tense form of *be*. Use *were* to tell about more than one person or thing. Also use the word *were* with *you*.** Hana and her friend were both unhappy. Were you home yesterday?
has	**Use *has* to tell about one person or thing.** Rory has a stamp collection.
have	**Use *have* to tell about more than one. Also use *have* with the pronoun *I*.** David and Lin have a rock collection. I have a bottle cap collection.
who	***Who* is in the nominative case and should be used as the subject of a clause. Use *who* to refer to people.** The man who picked me up is my father.
whom	***Whom* is in the objective case and should be used as a direct or indirect object or as the object of a preposition. Use *whom* to refer to people.** To whom am I speaking?
which	**Use *which* to refer to things.** His rear tire, which was flat, had to be repaired.
that	***That* can refer to people or things. Use *that* instead of *which* to begin a clause that is necessary to the meaning of the sentence.** The picture that Stephen drew won first prize.
very	***Very* is an adverb. It means "extremely."** I was very tired after the hike.
real	***Real* is an adjective. It means "actual." Never use *real* in place of *very*.** **Incorrect:** The hike was real long. **Correct:** I used a real compass to find my way.

less	***Less* can be used to refer to a *smaller amount* that is not a sum of items.** If you want to use **less** gasoline, buy a hybrid.
fewer	***Fewer* is used to refer to a *smaller number* of items.** Be aware that there will be **fewer** cars from which to choose.
over	***Over* can be used to refer to a *larger amount* that is not a sum of items.** We drove **over** 30 miles, then biked the rest of the way.
more than	***More than* is used to describe a *larger number* of items.** **More than** 20 cars remained on the lot.

In academic writing, avoid *contractions; shortened forms* of words (*gonna, gotta, wanna*); *slang* or *informal language* (*stuff, cool, guy, way* or *totally* for *very, lots of, okay*); and *vague words* (*thing, nice, good, bad*).

Section 33 Homophones

Homophones sound alike but have different spellings and meanings.

are	***Are* is a form of the verb *be*.**	We **are** best friends.
our	***Our* is a possessive pronoun.**	**Our** favorite color is green.
hour	**An *hour* is sixty minutes.**	Meet me in an **hour**.
its	***Its* is a possessive pronoun.**	The horse shook **its** shaggy head.
it's	***It's* is a contraction of the words *it is* or *it has*.**	**It's** a beautiful day for a ride.
there	***There* is an adverb that usually means "in that place." It can also be used in the expressions "there is" and "there are."** Please put the books **there**. **There** is an aquarium nearby. **Note:** Using the expressions *there is, there are,* and *it is* sometimes weakens sentences; try to avoid these expressions in academic writing.	**There** are three books on the table.
their	***Their* is a possessive pronoun. It shows something belongs to more than one person or thing.** **Their** tickets are in my pocket.	
they're	***They're* is a contraction made from the words *they are*.** **They're** waiting for me inside.	
two	***Two* is a number.**	Apples and pears are **two** fruits I like.
to	***To* can be a preposition meaning "toward." *To* can also be used with a verb to form an infinitive.** I brought the pot **to** the stove. (*preposition*)	I like **to** cook. (*infinitive*)
too	***Too* means "also."**	I'd like some lunch, **too**.
	***Too* can mean "more than enough."**	That's **too** much pepper!
your	***Your* is a possessive pronoun.** Where are **your** socks?	
you're	***You're* is a contraction made from the words *you are*.** **You're** coming with us, aren't you?	
whose	***Whose* is a possessive pronoun. It can refer to people or things.** **Whose** raincoat is this?	The raincoat **whose** buttons are blue is mine.
who's	***Who's* is a contraction made from the words *who* and *is* or *who* and *has*.** **Who's** at the front door?	**Who's** taken my book?

than	***Than* is used to make comparisons.** We waited for more <u>**than**</u> an hour.	She is taller <u>**than**</u> you.
then	***Then* can be an adverb that tells about time. It can also mean "therefore."** <u>**Then**</u> I went home. If you like mangoes, <u>**then**</u> you should try this mango ice cream.	
principal	**A *principal* is a person with authority.** The <u>**principal**</u> made the rule.	
principle	**A *principle* is a general rule or code of behavior.** He lived with a strong <u>**principle**</u> of honesty.	
waist	**The *waist* is the middle part of the body.** She wore a belt around her <u>**waist**</u>.	
waste	**To *waste* something is to use it in a careless way.** She would never <u>**waste**</u> something she could recycle.	
aloud	***Aloud* means "out loud" or "able to be heard."**	He read the poem <u>**aloud**</u>.
allowed	***Allowed* is a form of the verb *allow*.**	We were not <u>**allowed**</u> to swim after dark.
raise	***Raise* is a verb that means "lift up."**	We <u>**raise**</u> the American flag each morning.
raze	***Raze* is a verb that means "destroy."**	Bulldozers <u>**raze**</u> old buildings so that new ones can be built.

Letters and E-mails

Section 34 Letters

A *friendly letter* is an informal letter written to a friend or a family member.
In a friendly letter, you might send a message, invite someone to a party, or thank someone for a gift. A friendly letter has five parts.

- The ***heading*** gives your address and the date.
- The ***greeting*** includes the name of the person you are writing to. It begins with an uppercase letter and ends with a comma.
- The ***body*** of the letter gives your message.
- The ***closing*** is a friendly or polite way to say good-bye. It ends with a comma.
- The ***signature*** is your name.

35 Rand Street
Chicago, IL 60606
July 15, 20__

Dear Kim,

Hi from the big city. I'm spending the summer learning to skateboard. My brother Raj is teaching me. He's a pro.

I have one skateboard and hope to buy another one soon. If I can do that, we can practice together when you come to visit.

Your friend,

Art

A *business letter* is a formal letter.
You would write a business letter to a company, an employer, a newspaper, or any person you do not know well. A business letter looks a lot like a friendly letter, but a business letter substitutes a colon for a comma after the greeting, omits paragraph indentations, and aligns all of the letter parts along the left-hand margin.

35 Rand Street
Chicago, IL 60606
July 15, 20__

Swenson Skateboard Company
10026 Portage Road
Lansing, MI 48091

Dear Sir or Madam:

Please send me your latest skateboard catalog. I am particularly interested in your newest models, the K-7 series.

Thank you.

Sincerely yours,
Arthur Quinn
Arthur Quinn

The envelope below shows how to address a letter. A friendly letter and a business letter are addressed the same way.

ARTHUR QUINN
35 RAND ST
CHICAGO IL 60606

KIM LEE
1555 MONTAGUE BLVD
MEMPHIS TN 38106

Section 35 E-mails

An *e-mail* is a note sent from one person to another person, a group, or a company through a computer network. Today, many people use e-mail to stay in touch with friends and family. An e-mail should contain five parts, like a letter does.

- An e-mail contains a *greeting,* a *body,* a *closing,* and your *name.*
- An e-mail *header* contains your e-mail address, the e-mail address of the person you are writing to, the date, and a subject line.

Send | Save as a Draft | Cancel

From: arthur_quinn@communicago.net

To: info@swenskate.com

Date: July 15, 20__

Subject: Skateboard catalog

Attach Files

Dear Sir or Madam:

Please send me your latest skateboard catalog. I am particularly interested in your newest models, the K-7 series.

My address is 35 Rand Street, Chicago, IL 60606. Thank you.

Sincerely,
Arthur Quinn

Research

Section 36 Library Research

You can find information for a report or a project in a library.

- Many libraries have an information desk. The person at the desk can help you look for information.
- Libraries have many reference books, including dictionaries, thesauruses, and encyclopedias. You can use these to find information about words and basic information about topics.
- Libraries have nonfiction books about all kinds of subjects. You can find books on a particular subject by entering that subject into a computer connected to the library's database. This database lists all the publications in the library. The computer will usually list several books on the subject you entered. Each listing will have a code that tells where in the library that book can be found.

Section 37 Internet Research

You can use online dictionaries, thesauruses, and encyclopedias to find basic information about words and topics. You can also find information for a report or a project by using an Internet *search engine*.

- Think of **key words** that describe what you are looking for. For example, if you need information on animals that live in the rainforest, you might use the key words **rainforest animals**. Type these words into the search engine's text box.
- The search engine will provide you with links to **websites**. You can click on a link to visit a website.
- When you get to the website, you need to judge whether it will be a good source of information.
  —Notice the last three letters of the website's Internet address. Sites with **.gov** and **.edu** are usually more reliable than sites with **.com**.
  —Think about who has written the information. Is the writer an expert on the topic? Is the writer giving facts, or just expressing opinions?
  —Check to see if the information is up-to-date. The site should tell you when it was last updated.

Internet Safety

Be sure to follow safety rules whenever you use the Internet. These rules will help you keep personal information private.

- When you log on to a school computer, you may type your own name as a username. However, when you go on the Internet, you use a screen name. That should never be your real name or nickname. You will also use a password, a secret word or symbol that identifies who you are. Keep your password safe. Do not share it with anyone. Never use your address, birthday, phone number, or pet's name as a password. Those are too easy for someone else to figure out.
- Have you ever received e-mail with an attachment? Usually you must click the attachment to load it into your computer. Never download attachments from strangers. These may harm your computer.

Section 38 Bibliographies

A *bibliography* is an alphabetical list of all sources used when gathering information for a report or an essay. The models below demonstrate how to create bibliographic entries.

- **Encyclopedia Article or Dictionary Entry**
  "Asteroid." The Columbia Encyclopedia. 6th ed. 2007.
- **Magazine or Newspaper Article**
  Bridges, Andrew. "Deadly Space Threats Get More Attention." The Columbus Dispatch. 13 May 2010: C4.
- **Website**
  Britt, Robert Roy. "Asteroid Discoveries May Outpace Ability to Assess Threat to Earth." Space.com. 19 Oct. 2001. Imaginova Corp. 1 Apr. 2008 <http://space.com/scienceastronomy/solarsystem/asteroid.html>.
- **Book**
  Miller, Ron. Asteroids, Comets, and Meteors. Twenty-First Century: Minneapolis, 2006.

Guidelines for Listening and Speaking

Section 39 Listening

These steps will help you be a good listener:

- **Listen carefully** when others are speaking.
- **Keep in mind your reason for listening.** Are you listening to learn about a topic? To be entertained? To get directions? Decide what you should get out of the listening experience.
- **Look directly at the speaker.** Doing this will help you concentrate on what he or she is saying.
- **Do not interrupt** the speaker or talk to others while the speaker is talking.
- **Ask questions** when the speaker is finished talking if there is anything you do not understand.

Section 40 Speaking

Being a good speaker takes practice. These guidelines can help you become an effective speaker:

Giving Oral Reports

- **Be prepared.** Know exactly what it is that you are going to talk about and how long you will speak. Have your notes in front of you.
- **Speak slowly** and **clearly**. Speak **loudly** enough so everyone can hear you.
- **Look** at your audience.

Taking Part in Discussions

- **Listen** to what others have to say.
- **Disagree politely.** Let others in the group know you respect their point of view.
- **Try not to interrupt** others. Everyone should have a chance to speak.

(you) | Diagram | sentences

Section 41 Diagramming Sentences

A sentence diagram is a map of a sentence. It shows how the parts of a sentence fit together and how the individual words in a sentence are related. Sentence diagrams can represent every part of speech and every type of sentence. The models below demonstrate how to create sentence diagrams, beginning with the simplest kinds of sentences.

- In a sentence consisting of a subject and an action verb, the subject and the verb are separated by a vertical line that bisects the horizontal line.
  Rain fell.
  Rain | fell

- An adjective (or article) that modifies a noun or pronoun belongs on a slanted line below the word it modifies.
  A **cold** rain fell.

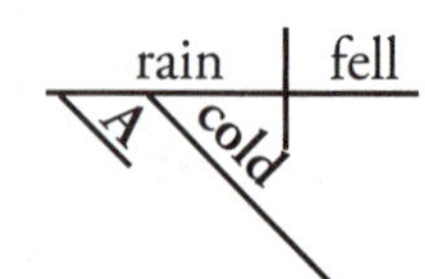

- An adverb that modifies a verb belongs on a slanted line below the verb it modifies.
  A very cold rain fell **steadily**.

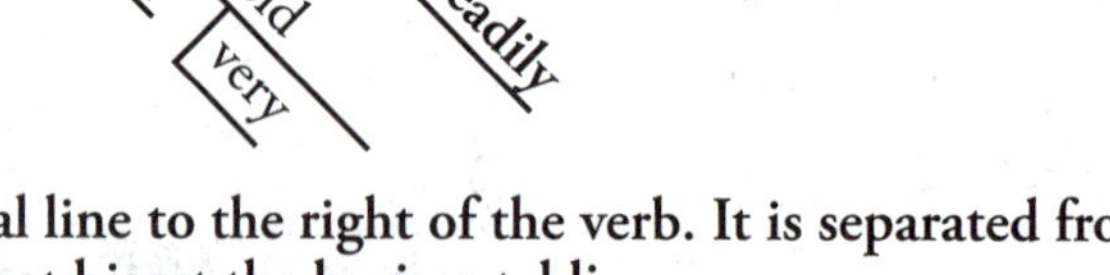

- A direct object is placed on a horizontal line to the right of the verb. It is separated from the verb by a short vertical line that does not bisect the horizontal line.
  The downpour drenched the **land**.
  downpour | drenched | land
  The
  the

- An indirect object goes below the verb to show *who* or *what* receives something.
  It gave the **crops** a welcome soaking.
  It | gave | soaking
  crops
  the
  a
  welcome

- Two separate horizontal lines show a compound predicate. The conjunction joins the verbs.
  Seedlings **uncurled** and **grew**.
  uncurled
  Seedlings
  and
  grew

- A compound subject is placed on two horizontal lines with a conjunction joining the subjects.
  Leaves and **flowers** glistened.
  Leaves
  and
  glistened
  flowers

- A compound sentence is diagrammed as two sentences with a conjunction joining them.
  The rain stopped and the sun appeared.
  rain | stopped
  The
  and
  sun | appeared
  the

- **A demonstrative pronoun takes the place of a noun. It belongs wherever the noun it replaces would go in the diagram.**

  This prompted a collective cheer.

- **A possessive pronoun belongs on a slanted line under the noun that is the possession.**

  The children left **their** homes gleefully.

- **An indefinite pronoun, a subject pronoun, or an object pronoun also belongs wherever the noun it replaces would go.**

  Someone started a soccer game.

  I watched it.

- **The understood *you* belongs where the subject of the sentence would go. It is written in parentheses.**

  Remove your muddy shoes.

- **A linking verb has the same position in a diagram that an action verb has, but the linking verb is separated from the predicate adjective or predicate noun by a diagonal line instead of by a vertical line.**

  Your clothes **are** incredibly muddy.

  Soccer **is** a rough sport.

- **An adverbial prepositional phrase that modifies a verb is connected to that verb.**

  Leave your shoes **on the porch.**

- **An adjectival prepositional phrase that modifies a noun is connected to that noun.**

  The mud **in the field** is quite deep.

- **When *there* begins a sentence, it is placed on a separate line above the rest of the diagram.**

  There are fresh towels inside the house.

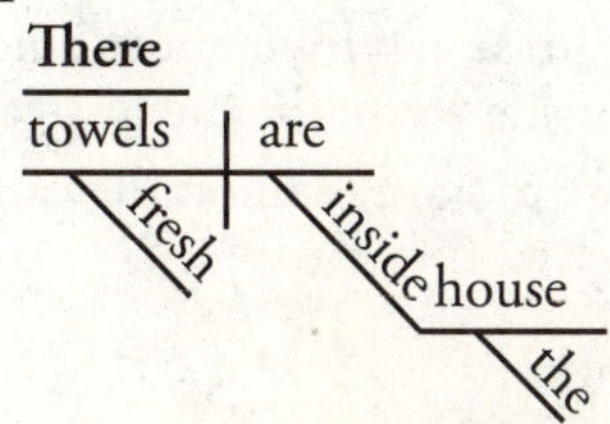

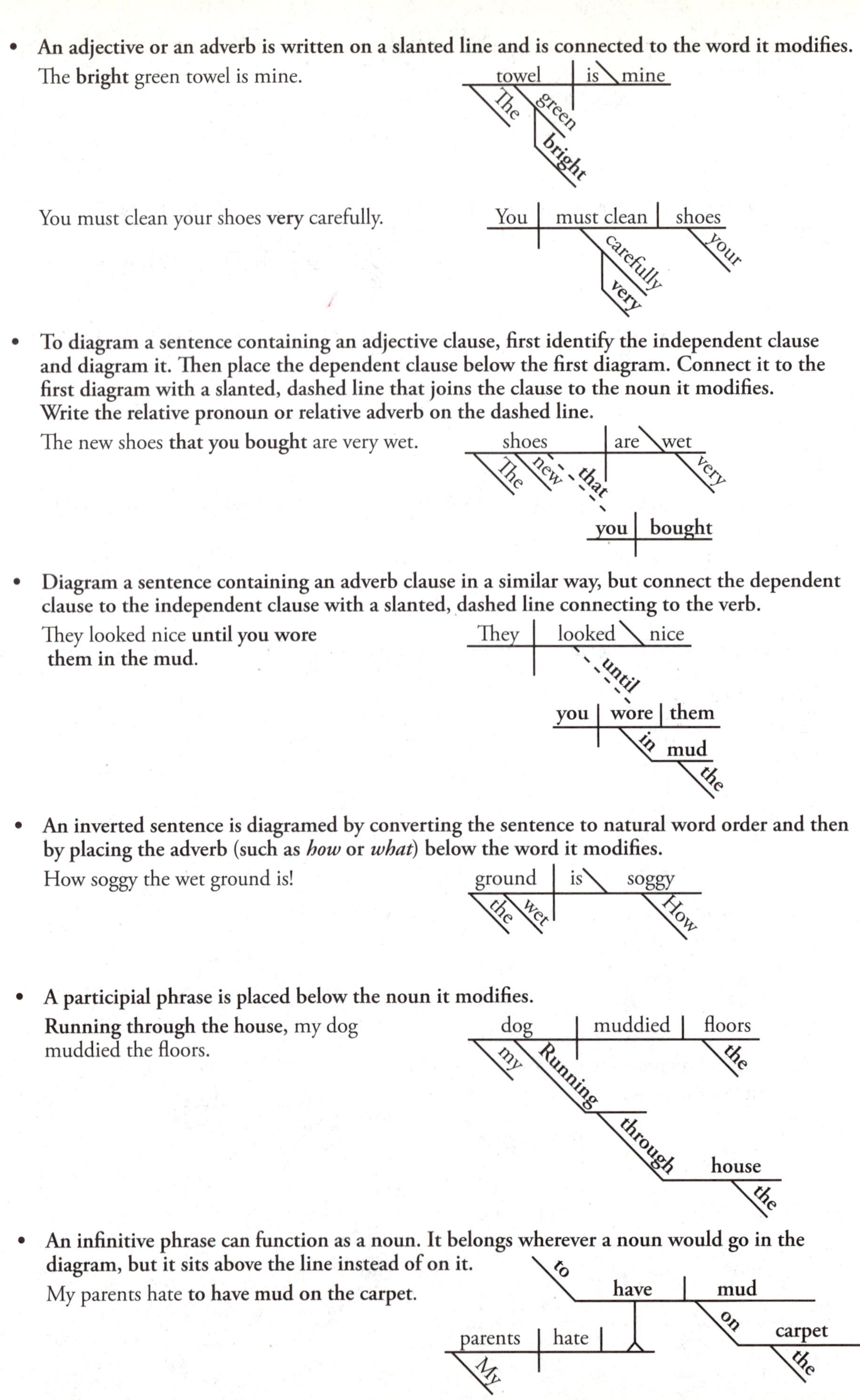

- **An adjective or an adverb is written on a slanted line and is connected to the word it modifies.**

  The **bright** green towel is mine.

  You must clean your shoes **very** carefully.

- **To diagram a sentence containing an adjective clause, first identify the independent clause and diagram it. Then place the dependent clause below the first diagram. Connect it to the first diagram with a slanted, dashed line that joins the clause to the noun it modifies. Write the relative pronoun or relative adverb on the dashed line.**

  The new shoes **that you bought** are very wet.

- **Diagram a sentence containing an adverb clause in a similar way, but connect the dependent clause to the independent clause with a slanted, dashed line connecting to the verb.**

  They looked nice **until you wore them in the mud.**

- **An inverted sentence is diagramed by converting the sentence to natural word order and then by placing the adverb (such as *how* or *what*) below the word it modifies.**

  How soggy the wet ground is!

- **A participial phrase is placed below the noun it modifies.**

  Running through the house, my dog muddied the floors.

- **An infinitive phrase can function as a noun. It belongs wherever a noun would go in the diagram, but it sits above the line instead of on it.**

  My parents hate **to have mud on the carpet.**

- **A gerund phrase functions as a noun. It belongs wherever a noun would go in the diagram, but it sits above the line instead of on it.**

  Cleaning the carpet is never a fun chore.

  Cleaning
  carpet
  the
  is
  chore
  never
  a
  fun

- **An appositive is a phrase that identifies a noun. The noun in an appositive is placed in parentheses next to the noun that the appositive identifies.**

  My dog hid in the garage,
  his favorite hideout.

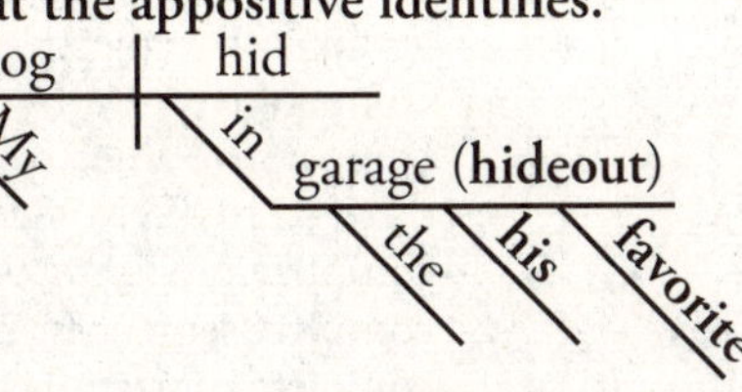

Language Index

Conventions of Standard English